D0812656

BROOKS

Doug Wilson

BROOKS

THE BIOGRAPHY BROOKS ROBINSON

THOMAS DUNNE BOOKS
ST. MARTIN'S PRESS   NEW YORK

THOMAS DUNNE BOOKS.
An imprint of St. Martin's Press.

www.thomasdunnebooks.com
www.stmartins.com

Library of Congress Cataloging-in-Publication Data

Wilson, Doug.
    Brooks : the biography of Brooks Robinson / Doug Wilson.
      p. cm
    Includes bibliographical references and index.
    ISBN 978-1-250-03304-8 (hardcover)
    ISBN 978-1-250-03303-1 (e-book)
    1. Robinson, Brooks, 1937– 2. Baseball players—United States—
Biography. 3. African American baseball players—Biography. I. Title.
    GV865.R58W55 2014
    796.357092—dc23
    [B]

2013031434

St. Martin's Press books may be purchased for educational, business, or promotional use. For information on bulk purchases, please contact Macmillan Corporate and Premium Sales Department at 1-800-221-7945, extension 5442, or write specialmarkets@macmillan.com.

First Edition: March 2014

10 9 8 7 6 5 4 3 2 1

Contents

Preface

THERE ARE A FEW PLAYERS in each sport whose deeds and aura were so pervasive that they defined the era in which they played. For me, Brooks Robinson was one of those players. He was a ubiquitous presence in the baseball of my youth, leaving an indelible impression on both All-Star Games and the postseason. His 23-year career spanned an epic period of change in baseball. It started in the mid-1950s, a time of sporadic black-and-white televised games and daytime World Series; a time when a prospect could sign with any team, outrageous bonuses were considered to be $4,000, and players were bound for life to the team that signed them. It lasted through the mid-1970s with the dawning of the Players Association, the fight for free agency, exploding television rights, agents, and big money. He not only was there, but more often than not played an important role in shaping the way the game was played and presented to the public.

Yet very little has been written about Brooks Robinson in the past 30 years and his life has never had the full-length, comprehensive biography treatment. I believe the reason for this is that there was a notable lack of conflict or controversy. There were no tragic humiliations; no arrests, no public brawls with spouses, no hints of cheating, substance abuse, or scandal. In other words, none of the things that drive book sales. He was unquestionably viewed as a squeaky-clean good guy in a time when attitudes were changing and other attributes were more celebrated, and consequently, his character was taken for granted. It is precisely for these qualities that I decided to pursue this book, however. Brooks exhibited many of the values that we now regret as lost. As time has gone by, his public persona stands as the role model we would want for our children. The present generation of fans is constantly reminded of the failings of its heroes. Much is written about how we are let down by cheaters and liars, by overpaid bores with little regard for their fans. This makes a man of Brooks Robinson's reputation even more important to revisit.

I should state at this point that I was never a particular fan of Brooks Robinson's while growing up. My heart belonged to Harmon Killebrew and the Twins and later, after my family moved, to the Big Red Machine of Cincinnati. The fact that Brooks seemed to enjoy inflicting postseason pain and misery on both of my teams did not make me dislike him, however. He played with a style and a flair that were impossible not to appreciate. I invariably found myself in the yard throwing a rubber ball against the side of the garage in such a way that I would be forced to dive to catch it, attempting to replicate his plays, although admittedly more than a few redos were required.

I communicated with Brooks Robinson, out of courtesy, to let him know of my intentions, but he was not involved in this project in any way. This was by design. I had previously learned that he had been battling serious medical problems which had forced him to curtail public appearances and he had turned down several book offers due to time constraints. He obviously needed to spend more time with his family.

More importantly, I feel that an inherent weakness of authorized biographies is that the subject has ultimate editorial control. Therefore, the author may not be able to critically evaluate sensitive topics. In choosing this subject, I knew that much of the material would be flattering. I did not want there to be a perception that I was influenced or felt a debt. I wanted the reader to be sure that the facts were presented based on research and interviews.

In my search for the Brooks Robinson story, I talked to people from all aspects of his life. I visited Little Rock to view Brooks Robinson's childhood homes, schools, playing fields, and even the firehouse in which his father worked. I listened as a group of his childhood friends traded stories. I talked to teammates, managers, and opponents from throughout his career, as well as those peripheral to the game. I talked to fans who met him as a player and those who met him in his later years. I talked to a scout and a newspaper reporter who witnessed his first workout with the Baltimore Orioles. I sifted through a mountain of microfilm and a gaggle of Google News Archives articles in addition to searching through old editions of the *Sporting News*, *Sport*, *Baseball Digest*, and *Sports Illustrated* to fact-check numbers and accounts of events as well as to find out what his contemporaries said about him.

Over the years, Brooks freely gave information about his life to numerous articles and book chapters, and wrote two autobiographical works. *Putting It All Together*, published in 1971, focused mostly on the 1970 World Series but also included anecdotes from his life. *Third Base Is My Home*, published in 1974, was more comprehensive. This book will fill in the gaps and will cover his entire career along with his post-baseball life. Also, a large part of the present book will deal with Brooks Robinson's character and treatment of fans— subjects that are impossible for a man to objectively write about himself.

I did not set out to blindly apply another coat of polish to the statue of a legend. In a closing scene of the classic western *The Man Who Shot Liberty Valance*, the reporter states, "When the legend becomes fact, print the legend." It was my intention to do just the opposite; I wanted to find out if the legend was indeed fact, and print whatever I found. If after reviewing the results of the research, another coat of polish is applied, then so be it.

BROOKS

Prologue

IT WAS JUST A MATTER OF TIME before the Big Red Machine started rolling. Going into the bottom of the sixth inning of the first game of the 1970 World Series, the powerful Reds were tied with the Baltimore Orioles, 3–3. Lee May, the Cincinnati first baseman, took his place in the right-handed batter's box. A strapping man known as a dead pull hitter, May had hit 72 home runs in the past two seasons. He focused intently on the pitcher, Jim Palmer, and paid no attention to the man standing roughly 100 feet to his left. That man, Baltimore third baseman Brooks Robinson, was studying him closely, however. A 33-year-old veteran with droopy shoulders, a doughy body, and a rapidly receding hairline, Robinson did not look like a professional athlete when seen out of uniform; but looks could be deceiving.

Robinson held his hands close together in front of his chest and crouched, not unlike a cat before pouncing on a mouse. On his left hand he wore an ordinary-looking piece of leather that held the words "Rawlings Pro Model." The glove was stained brown, stiff and cracked. The fur under the wrist strap was worn and frayed. A small piece of tape bearing Robinson's name covered the name of the glove's original owner, a young Oriole outfielder from whom he had obtained it in a trade a few years earlier because he liked the way it felt. This glove was not the only glove Robinson possessed. He had two other gloves in his locker that he used during pregame practice to break in for future use. He also had some gold ones at home—he had been the winner of the past 10 Gold Gloves for American League third basemen. Brooks Robinson had been one of the best players in baseball over the previous decade and was appearing in his third World Series in five years, but in the days before daily television highlights, he was still underappreciated by casual fans outside Baltimore. That was about to change. As Palmer went into his long-armed windup, Robinson did not realize that the next pitch would be the start of a series of events over the next five days that would ensure that the unappealing piece of leather on his hand would wind up in the Baseball Hall of Fame a good 10 years before its owner would.

Palmer threw an off-speed pitch that hung a bit more than he would have liked. May kept his weight back, and then unleashed a vicious swing that met the ball squarely, sending it rocketing down the third base line. May, as all baseball players are taught on similarly hit balls, was thinking two bases as he left the batter's box. The ball took two bounding hops off the artificial turf—1970 artificial turf that was little more than green carpet laid on concrete—and shot over third base like a golf ball skimming over an airport runway.

From his original position 10 feet off the line, on the back edge of the infield, Robinson took four quick steps and lunged to his right, reaching as far as possible with his gloved left hand. He backhanded the ball behind third base, spearing it just as the umpire on the edge of the outfield waved his hand indicating that it was a fair ball—a great snag that would hold May to a single. But Robinson wasn't finished. He took one more step with his left foot and, with his back to the infield and his momentum carrying him well into foul ground, turned in midair and, throwing across his body, seemingly without looking, launched the ball in the general direction of the Ohio River. Incredibly, the ball arrived at first base on one hop just before May did. The first base umpire jerked his closed fist into the air and 50,000 fans watching the game in the stadium and millions more watching on television gasped at what they had just witnessed.

This one play, which would be replayed many times in the coming decades and be regarded as one of the top fielding plays in World

Series history, was only a preview of the next four games. The Reds would be continually flummoxed in attempts to drive the ball through the left side of the Orioles' infield, stopped by an endless series of unbelievable plays by Robinson. By the end of the week, Brooks Robinson would be the most celebrated fielder in baseball history. He would be selected as the Most Valuable Player of the World Series, and the fact that he hit .429 with two home runs and six RBIs was almost superfluous. It was more than just the most dominating performance of an entire World Series by a single player; it was transcendent, sublime. Even Reds fans, who hated what he did to their team, had to admire the sheer artistry of it all. Forty years later, an entire generation of baseball fans would still smile when they remembered it, and Brooks Robinson would remain the standard for fielding excellence.

Amazingly, after the Series the Oriole players and coaches acted like they didn't know what all the fuss was about. They said they had been watching the same thing for years and these weren't even his best plays. And the thing about it was, they were telling the truth.

Brooks Robinson would go on to complete a 23-year Major League Baseball career, all with the Orioles, and would join his glove in the Baseball Hall of Fame in 1983. He would participate in 18 All-Star Games, accumulate a record 16 consecutive Gold Gloves, set records for fielding percentage, and be selected to the All-Century Team. As great as he was on the baseball field, however, the singular way in which Brooks Robinson conducted himself off the field was as important as anything he did on it. He was universally acknowledged as baseball's nice guy; a man friendly to writers, fans, and opposing players; a man who always demonstrated class and regard for others. Thirty-five years after he played his last game, Brooks Robinson remains an unquestioned icon in Baltimore. His genuine, humble demeanor, friendliness, and, above all, ability to remain a great role model have somehow grown in significance over the years as fans are continually disappointed by sports figures who are rude, selfish, and inaccessible. Brooks Robinson exhibits the exact opposite of all the traits that modern fans hate in their sports idols. And, no matter how much fame and adoration he achieved, he never lost the sense of who he was: just a regular guy who loved the game of baseball. It was his great character, rather than his athletic ability, that prompted a writer to remark, "Nobody's ever named a candy bar for Brooks. Around here we name our children after him."

1. Little Rock

WATCHING THE FINAL GAME of the 1970 World Series, famed sports-writer Red Smith, in the twilight of a 60-year career, commented on Brooks Robinson's uncanny ability to be where the ball was before it got there: "I can't recall any player in any sport who ever had such a knack for always being in the right place at the right time." It was not the first time someone had made such a remark about Brooks Robinson. Whether due to instinct, luck, design, or all three, Brooks made a habit of being in the right place at the right time throughout his life, even from the start.

Brooks Robinson always maintained that he never wanted to be anything other than a baseball player. For that purpose, he couldn't have picked a better place and time to grow up than Little Rock, Arkansas, in the 1940s and 1950s. Located near the geographic center of the state, Little Rock took its name from a description given by a Frenchman, Jean-Baptiste Bénard de la Harpe, who led an exploration party up the Arkansas River in 1772—noting an outcropping of rock on the banks and calling it *"la petite roche"* to distinguish it from a larger rock cliff across the river. Part of the Louisiana Purchase, Little Rock became the capital of Arkansas Territory in 1821 and remained the capital as Arkansas became a state in 1836. The city experienced slow, steady growth as people moved in from the countryside in search of better living conditions and jobs, but by 1930 the population barely exceeded 80,000. As the state's capital and largest city, however, Little Rock possessed the culture and potential afforded by being the political, economic, and educational center. It was by no means a metropolis, but compared to the rest of the mostly rural, agrarian state, it was downright bustling and equaled the larger cities of the United States with every modern convenience. A few early skyscrapers were beginning to dot the skyline, some as high as 14 stories, and the large, beautiful capitol dome could be seen from miles away. Electric streetcars and trolleys ran through the city, bringing citizens to the active downtown area, which held all the major department stores, banks, and numerous theaters. In other aspects, Little Rock retained a certain small-town, country atmosphere with mom-and-pop grocery stores and drugstores scattered on corners in most neighborhoods and a lot of open space.

Most important for Brooks, Little Rock was a hotbed of sports, particularly baseball. There were well-organized baseball leagues for players of all ages and they were actively supported. The daily newspapers regularly printed scores and highlights from the Pee Wee Leagues, semipros, and the minor league Little Rock Travelers, who had been members of the Southern Association since 1902. The American Legion baseball program was one of the best in the region, a fact not lost on professional scouts.

If not for some economic and meteorologic bad luck, however, Brooks Robinson would likely have grown up on a farm in rural Arkansas and missed out on the opportunities Little Rock provided. The future baseball player's father, Brooks Calbert Robinson (he would later have a senior after his name), was born in 1914 in Pope County, Arkansas. The nearest town was Atkins, a small community of about a thousand, 60 miles northwest of Little Rock. Brooks Sr.'s father, Bruce, like most of the inhabitants of Pope County, was a farmer. Robinsons had farmed in southern Pope County since Samuel Calbert Robinson had moved to Arkansas from North Carolina in the 1840s with his wife and two small children—traveling in a wagon train with other settlers.

Although the Robinsons were not among the most prosperous farmers in the county, they made a good living. Pope County, particularly the Arkansas River bottoms, which formed the southern border of the county, had some of the best farmland in the state, growing cotton, corn, wheat, apples, and peaches in abundance. Grapes were said to be so plentiful they grew without cultivation. The ample supply of running water provided good irrigation for crops and stock even in the driest seasons. But no matter how good the land was, life for rural Arkansas farmers in the early part of the twentieth century was not easy. Brooks, the youngest of five children, certainly learned the value, and necessity, of hard work.

Life became harder for Pope County farmers in the 1920s. The cotton market, which drove the economy for the entire state, nearly crumbled under the burden of a precipitous drop in cotton prices following World War I. By 1920, the price had fallen from 37 cents a pound to barely six. A blight on the orchard industry soon followed. Many farmers left Pope County for California and other lands of opportunity. Those who stayed were in for more bad luck.

While the rest of the country was roaring through the 1920s, storm clouds were forming over Arkansas in the spring of 1927. The previous winter had been particularly wet across the Midwest, and early snow melts in the north had swollen the Mississippi River and its southern tributaries. Then, in April, the rain came. Torrential rain; rain that seemed like it would never stop. Seven inches were recorded in Little Rock in less than a day. Every levee in the state west of Little Rock failed as the Arkansas River poured over its banks. Residents watched helplessly as towns and farms along the river were buried within hours. In an instant, generations of work were lost.

The Great Flood of 1927 is still considered one of the three major floods in North American history. Some towns and farmland stood beneath more than six feet of murky water. Dead animals floated everywhere. With nowhere for the water to go, thousands of residents were displaced and many were unable to return home until September. Red Cross camps and tent cities provided the only resource for families. Typhoid, malaria, and pellagra became epidemic. Secretary of Commerce Herbert Hoover, who rose to national prominence while leading the recovery effort, called the flood "America's greatest peacetime disaster" and said that "the disaster felt by Arkansas farmers, planters and residents of river lowlands was of epic proportions." And farms in the Arkansas River bottom were a particularly bad place to be.

Bruce Robinson died in Little Rock in 1928 at the age of forty-eight, leaving his wife, Bertha, a widow with five children, aged fourteen to twenty-two. By 1930, as the Great Depression was getting into full swing, Bertha Robinson was residing in Little Rock, in a house that rented for $25 a month, with all five children still living at home.

Times were tough, especially for a boy who had to face his teen years without a father. It was the type of situation that could make or break someone. Without a male role model of his own, how would Brooks learn to be one himself? Also, he had to become a city kid—the Robinsons' farming days were over. This couldn't have been an easy period but the effect it had on him can only be estimated, as he rarely talked about it over the years. If it affected him negatively, it didn't show—he got over it.

Brooks developed into an excellent athlete, eventually starring in basketball and football at Little Rock Central High School. In the summers, he played American Legion baseball, playing on the first Little Rock Legion team to be known as the Doughboys in 1930. It was a good team. One of his teammates, Skeeter Dickey, had an older brother, Bill, who was an All-Star catcher for the New York Yankees. As a second baseman and leadoff hitter, Brooks helped the 1930 team to the Arkansas State Championship, scoring four runs in the title game win over Blytheville.

Brooks met Ethel Mae Denker in high school. She had grown up in Little Rock as the only surviving child of August and Maurine Denker, who were in their late 30s and had been married 18 years when she was born. Although not rich, the Denkers were more comfortable than most at the time, living in a house they owned, which was valued at $10,000 in the 1930 U.S. Census. Brooks and Ethel married soon after she graduated high school in June 1935. Their first child, Brooks Calbert Robinson, Jr., was born May 18, 1937. They would add another child, Gary, five years later.

Brooks Sr. worked at the large Colonial Bakery, then got hired by the Little Rock Fire Department in 1941. He would become a career fireman, eventually rising to captain. Gary and Brooks had two working parents before that became common. Ethel worked for Sears, and then as a longtime administrative and clerical assistant in the state capitol. She still had time, however, to get fried chicken and biscuits and the like on the table for dinner every night.

The Robinson family lived in a tiny house on Lloyd Court. When Brooks was in junior high, they moved up to a larger two-story house nearby on Dennison Street. They lived in the Capitol View/ Stiff's Station district, a solidly middle-class, older, well-established, rolling, tree-filled neighborhood in west-central Little Rock, not far from the capitol. The houses were close together, small, single-family dwellings, mostly built in the 1920s, and as a rule contained two-parent families. Everyone knew everyone else. People left their doors unlocked. There were lots of kids around and they enjoyed the free-dom to play and explore at will with little concern about crime or other bad things that modern parents worry about. Both grand-mothers lived in the neighborhood, but otherwise there were few relatives around. As Ethel's father had died at age fifty-four in 1933, Gary and Brooks never knew either of their grandfathers.

The Robinsons grew up relatively unfazed by the horrors of the Great Depression and World War II that affected some of their neigh-bors. Brooks Sr. had a steady, respected job, and with the addition of Ethel's salary, they had enough money to be comfortable—certainly not frivolous, but comfortable. By all accounts, it was a happy, loving family atmosphere fostered by Brooks Sr. and Ethel. Both were gen-erally soft-spoken; there was little yelling in the Robinson household. Brooks and Gary learned about honest work and treating people with respect from example.

Ethel, much more outgoing than her husband, was the type of po-lite, pleasant southern woman who had surprising steel when she needed to make a point, such as with disciplining her children or making sure everyone got to church on time. Brooks Sr. was laid-back and low-key, sometimes enjoying nothing more than sitting on the porch and chewing tobacco or having an occasional cigar. Work-ing as a fireman, he had an irregular schedule—frequently two or three full days on, then two or three days off—which gave him a lot of time to be at home. And he used that time to be with his kids.

"We were a middle-income family," says Gary. "We grew up in a good family. We didn't have fancy cars or things like that, but our parents taught us good values. I think I appreciate that more now that I'm older. You don't realize it so much when you're growing up, but later when you have a family of your own, you look back and think, 'Hey, I'm glad I was taught good values growing up.'"

"I spent a lot of time at their house in junior high and high school," says Buddy Rotenberry, one of Brooks's best friends. "His parents were good people; common, down-to-earth, unassuming, kind people. I really respected the kind of man Brooks's father was. Mr. Robinson was a model father in my opinion. I envied Brooks so much for having a mother and father who created a happy environment."

"They were both just nice people," says Harold Ellingson, a teammate on Legion baseball teams. "It wasn't an accident that Brooks and Gary turned out so well. They had a good upbringing."

Part of that good upbringing was discipline and respect. "Although Mr. Robinson was a man of few words, you didn't want to mess with him," says Rotenberry. "He could be very stern. Brooks's mother, Ethel, was very nice, but she also laid down the law to Brooks and Gary when it needed to be done. They taught them good values and if they strayed, they jerked them back in line pretty quick."

Sometimes, that included applying a belt to the butt, such as the time when Brooks was 12 and he and Gary took a trolley downtown to watch a movie. After the movie, Gary, as younger brothers are wont to do, was making such a pain of himself that Brooks left him downtown, telling him, "Find your own way home." Even though Gary did indeed find his way home safely, this did not sit well with their parents, and Brooks received one of his worst spankings from his father.

Usually the punishment was less traumatic, but more unbearable—having to endure a lecture. Recalling one discourse, Brooks said, "My dad should have been a lawyer. What he was, was a good parent. Both he and Mother were. Though Gary and I may have gotten our share of spankings as kids—all deserved—more often than not Dad's method was to sit down with us 'and reason together.' After discussing some misbehavior, he might say, 'What kind of punishment do you think you deserve?' The end result was often a loss of privileges, such as seeing a movie or playing ball for a couple of days. There was also a loss of face at such times. When I did something I shouldn't and then confronted Dad or Mom, I always felt ashamed that I let them down. A spanking would have been so much quicker, but usually I was made to suffer through a discussion of the offense."

Brooks didn't suffer too often though, as he was generally a good-natured, agreeable, trouble-free kid. "He was always a well-organized boy and you could talk and reason with him," Brooks Sr. would tell reporters in 1964. The influence of his parents was immeasurable in contributing to the foundation of Brooks Robinson: personality and character; responsibility and sense of duty; politeness, and the easy acceptance of authority. These traits would only grow over time.

Brooks's recollections of his parents in his autobiography and interviews paint a portrait reminiscent of a 1950s black-and-white family television show, like *Leave It to Beaver* or *Father Knows Best*. And that's not too far from the truth. There were no demons in Brooks Robinson's past that needed to be wrestled into adulthood. There was no timidity in the Robinson household—no fear of a stray comment causing an explosion. There was no apprehension of mistakes. If there were skeletons in the Robinson closet, they were buried deeply. It was a good environment in which to cultivate a happy, outgoing, trusting personality. The Robinson kids were confident of dinner being on the table every night and of their father coming home from work and spending time with them.

While he took his outgoing personality from his mother, Brooks Jr., called Buddy by his parents growing up, was very much the product of his father. Sports created an indelible bond between father and son. Brooks Sr. was still athletic and played a lot of fast-pitch softball and semipro baseball. The fire department had a baseball team as did the Methodist church. In 1937 he was on an International Harvester softball team that went to the world championships at Soldier Field in Chicago, losing to a team from Cincinnati 2–1 in the finals. When Brooks was still a toddler, his father started him out playing catch with tennis balls so the ball wouldn't hurt. He taught him how to hold the ball, how to throw, how to hold a bat, and how to hit. But he was not a taskmaster—it was all done as fun. And the little kid loved it; he couldn't get enough of it. "He'd wake up every morning saying, 'Play ball, Daddy,'" said his mother in 1970. As Brooks got older, he tagged along to games with his father as often as possible to be the batboy. They spent a lot of time in the yard playing catch. For Brooks, it was the start of a love affair with the game of baseball that would last a lifetime.

Often Brooks, either alone or with a friend or two, would visit his father when he was on call at the fire station. They would enjoy a quiet game of catch or pepper in the grassy area behind the small, two-garage station or shoot baskets on the goal near the parking lot. When older, they would join in basketball games there with the other firemen. Brooks Sr. would get his son out of school to go to the Little Rock Travelers Field every year when the St. Louis Cardinals came to town to play the Chicago White Sox in the last exhibition game before the season opener.

Brooks's friends enjoyed the attention of his father as much as he did. "His daddy had been, in his own right, one of the best school-boy athletes growing up in Little Rock," says Rotenberry. "He spent a lot of time playing with us. They lived in an old two-story white frame house on kind of a hilly lot. Out in the backyard, attached to the garage, was a basketball goal. When his dad was home, we were always out there. We would play HORSE and 21. His dad was a great shooter. He would sit out there at sixteen to eighteen feet with his two-handed set shot and just make shot after shot after shot. When we were in high school, and you have to understand that Brooks was an All-State basketball player in high school, he still couldn't out-shoot his daddy."

Brooks recalled that his father had the perfect attitude for a sports parent. "My dad had the great insight to keep just the right balance between play and practice," he said in 2007. "He never put any pressure on me, and he never corrected me about how I played in a game unless I asked. If I wanted to field some grounders, he'd drop everything to go out and hit them to me. Then he'd pitch me hours of batting practice. But he never told me, 'You've got to do it this way.' It was always, 'Why don't you try this?' "

"He's the one responsible for my love of baseball and especially my desire to do the best I can every day," Brooks wrote in 1974. "He's also the one who instilled in me the ability to forget today's game and prepare for tomorrow."

Mr. Robinson was restrained in his praise when Brooks did well. This was important to help keep him grounded because it became obvious at an early age that Brooks had exceptional ability. He did not grow up on a pedestal because he had athletic talent; there was no hint of the spoiled, privileged athlete. Dad was just as reserved with criticism when son failed. "Some parents get their values confused and emphasize winning and individual accomplishment over everything else. They could learn a lot from my father," Brooks later noted.

"Brooks's father was not a sports parent from hell," says Rotenberry. "He rarely instructed him or corrected him in sports in front of his peers. He always picked a quiet time alone, in the backyard or behind the fire station, for instruction. He was very thoughtful and helped Brooks achieve his goals but didn't yell and wasn't overbearing or pushy. And he left Brooks's coaches alone and let them coach his kid. You don't see that with a lot of parents of good athletes unfortunately." The remarkably close bond between father and son would only grow through the years.

Young Brooks became an ardent fan and student of the game of baseball and its history. He devoured the box scores in the *Arkansas Gazette* each morning. Since there were no major league teams in the South at the time, Brooks followed the St. Louis Cardinals, as did most in the area, listening to their games every night on his Philco radio over the powerful KMOX. The Cardinals won National League pennants in 1942, 1943, 1944, and 1946 and were the dream team of all midwestern boys. Brooks idolized Stan Musial, and also followed players from Arkansas such as Dizzy Dean, George Kell, Preacher Roe, and Johnny Sain. He kept a scrapbook with pictures of his favorites and cut out articles of momentous occasions, such as when Babe Ruth died. He was much better at calculating batting averages than he was at doing math word problems in school.

Brooks spent hours behind his house hitting rocks with a cut-off broomstick. By the time he was seven or eight, he was strong enough to reach the woods across the meadow from the gravel road behind his house—envisioning he was hitting one out for the Cards at Sportsman's Park. His mother could always tell where he was by the ping of rocks hitting the broomstick out back. Or from the thud of a ball hitting the front steps. Brooks put in a lot of time throwing a golf ball or tennis ball against the steps—making grounders or flies depending on how he threw them—inventing baseball games and dreaming of playing with his heroes (all the while helping his hand-eye coordination).

But Brooks was not a loner. He was friendly and always had plenty of kids to play with. He enjoyed both the competition and the camaraderie that sports provided. Sports dominated the boys' childhood; whatever was in season—baseball, basketball, or football—that's what they played. During winters the Boys Club, situated in a three-story brick building downtown, had well-organized basketball leagues, and the kids played one-on-one and shooting games on the backyard goal. As they got older, Brooks and a few friends would play basketball at the nearby Arkansas School for the Deaf gym—and not always when it was open. "Brooks was a good guy, but he was not an angel," says Rotenberry. "Sometimes when the Deaf School gym was closed, we were not above breaking out a small pane and lifting a latch on a window to get in to play. Eventually Houston Nutt, Sr., who was the athletic director, talked to Brooks—I guess he figured he was involved—and just gave him a key. That was easier than fixing the windows."

While they enjoyed basketball and football, it was baseball that held the most interest. At the time, baseball was the only professional team sport that mattered; unquestionably the national pastime. All the kids were crazy about baseball. There were endless games of pepper, hot box, workup, and other variations when there weren't enough for a game—anything to hit and catch a ball. They all dreamed of the day they could be on a real team and wear a uniform.

It's hard for someone not from Little Rock to understand what a big deal Lamar Porter Field was. The field's namesake, Lamar Porter, had been the son of a wealthy Little Rock family who had been killed in a car accident at the age of twenty-one while attending college in Virginia. The family donated the land to the Boys Club as a memorial to their son. The park was constructed at a cost of $120,000 by the Works Progress Administration, part of President Franklin Roosevelt's plan to put Americans to work, and was completed in 1937.

Lamar Porter became a community center for all ages. There was a large playground with slides and swings; little kids played in a sandbox or skipped rocks on a nearby creek and hunted for crawdads and tadpoles. There were clay tennis courts, areas for shuffleboard, marbles, horseshoes, and volleyball, and a picnic grounds. The prize jewel of Lamar Porter, however, was the baseball diamond. It had built-in, sunken dugouts complete with lockers and showers, and a covered grandstand that extended well beyond first and third bases and seated 1,500, and it was the only field in the state to have lights at the time. Kids couldn't help but feel like big leaguers when they trotted out on the Lamar Porter baseball field. The field was in near-constant use by all ages. The youth leagues were coordinated by the Boys Club, as Little League did not start in Little Rock until 1951.

Brooks Robinson spent most of his youth at Lamar Porter Field. He lived only a short bike ride away and it was right across the street from his elementary school. When not playing, he was making money. Employment opportunities for youths at the field started at seat duster for a quarter a day and worked up to ball shagger, concession worker, and finally, the prestigious job of scoreboard operator—paying 50 cents a game. The scoreboard was a giant steel monster located in left center field about 400 feet from home plate. The scorekeeper climbed a ladder, sat on a catwalk, and hung large metal number signs onto pegs, frequently performing this duty while dodging rocks and dirt clods flung by well-wishing friends.

The entire city supported baseball. Youth and American Legion games were carried on the radio. Crowds of adults would watch the kids, to enjoy the game and to see who the stars of the future would be. "Little Rock was a great place to grow up back then," says Tommy Lauderdale, a Legion teammate of Brooks's, "especially if you loved baseball. It would have made a good Norman Rockwell picture—us kids walking to Lamar Porter Field, carrying our gloves, with our bats over our shoulders."

The kids learned the value of competition at an early age. There were only so many spots available on the Pee Wee League teams. Those who didn't make it knew the only way to get a uniform next year was to work hard and get better. There were certainly no participation awards in those days; no trophies just for showing up. It was the ideal environment for the development of a professional baseball player.

Brooks's future American Legion coach, George Haynie, long

remembered the first time he ever saw him play in a Midget League (eleven- and twelve-year olds) game. Brooks pitched and lost 1–0. "I've never seen anybody so mad at himself in my life," Haynie said. "I told a friend that [Brooks] had the makings of a good player because [he] hated to lose." But he didn't lose often. Brooks played on a Midget team that won the Boys Club State Championship in 1948. His 1949 team won the city title, and his Standard Paints Company fourteen-and-under Boys Club team won the State Championship in 1950.

His play left a lasting impression on those who watched. Tommy Lauderdale, a teammate from the Pee Wee League through Legion ball, recalls, "He was always a great fielder. He could play any position. Even when he was a little kid, he had a great glove." The ability to catch a ball, to handle anything hit his way—Brooks seemed to have had that from the earliest age. Was there a secret to the development of his great fielding? Something a father could use to teach his son to become another Brooks Robinson? One thing that certainly helped was that Brooks was naturally left-handed—he wrote, played Ping-Pong and tennis, and did most other activities with his left hand—but played baseball right-handed. This allowed him to wear his glove on his dominant hand, improving the coordination he was able to use in wielding it. Otherwise, there were the hours he spent in the yard fielding grounders from his father and catching a tennis ball bounced off the steps of the front of the house. But this only placed him in a select group of perhaps one million other kids at the time who did the exact same thing, all dreaming of a professional baseball career. None of them went on to win 16 Gold Gloves.

Unfortunately, there was no real secret; nothing that can be replicated. While Brooks definitely put in the time and worked at it, he also possessed a magical, special talent; a unique combination of hand-eye coordination, reflexes, and body control. While Brooks often shared his methods with reporters over the years, those tips could not help anyone else become a great fielder. Just like Ted Williams, who possessed an inimitable ability for hitting but, although he became a prophet for the science of hitting, could not teach anyone else to hit .400, Brooks could not pass on his secret by mere words. The supernatural ability was there; it was honed and improved through constant repetition and would evolve over the years, but it was there from the start. It was something that would always make him different from everyone else.

As he grew, Brooks became known around town as one of the better athletes. He showed that he had a better arm than most kids his age when he won a prize in the junior distance softball throw in a Fourth of July contest when he was ten. Buddy Rotenberry recalls Brooks's reputation among the local kids: "We first met in grade school. We went to different schools. Back then, the elementary schools competed against each other in different sports. We played a touch football game against Woodruff, where Brooks went. Brooks played tailback in a single wing; kind of like a quarterback position. During pregame warm-ups, somebody came over and pointed him out, 'Look out for that guy throwing passes, he's really good.' We found out during the game that the guy had been right. He could throw the football 50 yards in sixth grade."

"His athletic ability in every sport was very obvious to everyone," says Robert Baird, one of Brooks's best friends in junior high and high school. "Everybody knew who he was going into junior high because of that."

In the ninth grade at Pulaski Heights Junior High, some friends on the football team talked Brooks into going out for the team. Coach Winston Faulkner, a tall, calm, slow-speaking man nicknamed "Preacher" by students, saw the talent and made Brooks the starting quarterback. Arkansas at the time was a football-mad state. The coaches usually picked the best athlete and groomed him to be quarterback—they didn't give the keys to the offense to just anybody. Brooks was a good quarterback, calling his own plays and helping the team to a 9–0–1 record and the junior high State Championship.

"He was smart and he could really throw the football," Faulkner recalled in 1978. While the team had two good backs for running the ball and didn't need Brooks to run, "we threw an awful lot, especially for a junior high team. We had a lot of stars . . . but we couldn't have done it without him."

Brooks was popular in junior high for his likable personality as well as his athletic talent. The first issue of the school paper in October

1951 had Brooks's mug gracing the front page in two separate spots: once, along with two other kids who were elected student council officers, and once as the paper's choice for the "Hall of Fame." The caption read, "For the first issue of our Tip Top Times this year, Heights has chosen for the Hall of Fame a boy who needs no introduction. He has made an outstanding record in his school work and athletics. . . . This last summer he played on the American Legion Doughboys, and last year he was on the Panther Basketball team. He was also president of Mr. Romine's boys in the eighth grade, and has done monitor's service for the school. . . . Yes, you're right; it is none other than Brooks Robinson."

2. "Everyone Liked Brooks"

LITTLE ROCK CENTRAL was no ordinary high school. Although the events of 1957 would permanently cast it in a certain light in history's eye, it was one of the most impressive schools in the country. When the majestic 600,000-square-foot, five-story building of brick and cast stone trim was constructed in 1927 at a cost of $1.5 million, *The New York Times* declared that it was the most expensive school building ever built in the United States. Originally called Little Rock Senior High School (the name was changed to Central in 1955 when construction was started on a school in west Little Rock), it was hailed as "America's Most Beautiful High School" by the National Association of Architects. Its opening was a nationwide media event, drawing reporters from both coasts. With nearly 3,000 students, it remained the largest high school in the country until the late 1940s. The architects of the school prominently placed four statues of Greek goddesses over the front entrance. Carved under them were the words *ambition, personality, opportunity,* and *preparation*. It is doubtful that any student ever represented these four traits better than Brooks Robinson, Jr., class of '55.

Brooks stood out. He was popular and outgoing, and possessed the kind of Pat Boone, clean-faced good looks that were valued at the time. He liked to have fun and he could tell a good story—frequently with himself as the butt of the joke. In addition to sports, he was thoroughly involved in other school activities, such as the Key Club and the student council. As a senior, he was voted "Best All-Around." In a southern town where reputation was held as gospel, Brooks's was sterling. He was the kind of guy fathers didn't mind too much when he showed up to take out their daughters.

"He was a happy guy," says Marshall Gazette, a close friend. "He had a good sense of humor. He liked the girls. He always had a girl-friend. He was always a guy who was just nice to everybody, whether the guy had money or didn't have any money. He knew everybody."

"He was always just so nice," says Glenda Gazette, Marshall's wife, who was a year behind them in high school. "Everyone liked Brooks."

"We had a group of friends of about 10 to 12 guys who were close-knit," says Buddy Rotenberry. "Our group of friends did not include just athletes. Brooks did not draw distinctions between athletes and nonathletes. His friends included people he thought had good character traits. You didn't have to play a sport to be his friend. And he was really just a regular teenager who liked to hang out with his friends, go on double dates, go to dances, and do the things regular teenagers did back then."

High school in Little Rock in the mid-1950s was typical of life everywhere in the United States in that era. Female teachers wore the Harlequin, pointy-rimmed glasses, males dark horn-rims. Girls wore skirts with blouses or sweaters to school—never pants or shorts. Cheerleaders wore long skirts that nearly reached their ankles; the only skin showing was from the crew neck up and below their elbows. Boys wore jeans with the bottoms rolled up a few inches above their penny loafers, exposing white socks. Most girls had short, curled hair, rarely longer than their shoulders. Boys had either crew cuts, like Brooks, or short hair parted on the side and combed straight back. Either way, it was cut very tight on the sides and never, ever strayed anywhere near their ears. There was no facial hair anywhere. Drug use was unfathomable.

The kids—and the community—had immense pride in their school, which had a reputation for sending outstanding students to top colleges around the country, often on scholarship, and routinely competed for state championships on the athletic fields. Not only was the Pledge of Allegiance repeated during homeroom each morning after the daily bulletin, but there was a short reading from the Bible as well. There were almost 550 students in Brooks's senior class, and, when viewed in the yearbook, they all seem homogeneous. Individuality was not particularly celebrated in 1955. The only thought given to diversity was whether or not to have green beans with their Tater Tots at lunch.

Popular music charts were dominated by Perry Como, Frank Sinatra, and Doris Day, but a new type of music, called rock 'n' roll, was catching on. Bill Haley and the Comets had a hit with "Shake, Rattle and Roll" in 1954 and then reached number one with "Rock Around the Clock." A little over 100 miles to the east, in Memphis, a young singer was rapidly gaining a large regional following with a revolutionary brand of music, hair, and swiveling hips. Elvis Presley would play in Little Rock twice in 1955 to moderate interest, but would not release his first national single, "Heartbreak Hotel," until January of 1956. Thereafter, teenagers, music, and hair would never be the same.

A favorite hangout in Brooks's neighborhood was Winkler's Drive-In across the street from Lamar Porter Field, but there were lots of similar drive-ins across the city. Carhops brought food to the cars, large jukeboxes blared hits for a nickel, and the pinball machines were always in use. Brooks and his friends didn't have cars, as most were in one-car families, and they usually walked to school. If someone got the family car for a day, it was a big deal and as many as six of them would pile in and drive around looking for fun.

Brooks was the kind of guy other kids naturally wanted to be around. "He had a way about him that just drew people to him," says Robert Nosari, a friend and Legion teammate. He was comfortable with his popularity and talent, but not conceited. The cup was always half full. That mixed with a natural, easygoing sense of humor and social confidence made him someone to look up to; someone coaches and teachers always picked out. Whereas in some teenage circles, these attributes could be annoying, or even provoke jealousy or ridicule, Brooks was able to pull it off as effortlessly as he turned ground balls with men on first into double plays. It was a different era with different values to be sure—a time when optimism, ambition, and regard for rules were acceptable—but also kids, who normally are acutely aware of hypocrisy, realized that with Brooks it was genuine, not an act.

"He had so much talent and so much going for him, but he was very humble," says Robert Baird, who grew up to be chairman of the Department of Philosophy at Baylor University. "He was not arrogant or presumptuous and that's why everyone liked him so much. You just naturally cheered for him and wanted him to do well. I think he saw his having been born into the family he was and the opportunities he had with good coaches and things and he saw these as gifts—maybe not articulated as such at that age—but he realized he was fortunate. I'm sure his parents had a lot to do with that."

While generally trouble-free, Brooks was not above a little mischief. He just knew how to pick his spots. Like the Great Lovers' Lane Boulder Caper. "The statute of limitations has run out on this now, so I guess it's okay to tell it," says Rotenberry, who recently retired after a forty-year career as a lawyer. "One night we were hanging around at a drive-in and someone came up with the big idea to have some fun at a local lovers' lane on Palisades Drive. It was a cul-de-sac in a new housing development that was going in over in west Little Rock. Couples would drive back there and park. Well, we rolled about three or four big boulders out of the construction area across the road, blocking the cars back in there—they couldn't get out. We probably knew most of the guys who were back there. I guess we made so much noise that someone called the cops and they pulled up just as we were finishing.

"Now, Brooks is a junior, named after his father who was on the fire department, and I was a third, and my grandfather had been chief of police in Little Rock for 13 years a while back. Little Rock was kind of a small city back then, so all the police knew who my grandfather was and most of them knew all the firemen. Neither of us went by our given name much back then, but when the police shined the flashlight in our faces and asked who we were, we both gave our complete names, hoping that they would go easy on us." He pauses. "It didn't work."

"You two in particular should know better," they were told.

"Well, maybe it did save us a trip downtown," Rotenberry continues. "Anyway, they made us move all the boulders back and told us to get home and not cause any more trouble. And that's about as deep in trouble as we ever got."

In many ways, Brooks and his classmates experienced a certain type of simplicity and innocence that is totally foreign to kids today. The country was in a period of unquestioned patriotism and prosperity. There was little opportunity, or seeming need, to question authority. Their heroes, like John Wayne and Audie Murphy, always wore white hats. There was no hint or fear that traditionally held virtues and beliefs would soon slip away. Vietnam was a little-known French colony on the other side of the world. Words and phrases like *civil disobedience, war protest, youth rebellion, the counterculture,* and *race riots*—words that would dominate the next decade, at the cost of the next generation's innocence—were never uttered.

Like the rest of the South at the time, the Little Rock that Brooks Robinson grew up in was a totally segregated society. Jim Crow dictated the accepted law of the land. There were as many as seven actual laws in Arkansas that mandated the separation of the races in virtually every aspect of life—from schools to prisons the races were physically separated by law.

African Americans, who made up 20 percent of the population of Little Rock in the 1930s, had what amounted to a separate city within a city on West Ninth Street, where black-owned businesses and culture flourished with pride. The high school, Dunbar, was the best "colored" high school in the state. Many African Americans moved into Little Rock seeking the educational opportunities afforded by Dunbar and nearby Philander Smith College.

Little Rock had a Negro minor league baseball team, the Little Rock Black Travelers. While both races enjoyed baseball, they supported their own teams. The park would be filled with a totally African American crowd when major league Negro teams, such as Willie Mays's Birmingham Black Barons or the always entertaining Indianapolis Clowns (who briefly had Hank Aaron), came to town for exhibitions. White fans seemed to have little interest in the Negro Leagues, unaware of the players who would shape the major leagues in the 1950s and 1960s. While Jackie Robinson's integrated barnstorming team of major league players was allowed to play in Little Rock in the early 1950s—the four white players had been forced to sit out games in Birmingham and Memphis due to strict prohibition of integrated play—sections in the stadium were roped off to ensure the fans remained seated with their own kind.

There was very little interaction between the races in everyday life in Little Rock. The only African American many of Brooks's contemporaries talked to on a regular basis was Sonny, the 250-pound maintenance man and groundskeeper at Lamar Porter Field. Sonny, who lived in rooms below the stadium, was generally quiet as he went about his work, but would sometimes provide kids with equipment that he had found lying around the field, and, for the ones who took the time to get to know him better, would even supply "simple but important lessons of life," according to Norris Guinn, a Lamar Porter Field diamond rat two years younger than Brooks. Once Guinn let the "n" word slip around Sonny and later felt bad and returned to apologize. "Sonny gave me instant forgiveness and then we had a long talk about colored people. He pointed out to me that he was a creature made by God just as I was and that the difference in our skin color did not matter. We talked about manners and respecting one's elders." Conversations between the races such as this were rare, however.

While they were prohibited by law from playing organized, integrated games, kids—especially grade-school-aged—occasionally played pickup games together. No adults interfered. "Sometimes we played against black kids from the other neighborhood in football games on the capitol grounds or the large field at the Deaf School," says Rotenberry. "Since our schools were segregated, that was about the only social contact I can remember either Brooks or myself having with kids of African American descent. They always wanted Brooks on their team. It didn't take another kid, black or white, long to recognize that Brooks was a bit more talented than most of the other kids. Brooks was friendly with the black kids, the same as with everyone else." But once the games were over, they went their separate ways.

Little Rock was a bit more progressive than other southern cities— the public libraries were integrated in the early 1950s without a peep. The *Brown v. Board of Education* ruling, which would end segregation in public schools, had been passed down in 1954, but states were still deciding how to implement it, and its impact on life in Little Rock was still two years away when Brooks and his friends graduated in 1955. Similarly, it was in December of 1955 when Rosa Parks refused to give up her seat on an Alabama bus and the civil rights movement began to become news—after the class of '55 had graduated and moved on. The amount of actual racial tension in the city of Little Rock depends on who you talk to, but it was rarely overt, even up until the mid-1950s. While it was something African Americans faced every day, most of the white kids gave it little thought. Brooks and his friends didn't cross the line and didn't know of the pain on the other side. They certainly noticed that "Negroes" had to enter the movie theater through a separate, side door and sit in the balcony, that they were never served at the drugstore counter, had to sit in a cramped, separate waiting room at the bus station, couldn't dare drink from the "Whites Only" drinking fountains or use the "Whites Only" restrooms. They might have sometimes realized that things weren't fair and that while, certainly separate, the facilities were by no means equal, as the law stated. But, for the most part, they rarely considered it. It was just the way things were, and had seemingly always been.

"I've thought back a lot on the subject," says Robert Baird, the philosophy professor. "I think at a young age you just take your environment as it's presented."

"We simply accepted segregation as a way of life without musing too much about the moral ramifications of it," says Buddy Rotenberry.

"Maybe we were just naive," says Robert Nosari, "but I don't think we really thought about it. It just didn't come up. We were busy playing and going to school and there was no sign of trouble. We were really totally separate with very little interaction. Of course, looking back, it's obvious that things weren't fair and that the system needed to change, but we just didn't think about it when we were growing up."

"After we left high school we confronted it," adds Baird. "We became more aware of the injustice of it all."

"With age, and the fact that everything was happening, our social conscience finally emerged," says Rotenberry, who in the 1960s left a successful law practice to form the first integrated law firm in the state and specialized in a broad spectrum of civil rights cases.

While some of Brooks's teammates and friends may have had

parents who zealously defended the system, including at least one teammate whose father was a "night rider" and a member of the Klan, many of them had parents who taught them that they shouldn't look down on "Negroes," or anyone else who was different. Brooks never showed any evidence of prejudice. He wrote in 1970, "I've just never believed in judging a man by such superficials as his skin." He recalled that once, when he mentioned to his mother that he had originally been afraid to meet some of the kids from the Deaf School because they were different, but later discovered that they were just regular kids who enjoyed playing sports, his mother (sounding like Atticus Finch) explained, "Most of us are afraid of what we don't know." Brooks, to the surprise of some future sportswriters who just assumed anyone from his high school would be a racist, never had trouble with future African American teammates. Somewhere in his upbringing, he had learned to treat everyone with respect.

While Brooks was a nice guy off the field, on it he was intensely competitive, a cold-blooded killer. He had a burning desire to be the best and to come out on top. It wasn't good enough to play well, he had to win. "We competed in everything," says Rotenberry. "Basketball, wrestling, you name it. He was the most competitive person I ever met. He had that ability, and I recognized it over the years in basketball in high school and baseball later, to rise to the occasion when things were tight. Maybe it was concentration or confidence or whatever, but he always seemed to do what it took to win."

Although he was encouraged by the coach, Brooks decided not to play football in high school. This was not a small decision at the time. Central's football team was in the middle of a string of state championships, led by a future Arkansas Hall of Fame coach. Brooks and his father were wary of an injury that might hurt his baseball career. "Brooks would have been a star in football," says Rotenberry, who was the center on the junior high football team. "He would have been the starting quarterback on a team that won the state championship and he would have been All-State. He had the agility and talent. The high school coach, Wilson Matthews, tried everything he could to get him on the football team, but it didn't work."

During the winters, Brooks played on the Central basketball team.

As a sophomore, he spent a lot of time on the bench in varsity games, but was a star for the junior varsity. "Our B-team [junior varsity] went 33–0," said Winston Faulkner, the JV coach. "Brooks was a natural. The only thing he lacked was speed. But he was quick. He was loose as a goose, and had some great moves. He was a good driver and had a good shot."

The next two years, Brooks was the leading scorer for the varsity, averaging around 17 points a game, and made first-team All-State. A guard with skinny arms and legs—made more prominent by the short-shorts, high-top canvas shoes, and droopy white socks of the time—he was a good ball handler and possessed a deadly shot from the corner. Not shy about contact, he usually was in the thick of things under the basket also.

While Brooks did not possess an impressive vertical game, he was a quick jumper with good hands and a natural sense of timing that helped him rebound. "He was the kind of guy who was always in the right place at the right time," says Harold Ellingson. "A rebound could bounce all the way to midcourt and he would just happen to be there."

"He wasn't big, but he was a good rebounder," said varsity coach George Haynie in 1978. "And he was cat quick. He was a smooth ball handler; he had good control of his body. And he could shoot." Although a lot of teams then played slow, pattern offenses, Central often picked the pace up. "We liked to fast break; run. Don't laugh. Brooks could get up and down the floor about as quick as any of them."

In Brooks's junior season, 1953–54, Central had a very good team. Unfortunately, rival Jonesboro had one of the best teams ever to come out of Arkansas up to that point. The undefeated Jonesboro team beat Central twice during the regular season, once by only one point in Little Rock. Central got hot thereafter and breezed through the rest of the season and the early rounds of the state tournament. The two teams met again in the semifinals. Down by 10 in the second half, Little Rock put on a furious rally and moved ahead by one point with a minute to play. Two late missed shots proved fatal, however, and they lost by a single point. Although he had scored several key baskets during the rally, Brooks missed a layup late in the game and was crushed with disappointment. He later wrote that after the game, Coach Haynie, although disappointed also, consoled him and said, "Brooks, remember that one shot doesn't make a game or one game a season. Now take a shower; you've got a lot more big games ahead."

"On the bus coming back, Brooks told me that he'd lost the game for us," recalled Haynie in 1978. "He didn't lose it, I did. Brooks has never lost at anything."

In the Dell 1954 preseason basketball yearbook, the name Brooks Robinson appears as one of the 500 high school basketball players to watch in the country. Central had lost several starters and had a new coach, Lawrence Mobley, for the 1954–55 season but they were still good. A picture in the *Arkansas Gazette* of Brooks and fellow guard Ray Wilson noted, "[Wilson and Robinson] are among the best hereabouts at bringing the ball down court, but they don't stop there. The senior scrappers are also the Tigers' best scorers and ballhawks, just about the best guard twosome since the title teams of 1944–47." Their harassing defense frequently made life miserable for opposing ball handlers trying to get the ball into the frontcourt. In the end-of-season tournament, Brooks scored 46 points in leading the Tigers to wins in the first two games, but fouled out, along with three other starters, in a 51–47 semifinal loss to Fort Smith and his high school basketball career was over.

"The thing that sticks out in my mind [that season] was the way Brooks adjusted to me," coach Mobley later said. "We were putting in a new system and a new style of play. The only thing I ever heard out of Brooks was 'yes sir' or 'yes coach.' Whatever I asked, and I asked a lot that first year, Brooks never questioned. And that's not always the case with a new coach and a successful athlete." This ability to accept authority would be a Brooks Robinson characteristic that would be recognized and appreciated throughout his athletic career. It would benefit him greatly as he progressed professionally.

Brooks played basketball well enough to attract a full scholarship offer to attend the University of Arkansas. Had he been interested, there were other suitors throughout the South as well. "I know he could have gone to Arkansas and LSU on scholarships," said Haynie. "He would have been the quarterback; the ball handler."

While he enjoyed basketball, Brooks never had any doubt that baseball was to be his future. When he was in the eighth grade his English teacher had assigned a term paper in which the students were to write about their future careers. Brooks titled his paper "Why I Want to Play Professional Baseball." He explained why he thought the life of a ballplayer was desirable: "the hours are good" and "ballplayers are paid very well." He added, "In playing baseball you will meet many people, sportswriters from leading newspapers, leading baseball players, umpires and few of the fans." Part of the assignment was to evaluate their dispositions, and Brooks wrote, "Slow to anger, not easily discouraged, enthusiastic, happy, calm, and active." The impressive thing about the paper is not the prose or grammar skills, but how accurately Brooks assessed his personality traits at 13 and how much those traits remained with him as an adult, along with his enjoyment meeting writers, players, umpires, and fans.

3. The Doughboys

AS SOMEONE WHO WANTED a future in baseball, Brooks was lucky in that Little Rock possessed one of the best American Legion baseball programs in the region. The Doughboys of M. M. Eberts Post No. 1 were a Little Rock institution. Started in 1930, the team was named after the American infantrymen of World War I. George Haynie, who had played for them in 1933 and 1934, coached the Doughboys from 1947 to 1953. An ex–Louisiana State University athlete, he was personable and had a good way with kids. He was also the basketball and track coach at Little Rock Central. Haynie would become one of the most important men in the development of young Brooks Robinson.

George Haynie was a winner and a role model. "Everybody who played for George Haynie respected him," says Robert Nosari. "He was a great coach. If you played for George Haynie, you knew the fundamentals of the game." Haynie was strict but fair and believed in hard work. He preached an aggressive, hitting-and-running, bunting style of baseball and was serious about the small details.

There was no time for regular summer jobs for the members of the Doughboys. They practiced at Lamar Porter every day they didn't have a game. The three-hour practices, starting at noon, were efficiently organized with no wasted time as Haynie put the boys through continuous drills. The only relief from the midday heat was 100 pounds of chipped ice purchased at a nearby gas station. But the players didn't mind all that practice too much. "Most of the boys on the team were hardworking boys," says Tommy Lauderdale, who played in 1952 and 1953. "You didn't get no free ride back then. My daddy was in the roofing business—I had plenty of work to do when I wasn't playing ball. I played baseball to get away from working. Let me tell you, those roofs got awful hot in Arkansas in the summer."

"George Haynie was a very knowledgeable baseball man," says Harold Ellingson, who played on the 1952 and 1953 teams. "He was a stickler on fundamentals. He taught me things that when I signed with the Yankees and went to spring training, the guys there had never heard of. The play Brooks later made famous, coming in from third full speed and barehanding the ball and throwing to first in the same motion, Haynie taught us that. He'd have us there at third on a 100 degree day at high noon and he'd drop balls along the third base line and make us charge them and throw to first and do it again and again. That's where Brooks learned that play. Back then, there weren't that many good coaches, probably a lot less now. We were lucky to have a guy like George Haynie."

"Coach Haynie was one of the best guys I ever met in my life," adds Lauderdale. "Just an all-around good guy. We called him the Gentleman Genius of the South or Gentleman George. He was a good coach. He wanted you to work hard but he didn't scream and cuss or raise hell to get his point across. He was more of a tactical trainer. He had been a great athlete in his day. He was only about 10 years older than us and he could still run faster backwards than most of us could run forwards. He had a very nice wife who would come to a lot of the away games with us and help."

In addition to learning to play great baseball, the players had a lot of fun and developed lasting friendships. Being normal teenage guys, they didn't always follow the rules, but their transgressions seem mild compared to modern-day troubles. Haynie tried to impart wisdom and guidance. He didn't like his boys to chew tobacco, though one player famously puked after sneaking it during a game, and another, who could hold it better, was known to teammates as Slobberface Joe, because it sometimes dribbled down his chin. Once, on the team bus, Haynie lectured the boys on the evils of alcohol, telling them, "Drinking beer is just like drinking horse piss." From the back of the bus, one of the kids with a known appetite for the stuff yelled, "Somebody pass me some horse piss."

George Haynie had a way of inspiring loyalty and respect in his men and had a tremendous influence on them that lasted a lifetime. "Coach Haynie always tried to push us to be better," says Ted Rogers, who played in 1952–53. "You really wanted to please him. Even years later, after the 1970 World Series, someone got a film of highlights and some of us got together to watch them. Coach Haynie was there and some of the guys had a beer or two, but I was ashamed to let him see me drink a beer—I was only thirty-four at the time."

There was a lot of baseball talent in Little Rock and the Doughboys were the only Legion team in town. At the time in Arkansas, large schools that had football programs did not have baseball teams, so Legion ball was the only opportunity for high school–aged kids. The Doughboys regularly had players sign to play professional baseball. The 1952 team, for instance, had 11 players who eventually signed and the 1953 team had seven. "It meant something to be a Doughboy," Haynie said in 1988. "It was as competitive as heck. There was a lot of pride and a lot of winning tradition." Winning tradition? The Doughboys won 15 state titles in 25 years—six in Haynie's seven seasons.

"We played all over," says Lauderdale. "A lot of teams in the state didn't want to play us because we were so good. We had a bus, an old school bus, it had M. M. Ebberts Post No. 1 on it. Coach Haynie drove the bus—he was a jack-of-all-trades. We went out of state a lot to find good teams to play."

Brooks Robinson first made the Doughboys in 1951. Easily the smallest player on the team, he wasn't quite fourteen years old. Most of his teammates were sixteen or seventeen. In the team picture, Brooks, barely 5-foot-5, looks like the batboy. But he certainly earned his way on the team. A good coach can spot details others might miss; he can see the potential that a year of growth and maturity will bring. Haynie knew what Brooks could become. He also knew Brooks's reputation. "We picked him up early," Haynie said later. "Brooks always had a lot of natural ability. No one was quicker the first two or three steps."

A big event for the Doughboys each year was the 470-mile drive to Altus, Oklahoma, for the annual Tri-State Fourth of July Legion Tournament, featuring teams from Oklahoma, Arkansas, and Kansas. The Little Rock boys traveled by bus and stayed a week in the Hotel

Altus—the first time many of them had ever been away from home. Altus had a great Legion program at the time, featuring future major league pitchers Eddie Fisher and Lindy McDaniel. In the first round in 1951, with McDaniel shutting down the Doughboys, Haynie sent Brooks up to pinch-hit. Though surprised since he hadn't seen much action to that point, Brooks hit a double down the left field line, one of the high points of his season. Although Brooks didn't play a lot that year and the Doughboys failed to make the state tournament for the first time in 10 years, it was a valuable season of experience.

Sometimes the youngest, smallest member of a team can be in a precarious position—especially when there is such a disparity in size and age as Brooks faced that year. Sometimes the older kids, through jealousy or just plain meanness, pick on the younger kid or lure him into bad habits. But there was little of this on the Doughboys. "The older guys on the team looked after him," says Rotenberry. "Now, there were a few known hell-raisers on that team, but for the most part they knew Brooks was a straight arrow and they didn't try to lead him astray."

The next season, Brooks was a regular and the Doughboys were a strong team. They beat the host club in the early round of the Altus Tournament to break Altus's 31-game winning streak. They won the Arkansas State Championship and traveled to Ponchatoula, Louisiana, for the regional tournament. They made it to the finals before losing to Austin, Texas, 3–2. Brooks hit well over .300 and was beginning to find that he was one of the better all-around players in that part of the country for his age.

He made an impression on Eddie Fisher, who would later be a teammate on the 1966 Orioles, in his yearly trip to Altus. "We saw a lot of good players," says Fisher. "I think the competition overall was tougher back then—things seem more diluted now, but Brooks stood out. After watching a few games of the tournament, everyone knew who the best players were. You could just tell that Brooks was a good natural athlete. He had all the moves. He was a very intelligent athlete, very mature for his age, I remember that." A dozen years later, while a member of the Orioles, Fisher would tell reporters, "Brooks was as good a third baseman [then] as he is now."

In 1953, the Doughboys were even better. Coming out of the losers' bracket in the Altus Tournament, they won the title by winning two games from Topeka, Kansas, the last day, with Brooks getting two doubles and a single in the first game and a double and a single in the finals. The Doughboys won the Arkansas State Championship for the second consecutive year. They advanced to the regionals, traveling once again to Ponchatoula, Louisiana. They went undefeated through the early rounds of the tournament, needing only one more win to advance to the sectionals in South Carolina, but lost two games the last day to Monroe, Louisiana. It was a bittersweet end to a great season.

The year 1954 marked the end of an era of sorts for Little Rock American Legion baseball. The organizers instituted drastic changes, forming a local league of eight teams. While this gave many more boys a chance to play, it hurt the team's chances of going far in the state tournament. Also, Coach Haynie had left town to take a job with Johnson & Johnson. Brooks played on a collection of All-Stars from the league called the Radio Center Videos, which was thrown together shortly before the tournaments started.

By this time, having just finished his junior year of high school, Brooks had filled out and possessed legitimate home run power, several times hitting two in one game. He was now easily the best player on the field most games. Brooks hit cleanup and also pitched quite a bit. As a pitcher, he was described in the *Arkansas Gazette* as a "hard-throwing righthander," after he beat a team from Oklahoma 6–2 with 10 strikeouts.

Brooks dominated the Altus Tournament in 1954 as Little Rock won it for the third straight year. "Robinson Dazzles Altus with Slants, Slugging in 18–6 Win," the *Gazette* blared after Brooks pitched a five-hitter to beat the home team. He had a three-run triple in the third inning and a grand slam in the fifth. The next day, in the championship game, Brooks hit a drive off the boards in left center, 370 feet away, for a two-run double to cap a four-run ninth-inning rally in an 8–7 win over Topeka. Brooks was named the tournament MVP after hitting .647 with 12 RBIs. Brooks's American Legion career soon ended as the Little Rock team fell in the state tournament.

Brooks played more second base than he did third base in American Legion ball. Haynie felt he was the best on the team at making the double play pivot at second, but his talent was evident no matter where he played. The memory he left on his teammates has as much to do with his attitude as with his glove. "I have lots of funny stories about some of the other guys on the team who were a little less interested in following rules," says Ted Rogers. "But I don't have any good ones on Brooks because he always did what he was supposed to. There were some guys who might have had more talent and physical ability on our team but Brooks was by far the most dedicated. He did the right things and got better. Coach Haynie would always hold Brooks up to us. Once he was lecturing us on not being dedicated enough. He asked me how I got to practice and I said, 'I rode my motorcycle.' And he said, 'See there. Brooks walks or runs to practice.' But we laughed at Brooks because he only lived a few blocks away."

"In Legion ball, Brooks was good, he could play any infield position," says Harold Ellingson. "He was very versatile and very talented. He was a great fielder; that was his strong point. He had quick hands and reflexes. He got rid of the ball so quick. That was all there in Legion ball. He was a good hitter too."

"I'm not sure Brooks was always the best player on our teams," says Tommy Lauderdale, who signed with the Brooklyn Dodgers. "There were a lot of good players there. Most of them signed professionally. We had some big boys on the Legion team. A lot of the guys had more physical strength than he did. You certainly wouldn't have picked him to be a future Hall of Famer at that age. I would definitely say that he was more dedicated and more persistent than anyone else, especially after he left Little Rock for the pros. But he always had a good glove, regardless of what position he played. He made a lot of great plays in the field as a kid. I saw him make every kind of play that he later did in the majors—he made the same types of plays with the Doughboys."

"Nobody could field like Brooks," says Rogers. "Nothing got by him. Even in Legion ball you could see that he was a better fielder than anybody else we played."

Looking back at his time managing American Legion ball, in 1988 Haynie said, "Of course, times have changed. The thing now is to play to win. We didn't play to win, we played to learn. We played to have fun. That more than anything else, is my coaching style— you've got to learn and have fun. . . . I think the big difference is that most of the young folks then had a role model. I'm not sure the kids today do."

The importance of role models was not lost on Brooks Robinson. In later years, when he achieved professional success, he was acutely aware of his image and vocal about his obligation as an example for youngsters. There had been a number of great role models in Little Rock when Brooks was growing up. Kids only needed to listen to them and take their messages to heart. In addition to Brooks's greatest role model, Brooks Robinson, Sr., and George Haynie, there were many others. Like Mr. Breezy, the enormous ex–professional wrestler who ran the concession stand at Lamar Porter Field. Kids had to stay on his good side to get the choice jobs. An imposing man with cauliflower ears and arms covered with tattoos, Breezy loved to joke and laugh and was actually "a gentle giant who took kids under his wings" and helped keep them in line, according to Norris Guinn. There was Billy Mitchell, who ran the Little Rock Boys' Club for decades. There was Lee Rogers, who owned Spaulding's Athletic Store downtown. Rogers had been a great athlete in his youth, pitching for the Brooklyn Dodgers after playing football for a University of Alabama team that featured two other Arkansas boys of note, Paul (later known more widely as Bear) Bryant and Don Hutson. Rogers became a driving force behind amateur baseball in Little Rock, loved to teach young players about sports, and always made sure kids, even the ones who couldn't afford it, had the right equipment.

On the air, there was Benny Craig, the Colonial Bread Man. In the early days of Little Rock television, Benny, who frequently coached youth baseball teams in his spare time, read the nightly sports for Channel 11 dressed in a bread truck driver's uniform with a policeman's hat with the Colonial Bread insignia on top. He also sat on the windowsill of the station and broadcast a sort of play-by-play— reenacted from a ticker tape report—for the Travelers baseball games over the radio. He frequently told his audience, "And remember boys and girls, it never costs an extra cent to be a good sport," and always gave his signature sign-off, "This is the Old Bread Man say-ing good-bye, and remember, no one ever stood as straight as the one who stoops to help a child."

Role models—many kids passed these men every day and never took the time to learn from them. Others accumulated their advice somewhere deep in their subconscious and applied it to their charac-ter. Brooks Robinson was certainly in the right place at the right time for a boy who wanted to be a baseball player; and also for a young man to build great character. And, unlike the player who is in the way of a hard smash but fails to field it cleanly, Brooks took advan-tage of the opportunities his environment provided.

Brooks attracted quite a bit of attention from scouts for his play in American Legion ball. In the early 1950s Major League Baseball was still more than a decade away from instituting an organized player draft. Any amateur player could sign with any team. There was a well-orchestrated dance between prospects and their suitors. First, the bird dogs showed up. These were men, often retired, who had played or coached or both in their younger days and who still loved the game. Often, they were only paid a bounty if players they recom-mended made it. Sometimes they weren't paid at all, gladly perform-ing their chores as a labor of love. Bird dogs were at most of the Doughboys' games. The kids knew who they were and could pick them out in the stands, such as the massive Yankee rep who always sat down the third base line.

The bird dogs dutifully passed on news about potential players and then the real scouts took over. The scouts got to know the player and his family, often becoming a semipermanent fixture over the course of a season for players they liked. They wined and dined the prospect and the good ones found out which parent needed to be but-tered up the most. Successful scouts became quite accomplished at this routine; many kids ended up signing with a team based on the fact that they liked the scout. Of course when there was doubt, a bo-nus helped seal the deal.

By the early 1950s, major league owners realized that they were wasting an ever-increasing amount of money on bonuses to kids who did not pan out and admitted to the fact that they could not control themselves in their zeal. To remedy this, they instituted the short-lived, much reviled bonus baby rule. This rule stated that if a prospect signed for a bonus of more than an outlandish amount (outlandish in the 1950s was defined as $4,000), the player had to spend two years on the active major league roster before he could be sent to the minors. While this rule may or may not have slowed the payment of large bonuses (there were many tales of extra money being given under the table), it had one very bad side effect: the bonus babies often wasted away on the major league bench instead of getting the training they needed playing against players their own age in the minors. Many bonus babies never made it due to this fact.

In February of 1955, Paul Richards, new general manager and manager of the Baltimore Orioles, received a letter from a former teammate on the Atlanta Crackers named Lindsay Deal who lived in Little Rock. Deal informed Richards of a prospect who just happened to attend the same church, Capitol View Methodist. "Dear Paul," he wrote. "I am writing to you in regard to a youngster named Brooks Robinson. I think he measures up to having a chance in major league baseball. I think he is a natural third baseman although he has been playing both second and third. He will be 18 years old May 18 and graduates from Little Rock Senior High School on May 27. He is 6-foot, one-inch in height and weighs 175. His physique is outstanding for a boy this age. . . . He is no speed demon but neither is he a truck horse. I believe in a year or two he will be above average in speed. He hit well over .400 last year in American Legion baseball. . . . Brooks has a lot of power, baseball savvy, and is always cool when the chips are down. This boy is the best prospect I've seen since Billy Goodman came to Atlanta to play when I was playing there. . . . This boy can go to most any university in the Southwest on a scholarship and will do so if he doesn't receive a contract in major league baseball. I know his parents well; in fact, we attend the same church.

"He has been bird-dogged by scouts for the past three years. . . . Hope this finds you and your family in good health. Best wishes for a successful season."

After Brooks became a major league star, the letter was reprinted often, appearing in *Baseball Digest*, the *Sporting News*, *Sports Illustrated*, and Brooks's 1971 and 1974 autobiographies. While it was a nice gesture and makes a quaint story, in reality if the Orioles did not already know about Brooks Robinson, they were in the distinct minority. As the best player on the best Legion team in a state known for baseball, Brooks was a recognized quantity. He had been more than bird-dogged, as he had been contacted by at least 12 of the 16 major league teams.

Although he was considered to be one of the top players in the area, and it was obvious from games that he could play baseball, there were some doubts, mainly about his physique, arm, and speed. "If you saw Brooks in the locker room without his shirt on, he was not impressive," says Rotenberry. "There were no rippling muscles and no six-pack abs. He didn't have a lean muscular build. Actually, our gang had a nickname for him, Jugbutt, because he had what you could call a protruding derriere."

"You'd want Brooks running behind you if a bear was chasing you," says Tommy Lauderdale. "It'd catch him before it got to you."

"Brooks had kind of a distinctive run," adds Rogers. "We used to joke that you could always tell it was him because he was in the same place so long."

Brooks possessed the type of speed that would one day allow him to steal as many as two bases in a single major league season (actually three in 1962 and 1965). Jokes aside, while Brooks's speed did not impress anyone, he was definitely not a turtle. In the spring of his senior year, Brooks went out for the track team solely for the purpose of improving his speed for baseball. He ended up running the 880 and came in second in the state with a time of 2:05, five seconds off the state record at the time.

But given scouts' reluctance to take a chance on someone who doesn't fit the charts, Brooks was lucky to be so highly regarded. In 1963 Oriole scout Ray Scarborough told reporters that Brooks might have trouble being signed in modern times. "A boy like Robinson throws scouting procedures into a cocked hat because the first things they tell you to look for in a prospect are the two natural things— running and throwing." Scarborough added that every once in a while a player comes along who turns out to be so outstanding at the major league level, it makes a scout wonder if he shouldn't deviate more often in what he thinks are the most important prerequisites.

One thing the Orioles had in their favor that made them appreciate the true baseball qualities of Brooks Robinson was the philosophy of their scouting director Jim McLaughlin, who was clearly ahead of his time. McLaughlin became the central figure in helping the Orioles construct championship teams built largely on home-grown talent. He pioneered the use of the cross-checker, a second scout brought in to test the opinion of the first scout. He was also one of the first baseball executives to judge players mentally as well as physically. In the Orioles' scouting book, each player was represented by a circle, with the physical tools listed in the upper half and the mental abilities in the lower half. "The lower half was guts, competitiveness, work ethic, integrity," longtime scout Jim Russo said in 2004, "and McLaughlin believed that half was just as important. That was an original thought for back then." Brooks certainly maxed out on the lower half of the chart.

As Brooks's senior year of high school progressed, many baseball clubs talked to him and it became apparent that he would be getting professional offers. He was torn between accepting the baseball offers, which he had been dreaming of his whole life, or taking the basketball scholarship and becoming the first in his family to attend college, as he felt his mother wanted him to do. The family had frequent conferences at the dinner table. While his parents made sure Brooks was aware of their opinions, the decision was ultimately left to him.

The Arkansas basketball coach did not help his own cause. "Glen Rose was famous for being a bad recruiter," says Rotenberry. "He felt Arkansas kids should just naturally come to him. He wouldn't usually walk across the street to get to them. But he made an effort to go get Brooks. He told Brooks that he had talked to Fred Hahn, who was the Cardinals' chief scout for the area, and Hahn said that Brooks wasn't good enough in baseball to make the majors, that he would be lucky to top out at Double or Triple A. Rose told Brooks that he should go to the university on the basketball scholarship and get an education so he could support a family later. I think that hurt Brooks's feelings."

"Glen Rose, the basketball coach at Arkansas, really wanted Brooks," says Brooks's brother, Gary. "When I went to Arkansas on a football scholarship in 1960, Coach Rose saw me and said, 'Gary, I offered Brooks a basketball scholarship and I told him he was making a mistake going to play baseball. But I guess I was wrong.'"

In reality, Brooks had been set on a career in baseball for a long time. It was just a question of where. And that was a big question. In some ways, the modern draft makes it easier for kids—they just go where they are picked. It could be a daunting task for an eighteen-year-old who had rarely been away from home, except for team trips, to make such an important decision. Once again, Brooks Sr. came through for his son. The role he played in guiding Brooks and helping him intelligently evaluate the options cannot be overstated. He studied and became thoroughly familiar with the teams and the rules to help make the correct choice and to avoid the pitfalls that affected the careers of so many other prospects. "Brooks really got some good advice from his father," says Ellingson. "He really helped him out in making the right choice in so many ways. I wish I could have had someone like that to advise me." Ellingson became buried in the overstocked Yankee farm system as the parent club regularly picked up veterans to bolster its perennial championship drives.

Teams were not allowed to sign a player until after high school graduation. Brooks and his father had dinner with many of the scouts, listened to their spiels, and knew the level of interest and how far each was willing to go. While Brooks had a high opinion of his abilities, he also knew his limitations, and both he and his father agreed that he needed some time in the minors to develop properly and so he didn't want to sign for more than $4,000 and be confined to a major league bench for two years. At the same time, they decided that if a ridiculous amount was offered, say over $30,000, they would have to consider that.

The other thing they wanted, though, was a major league contract. Under the rules at the time a player signed to a minor league contract could yo-yo between the big club and the minors for six years.

The team had three options in the minors and three more after the player had made the majors. Signing a major league contract meant that the team had only three options; then another club had a chance to pick the player up—this lessened the chance of withering in the minors.

After talking and studying, the Robinsons felt the Reds, Giants, and Orioles held the best prospects for Brooks. As graduation—and the time for a decision—neared, Brooks and his father decided to give each team representative 45 minutes to make his best offer. They met the scouts one at a time in their living room; Mrs. Robinson put on a pot of coffee, and each man gave his pitch.

The Giants went first and offered $4,000 but only a minor league contract. Next was Paul Florence, representing the Reds. He offered $4,000 and a major league contract. The Robinsons listened as Florence detailed the Reds' plans for Brooks in their development program. The Reds had been a weak team for a number of years and didn't possess a large amount of talent. That was a good thing for a young prospect who wanted a less impeded road to the big leagues. Florence was a likable man with a good living room manner, and as he left, the Robinsons felt Cincinnati would be a good fit.

Art Ehlers for the Orioles went last. The Orioles had shown more interest than anyone else that spring. Ehlers explained that the Orioles would offer a major league contract but apologized that, although they were very high on Brooks, the biggest bonus they could offer was $4,000. The Oriole bonus money would be going to Wayne Causey from Monroe, Louisiana, whom Brooks had played against twice in the Ponchatoula regionals. Causey, who had been MVP of the regionals in 1953, was stronger and more physically mature at that point and would command a bonus in the $30,000 range. Ehlers explained that the Oriole system was almost bare of young talent—much more bare than Cincinnati's—and that if Brooks showed what they expected in the minors, he would have a much better chance of moving up to the majors with Baltimore than any other team. This was what Paul Richards had also indicated when he had talked to Brooks on the phone earlier.

Brooks and his parents informed the scouts that they would discuss the offers and make a decision. The scouts retreated to their hotels to wait. The next day, Brooks called the Giants' and Reds' representatives and thanked them for their offers but turned them down (one of them thanked him for at least calling, noting that very few prospects took the time to extend that courtesy). Then he called Ehlers to inform him of the good news. Ehlers quickly returned to their house and the deed was done. Brooks Robinson, Jr., was now property of the Baltimore Orioles.

4. Welcome to the Baltimore Orioles

THE ORGANIZATION BROOKS ROBINSON had joined was a new product. The glory days of Baltimore Major League Baseball had been in the 1890s with the National League Baltimore Orioles of Wee Willie Keeler hitting them where they weren't and John McGraw and his band of ruffians. The Orioles had been one of the National League teams dropped after the 1899 season. In 1901, the team was revived, this time as a member of the start-up American League. After two seasons, however, the franchise moved to New York and the name was changed to the Highlanders. They soon became successful in the Bronx and changed their name again, this time to the Yankees.

Thereafter, Baltimore was a minor league baseball city. Playing in the International League, the Orioles had their moments. They signed a rambunctious left-handed pitcher named George Ruth out of a local orphanage. Although the kid, later known more widely as Babe, played less than a full season in Baltimore before being sold to the Red Sox, he left quite an impression. The Orioles later won seven straight pennants in the 1920s.

In 1944, Oriole Park burned to the ground. Good fortune arose from this tragedy, however, as the mayor of Baltimore, seeing the possibilities, convinced the team to move into Municipal Stadium, a much larger facility on 33rd Street. Baltimore, wanting to bill itself as a major league city after World War II, further renovated and enlarged the park (renaming it Memorial Stadium to honor the war dead) to accommodate pro football. Playing in the expansive Memorial Stadium, the Orioles drew more fans than several major league teams, a fact that did not go unnoticed, particularly by poor-drawing, losing clubs in two-team cities, such as the Boston Braves, Philadelphia A's, and St. Louis Browns.

The St. Louis Browns had been in the American League since 1902. They were always easy to find—one only had to look at the bottom of the standings. The Browns finished in last place 14 times and second-to-last another 12. It had taken a world war to get the Browns into the World Series. In 1944 when most able-bodied baseball players were in the military, the Browns swept into the postseason for the lone time in their existence, only to lose. Once the war ended and the real players returned, the Browns returned to their customary place in the basement.

Playing in miserable Sportsman's Park, the Browns could never get fans to come to their games—they rarely drew more than 300,000 a year. From 1902 to 1953, the Browns had exactly one sold-out crowd of 35,500 at home—the last day of their pennant-winning season. According to one story, the Browns' Charlie DeWitt once went to give the visiting Yankees their share of the gate from a game in St. Louis. The Yankee road secretary looked at the three dollars and fifty cents and, with pity for DeWitt, said, "Keep it."

Maverick owner Bill Veeck purchased the Browns in 1951 with visions of running the Cardinals out of town and taking over St. Louis. Unfortunately, beer baron August Busch soon purchased the Cardinals, and Veeck, hopelessly outgunned by the deep pockets of Busch, knew the Browns were doomed. Seeing opportunity, a group of businessmen from Baltimore organized and lobbied hard to get the team for their city. At the end of the 1953 season, Veeck sold out and Baltimore was back in the big leagues. The last game in St. Louis, the Browns fittingly used up all of their remaining game balls in an extra-inning affair and were forced to use dirty batting practice balls to finish the game—the St. Louis Browns were literally out of the baseball business.

Meanwhile, the city of Baltimore was ecstatic at the prospect of the return of Major League Baseball. The arrival of the NFL franchise in Baltimore earlier in 1953 had excited local fans, but at the time, pro football was not yet popular and the Colts drew only 28,000 to their first game. Baseball was unquestionably the national pastime, and with only 16 major league teams, having one was a significant status symbol for a city. "It was a major turning point in Baltimore's development," Thomas D'Alesandro III, the son of the mayor who was instrumental in bringing in the Orioles and also a mayor himself, said in 2003. "Not only was it important economically, but also in terms of the spirit of the city. It provided common ground. White, black, fat, thin, healthy, sick: Everyone could relate to them."

The Baltimore ownership group was eager to make the team its own—it became essentially a new team. Of the five baseball franchises that moved in the 1950s (the Dodgers, Giants, Braves, and Athletics were the others), only the shift of the Browns to Baltimore resulted in a new team name. A single member of the front office of the Browns made the move, farm director Jim McLaughlin; otherwise, they were starting from scratch.

The new Orioles were given a hero's welcome in Baltimore. An estimated 350,000 people turned out for a parade before the 1954 home opener. Players sat on the backseats of convertibles amid twenty-two bands and thirty-three floats. The fans treated the last place collection of rag-armed pitchers and castoffs as though they were World Series champs. The city was awash in the team's colors. Vice President Richard Nixon, who had ridden in the parade with his wife and two daughters, threw out the first pitch. After the Orioles won their opening game, a *Baltimore News-Post* editorial called it "the most thrilling day in Baltimore history since the bombardment of Fort McHenry in the War of 1812."

The club leadership picked fifty-seven-year-old Jimmy Dykes to manage the Orioles in 1954. Dykes had a good sense of humor and excellent baseball knowledge. Saddled with little talent, he needed the former much more than the latter to get through the season. The team finished with exactly the same won-lost record as the year before, 54–100. Dykes's most memorable contribution was to tie mistletoe to the back loop of his pants late in the season to give his detractors a suggestion for something to kiss.

The citizens of Baltimore, still giddy over having a major league team, were mostly forgiving for the on-field product, hoping that better days were ahead, and the team drew over a million fans the first season. Oriole ownership realized that the good graces would soon wear out if a decent team was not put forth, however. They fired Dykes after the 1954 season and decided to bring in someone who could build an entire organization from scratch. They found the perfect man in forty-seven-year-old Paul Richards and turned over the keys. As the first combination manager–general manager in baseball since John McGraw, Richards had free rein over all baseball decisions. Few men in baseball have ever wielded the power Paul Richards had over the Orioles—he controlled everything; the undisputed king.

A tall, thin, square-jawed Texan with brown, steely eyes and a constant tan, Richards had gotten his start in professional baseball in the late 1920s. After a career as an excellent defensive catcher with the Dodgers, Giants, A's, and Tigers, Richards had started managing in 1938 with the Atlanta Crackers, soon moved to the majors, and, over those years, had never been fired—a unique accomplishment for a manager. Hired by the White Sox in 1951, he had turned that perennially losing franchise into a consistent first division team by emphasizing speed and defense.

A taciturn man, Richards was viewed by the men who played for him as withdrawn and aloof. He would get on an elevator with a player and not exchange even a simple acknowledgment. Or he would get up from the bench, walk over to a coach, and tell him to pass on instructions to a player who was sitting next to him. Or, walking through a hotel lobby late at night with the coaches and seeing a wayward player coming in after curfew, rather than address the player himself he would turn to pitching coach Harry Brecheen and say, "Brecheen, is that one of your pitchers?"

Gus Triandos voices what many players thought about Richards when he says, "I always liked Richards. I don't know if he liked me. It was hard to tell what he thought."

Aware of his reputation, Richards explained to reporters, "No manager ever tries to win the love of his players. All he needs is their respect."

There was no doubt that Paul Richards had the respect of his players. All marveled at his baseball knowledge and preparation. Richards was a renowned rehabber of pitchers, usually teaching them his favorite, the slip pitch (a version of the palm ball), allegedly along with a more damp pitch that he sometimes favored. There was a cool sureness in his manner that left no room for second-guessing. During games, in addition to being an expert tactician, Richards was known to be a fierce competitor and relentless umpire battler. One umpire, in naming Richards as the number one enemy of his colleagues, said, "No one ever used more profane language. This fellow thought up words of his own."

There was never any doubt about who was in charge when Paul Richards was around—he ruled his team with an iron fist. One exasperated pitcher, upon leaving Richards's office after a good butt chewing, slammed the door and announced to the clubhouse, "He thinks he's God." And that was about right. Paul Richards *was* God as far as the Baltimore Orioles were concerned—and if a player didn't believe it, Richards would gladly walk across the water of the whirlpool and explain it to him.

Richards was a fanatic about fundamentals and especially believed in the importance of teaching young players. He frequently said that when he had come up as a player, there had been essentially no instructions—they were on their own to fight for scraps of knowledge in the dog-eat-dog world of too many prospects for too few major league slots. As ruler of the entire system, Richards trained the managers and coaches for his farm teams to ensure they could listen to a single authority (him) and made it a specific point that young players throughout his system were taught the same way to play—laying the foundation for what would one day be known as the "Oriole way."

Paul Richards was also a mad scientist in a baseball uniform. He knew the rule book forward and backward—not because he wanted to follow the rules, but because he wanted to test the limits and stretch the boundaries. He was an innovator not afraid to try new things or take chances if he felt it might give his team an edge. He was one of the first to use the Iron Mike pitching machine in spring training. He pioneered the double switch in which he would remove a pitcher and send him to a defensive position for one batter, then put him back on the mound. When Oriole catchers were driven crazy trying to corral the knuckleballs of Hoyt Wilhelm in the late 1950s, Richards went to his lab and concocted an enormous catcher's mitt. The mitts eventually reached as large as forty-five inches in circumference—making the catcher look like a waiter carrying a large pizza platter—before the league passed a Richards-specific rule limiting the circumference to thirty-eight inches.

Not all of Richards's ideas were successful, however. Because the large catcher's mitt made it difficult to field throws from the outfield on plays at the plate, Richards came up with the solution to have the pitcher and catcher switch gloves on these plays. In an early attempt, the pitcher gave up a hit with a man on second and ran to back up the plate, quickly tossing his glove to the catcher as planned. The throw came in to the catcher, who dropped it, and the run scored. The catcher threw down the pitcher's glove in disgust—they had forgotten that the pitcher was a lefty. Once, in order to discourage a pitcher whose alcohol, as they say, had a low blood content, Richards forced him to drink a quart of water in the clubhouse each night before he could leave, thinking that by filling his stomach with benign water, there would be no room left for spirits. (It didn't work.)

Paul Richards realized that the Orioles had inherited from the Browns a team and a farm system that were barren of kids with talent. With this in mind, he traded a lot of older players prior to the 1955 season in order to start fresh. He announced that his plan was to have an entire new team in place that would be ready to compete for the pennant within five years. His biggest deal involved sending his only two young players with talent, pitchers Bob Turley and Don Larsen, to the Yankees as part of a 17-player trade that remains the biggest in baseball history. While Turley became a vital cog in the Yankee rotation and Larsen had one good game in the 1956 World Series, Richards got several solid players in return, including Gene Woodling, Gus Triandos, and Willie Miranda, immediately allowing him to field a respectable team.

Once again, Brooks Robinson was in the right place at the right time. The Orioles, being a new team in a new city, had no well-known stars—the situation was wide open for a young talented player to come in and establish himself, both on the team and in the city. Even more significant was the fact that, as the most important man in Brooks's professional life, Paul Richards held two principles that were beneficial to the youngster. First, in the deepest recesses of his heart, Richards firmly believed that pitching and defense were the most important facets of building a winning baseball team. Thus, he would be more tolerant of a sure-handed infielder's slowly develop- ing bat than a manager who loved a high-scoring offense. Second, Richards did not believe in coddling youngsters and bringing them along too slowly. He once told reporters, "If he's got ability, put him in there and let him play . . . to hell with this bottle-feeding. Let's put him on steak and hot tamales."

After successfully obtaining Brooks Robinson's signature on a con- tract, Art Ehlers informed the family that he was booking himself and Brooks on the afternoon flight to Baltimore. Brooks packed his things, using the big suitcase because he was going to be away for the first time in his life (he'd always used the small one for American Legion road trips), endured a quiet ride to the Little Rock airport with his family in their blue Nash, said a teary good-bye (noting as they shook hands that his father called him Brooks for one of the first times instead of the usual Buddy), and boarded his first com- mercial airline flight.

The signing of Brooks Robinson did not generate excitement back in Baltimore—it was buried in the *Baltimore Sun* at the bottom of an inside page of the sports section. Two other third base signees that year were much more heralded: bonus babies Wayne Causey and Jim Pyburn. Pyburn was a rugged twenty-two-year-old who had been an All-America end at Auburn after setting a school record with 460 yards on 28 receptions. He had also led the Southeastern Conference in hitting in 1954 with a .432 average. After leaving school early, Pyburn had been with the Orioles all season.

After an anxious night at the Southern Hotel, not far from Memo- rial Stadium, Brooks showed up in the Oriole clubhouse and found Ehlers, who introduced him to Paul Richards. Although Brooks rec- ognized Richards from pictures, they had failed to do justice to the reptilian eyes that gave pause to strong men. Those eyes could cer- tainly intimidate an eighteen-year-old. "I was scared to death of that man," says Wayne Causey, who had signed and was on the major league bench due to the bonus rule—signing one day and appearing in a major league game, and going 0-for-1, the next. "He just looked evil to me. You sure didn't want to make a mistake around him. One time early I let a pop fly drop in and he hissed, 'If that ever happens again I'm going to get some of that bonus money back.' "

Contrary to his reputation, Richards was downright loquacious with Brooks when they were introduced: "Son, go see if Whitey has a uniform for you, then go out and take some infield."

Brooks was given a uniform by the clubhouse man and walked down the runway to the dugout. He gasped as he stepped onto the field for the first time, viewing the enormous, mostly empty, stadium from the infield. He tried to look nonchalant as he moved among the major league players who were busy preparing for the game. He recognized the faces and names of men he had followed in the newspapers. Brooks's skinny legs and arms made the normally loose-fitting uniform of the era appear even more baggy than usual. With his freshly crew-cut hair and shiny, smooth-skinned face, he was a stark contrast to the older men with dense five-o'clock shadows; men who smoked and drank and chewed tobacco and worked for a living. He looked more like a batboy, or maybe somebody's kid brother, than a major league baseball player. That is, until he picked up his glove and moved out to second base to take some grounders.

The hands were the thing. There was no mistaking the hands, even at that age; soft, confident, quick hands. There was a graceful fluidity to his movements around the infield. A coach hit balls to him, easy at first, then progressively more difficult—to the left, backhanders to the right, slow rollers that needed to be charged, hard shots. Brooks swallowed them all. Paul Richards made his way onto the field and now got his first look at his new signee. He had heard and read the reports from his scouts, but words didn't do justice—how do you describe a Picasso in a few words? The Orioles had worked out an endless array of young prospects in Memorial Stadium that year as Richards scoured the country for help. Many of them hit the ball harder and farther than Brooks, but none of them looked as good in the field; none looked as sure of themselves, as if they belonged there, as if they had been born there. Richards's mind went through the scout's checklist as he watched Brooks work around the infield: the natural flow of how his body worked, how he got to the ball, what position his feet were in when he caught the ball, the exchange of the ball from the glove to the throwing hand, how quickly he got to the throwing angle, the ability to throw from all angles. He was impressed with what he saw; especially those hands. The hands couldn't be missed by the seasoned eye of a professional. Hell, they couldn't be missed by the lady in the third row seeing her first baseball game.

"I was watching that first day," says Bob Maisel, who was a thirty-three-year-old writer for the *Baltimore Sun*. "They had Willie Miranda at short and Eddie Waitkus [the regular infielders] at first and they were taking infield with Brooks. The field was in pretty rough shape. It hadn't been drug yet for the game. But Brooks just caught everything. When it was over, Waitkus came over and said, 'I know this sounds ridiculous, but that kid may have the best hands I've ever seen.'"

George Henderson, a twenty-year-old part-time scout, was standing next to the coaches as they watched. "There were a few other guys working out at the same time," he says. "Brooks caught everything. He looked better than anybody else on the field. Richards was standing right next to me and Luman Harris, one of the assistant coaches, and he pointed to Brooks and said, 'That's the one I like.'"

"After that one workout, Richards had seen enough," says Maisel. "He knew. He said, 'Take a look, boys, that might be the best third baseman I've ever seen.'" Richards decided to take Brooks on the upcoming road trip with the team to show him what Major League Baseball was all about, telling him he would watch the team for about a week, and then be sent down to play at York in the Class B league. This sightseeing trip was not one afforded to most new signees. Richards had seen something. Brooks was indeed the one he liked.

The Orioles soon left for Cleveland. Brooks roomed with veteran Hoot Evers on the trip. Evers, in the last stages of a 12-year career that had started with the Tigers, was nice to Brooks, explaining how to live on the road in the big leagues. They took a taxi to the stadium the first day and Evers sprung for the fare.

Evers was apparently the veteran Richards liked to use to make rookies feel welcome. He roomed with Causey most of the year. "They couldn't have put me with a nicer guy," says Causey. "He treated me like one of the team. He taught me a lot about life in the big leagues. He sort of looked after me on the road."

After about a week with the team, it was time to start playing again. Brooks was sent fifty miles away to York, Pennsylvania, to join the York White Roses of the Class B Piedmont League. This was the tail end of the golden age of minor league baseball. In 1955, there were 32 minor leagues across the country from Class D to AAA, 243 teams in all. These 243 teams were stocked with eager players, including quite a few rugged men who were veterans of the war and many who had previously played in the majors and were trying to fight their way back. They were all competing for a spot on one of the 16 major league teams. The simple math was not good for most of them.

They had been playing minor league baseball in the pleasant town of York since 1882. The team was managed by thirty-nine-year-old George Staller, a man who had spent more than half of his life in the minor leagues. He had played in places such as Beatrice, Nebraska, Martinsville, Virginia, and Aberdeen, South Dakota, compiling a .309 lifetime average in 1,523 minor league games. After leading the International League in doubles and triples at Montreal in 1943, he had finally been promoted to the majors and played 21 games for the Philadelphia A's in September. After the season, with World War II on, he had joined the military. Once the war was over, Staller never got another chance at the majors; his time had passed. By 1955 George Staller was in his seventh year of managing in the minors. He had the reputation of a hard-driving, spirited leader, but one who showed an interest in the boys' futures rather than furthering his own ambition.

The White Roses played their games at Memorial Stadium, which had been constructed in the middle of farmland after World War II to honor those who served and died. A good crowd for the team was about a thousand; they drew 1,154 on June 15 for a special Knothole Club and Dentist Supply Company Day. They were a .500 team in 1955 (64–65), good for fourth place. The first place team that year was the Newport News Dodgers, who boasted 6-foot-4, 18-year-old fireballer Stan Williams, who set a league record with 301 strikeouts and would go on to a 14-year major league career. A total of 44 players suited up for York at one time or another in 1955, and although it was relatively low-level minors, there were a number of grizzled veterans on the team, seven of whom had major league experience. Ken Raffensberger was a thirty-seven-year-old pitcher who had won 119 games in the majors (including four one-hitters), mostly with bad Phillies and Reds teams, from 1939 to 1954. A York hometown guy, he went 11–2 in 1955. The average age on the team in 1955 was 22. Brooks Robinson was the only teenager.

The season was already well under way when Brooks joined the team. His was not exactly a highly anticipated arrival. "We had heard there was somebody coming," says George Trout, who was a twenty-four-year-old public address announcer for the team at the time, "but we didn't know what day or even know his name." Brooks took the field at second base in the late innings on Friday, June 3, 1955, for his professional debut in front of 939 fans. Up in the press box, Trout found himself running out of time to announce the substitution. The inning was about to start, but all he had on the new guy was a slip of paper that said "B. Robinson." Someone in the box suggested, "Just try Bob, almost everybody's named Bob," and so Trout went with it: "Now playing for the York White Roses, Bob Robinson."

The batboy soon ran up to the press box and informed Trout that it was Brooks, not Bob. Embarrassed, Trout went down to the clubhouse and introduced himself to the new player after the game and apologized. Although Brooks hadn't heard the announcement, he thought it was funny and laughed it off. Brooks had only fielded a few routine plays at second and had gone hitless in his one at bat, but he was the happiest player in the clubhouse after the game. It was one of those dingy, cramped, low-minor-league clubhouses in which the players hung their clothes on a nail, but to Brooks, it might as well have been the Taj Majal. "He was like a kid who just looked under the Christmas tree and found every gift he ever wanted," recalls Trout. "All he ever wanted to do was play baseball. He said that nothing bothered him; he was in a professional uniform and he didn't care about anything else that happened after that."

"Rookie Bob Robinson joined the York club last night and saw brief service at second base," the *York Gazette and Daily* reported the next day. Although informed of the mistake, the two local newspapers kept the citizens apprised of the exploits of Bob Robinson for another two weeks. "Bob Robinson homered over the centerfield wall for the White Roses," they announced June 10. The papers eventually changed the name of the White Roses' second baseman to Brooks without explanation.

Staller, who became a coach for the Orioles in the 1960s, would later tell reporters that Brooks's amiable personality was there from the start, and never changed over the years. When Brooks arrived, he was given the newest kid's traditional assignment of carrying out the bats. Although he quickly established himself as one of the best players on the team, he continued to perform the bat duty as eagerly as he performed any other.

After the first game, Brooks was made the everyday second baseman. Whereas low minor league play is often punctuated by a plethora of errors, Brooks showed immediate skill in the field and it was nine days before an *E* appeared next to "Robinson" in the box score. He would commit only 14 errors in 95 games for York. June 20, the *Gazette and Daily* reported that Brooks participated in four double plays and "he started two of the twin kills with incredible leaping catches." He also hit well, right from the start, slamming three home runs in the first two weeks. Initially he hit in the seven or eight spot in the order, but he soon moved up to three or four. There were several big days at the plate, such as June 26, when he had a single, double, and home run at Norfolk, and July 11, when he was 7-for-9 with a homer, two doubles, and four RBIs against Portsmouth in a doubleheader.

In midseason, the Orioles paid a promotional visit to York and played the White Roses in an exhibition. The largest crowd of the year (3,495) turned out to see the major leaguers. Baltimore, in the A.L. cellar at the time, did not impress the fans. Raffensberger took the mound for York and stymied the big club. Brooks lined a 380-foot first inning three-run home run off veteran pitcher Joe Coleman and added another hit later. York won 13–1, illustrating the type of team Richards had with the Orioles.

During the season, Brooks found himself in the center of some potential trouble. One day while they were in Lynchburg, Virginia, for a game, someone from Major League Commissioner Ford Frick's office paid him a visit and asked details about his signing. A few weeks later word came that Brooks, Paul Richards, and scout Claude Dietrich were to report to Frick's office for a hearing. Brooks was brought into Frick's office alone, asked to sit down and place his hand on a Bible someone produced, and told to swear to tell the truth, the whole truth, and nothing but the truth. It seems that some-one from the Cincinnati Reds had suggested to the commissioner's office that foul play may have been involved in Brooks's signing. Richards was indeed known to give some players extra money un-der the table to avoid the $4,000 limit, but in Brooks's case everything was on the up-and-up. Apparently, the commissioner believed them, and nothing ever came of it.

Later, Brooks received a visit from an IRS agent who informed him that an investigation of his taxes had been initiated. They had a re-port that he had been given $4,000 plus an annual salary of $4,000. After investigating him—and scaring out what wits were left after the commissioner's office had finished—they were convinced by the Oriole management that it had only been an annual salary. Such were the legal trials of the innocent young infielder, out in the real world for the first time.

On the field, Brooks had a good year at York. He was second on the team with a .331 average and hit 11 home runs in 95 games. He played second base for the first 50 games, then Staller moved him to third. Good baseball men could easily see the potential of Brooks's defense, but they could also see the angles—a second baseman needs to be able to cover more territory than a third baseman, where the ball gets to the fielder so fast that only a few steps are possible. Third base is a reflex position and few people had better reflexes than Brooks. Second basemen of the era tended to be feisty, annoying little guys—think Billy "the Kid" Martin and Eddie "the Brat" Stanky—and at six-foot-one Brooks was much bigger than most. While Brooks liked to joke later that the move saved his life because he was getting killed while turning double plays, that was misleading. He was a very good second baseman, but third was even better for him.

While both George Staller and Paul Richards would take credit for the move over the years, it was apparently Richards's plan all along. "I later asked Richards, 'If you thought he would be such a great third baseman the first time you saw him, why did you have him at second initially?'" says Maisel. "Richards had a real good eye for baseball. He explained that he didn't think that Brooks had the lateral speed to be a great second baseman, but for two or three steps, he was real quick and would be best at third. He had been playing mostly second base in Legion ball, though. Richards said, 'We wanted to let him get his feet on the ground for a while at York, then move him to third.' He didn't want to mix him up by making changes too quickly. And that turned out to be a pretty good plan."

"It became evident pretty quickly that it was a good move, to move Brooks to third," says Trout. "Very quickly there were two things that you noticed: although he wasn't fast, he was very quick, and he just seemed to have a way of positioning himself perfectly. And, of course, he had great hands. Nothing got through him. You knew third base was going to be his home."

Paul Richards regularly kept in touch with his minor league managers, receiving progress reports on all the encouraging players. In August, speaking to reporters about young prospects for the Orioles' future, Richards touted pitcher Mel Held, outfielder Jim Pisoni, Wayne Causey, and York farm hand Brooks Robinson as the most promising in the system. By the end of the 1955 season, by cup-of-coffee time, Richards knew—out of all the Orioles' minor league third basemen—who he wanted to watch in Baltimore. Brooks was called up to the Orioles when the York season concluded in mid-September. This immediately vaulted him over all the guys languishing in the farm system—not a small thing for an eighteen-year-old. He was viewed as a prospect.

While Brooks had been at York, the Orioles had been battling Washington to stay out of the American League cellar (a battle they would eventually win by four games while losing 97). The slick-fielding ex-Dodger Billy Cox had opened the season at third base, but was traded to Cleveland in June after hitting only .211. The Orioles had used a total of 12 men at third base, with Causey playing the most at 55 games while compiling a .194 batting average. Pyburn, also not hitting well, .204, had been moved to the outfield.

Brooks arrived in Baltimore as a player on September 17, 1955. Upon hitting town, he went straight to the stadium for the Oriole game against the Senators. He dressed in his baggy wool uniform and selected a spot in the dugout, expecting to have a nice view of the game. He was surprised when coach Lum Harris walked by and informed him that he was starting at third. Chuck Diering, one of the more reliably hitting veterans, had been taking most of the playing time at third the previous few weeks but was moved to center field, where he would spend the rest of the season.

In his first major league at bat, against Chuck Stobbs, Brooks hit a routine grounder to short for an out. The next time up he lined a single over the third baseman. It was the hit he had worked for his whole life. As he returned to first after rounding the bag, the Senators' first baseman, Mickey Vernon, said, "Nice hit, kid. Welcome to the big leagues." Brooks wasn't done. With the Orioles leading 2–1 in the eighth, he singled to center to drive in a run to make it 2-for-4 in his first major league game. Later, Brooks would frequently tell reporters that he rushed back to his room, called Little Rock, and told his parents, "I went two-for-four. I'm here in the majors to stay. This is my cup of tea. I don't know what I was doing in the minors this year." As Brooks would tell the story, he proceeded to go 0-for-18 after that with 10 strikeouts, learning that he still had a little ways to go before he was truly ready to be in the majors to stay.

Richards wanted to get a good look to see how the kid would conduct himself in the big leagues. He started him for six straight games, then, to spare him further pain after the 0-for-18 skid, mercifully sat him the last two games of the year. In his brief look at the majors, Brooks was particularly bad at the plate against slow breaking balls. But he showed definite flair in the field. It was reportedly after working a series during this period that veteran umpire Ed Hurley, impressed by the defensive skill of the recently called up Robinson, uttered the quote that would be repeated often over the years: "He plays third base like he came down from a higher league."

Rookies were treated rudely, or completely ignored, on many teams of the era. Since the addition of a youngster often meant that one of their older teammates, often a friend, had to be let go, new guys were met with resentment. There was little of that on the Orioles, however. The players were used to the revolving door on the clubhouse—Richards had made over 60 roster moves by midseason and of the 45 men on the spring training roster March 1, only 11 remained by season's end—so a new face was nothing unusual. Also, since there were several bonus babies, Brooks wasn't the only teenager on the club. "I really only had one guy who gave me a hard time," says Wayne Causey. "You know, 'Bonus baby this,' and 'Bonus baby that,' and 'Hey moneybags.' But I later found out that was just his personality. He was that way to everyone. Most of the guys on the Orioles were pretty good to us new guys."

With all the roster changes, the Orioles weren't cliquish like some teams that have a core of veterans together for years. Large groups of players would go out to dinner together after games. They were also a fairly loose team: there was certainly no pressure by that point of the season—they were just playing out the schedule. As big a wide-eyed country hayseed as ever landed in a major league clubhouse, Brooks had an easygoing, friendly way about him that made the veterans want to treat him well. He was appropriately deferential and respectful of the older players but was not shy and didn't keep his distance. He acted like he belonged and was eager to engage in a laugh. The veterans, who could all see his potential, took an immediate liking to him.

Catcher Gus Triandos said in 2001, "Brooks was a nice kid with a nice twang, but he was overmatched when he first got there. It scared the hell out of him. I kind of felt bad for him. You're eighteen, you grew up reading about the major leagues, and suddenly you're right there on the field. . . . I can't think of anyone who would have command of himself at that age."

"But you could tell that he was going to be a good player," Triandos adds. "He was already a great fielder then, you could see that. They were hoping he would become a good hitter. He got along with everybody. I don't remember anybody who ever had a problem with him. But put it this way: if you had a problem with Brooks, it was only because there was something wrong with you."

Veteran Joe Ginsberg later said, "He [Brooks] couldn't have a beer with us. He was too young. We'd take him with us and he'd drink a Coke. And he had that high voice. I said to him, 'How in the world are you going to be a big-leaguer with a voice like that? You better catch a cold or something.' "

Announcer Ernie Harwell, who would soon move to the Tigers, recalled, "He was sort of a skinny kid . . . he was pretty easy prey for the pitchers. They'd just blow him down at the bat. . . . But he was a terrific kid. . . . He'd come out to our house and play catch with my kids. One of the nicest ballplayers I ever met."

"Brooks was always nice; a polite kid," says Maisel, who would be promoted to sports editor of the *Sun* in 1959 and would finish a 40-plus-year career in the early 1990s. "He had that big southern accent when he first got here. You just found yourself immediately liking him. He was young, single, and didn't run around a lot. He would come over to our house a lot of times after games and my wife would cook dinner for him—he ended up doing that for several years until he got married. We got to be good friends. You could do that back then because the kids weren't hardly making anything."

While Brooks Robinson was getting his feet wet in Baltimore in September of 1955, another drama was taking place just up the road in Pittsburgh that would affect the fortunes of Baltimore and, indirectly, the Orioles in the coming years. A funny-shaped football player with a funny-sounding last name was being cut from the Pittsburgh Steelers without ever getting into a preseason game and would join a local semipro team, the Bloomfield Rams, earning 15 bucks a game. Johnny Unitas would be signed by the Baltimore Colts in the spring of 1956 as a backup to 1955 NFL Rookie Quarterback of the Year George Shaw. He would take the field in the fourth game of the 1956 season after an injury to Shaw and, with his first professional pass, throw an interception resulting in a touchdown for the other team. He would get better.

In a rare convergence of two true icons of their respective sports, living in the same city (same neighborhood for years) at the same time for over a decade, Brooks Robinson and Johnny Unitas would become friends and mutual admirers. Although Brooks played in Baltimore first, Johnny U and the Colts experienced success much sooner by winning the NFL Championship in 1958 and 1959. Baltimore would be a football city for the next 20 years. The Orioles would eventually have their championships, but, by then, the hearts of the citizens undeniably belonged to the Colts, affecting both attendance and fame for the city's baseball players.

After the 1955 season, Brooks returned to Little Rock. He had considered attending Little Rock Junior College in the fall, to please his mother, but he soon got word that Richards wanted him to go to Colombia to play in the Colombian Winter League along with 12 of the Orioles' other prized prospects such as Marv Breeding, Bob Hale, Tito Francona, and Wayne Causey. This was an honor—these were the guys the club's management felt had the potential to be major leaguers. The players met in Miami and flew together to Colombia. All unmarried, they lived in a big house with a couple of maids to take care of them and keep them well fed. The Orioles sent a coach down to stay with them and provide guidance (as well as to try to keep them out of trouble). Brooks, like most of the others, had never been out of the country. They were ready for new experiences—like getting seasick. "One night, we rented a boat and went out on the ocean fishing," says Causey. "I've never been so sick in my life. Bob Nelson was the only one able to eat and drink what we took out there. The rest of us were hanging over the side of the boat puking. We had rented it until midnight, but we didn't make it until ten, we were all so sick.

"That was the first time I really got to know Brooks," continues Causey. "He was one of the best guys I ever played with; a lot of fun, just a really good guy. Of course, over the years I heard a lot of people who played with him say that. Later, when I was on the A's in the 1960s, we would talk before batting practice or when one of us got on third and I could tell he hadn't changed a lot from the time we were playing down there."

The four teams in the Colombian League played a 66-game schedule. The Oriole players were on a team based in Barranquilla called the Willard Blues. The second largest city in Colombia at the time, Barranquilla was an industrial port city with a population of nearly half a million. Baseball was the number one sport and enthusiastic

crowds turned out for the games. Francona, a 21-year-old first baseman, led the league in home runs, and Breeding and Robinson were
in the top three in batting average, both hitting around .315.

Brooks's play did not go unnoticed. In an article in the *Baltimore
Sun* in mid-December entitled "Birds May Be O.K. at Third," Bob
Maisel wrote, "Ever since the end of last season Paul Richards has
designated third base as the spot the Orioles must strengthen, but
according to the latest information from the Birds' Winter League
operation in Colombia, South America, his hot corner worries may be
solved by a youngster already on the roster. This was brought to light
late yesterday by Farm Director Jim McLaughlin after the Oriole office had received a letter from scout Fred Hofmann, who is managing
the Willard club. 'According to Hofmann, Brooks Robinson is pro-
gressing so rapidly he may be able to stick as the Oriole third baseman next season,' says McLaughlin. 'He's looking better and better
all the time and he appears to be a cinch to eventually make the grade
in the majors.'"

Baseball south of the border was not entirely safe for American
players in those days. In Venezuela that winter, a group of men broke
into Pirate Clem Koshorek's living quarters and beat him in the aftermath of an on-field argument. In Cuba, a group of baseball players
were walking home from dinner when they were accosted by troops
at gunpoint. Informed that the government of dictator Fulgencio
Batista had outlawed more than two people being together in public
as a result of the revolution, the players were saved by the fact that
only one of them spoke Spanish and the troops figured that since
they were all Americans, they could not be plotting a takeover and
released them.

For Brooks, the only real danger he faced that winter was on the
baseball field—but it was considerable. One of the toughest pitchers
in the league was Red Sox farmhand Earl Wilson, a hulking speci-
men, built like Jim Brown, who pitched for Kola Román. One game a
Wilson fastball plunked Brooks on the head, dropping him in the
dirt. Willard teammates ran toward the motionless body fearing the
worst. "Wilson threw really hard," says Causey. "He hit him right in
the head." Luckily, in an era in which batting helmets were not often
used, the Willard team had been experimenting with a new hard

plastic liner. "It destroyed that helmet," adds Causey. "If he hadn't had that helmet on it would have killed him." As it turned out, all Brooks got out of the ordeal was a bad headache, a knot on his forehead, and an appreciation for Wilson's major-league-ready fastball.

The season ended in early January and Brooks returned to Little Rock. His first year of professional baseball had taken him from York to Baltimore to Colombia. He had impressed at every stop and given indications that the Birds indeed might be okay at third for years to come.

5. Glove Wizard

BROOKS WAS ONE OF 42 PLAYERS invited to the Oriole advance camp in Scottsdale, Arizona, ahead of the regulars in the spring of 1956. Considered the best players in the farm system, the players reported February 15 and were put through an intense program by Richards and his coaches. These weren't just two- or three-hour sessions; they were daylight to dusk. Every moment of camp was strictly regimented by Richards. They worked on all aspects of the game—cutoffs, pick-offs, base running—no detail was too small. It was all part of Richards's accelerated program to get his youngsters ready for the majors. The prized innovations from the Paul Richards lab for 1956 were a tackling dummy, nicknamed "The Thing," that he set up at second base for players to practice breaking up double plays, and the use of a video camera (one of the first in baseball) to record his players for later critique.

Once the exhibition season started, some of the young players left to work out with minor league teams; Brooks, however, remained with the big club. Richards continued the process of converting the Browns into the Orioles; of the 41 players on the spring roster, only 17 had been with the club in 1955 and only Diering remained from 1954. In March, Richards told reporters he was committed to the long-range building program and that the most impressive youngsters in camp were Brooks Robinson and Tito Francona.

Although he was high on Brooks, Richards realized that he was not quite physically ready for the majors. Third base at the Oriole camp seemed to be the busiest piece of real estate in Arizona. The Orioles tried a number of veterans at third, including Diering and

Bob Kennedy, as well as Causey and Pyburn. They soon traded for 34-year-old third baseman Bob Adams. Nevertheless, Brooks was the starting third baseman in the first game of spring training.

The *Sporting News* stated after the first game that "while uncorking a dashing brand of defensive play, [Brooks] went hitless in four times up." His glove had them talking. The *Baltimore Sun* reported February 23, "Brooks Robinson's sure handed glovework again impressed." A virus infection shelved Brooks a few weeks into the exhibition schedule, however, and he lost 10 pounds and precious time on the field. Richards optioned him to San Antonio of the Class AA Texas League on March 21, but told reporters, "He'll be back up one of these days as our regular third baseman."

Brooks joined the San Antonio team in Dunedin, Florida, where they were preparing for the season. The San Antonio Missions were managed by 38-year-old Joe Schultz. The round-faced, chrome-headed Schultz had been a major league catcher with the Pirates and Browns from 1939 to 1948, and was in his seventh year of managing in the minors. While maintaining a tough exterior, Schultz, who would later incur literary note as Jim Bouton's 1969 Seattle Pilots manager in *Ball Four*, liked to keep a loose clubhouse. He rarely yelled at players for mistakes and his zany countenance while spouting nonsensical sayings with his high shrill voice kept the players laughing. His favorite advice before a game was, "Let's kick their tails and get back here and pound that Budweiser." His remedy for a loss? "Pound that Budweiser and forget it."

Schultz had played with Arkansas native Arky Vaughan in Pittsburgh; therefore, anyone from Arkansas was automatically "Arky." When Brooks reported, Schultz's first words were, "Arky, you're playing third base for us, so get your glove and get out there." Later, after a workout, Schultz caught Brooks in the clubhouse eating an ice cream bar and drinking a Coke. "Arky, I want to tell you one thing. You can't get to the big leagues eating ice cream and drinking sody pop." The rest of the year, Schultz joked with him about ice cream and sody pop.

More important than dietary advice, however, was the help Schultz gave Arky with his hitting. After poking a home run and a single in the first game, Brooks slumped at the plate. He approached Schultz and asked for help. The next morning in a private session on the empty field, Schultz talked to him about going with the outside pitch to right and not trying to pull everything, as had been his habit; just hit the ball hard wherever it is. The two spent hours working together the next few weeks and Brooks gradually began improving.

His batting average soon received a further boost when his father came to visit, bringing him a car, a 1956 maroon Buick Special. Brooks got the game-winning hit in the eighth inning that night, then contributed a home run and a double the next day and two singles to right the game after that. His hitting was solid the rest of the season. May 24 he ended a game against Fort Worth with a 13th-inning, three-run homer. He hit two home runs against Shreveport June 10.

There were sporadic reports in Baltimore throughout the summer that Brooks Robinson was high on the Orioles' list of prospects, along with comments about his unusually impressive fielding; he was often referred to as a "third base phenom."

In addition to his glove work, Brooks's unusual work habits drew notice. "In 1956, I had just finished high school and me and some friends went to a baseball game in Houston," says Vic Roznovsky, who later played with the Orioles in 1966 and 1967. "Back then Houston was a minor league team in the Texas League. That night they were playing San Antonio. I distinctly remember seeing this guy out there early, before anyone else, taking ground ball after ground ball at third base. When it was his turn for BP he went in, took his cuts, then went back out there and took some more ground balls. And I thought, 'Who is this guy?' Nobody else did that. It turned out to be Brooks Robinson. Of course, at the time we had no idea we were looking at a future Hall of Famer, but maybe that's what helped him get there. And later when I got to Baltimore, he was still doing the same thing."

Late in the season, on a rainy night in Shreveport, Brooks singled to right center and tried to stretch it into a double when the ball bounced away from the outfielder. Coming into the bag, his spikes hung up in the mud as he slid. He heard something pop in his right knee and then experienced severe pain. The trainer examined the knee and said it looked like torn cartilage. The next day, the knee had swollen and Brooks could hardly walk. He feared that he would need season-ending knee surgery. After a few days of heat and whirl-pools, however, the swelling went down and he was able to get back into the lineup. Although the knee bothered him on and off the rest of the season, especially when making quick starts, it held up and he didn't miss any more games.

San Antonio ended up with a 76–78 record, good for fifth place. Brooks hit .272 with 28 doubles, nine homers, and 74 RBIs. He also led the league in defense at third base with a .957 fielding average and earned the nickname "Octopus," which years earlier had been bestowed on future Hall of Famer Marty Marion when he had played in the Texas League. When San Antonio was finished, Brooks was called up to the Orioles September 9.

The 1956 Orioles still had an opening at third base. Causey had started out there, played in 53 games, and hit .170. Veteran third baseman and future Hall of Famer George Kell was picked up in a trade in May and held down the job for 102 games, but he battled nagging injuries in September. Richards put Brooks in the lineup and played him 15 games from September 12 to September 30. Reporters noted that he played third base like a veteran and Richards remarked that he couldn't believe what his eyes were seeing. Brooks was still far from impressive at the plate, however, as he hit just .227 in 44 at bats.

When Brooks Robinson arrived in Arizona for spring training in 1957, he had ideas of sticking with the Orioles the whole season. George Kell was back, telling everyone it would be his last year as a player. In camp, it was widely reported that Brooks was being groomed as Kell's replacement.

George Kell was 34 years old in 1957, a veteran of 15 major league seasons. An excellent hitter, mostly with the Tigers, he had hit over .300 nine times and would finish with a .306 career average. He had a lot in common with Brooks Robinson. Kell was also from Arkansas—from the small town of Swifton—and remained, at heart, a good ole country boy. As kids, they had both wanted nothing more than to be big league baseball players. They had both grown up in the Methodist Church and were firm believers, regular churchgoers, and levelheaded noncarousers. An intelligent, naturally friendly person, Kell was nice to fans and was always gracious and cooperative with the media, "because I thought that was just the way any good person was supposed to act," he later wrote. After home games, Kell went straight home to his wife. His idea of living it up on the road was dinner, returning to the hotel, and maybe taking in a good book.

Whereas some veterans may have been annoyed by a talented, young, eager replacement obviously waiting for the demise of the elder, Kell was welcoming and helpful. "Sure, he's trying to steal my job," he told reporters. "I'd kick him in the pants if he wasn't. . . . I can't last forever." Brooks had admired Kell as a youngster and was thrilled to have him as a teammate. Making $6,000 a year, Brooks was amazed when he found out that Kell was pulling in the grand sum of $30,000—he resolved to work until he could be rich like that. The two men hit it off and would maintain a friendship for the next 50 years. Kell would later write in his autobiography: "There never was a finer fielding third baseman than Brooks. I don't believe there ever will be. It's not humanly possible. . . . Off the field, you have to walk two country miles and then skip through a row of cornfields to find a nicer person."

In addition to helping Brooks with tips on the field, Kell took him under his wing and taught him how a big leaguer was supposed to live. He showed him the good restaurants around the league and took him to see his first stage play when they were in New York. He related his experiences as a young ballplayer. While there had previously been few leaders on the Orioles who had played for winning teams, here was a man with Hall of Fame credentials to help the youngster. Although he soon began a long-running career as a broadcaster, mostly with the Tigers, at this point in his career Kell was entertaining notions of becoming a manager or coach. He assumed the role and acted as sort of a player-coach with the Orioles. He was quick to help all the players with hitting or fielding tips.

Reporters noted that Kell spent time on the field with Brooks each day. "We do something together whenever the time affords," Kell told them. "He can't miss. It's just a matter of experience." While helping him with hitting and life in general, fielding was another matter. Kell laughed when Richards suggested he help Brooks with his play at third. At one point Richards thought he had detected a flaw in his backhand mechanics, and told Kell to correct it. Kell refused, noting that Robinson hadn't missed a backhand ball in six weeks of spring training. "When I first saw Brooks Robinson I could see that he could play third base," Kell said in 2004. "He had all the moves and the instincts. Many third basemen just grab the ball and can't wait to get rid of it. Even as a youngster, Brooks never hurried his throws. He was already so good [in the field] that there wasn't much I could tell him." Kell was also impressed with the work ethic and single-minded resolve to improve his hitting. "He was determined to be a good ballplayer."

Though he wouldn't turn twenty until May 18, Brooks was ready to challenge for a regular job with the Orioles. His glove had them talking again. "Brooks was impressive at the hot corner after joining the Birds at the close of the season," reported the *Sporting News*, adding that the "glove wizard" was also a "handsome, All-American-boy type." He was "a finished fielder after only two years in the minors," according to *Sports Illustrated*. In addition to the printed remarks, his play sparked comments of the unprintable variety from opposing dugouts after he robbed certain base hits. People were starting to take notice. Yankee manager Casey Stengel said, "That Robinson sure looks good to me. Baltimore has a real prospect there."

"Defensively, he looks ready for the big leagues now," announced Richards. He added that Brooks possessed "the best pair of hands I've ever seen on a third baseman."

Joe Schultz told another reporter in camp that Brooks had the "finest pair of hands I have ever seen on any third baseman." That was rapidly becoming the consensus.

Brooks was noted to be "turning in a thrill a day at third base" once the exhibition season began and made the play of the week on March 24 when he backhanded a smash behind third base, fell to his knees, got up, and threw out the runner to the roaring cheers of 3,000 fans in Scottsdale. And he was hitting—he was at .357 after 20 exhibition games, was voted top rookie by a press-radio poll, and received a silver tray from Scottsdale mayor Malcolm White before the final home game. When the Orioles broke camp, Brooks was listed as the starting third baseman with Kell slated for duty at first.

Brooks's elation at being in the starting lineup was short-lived, however. Two weeks into the 1957 season, disaster struck. Hustling down the line after hitting a routine ground ball to short, Brooks saw the first baseman come off the bag to field a bad throw and he swerved to avoid the sweep tag. As he did, his knee collapsed. He was carried to the clubhouse on a stretcher.

It was the same knee that had been injured the previous August in Shreveport. This time the diagnosis was bad: completely torn cartilage. Dr. Edmund McDonnell operated on the knee at Baltimore's Union Memorial Hospital May 4 and Brooks was out two months; out before the season had really started—he had played in nine games and was hitting only .200 (5-for-25). The season that had held so much promise was now ruined. Once the knee had been rehabbed, Brooks was sent to San Antonio in early June to play back into shape.

Schultz greeted him upon his arrival in the San Antonio clubhouse: "Okay, Arky, they sent you down here to get back in shape, so you'd better be ready because I'm going to be all over you." Brooks played in 33 games over the course of the month, hitting .266. Schultz ran him in the outfield and hit fungoes back and forth at third. The knee held up. By the end of the month he was ready to return to Baltimore.

Coming back from San Antonio, Brooks traveled all day, arrived in Baltimore, and walked the two blocks to the stadium, getting there as the game was in the third inning. He found Richards in the dugout and was told to suit up. In the fifth inning with the bases loaded, Richards sent him up to pinch-hit. In his dramatic reappearance in an Oriole uniform . . . he popped up. "But it made me feel good to be put in the ball game right away," Brooks later said. "I felt like he was really glad to see me."

Richards wrote Brooks in the lineup the next day and told him, "I don't want you to worry about a thing. I don't care what your batting average is. All I want you to do is do your best and the rest will take care of itself."

But someone needed to take care of Brooks. August 2, against the Kansas City A's, Brooks stepped to the plate in the fourth inning against Ned Garver. An old pro, Garver was a nibbler with excellent control. He had worked Brooks outside the first time up and gotten a foul out to the catcher. Watching for the outside pitch this time, Brooks leaned over the plate. Garver came inside with a side-armed fastball that broke up and in. The pitch caught Brooks flush on the brim of his helmet over his left eye, broke a four-inch hunk out of the helmet, and opened a gash on his forehead that would require 10 stitches. A hush fell over the crowd. Brooks never lost consciousness, but was carried off the field and taken straight to Union Memorial Hospital, where a concussion was diagnosed. X rays showed no fracture, however. Dr. Edwin Mayer told reporters that Robinson "probably would not be alive if he hadn't been wearing a hard-top head gear. As it was, the ball struck Robbie in the temple, a delicate place, but the blow was cushioned enough that no serious damage was done."

"I feel very bad," said Garver. "It was an accident. This is the first time in my life I ever hit anybody in the head." Brooks told reporters that he saw the ball coming but "couldn't get out of the way of it."

Despite the scare of his second serious beaning in two years, Brooks didn't show any signs of being gun-shy when he returned to the lineup five days later, and he proceeded to have some memorable games. He hit his first major league home run, off Pedro Ramos, August 14 and got four hits September 25 off the Yankees' Whitey Ford.

Brooks was playing every day now, living the dream. It was hard for friends to believe how far he had come in just two years. "Late in the summer of 1957, Bob Baird, Marshall Gazette, and I took a trip to Baltimore to see Brooks," says Buddy Rotenberry. "We drove in Bob's parents' car. We stayed with Brooks and slept on the floor of his apartment. One night after a game with the Yankees, the four of us went to a neighborhood tavern not far from the stadium. We were sitting there eating burgers and we looked and four Yankees came in. We recognized them: Mickey Mantle, Billy Martin, Whitey Ford, and Hank Bauer. They saw Brooks and came over and spoke to him and shook hands. When the check came, they were still there. Brooks said, 'Let me have that,' and reached for the check, but the waitress said, 'Yours has been taken care of by those gentlemen over there.' So we thought he was a big shot now."

"I was struck by his confidence," says Robert Baird. "Seeing him on the field, he just seemed to have remarkable poise for a guy his age. But he handled the success and celebrity very well—he was the same guy off the field."

"After one of the games in Baltimore, we were waiting for him outside the stadium," says Marshall Gazette. "There was a crowd of fans and Brooks was talking to them and signing autographs. All of a sudden, he pointed his finger at me and said, 'See that guy over there? We just signed that guy for one hundred thousand dollars. He's going to be our next star.' And all the kids came running over to me and before I knew it, I was signing 'Marshall Gazette' on their scorecards and baseballs. Brooks was just laughing—that's the kind of thing he liked to do."

But while Brooks was recognized by opposing players and Baltimore fans, he was still far from a household name. "On an off day, the four of us drove up to New York City," says Rotenberry. "None of us three country boys had ever been there and Brooks had only been there playing baseball. Our mission was to see all the sights. We went to the top of the Empire State Building; went to Coney Island and rode the big roller coaster, all the stuff like that. One of the things the three of us wanted to see was Yankee Stadium. The Yankees were playing the Indians when we got there but the game was in the seventh inning. We went up to the gate and there was a big guy standing there. We asked him if we could just stick our heads in and look around. He was going to charge us for a general admission ticket. Finally, Brooks decided to pull rank. He stepped up and said, 'I'm Brooks Robinson and I play third base for the Baltimore Orioles.' And the guy just looked at him and said, 'Nice to meet you. I'm Babe Ruth. But if you guys want to get in, you're still going to have to buy a ticket.'"

Although the Orioles were largely an older team, Brooks had plenty of company his age. Bonus babies Causey and Bob Nelson were still around, along with a couple of pitchers who would become Brooks's close friends over the next few years. Eighteen-year-old Milt Pappas was called up in midseason and he and Brooks roomed together on the road. "We were both underage and we couldn't go out with the rest of the team to a lot of places, so we hung out together a lot," Pappas says. "He was a great roommate. He was such a great guy, it was just a pleasure knowing him. He was so down-to-earth; had that southern accent. He was kind of quiet, especially around the older players. Brooks wasn't hitting great yet, he was still so young, but there was no doubt about his fielding—he was already a great fielder. He was so swift and smooth getting rid of the ball. I loved having him over there when I was on the mound."

"I came up to the Orioles in July of 1957 right out of high school," says Jerry Walker. "I'm from Oklahoma, so me and Brooks had a lot of things in common and became good friends. Also, being young guys, we hung around together most of the time. He was twenty when I first came up. He called me 'Rook.' If he sees me now over 50 years later, he'll still say, 'Hello Rook.'"

Playing the rest of the season at third, Brooks hit .239 in 50 games. The Orioles finished in fifth place—a marked improvement—only one game out of the first division. (Each of the four teams in the top half earned a share of the World Series loot.) Richards arranged for Brooks to play in the Cuban Winter League to make up for the lost time due to the injury.

Perhaps more than any other Caribbean country, Cuba had a love affair with baseball. Cuban baseball leagues dated back to 1878 and had survived political uprisings, severe economic depression, and the travel restrictions of World War II, which kept American ballplayers at home. The Cuban League had entered into an agreement with Major League Baseball in 1947 to be used for winter development of players under contract to big league teams. Top minor league and new major league players were sent there to play alongside Cuban major leaguers, making it the best winter league in baseball at the time. In 1957, the four teams played a 72-game schedule from October to February. Competition was stiff, especially the pitching. Almendares, based in Havana, had major league pitchers Mike Cuellar and Jim Grant. Brooks played for Cienfuegos, which was located on the south coast of the island on the Caribbean 140 miles southeast of Havana, and had big league pitchers Pedro Ramos and Camilio Pasqual as teammates. Because the team had already signed someone to play third base, Brooks played second the entire time he was in Cuba. Orlando Peña, a veteran Cuban pitcher, later told writers that Brooks was the best second baseman he ever saw. "He made fantastic plays every time we played against them," he said. "I'll never forget some of them."

Brooks hit slightly over .200 but led the league in home runs with nine and made an impression on observers. Pirate manager Bobby Bragan, who managed another Cuban team, told reporters back in the States, "He'll be a great one."

Baseball wasn't the only excitement. The Cuban Revolution had started in 1953, but really heated up in 1956. By the winter of 1957, open warfare existed between Fidel Castro's rebels and Batista's forces and the U.S. ambassador had been recalled. "Brooks wrote me letters from Cuba about every other week," says Gazette. "He would tell me about what was going on. Brooks wrote about all the problems in Havana with Batista and the revolution and the different things he saw. Brooks was a real good writer. We didn't know he was living through history."

"Brooks wrote that Cuba was a thrill a minute," says Rotenberry. One night, some of Castro's supporters interrupted a game with an explosion behind the field. Perhaps becoming accustomed to the dangers of the revolution, the players took it in stride and finished the game. "He said, 'You don't know how hard it is to concentrate at third base when someone sets off a bomb that blows down part of the outfield fence in the middle of a game.'"

When George Kell announced his retirement in January 1958, the Oriole third base job was officially ceded to Brooks Robinson. Brooks knew his hitting had to improve, however. In Arizona, he took advantage of Eddie Robinson, who was coaching after ending his career the previous season. "I worked a lot with Brooks on his hitting," says Robinson. "Everybody knew he had great potential. We all knew he was a great fielder. He could catch anything that was hit at him. But it was his hitting that was the question. Every day we would go down to the batting cage. Initially he was pulling everything. He was still kind of skinny and hadn't filled out yet in 1958, so he didn't have much power then. As a kid, he would lunge a lot because of his eagerness. I worked with him on using the whole field. He learned to stay back and hit the ball to right field and that's when he started to become a hitter. He was a hard worker. We would go down to the batting cage and I would throw to him. He would work as long as he felt like he could swing a bat. He would stay out there as long as you wanted to work with him—and enjoy it.

"It was evident pretty quickly that he was just a great guy," continues Robinson. "I enjoyed working with him. He always had a smile on his face; was always out to help people if he could. He was always exuberant. He enjoyed playing the game. He was just a great guy to have on a ball club."

One fan recalled watching him hit until a coach told him, "Both of your hands are covered with blisters." Brooks replied, "Maybe some day I can hit .300 and all of this will pay off."

Paul Richards was still ready to talk to anyone who would listen about Brooks's defense. Once he spotted a writer wandering around the field. Richards told him, "If you're looking for a story, why don't you write about the way Al Vincent [an Oriole coach] hits fungoes?" He motioned to the infield where Brooks was taking grounders. "Look, he's been hitting ground balls to Robinson for an hour and hasn't missed yet. Wherever Robinson puts his glove, Vincent hits the ball right into it." The writer stared, taken in for a moment, before Richards laughed. "I'm telling you," Richards continued, nodding at Brooks, "that boy is going to become a star."

Anxious to build a winner, Richards was spending copiously on prospects. He blew $250,000 in 1955 on bonuses and essentially got nothing back. There was a strong-armed high school pitcher who turned out to be paralyzed by a fear of crowds, a mammoth power hitter from Texas who never learned to hit off-speed pitches, and several players whose development was arrested due to the bonus baby rule and eventually became major league players, but not until years later for someone else. But the spending did accomplish one important thing: it showed that the Orioles were committed to trying to win, not just trying to stay afloat like the Browns. Richards struck pay dirt, while spending less money, in 1956 with Ron Hansen and Chuck Estrada and in 1957 with Milt Pappas, Jerry Walker, Jack Fisher, and Steve Barber—all players who would pay big dividends as soon as 1960.

Opening Day of the 1958 season, in Baltimore, Brooks went 3-for-3 with a triple and made several great plays at third. The next game he added two more hits. By the end of April, he was hitting .406, trailing only Rocky Colavito and Harvey Kuenn for the league lead. He was still hitting well in May and there was some talk that he might be named as a reserve on the All-Star team.

His seemingly endless array of jaw-dropping defensive moves was the talk of the American League. He put on an impressive fielding display during a late-April series against the Yankees, topped by a play in which he made a diving stop of a Gil McDougald bouncer between third and short, scrambled to his feet, and threw home to get Yogi Berra. Berra admitted that he took for granted that the ball would get through for a base hit. "That kid's got a great future," he told reporters.

Another eyepopper soon after that saw Brooks stumbling over a bullpen mound while catching a foul fly. Bob Addie wrote in the *Sporting News,* "Everybody who sees Brooks Robinson, the 21-year-old third baseman of the Orioles, labels him a future great. . . . Everywhere the Birds go, rival players and managers are acclaiming the whiz-kid from Little Rock as a glove man second to none." Less than a month later, Jim Ellis added in the *Sporting News,* "So dependably was he scooping up smashes down third base way that he earned the nickname 'vacuum cleaner.'" His glove definitely had them talking.

Just when it seemed as though Brooks was hitting his stride, a sharp slump caused his batting average to plummet. He developed a hitch, was swinging at high pitches too often and popping up just about everything. The slump arrived perhaps one week too soon—Brooks narrowly missed making the All-Star team, finishing second to Frank Malzone in the players' vote.

Brooks continued to struggle at the plate, and after a 2-for-39 stretch in August in which he also made several uncharacteristic errors, Richards sat him for a while and used Dick Williams at third. Brooks played a part in history September 28 when he replaced Williams late in the game while 36-year-old knuckler Hoyt Wilhelm had a no-hitter going against the Yankees. Brooks made two outstanding plays charging topped grounders on the damp misty field. In the ninth inning, right-handed slugger Hank Bauer stepped to the plate and dropped a bunt down the third base line. As Brooks charged the ball, he snuck a glance at Bauer sprinting down the first base line and determined that if he fielded the ball there was no chance to get his man at first. The only play was to let the ball roll and hope it bent foul, which it finally did, and then Brooks quickly snatched it up. Bauer trudged back to the plate and bounced one to the mound and the first Baltimore Oriole no-hitter was in the books.

While everyone loved to watch Brooks wield his glove, in truth, he was barely hitting enough to hold on to his job. The fact that the Orioles did not have a power hitter other than Gus Triandos and only one good-hitting outfielder (Gene Woodling) made it difficult to have the luxury of a light-hitting third baseman in the lineup. Brooks was swinging at too many bad pitches, often hacking away early in the count at anything close to avoid getting behind and striking out. The patience Richards was showing him seemed to make him press even more.

Brooks finished the 1958 season with a .238 batting average and three home runs in 463 at bats. The Orioles finished in sixth place, three games out of the first division. In spite of his weak hitting, Brooks was being touted as one of the brightest young players in baseball. "As a third baseman, he has made it clear around the American League that he takes a back seat to nobody," said Bill Tanton in a *Baseball Digest* article entitled "Baltimore's Future All-Star at Third."

"I think he's the best third baseman in the league right now," said Tiger manager Jack Tighe.

"I think Brooks is in a class by himself as a defensive third baseman," added Richards.

The future indeed appeared bright for Brooks Robinson. He could hardly wait for the next season. But first, he had to pay a debt to Uncle Sam.

6. Back to the Minors

THE GENERATION OF AMERICAN MEN who came of age in the 1950s had never known a time when there was not a military draft. In an era in which a major star such as Elvis Presley would report for duty at the peak of his career without a peep of protest, a struggling baseball player certainly had no room for complaint. The choice for Brooks was to risk being drafted for two years of continuous service or to spend six months on active duty with the Arkansas National Guard followed by five and a half years of reserve duty. He chose the second option and served time at Fort Chaffee and Fort Lynn after the 1958 season. While military life kept him in good physical condition, it was not baseball shape. He tried to practice with several other baseball players but it was difficult to work out regularly and there was no substitute for hitting against decent pitching. Brooks hurried to the Orioles' new spring home in Miami as soon as he was released, reporting March 29, but there was little time to get ready to play major league baseball.

As the team headed north to start the season, Brooks's play was still olive drab and veteran Billy Klaus, picked up in an off-season trade, won the third base job. The day before the opener, however, Klaus slipped in his hotel bathroom, fell, and jammed his side against a wash basin, suffering a hairline rib fracture. By default, Brooks opened the season as the starter, but he failed to hit. Klaus soon returned and Brooks went back to the bench. Journeyman Jim Finigan was picked up and began seeing time at third base.

Because of baseball's "returning serviceman rule" at the time, Brooks was carried by the Orioles without counting on their official roster limit. That status ran out on May 2. At that point Brooks had five hits in 25 at bats for an even .200 batting average. The team was in Chicago to play the White Sox and Brooks was in his hotel room when Coach Lum Harris called and said Richards wanted to see him for breakfast in the hotel coffee shop.

Brooks found Richards sitting alone in a corner, reading the paper and sipping coffee. Before Brooks could dig into his eggs, Richards spilled the news: "We want you to go to Vancouver. You need work and out there you can play every day." Brooks was speechless. "Go out there and play yourself into shape," Richards continued. "If you get your game together, I'll bring you back at the All-Star break."

The news hit the young third baseman like a bad hop to the kneecap. He had a hard time finishing his breakfast, fighting to keep his eyes from watering and struggling to force food past the lump in his throat. Two years on the major league roster as a regular and now he was being sent down? Emotions flooded in—anger, denial, pain—but he kept his thoughts quiet, excused himself, and slunk upstairs. What would people back in Little Rock think when they heard the news? Brooks somberly packed his bags and snuck out of the hotel. He sat on the street side of the bus to the airport so teammates coming out early wouldn't see him, not being able to bear the thought of answering the inevitable questions. It was the low point of his career. *I'll bring you back at the All-Star break.* Was Richards serious, or was he just saying that to ease the pain? He was an impossible man to read.

Did Paul Richards really feel that the Orioles were a better team with Billy Klaus and Jim Finigan playing third base instead of Brooks Robinson? "We [the writers] were all surprised when Brooks got sent out to Vancouver," says Maisel. "But Richards was smart. He saw that Brooks needed more work on his hitting. He couldn't hit high fastballs but was always chasing them—word got around, pitchers aren't stupid. Vancouver had a good team and a good manager. Richards told me later that day that the move would be good for him. He had every intention of bringing him back soon."

To say that Brooks Robinson was at a crossroads in his career would be not only a cliché but a gross understatement as well. He had spent parts of five seasons in the majors, accumulating 651 at bats, and had six home runs, 48 RBIs, and a .231 batting average to show for it. Major league benches were littered with similar-hitting, once promising, good-fielding prospects who had been turned into utility infield lifers. Brooks would be 22 years old in a few weeks; time was running out. One can only wonder what would have happened if Brooks had gone to Vancouver and sulked his way to a .230 season. How much patience would Paul Richards have had while he was regularly looking over busloads of new players?

If ever a player had a reason to sulk, it was Brooks Robinson, but if he did wallow in self-pity, he was finished by the time he got off the plane and never gave any outward indication. Vancouver manager Charlie Metro would later tell reporters that instead of moping and complaining about being sent down, Brooks acted like he had been promoted to Vancouver to help the team and raved about the scenery on Canada's west coast.

Brooks quickly made himself at home. He already knew quite a few of the players at Vancouver. Ron Hansen and Chuck Estrada, whom he had met and befriended in spring training, offered to share their apartment. Wayne Causey, freed from the restrictions of the bonus baby rule, was also there.

Forty-year-old Charlie Metro, the manager of the Vancouver Mounties, had a reputation as a scourge of wayward umpires. It was rumored that when he was hired to manage Vancouver in 1957, the owners took out an insurance policy from Lloyd's of London to cover the first $500 in fines he generated. He was equally harsh with his players. It was not uncommon for him to drag the team out for morning practice the day after a loss. He believed in keeping his players in shape. The whole team ran along the warning track every day before games. Once when a pitcher complained that Metro was running the players until they were sterile, he replied, "Well, your wife'll appreciate that."

"Charlie Metro was tough on everybody," says pitcher Wes Stock, who palled around with Brooks, Hansen, and Estrada. "You played the game hard or else. But he was a good man to have as a manager in the minors. You learned what it took to be a big league ballplayer. He got you ready for the majors."

Metro was an incurable optimist. He had an eye for talent, was an excellent teacher, and was a good baseball man in general. "I liked Charlie," says Estrada, a hard-throwing young right-hander. "He just put us out there and we played—he didn't bother us with little things that weren't important. You knew he was always there for us. He really wanted his guys to make it to the next level." And Metro's eye for talent was apparently color-blind—in 1958, he had trotted out a lineup featuring eight African Americans, possibly the first time that had happened in North America outside the Negro Leagues. Metro was well liked around baseball and was considered by many to be one of the best storytellers in the game. Most importantly, he had the confidence of Paul Richards, who sent him many of Baltimore's prized prospects. In 1957, Metro had taken over a Vancouver team that had finished 38 games out of first in the Pacific Coast League the previous season and turned it into a contender.

Vancouver was a beautiful city and a great place to play baseball. The citizens enthusiastically embraced the team. The booster club included over 1,000 members and was believed to be the largest such group in organized ball. The stadium was in the middle of a tree-lined park, with gorgeous mountains visible in the distance. The 1959 Vancouver Triple A team featured a half-dozen players who would soon make the Baltimore Orioles a contender. "We had a great team in Vancouver in '59," says Estrada. "There was a lot of talent there. Almost our whole infield [Brooks, shortstop Ron Hansen, second baseman Marv Breeding] formed the Orioles infield the next year."

Brooks was placed in the lineup the day after he arrived in Vancouver and he quickly made his presence felt at the plate—breaking up a no-hitter in the seventh inning by future teammate Dick Hall of the Salt Lake City Bees in his first game. "Robinson is a sparkling gem for the Vancouver infield," *The Vancouver Sun* reported the next day. "Manager Charlie Metro, who calls Robbie 'the best glove man I've ever seen at third base,' was grinning ear to ear [upon Brooks's arrival]."

There was soon a serious setback, however. Talk to anyone who was with Brooks at Vancouver and the first thing they mention is "the accident." May 17, the day before his 22nd birthday, almost turned out to be the last game Brooks ever played. The field was wet, as it usually was in the rainy Vancouver summer—so much so that the poorly draining outfield in Capilano Stadium was called "Laws' Lagoon" after owner Brick Laws. Brooks hit a home run early in the game against Portland and made a great play in the field by grabbing a pop foul out of the third base seats. In the fourth inning, he chased a high, twisting foul ball that kept drifting toward the Mounties' dugout. As he leaned over the dugout railing for the ball, which was just beyond his outstretched glove, his feet slipped and he fell into the dugout. He reached out with his right arm for support but his shirt got caught on a thick wire hook that was protruding from the guardrail. The hook dug deep into the muscle of his right biceps.

Caught, he hung there, suspended on his heels, almost sitting down, but not quite able to, as his own weight ripped the hook deeper into his flesh. Blood gushed out in spurts and ran down his arm, soaking his jersey. Teammates jumped up to help and Metro quickly grabbed Brooks, held him up, and kept his arm steady while they tried to carefully get him off the hook without any more damage. "I've never had one of these [situations]," the 91-year-old trainer, Doc Younker, remembered in 2011. "All I'm thinking of is how I'm going to get Brooks Robinson off that fence. I got a stepladder and took him down with help from some of the players. I got a bottle of Merthiolate and put that on and put a tourniquet on him and wrapped him up in my white towel. I called the ambulance but they never showed up. I said, 'I'm taking you to the hospital, I'm not waiting any longer.' I put on all the lights on my car and somebody called Nat Bailey's store on the corner and they went out and one of the guys stopped traffic." Younker would forever remember the amount of blood that covered the inside of his car by the time they reached the hospital.

"I was in the dugout," says Charles Metro, Jr., who was a thirteen-year-old batboy. "It happened right in front of me. I remember him hanging there. All the players got real quiet after they got him down. You could tell it was something serious. I've never seen so much blood."

"It was the worst thing I ever saw on a baseball field," says Causey. "I'll never forget all that blood."

"We were really worried," says Hansen. "It could have ended his career right there."

Younker was impressed by Brooks's demeanor throughout the drama. "He didn't even use swear words. I guess he hadn't learned them yet."

Brooks later recalled lying in the hospital emergency room while his arm was examined and looking at the exposed tendons of his arm, which had been filleted as if dissected on a cadaver table. He watched with detached amusement as the muscles and tendons moved when he wiggled his fingers. It was later reported that, while getting his arm treated, he joked with the nurses. "But this is serious," one said; "you might never bend that elbow again."

"In that case," Brooks answered, "I'll stay half-sober the rest of my life."

It was a very dangerous injury, but it could have been worse. The doctor told Brooks that a tendon had been severed but the nerve was intact. If the nerve had been cut, his playing career would have been over. Also, with a cut that deep on a dirty metal hook, there was a risk of infection.

But Brooks was lucky and the doctor was good. After successful surgery, he missed 25 games, then returned with no residual effects. They quickly fixed all the hooks on the rails in Capilano Stadium.

June 8, Brooks returned to the lineup with a two-run triple that led the Mounties to a 4–2 win. He then went on a hitting tear, raising his average well above .300. The team won 15 of the next 20 games and climbed into the pennant race with big crowds coming to every game. Their infield was touted as the best seen around the Pacific Coast League in years. Manager Fred Hutchinson of the Seattle Rainiers said, "Nothing goes through that side of the diamond [Robinson and Hansen]. You can't hit the ball on the ground and expect to win."

"Brooks was great with the glove at Vancouver," says Stock. "A lot of the other guys had seen him before and when we heard he was coming to Vancouver, they all talked about how good he was. It was funny, teams would come in to play a three- or four-game series. After he made a great play, the next day at the park, the guys on the other team would say, 'Gosh, did you see the play he made yesterday?'

We would laugh. 'He does that all the time.' We [the pitchers] would joke that we made so many mistakes, he had to learn to field all the hard-hit balls off of us, that's how he got so good."

In infield practice, Metro would try to get a ball past Hansen and Robinson. "I'd try to finesse them," Metro wrote in his autobiography. "I'd try to throw the ball way out there and then cut it back in, and then I'd try to cut it the other way, but I never could hit a ball through. . . . I told the writers that I had the best left infield in baseball, including the major leagues."

Brooks made an impression in more than the dugout wall that year. "Brooks was unforgettable, even if he had never made it big later," says Charles Metro, Jr. "He was just different from any other player I'd seen. He was so focused. He had such a great attitude. There were never any problems or complaints or negativity—he just focused on the game. It was like he was in another world. He had clear eyes, crystal clear, and there was no fooling around; just get in the game and play ball. He really was the best.

"He was also really nice, one of the nicest ballplayers," Metro continues. "I don't think he ever swore. He had kind of a quiet midwestern way about him. He was not a guy who said a lot in the clubhouse; he wouldn't yell and cheer a lot. But he was a lot of fun. My brother was four years younger than me and he hung around the field too. Brooks would play catch with us. We were also the clubhouse boys—we would sell candy bars and Cokes to the players. Candy was a nickel. Cokes were a nickel. They would mark down what they took, and at the end of the week they would pay their bill. Some guys wouldn't pay and we would have to track them down—not an easy thing for kids to do. Brooks always paid his on time and he always tipped us. That was a big deal for us."

"In 1959 you could see the talent; everybody could," says the manager's daughter Elena, who was 16 that year. "Dad would tell us, 'He's going to play in the major leagues a long time.'"

"Charlie thought the world of Brooks," says Charles Jr., speaking of his father. "He knew from the start he was the real thing and he would be a star. Brooks didn't seem to have any weaknesses that year."

"I'll never forget one play he made in Vancouver," the manager later wrote of Brooks. "The ball was hit to his left, and he went over and stretched his arms up way in the hole, almost back on the grass, angling back. He had his glove down near the ground because, as he always told me, he could bring the glove up more quickly than he could get it down. So the ball took a wicked hop, but he took the glove and put it back of his head, caught the ball, took a spin and threw the guy out at first base." In 1961, when asked about the best player he ever managed in the minors, Charlie Metro named Brooks Robinson.

According to Charles Jr., Elena had a huge crush on Brooks, "as did all the women from 12 to 60 who came to the games."

Chuck Estrada disagrees with the last statement. "I wouldn't limit it to 60, the old ladies loved him too."

"He might have become my son-in-law," wrote Charlie Metro in 2002. "I still catch heck about it from my daughter. She was sixteen or so when Brooks was at Vancouver. He asked her if he could take her to the show or have a date. When my daughter asked me, I said, 'Absolutely not. You're not old enough to go with him. By the time she was over 18, he was gone to the majors."

"It's true, I did have a crush on Brooks," says Elena. "I thought he was cute. He had great blue eyes; but also because he was so nice to everybody. He was very nice to me and my mother. He was always polite, always had something nice to say. I like to tell the story that Brooks asked my dad if he could take me out and my dad told him, 'Not if you value your baseball career.' I always told Dad, 'If it wasn't for you, you could have had a Hall of Famer for a son-in-law.'

"About 10 years ago, Brooks was in Denver for a card show," Elena continues. "I live outside Denver. My dad was there visiting and we went over to see Brooks. When he saw us, he got a big smile and greeted us—the first thing he did was come over and throw his arm around me and tell my dad, 'I'm still mad at you for not letting me take her out.' A little later, Dad got a postcard from Brooks saying how much he enjoyed seeing us. Then he wrote, 'But I still haven't forgotten that you wouldn't let me go out with your daughter.' Dad just laughed when he read that."

Brooks hit .331 in 42 games in Vancouver. He was recalled to the majors July 8, 1959—at the All-Star break, just as Richards had said. His picture appeared under the title "glove whiz" in the week's

Sporting News next to the headline of the accompanying article, "Bird Bobbles Bring Recall of Robinson: Infield Artist Brought Back from Vancouver to Help Bolster Orioles Defense." He was said to be a "prime favorite with Baltimore fans who remember him well for his exploits with a glove in previous years."

Although he was ecstatic to be back in Baltimore and had hits in eight of his first 10 games, Brooks still struggled at the plate the month of July. He was hitting .186 July 31, but his confidence never wavered and, just as important, the confidence of Paul Richards in Brooks never wavered. Then, everything changed. It was slow, almost imperceptible, at first—nothing earth-shattering; no epiphany; no burning bush event; just a gradual improvement in hitting that gained momentum, like a snowball rolling down a hill. August 1, Brooks had two hits. A week later he had another two-hit game, followed quickly by two consecutive two-hit games. Then, a week later, he had two hits in a game followed by two straight three-hit games. He raised his average over 50 points in a month.

Suddenly, the Orioles seemed like a new team. And Brooks Robinson seemed like a major leaguer. The confidence and spirit had always been there; the fielding certainly had been there; but now he was hitting. The *Sporting News* reported that Brooks was "displaying his old wizardry at third base" as the Orioles battled to stay in the first division. "Spectacular and sure-handed, Robinson clutches everything within reach. It's actually fun to watch the fellow field." More importantly, it was now becoming fun for Oriole fans to watch him hit. He was no longer overmatched by big league pitchers. In August, he had a 22-for-51 (.431) streak over 14 games and soon began demonstrating the late-game clutch hitting that would become a trademark. September 6, he homered leading off the ninth to tie a game with Washington 1–1. September 11, after Jerry Walker pitched 16 innings of six-hit ball, Brooks won the game with a two-out single in the bottom of the 16th. In a related note, which would make modern-day pitching coaches shriek in terror, Richards afterward told reporters that he would have cautiously taken the 20-year-old Walker out of the game had it reached the 17th inning. "He only threw 188 pitches, that's not many for 16 innings," added pitching coach Harry Brecheen.

Walker was Brooks's roommate that year. In 1959, he was having a solid year and had become the youngest pitcher ever to start an All-Star Game. He noticed the difference in his roommate. "After he came back from Vancouver he was a different player," he says. "He had always been a great fielder, but now he was hitting. He seemed more mature and sure of himself. Everybody started viewing him as a team leader."

Brooks continued to swing a hot bat the rest of the season. He carried the Oriole offense in August and September, hitting .343 (67-for-195) over the last two months—including two 4-for-4 days at Fenway Park—and ended the season with a .284 average as the Orioles finished in sixth place.

In only half a season Brooks had gone from banishment to the minors to being the Orioles' best player. His arrival as a major leaguer was undeniable. There would never again be doubt as to where Brooks Robinson belonged. Late in the year, Richards told reporters that Brooks was "the best player in the American League the last five weeks of the season." He was noted to be one of the only players on the team who was untouchable for trades.

Brooks recognized the change and what it meant. "He later told me that it was a big disappointment being sent out to Vancouver, but that it was probably the best thing that ever happened to him," says Maisel.

Off the field, Brooks's fortunes were taking a dramatic turn for the better also. Needing space-filler during the off-season, the *Sporting News* had placed a small paragraph in the February 4, 1959, issue in which Oriole general manager Lee MacPhail announced that 17 flights had been scheduled for the team for the 1959 season (as opposed to only seven in 1958). "There are many advantages to flying, not the least is that we can arrange our own departure times in most cases, arrive in the next city in time to have a full night's rest," MacPhail stated. Brooks didn't know it at the time, but the decision to fly more would play a major role in the rest of his life, as he discovered an advantage to flying even better than rest.

August 26, Brooks was in good spirits as he and his teammates boarded their United Airlines flight in Kansas City. They had just beaten the A's 6–3 and Brooks had contributed a two-run home run. As he stepped onto the plane, Brooks found himself suddenly entranced by an angel. Stewardess Connie Butcher, a former Homecoming Queen at the University of Detroit, was tall, blond, and stunningly attractive. If ever a young man was smitten with just one look, and maybe a smile, it was Brooks Robinson—he was, as the owl in *Bambi* said, hopelessly twitterpated. As he went back to his seat, his mind raced to come up with a plan to meet this gorgeous creature. He also immediately recognized an even greater problem—there were 24 baseball players on the flight, men who made their living based in part on their excellent eyesight—eyesight that would surely notice this lovely lady—and some of them would undoubtedly have the same idea as Brooks. He quickly jumped into an aisle seat. When Jerry Walker arrived, Brooks made him crawl over to the window seat. "What's going on?" Walker asked.

"I'll tell you later," Brooks replied.

Brooks soon stopped the stewardess going down the aisle, "Miss, could you please bring me a glass of iced tea?"

He promptly asked for another, then another. Finally, unable to hold any more tea, he summoned up the courage to make his move. He carried his glass back to the galley and returned it to her.

"Excuse me miss, have you got a moment? I want to tell you something," he said in a conspiratorial tone. He then clued her in: "If any of these guys ask you for a date, tell them you don't go out with married men. Every one of them is married. I'm the only single guy on the team."

She thanked him for this important piece of information, most likely smart enough to see through the ruse. They continued to talk and before the plane landed, Brooks had a phone number and a date lined up, much to the chagrin of the other bachelors on the flight— about half the team.

"That night, Brooks said something to the effect that he was going to marry her," says his roommate Walker. "He was definitely smitten from the start."

The right place at the right time? Connie wasn't even supposed to be on the flight. She had been on reserve, but was called at the last minute to pick up the baseball team. But Brooks also knew how to take advantage of a good thing when he saw it. In a little over a year, Connie Butcher would become Mrs. Brooks Robinson, a title she still happily carries over 50 years later.

The next day, Brooks had his first 4-for-4 day of the season, against the Red Sox. Maybe being smitten is good for the batting average.

7. Baby Birds

"WE HAVE A YOUNG CLUB with tremendous potential and I am more eager to see what is going to happen in this 1960 season than I have ever been in 34 years of baseball." The speaker was Paul Richards, addressing the preseason luncheon meeting of the Baltimore Sports Reporters Association. While many dismissed this as typical springtime blather designed to sell a few tickets, it was soon apparent that the 1960 Orioles would bear little resemblance to previous teams.

For four years, Richards's scouts had been signing top-quality talent that had then been trained in his personally directed farm system. He had made a conscious decision late in 1959 that the time had come to capitalize on his investments. The youth movement was now officially in full swing. During spring training, Richards had called a team meeting and, addressing the youngsters, told them, "This gang before me is the Orioles this year. You have the jobs. No one is going to take them away from you. This is your chance. Make the most of it." In other words, it was time to start with the steak and hot tamales.

"That kind of talk gave us confidence," Brooks Robinson said later in the summer, "not only in ourselves, but in Mr. Richards. It meant that we would have the time to correct our mistakes and to make good."

Other than Brooks, Gene Woodling, Gus Triandos, and pitchers Hoyt Wilhelm, Hal "Skinny," Brown, and Arnold Portocarrero, the roster held no one who had been with the team before 1959. Only Triandos and Woodling had been on the Orioles in 1955 when Brooks had first joined them. As stated in *Sports Illustrated*, there were two groups of players on the Orioles: the five veterans and "the large, noisy crowd which assembles each day in the Oriole clubhouse to watch [them] shave."

Although he wouldn't turn 23 until May, Brooks was suddenly one of the old hands. Early in the season he joked to a reporter, "I guess it will be up to Woodling, Hoyt Wilhelm and me to keep the kids in line." While Brooks's clubhouse presence was understated—amiably getting along with everyone but by no means dominating conversations and certainly never calling out teammates—and he still invariably referred to his manager as "Mr. Richards," his self-assurance on the field was contagious and inspired confidence in his abilities. He was now one of the acknowledged leaders.

He entered spring training in 1960 as a fixture at third base. No longer were there doubts as to whether he could hit major league pitching. And he was now making serious money. He had received what general manager Lee MacPhail termed a "good raise" to $10,000 as a reward for his stellar play the second half of 1959. Doug Brown wrote in the *Sporting News*, "There is no question that Robby deserved the boost since he alone on the Orioles was hot in September . . . and some of the 22-year-old youngster's sensational stops at third base already have become legends."

Brooks's play after returning from Vancouver had impressed everyone. *Sports Illustrated* stated in its preseason issue what was generally felt around the league: "Third base has been deeded outright to Brooks Robinson, who had made three previous unsuccessful bids for it. A tiger defensively, Robinson at last shows promise as a hitter as well."

Brooks was still far from being considered an All-Star, however. In a *Sport* article based on a preseason survey of American League managers rating the league's players, Frank Malzone of the Red Sox was the consensus choice as the best third baseman. Brooks was listed at seventh among league third basemen, just behind Bubba Phillips of Cleveland. The less than enthusiastic scouting report read: "Improved tremendously at bat toward the end of last season. Once considered an 'automatic out man.' Always battles the pitchers. An excellent fielder who gets remarkable mileage out of average arm and mediocre speed. Could move up right behind Malzone if hitting improves."

The backbone of the young 1960 Orioles team was the pitching staff. Three starters were 21: Milt Pappas, Jack Fisher, and Jerry Walker. The other two, graybeards Chuck Estrada and Steve Barber, were 22. Pappas had been 15–9 for the Orioles in 1959. He was brash on the mound and had the ability to back it up. Relying on two pitches, a fastball and slider, he had excellent control of both and was the most dependable member of the staff. Jack Fisher, who fought both control and weight problems, had an impressive array of off-speed pitches to set up his fastball. Estrada, who had spent the entire 1959 season at Vancouver, had a fast-breaking curve and a blazing fastball that exploded in any direction. Steve Barber was a left-hander with a heavy, sinking fastball and quick-breaking slider. He was just wild enough to make batters nervous. He had signed as a freshman off the University of Maryland campus in 1957 for $500. After a few years in the minors, he made the big jump to the majors from Class D ball for the 1960 season.

It was an unusual collection of very hard throwing young pitchers. This made the relief corps of veteran knuckleballers Hoyt Wilhelm and Skinny Brown a particularly vexing change of pace. The Oriole staff quickly proved to be one of the best in the league. "We had three power arms and two good pitchers," says Estrada. "Barber, Pappas, and myself were blessed with great talent. Walker was the control pitcher and Jack Fisher had good off-speed stuff. You couldn't have enough money to put together a young staff like that nowadays."

In addition to the neophytes on the pitching staff, the entire starting infield had been in the minors in 1959—all except Brooks for the whole season. Hustling second baseman Marv Breeding and shortstop Ron Hansen had been teammates at Vancouver. Twenty-six-year-old behemoth first baseman Jim Gentile had spent seven long years in the farm system of the Dodgers, hitting 208 minor league home runs for half a dozen teams while waiting for Gil Hodges to grow old. Despite the huge numbers in the minors, he was never given a shot by the Dodgers, who thought so little of him that they gave him to the Orioles on a trial basis for spring training in 1960 with the understanding that if Richards didn't like him, he could send him back for a partial refund, no receipt required. The man nicknamed Diamond Jim by Roy Campanella (who said he was a diamond in the rough) was a welcome addition to the Oriole team, which was in dire need of a power hitter. "I had met Brooks in the Texas League back in 1956," says Gentile. "When I got to the Orioles in the spring of 1960, he was the first guy I saw when I came through the door in Miami. He said, 'Where have you been? I've been waiting for you for four years to get here.'"

Even though Gentile was less than impressive in Florida, Richards decided to keep him. "I thought I was going to get sent out for sure," Gentile says. "Richards called me in and said, 'Son, you can't be as bad as you look. I need power. You hit 210 homers in the minors, so you must be able to hit. I'm gonna give you 150 at bats here to see what you can do.'" It turned out to be a wise decision. Gentile would hit 21 home runs with 98 RBIs in 1960 and became one of the best power hitters in the league the next several years.

The last name was one of the great misnomers of baseball, however. An intense competitor, he was anything but genteel on the field. Known for his volatile temper, he was given to splintering bats, flinging helmets, and storming umpires. Jim Gentile never got cheated on a swing in his life—his cuts were so violent that he occasionally bruised his own back by hitting it with the bat on his follow-through. Fans, who can sense indifference in players and detest it, loved Diamond Jim for his obvious competitive fire and also for his friendliness around town. He was popular with teammates as well. In August he was fined $50 by the American League for a dispute with an umpire after being thrown out on the bases. He promptly hung a donation box on the bulletin board in the clubhouse. Oriole players, perhaps afraid to walk past the hulking first baseman without at least making a show of digging in their pockets, dutifully contributed. Gentile happily informed reporters that he had collected $1.48 from his buddies to help pay the fine.

The Orioles outfield was bolstered by the addition of center fielder Jackie Brandt from the Giants. Brandt was a gifted athlete with great speed, a strong arm, and surprising power. He was also one of the original flakes, so much so that he was known to most of the league by the nickname "Flakey." He was a happy, carefree guy—as loosey-goosey as they came—who was almost impossible to make mad. His laid-back attitude and general contentment with life were sometimes mistaken for laziness. When writers complained that he seemed too nonchalant, Brandt vowed to improve his image: "This year I'm going to play with harder nonchalance."

Brandt seemed to have a special talent for driving managers crazy and was never bothered by incidentals like facts—he had an excuse for everything. Once when he came back to the bench after striking out with the bases loaded, Richards asked, "What pitch were you guessing? Fastball or curve?"

"Neither," Brandt replied. "I was guessing ball."

On a later occasion, after Brandt misplayed a fly ball, then manager Hank Bauer asked what happened. Brandt answered without hesitation, "I lost it in the jet stream."

As the team boarded a plane for Boston that was late due to bad weather, Brandt asked loudly, "What time is this plane scheduled to crash?" Standing nearby, catcher Clint Courtney, who was deathly afraid of flying anyway, was so unnerved by the comment that he left the airport and went to the bus station.

Once, tired of the minimal ice cream choices in the team's hotel, Brandt organized an expedition with other players to an ice cream place 20 miles away that offered multiple flavors. Upon arriving there, he was overwhelmed with the multitude of possibilities and ended up ordering vanilla, causing his angry teammates to consider making him walk back.

This new cast of characters did not impress anyone at the start of the season. Most observers felt that by jumping into the youth movement with both feet, the Orioles had potential to be a decent team in a few years—provided that most of the young players worked out. Few gave the team much chance for immediate improvement. After all, the Baltimore Orioles had never even had a winning season up to that point.

The assortment of rookies, add-ons, and veterans meshed well in the clubhouse, however. "The fun thing about the young guys was that almost all of us had come up together through the system," says pitcher Wes Stock, who moved up from Vancouver and augmented the bullpen. "We had started as kids just out of high school and had gotten to know each other either during spring training camps or on teams in the minors and had become friends, and now here we were in the majors playing together. So we were close as a team. A lot of us went out as a group on the road. We did a lot of things together. Later when we got families, we went to parties and cookouts together with our families. It was like a big club."

The veterans had been handpicked by Richards. They were hard-nosed players with good attitudes, not has-beens just putting in time. "Although we had a really young team for 1960, the older guys we had helped us out a lot," continues Stock. "Gene Woodling and Walt Dropo were like the dads. They would tell us if we did something wrong or even if we didn't have the right clothes on when we were getting ready to go out. They would send us back to the room to change, saying, 'You don't dress like that in the big leagues.' They kept us in line and taught us how big leaguers were supposed to act. Hoyt Wilhelm really was great to the young guys too. Away from the park his wife was like our mom, helping when we didn't know how to do things. That was really important for us. We respected their opinions because those guys had played for winners."

The Orioles, for the first time, looked like winners themselves. After going 1–5 to open the season, they quickly turned around and began winning major league baseball games at a rate not seen in Baltimore in the 20th century. May 16 in Kansas City, they beat the A's 2–1 to take sole possession of first place—the first day the team had occupied the top spot in the standings since the franchise had moved six years earlier. The fulfillment of Richards's five-year plan, timed perfectly, made the Wizard of Waxahachie, Texas, look like a genius.

The young Orioles were soon the talk of the sporting world. *Sports Illustrated* called them "pink-cheeked players too young to be called men, too old to be called cub scouts." They were called "Eager Young Birds," "Baby Birds," and "Richards' Whiz Kids." The pitching staff was tagged the "Kiddie Korps." Whatever they were called, they were playing great baseball and as the season progressed, instead of fading, as everyone expected, they hung right in there with the old-money aristocracy of the league. They were just young, brash, and optimistic enough to believe they could win. A string of late-game comebacks and narrow victories kept them in contention. By mid-June the team had won 18 of 22 one-run games. The change in attitude from perennial losers to contenders was contagious. "I don't think we even realized how good we were doing," says Estrada. "We didn't even think about it. We just went out and played and had fun." And nothing is more fun than being young and athletic, and winning.

Brooks, like most of the players, lived near the stadium, sharing a three-bedroom house with Hansen, Estrada, and Skinny Brown. "There was a family named the Grotens who had one of those tri-level row houses; the kind where the outside walls attach to the next house," says Estrada. "During the season, they would move downstairs and rent out the upstairs to ballplayers. They were wonderful people; just really great. Mrs. Groten took care of us like we were her kids. We had a lot of fun, we ran around a lot, did everything together, breakfast, lunch, and dinner."

Brooks roomed with Ron Hansen on the road. At 6-foot-3 the 21-year-old Hansen had legitimate power and was a forerunner of the large Cal Ripken–type shortstops that would populate the league twenty-five years later. Hansen and Brooks had met during spring camp in 1957 and became close friends. They had a lot in common and enjoyed joking with one another. In his 1974 autobiography, Brooks would still call Hansen his best friend in baseball. "We were close those first few years in Baltimore," says Hansen. "We ran around together most of the time, at home and on the road." There was little hell-raising—these were not the party guys on the team. "We didn't get into any trouble or stay out late—mostly we just went out to eat and went to a lot of movies. Of course after we both got married, we didn't run around as much when we were at home, but we still roomed together on the road. After I got traded in 1963 I still made my home in Baltimore and we always got together a lot in the off-season."

At home, the players walked to the ballpark every day, passing through the azalea-scented neighborhood, waving to kids and neighbors on the way. "The Baltimore fans were outstanding," says Stock. "Baltimore was really like a small city then. After a while, it seemed like everybody knew your name. You could walk down the street and fans would say 'Hi' and talk to you—not bothering you, just being nice. Policemen would stop you and say 'Great game.'"

"The best time was on Sundays at home during crab season," says Estrada. "Some guy would deliver a sack of crabs, already cooked, to our house and we would have a feast. He just wanted to be nice because we were ballplayers. Man, that was great. You never saw a bunch of guys get out of a ballpark so fast in your life as we did those days. We couldn't wait to get at those crabs."

Baltimore at the time was a unique place in the realm of sports communities. The population had peaked in 1950 at nearly one million but the city still had a smallish atmosphere and a characteristic identity, with middle-class people living inside distinct neighborhoods, predominantly in row houses, within the city. Athletes, who were not making much more money than most of the city's workers, were full-time members of the community—friends and neighbors—not secluded away in gated, guarded mansions in the suburbs. They were so frequently spotted around town that it was not a cause for a scene, it was just like seeing a local schoolteacher or mailman; the only difference was that on game day they would be out on the field. Fans and athletes interacted almost as equals—an atmosphere that modern sports economics prevents from being replicated.

After the Colts won championships in 1958 and 1959, the city was first and foremost a football town. Led by working-class, blue-collar heroes like Johnny Unitas, Art Donovan, Gino Marchetti, and Alan Ameche, the Colts were revered by the entire city. The baseball players, while not held on the exalted plane of the footballers, were similarly accepted and loved by the citizens. Players made Baltimore their home and found it easy to find employment and business opportunities around town. A player's name on a sign in front of a restaurant or store guaranteed a certain recognition and patronage—even more so if the guy was reported to be spotted there on occasion. The players were accessible in ways that modern fans would find unfathomable. The club would send players out for autograph sessions, paying them $50, and it was a big deal, for both the fans and the low-paid players, who appreciated the extra money. During the winter one season, the team came up with an interesting gimmick to stimulate interest in season ticket sales: Oriole players Gentile, Brandt, Pappas, and Robinson were available, by appointment, to meet with fans to discuss baseball. The fans merely needed to call the Oriole office to make an appointment with the player of their choice. The team held special picture days at Memorial Stadium in which fans could walk out on the field and take pictures with their favorite players.

And suddenly, everyone's favorite player was Brooks Robinson. The hard work on his hitting was finally paying off. He had now filled out to 190 pounds (up from the 175 he weighed when he first reported in 1955) and had matured into the key man in the Oriole batting order. He began the season in the six slot, but as his batting average steadily climbed he was moved up to five and then, after hitting .333 for the month of June and .351 for July, to third in the order. He developed a reputation for uncanny late-game clutch hitting that would continue throughout his career. And his fielding seemed, if possible, even better. The unbelievable plays came to be expected and "E-5" was spotted around Baltimore about as often as Bigfoot. Unlike some fielders who make great plays, then have a mental lapse on the routine ones, Brooks made them all. After so many false starts, the knee injury, the beanings, the demotion, the arm injury—he had withstood the misfortune. By midseason, he was the best player on the team.

As out-of-town sportswriters began making their way to Brooks's locker after games, they found out what Baltimore writers, who were beginning to call him Mr. Impossible, had known for several years: he was unfailingly polite, eager to please, patient with interviews, and always ready with a quote—albeit frequently laced with clichés and coach-speak. Not at all shy, he acted like he had been there all his life. His naturally outgoing personality and self-deprecating sense of humor made him engaging and his relaxed southern accent made conversations feel just like talking to an old friend, not a star athlete. He seemed to enjoy talking to them. He was soon on a first name basis with writers in every city. "He was that way with everybody," says Chuck Estrada. "If you met Brooks, the minute you talked to him, you liked him."

"He was friendly to everybody," says Gentile. "One of a kind. And he was never grumpy or rude after a bad game. He was the same win or lose."

Brooks quickly became one of the most popular players among writers, who relayed the scouting report on his personality to their readers. He was described in *Sport* as "quiet, good-natured, polite and modest," and, impressed with his obvious love for the game, another writer for *Sport* added, "In temperament, he's a rah-rah boy, after the other kids have settled down snug in their rocking chairs, Robinson will still have his boyish enthusiasm."

In a *Baseball Digest* profile, Charles Dexter wrote that Brooks was "clean-cut, good-looking, optimistic, out-going." He noted that he hunted birds and squirrel in the off-season, but otherwise didn't have a hobby, and that he "drives an old Chevrolet, lives with his parents in the off-season and is not overly interested in chicks or anything stronger than water."

By mid-July Brooks was being noticed by opponents as well as the media. He was named to his first All-Star team as a reserve behind Frank Malzone. During the years from 1959 to 1962, there were two All-Star games each year to help boost revenue for the players' pension fund. The first game in 1960 was in Kansas City at Municipal Stadium on July 11. Brooks traveled there along with fellow Oriole All-Stars Estrada, Gentile, and Hansen.

The All-Star Game was much less of a media extravaganza and more of a game then. The players arrived at their hotel, found a letter telling them what time to report to the field the next day, played the game, then left town. It was a tremendous honor since players were selected to the team by their peers (players, managers, and coaches made the selections from 1958 to 1969), and, since there were only eight teams in each league, the need to have at least one player from each team did not force managers to select a handful of unknown guys from bad teams to meet the rule, while leaving good players at home. In 1960, 17 future Hall of Famers took the field. Brooks shared a dugout with Luis Aparicio, Yogi Berra, Whitey Ford, Nellie Fox, Al

Kaline, Mickey Mantle, Early Wynn, and Ted Williams. Across the field sat Henry Aaron, Ernie Banks, Orlando Cepeda, Roberto Clemente, Eddie Mathews, Willie Mays, Bill Mazeroski, and Stan Musial.

The game afforded the chance to associate with the other All-Star players at the field and in the hotel. It was a great thrill for the young players walking through the hotel lobby, being recognized by fans, and spotting venerable heroes from their youth. Brooks got a special treat listening to Ted Williams expound on hitting to other players on the plane. They didn't need to attach artificial significance, such as home field advantage in the World Series, to the outcome of the All-Star Game. The game itself was meaningful to the players. With no interleague play, it was the only chance, other than the World Series and spring training, to see the other league and to judge who was the best.

Brooks entered his first All-Star Game at third base in the top of the sixth inning. In his first All-Star at bat, he grounded out to short against Pirate Roy Face. In the ninth, he faced Vern Law and flied out to center. The National League won 5–3. They flew to New York where the second All-Star game was played on July 13 in Yankee Stadium. Brooks was 0-for-1, and the Nationals won again, 6–0. It was reported in *Sports Illustrated* that during the All-Star Game the young third baseman made a startling discovery that tainted his sense of fair play while sitting in the home dugout of the stadium for the first time, "Hey, it's air-conditioned," he said with surprise. The visiting dugout in Yankee Stadium had always been unbearably hot and humid during New York summers—giving the Bronx Bombers an added advantage during dog-day pennant race games.

Just before the All-Star break, Brooks had hits in his last three at bats, a triple, a double, and a home run. The first game after the break, July 15 against the White Sox, he had a double, triple, and home run to go with two singles in a 5–2 victory. It would turn out to be the only time an Oriole hit for the cycle until 1994 when Cal Ripken, Jr., turned the trick (still the only two in team history). It also gave Brooks eight straight hits.

The hits kept coming as Brooks and the Orioles continued to top the standings. July 31, against the Indians, he had five RBIs, including his first grand slam. Facing the Indians a week later, he had another five-hit day.

Realizing that something special was happening, Baltimore fans flocked to see their team play. The Orioles broke a million in attendance in late August, the earliest in team history. Twenty-five-year-old John Hunter, the lucky one millionth fan of the season, received a free trip to New York for the Orioles-Yankees series September 16–18 and a 1961 season pass.

As August came to an end, the Orioles showed the world that they were no longer a surprising bunch of youngsters, but a legitimate contender, hanging in a tight three-team race with the Yankees and the defending champion White Sox. Giddy Baltimore citizens began thinking about the prospects for their first World Series.

On September 2, the Yankees arrived in Baltimore with a one-and-a-half-game lead, prepared to put the annoying Orioles in their place. It was the most important series in Oriole history up to that point. *Baltimore Sun* sports editor Bob Maisel summed up the mood, writing, "It is difficult to match the excitement generated by the fight for the top spot in a major league pennant race. . . . Hold on to your hats." These were the Yankees of Mantle, Maris, Ford, and Berra, winners of 10 of the last 12 American League pennants. The young Orioles were not intimidated, however. "We felt like we could beat anybody by that time," says Estrada. "That's what you go there for, to find out if you belong." The Orioles proved that they definitely belonged. The first game, 44,518 (an estimated 5,000 were turned away) watched the Orioles face Whitey Ford. Brooks doubled into the right field corner to score Brandt in the first inning to put the Orioles on top. He added a single and a run later. In the ninth, he fielded a Hector Lopez smash that had bounced off Milt Pappas's leg and threw the batter out. Pappas was brilliant, throwing a three-hitter and at one time retiring 18 in a row as the Orioles won 5–0. The win was their 77th of the season, setting a new team mark.

Another near-sellout crowd showed up Saturday, cheering every play. Once again Brooks sparkled with his glove and bat. In the third, he ranged far to his left to field Clete Boyer's slow roller and threw him out. In the fourth, he broke a scoreless tie, driving in the first run for the second day in a row. In the eighth, with the score 1–0, Casey Stengel brought in left-hander Luis Arroyo, who had emerged as one of the league's best relievers that season, confounding hitters

with his screwball. In the Oriole dugout, Richards told Brooks, leading off the inning, to be aware of the screwball breaking away from
him and try to hit the ball to right. In the on-deck circle, Gentile
stepped up and told Brooks, "Don't be fooled by his screwgie." Arroyo
crossed up the advisers by throwing a fastball on the first pitch, but
Brooks hit it into the left field seats to make the winning score 2–0
and the Orioles were in first place. The home run gave him a 3-for-4
day. After the game, Yankee manager Casey Stengel told reporters,
"The man at third base is hitting better than he has ever hit in his
life, and sometimes you think you are lucky to get him out at all."

The next day, Chuck Estrada pitched no-hit ball for six and two-
thirds before fading and needing relief help from Hoyt Wilhelm.
The Orioles won 6–2 to make it a three-game sweep. The Yankees
left town two games out. "We just stared 'em in the face and beat 'em
down," an elated Richards told reporters in the noisy postgame clubhouse.

It concluded an 11–2 home stand for the Orioles and spirits were
high. Newly acquired 40-year-old pinch-hitting specialist Dave Philley told reporters, "I believe this club has about as good an attitude
as I've ever seen. There's no big star, just a lot of good, solid ball players, and every one of them seems to be pulling for the other ones.
Nobody's out to be a hero, they just want to win."

Maisel remarked that during the series there was "no tension whatsoever in the Oriole clubhouse," as players were making wisecracks
and one was even singing before the game.

"We were so sky high after sweeping the Yankees it was pitiful,"
says Estrada. Suddenly Baltimore was a baseball city—at least until
football season started. The town was talking about nothing but the
Baby Birds. Players' pictures and Oriole pennants were everywhere.
The city was wild with pennant fever.

Unfortunately, Brooks Robinson had a fever of another kind. The
Baltimore Sun sub-headline September 5 read, "Robinson in Hospital
with Fever, Might Not Play Today." Brooks had shown up for the final game of the Yankee series with a sore throat, nausea, chills, and
severe pain in his neck glands. Though he played against the Yankees, he was clearly weakened and after the game was taken to Union

Memorial Hospital where his temperature was 103 and he was diagnosed with "infectious tonsillitis." He spent the next day in the hospital, while the Orioles split a doubleheader with Washington. It was the first time all season Brooks had missed a game.

As the rest of the team took a train to Cleveland, Brooks remained hospitalized. He was finally cleared the next morning, with the doctor telling him he could play if he guaranteed three hits. Brooks flew to Cleveland, arrived shortly before game time, dressed, went on the field, played a game of pepper, then told Richards that he felt well enough to play. "That's the way he was," says Estrada. "He was there every day to play, come hell or high water. An infection wasn't going to keep him out of the lineup." Despite the doctor's orders, however, Brooks only got two hits in the game.

The Orioles played gamely, but their luck seemed to be running out. They alternated wins with excruciating close losses. There was a string of bad breaks in critical situations such as when Philley was picked off first in the ninth inning of a 3–2 loss to Cleveland and a few days later when the Orioles lost 3–2 in 11 innings in Chicago as Triandos, the slowest man in the league, left in the game instead of being removed for a pinch runner, was thrown out at the plate in the last inning. Brooks, obviously bothered by the infection, had a 1-for-26 skid September 8 to September 14. Meanwhile, the Yankees were doing what Yankee teams did in those days: winning almost every day down the stretch.

Brooks broke out of his slump in a wild win over the Tigers in Detroit September 14. He hit a two-out, two-run triple to tie the game in the ninth and scored the go-ahead run when Hansen followed with a single. Earlier in the game he made what the *Baltimore Sun* described as a "great leaping backhand catch of a real screamer to save at least one run." The triple was the ninth of the year for the man reputed to be slow, setting a new team record.

The Orioles pulled into New York by train on September 15 tied with the Yankees and ready for the showdown series of the year. The whole baseball world seemed to be watching. The hotel lobby was filled with writers, not just from New York and Baltimore, but from every other major league city as well.

The players were well aware that another sweep would provide, as Richards told reporters, "the gateway to the rainbow." Richards added, "There's no question these next four games are the most important ones these youngsters have ever faced." He said he was not worried about his players being affected by the pressure, but was concerned about the tension of expectations causing them to be too eager.

"By that time, we all thought we could win it," says Stock. "We didn't seem to feel pressure on us. But the Yankees just didn't make mistakes in those days. They never beat themselves. You couldn't make mistakes against them. One bad pitch was all it took."

The Yankees, accustomed to the pressure of September pennant races, played like the veteran champions they were and beat Barber, Estrada, Fisher, and Pappas—the heart of the Oriole staff—in order. In the first game, Hector Lopez gave the Yankees an early lead with a fly that bounced off Brandt's glove and fell into the right field bleachers along the foul pole at the 296-foot sign. Whitey Ford took a 4–0 shutout into the ninth. The Orioles got two runs, but Bobby Shantz came on to close the door with two men on, giving the Yankees a one-game lead in the pennant race.

The second game was tied 3–3 in the eighth when Berra led off with a hard ground ball that took a bad hop, hit first baseman Gentile in the elbow, and bounded into right center for a double. Estrada then walked two batters. Bobby Richardson followed with a smash up the middle that looked like a certain double play. The ball bounced off Estrada's glove, however, and into right field—rolling through the second base hole Klaus had just vacated when he broke up the middle to field it. It went for a double and brought in the two deciding runs.

The next day, the Yankees won both games of a doubleheader—one when a crucial pop fly barely fell in safe between four scrambling Oriole fielders. The Orioles left town four games back. The clock had struck midnight on their Cinderella season. "The Yankees broke our back," says Gentile.

The Orioles didn't choke, they were just beaten by a better team that took advantage of a maddening number of breaks in their favor;

the cream had risen to the top. It was the first time in a pennant race for most of the Orioles. Would a little more veteran leadership have helped keep them focused? "I don't think we had what you'd call a team leader," Gentle said in 2001. "We just didn't have the guy to get in the middle of the clubhouse and say, 'Hey look, fellas.' And we needed it. The only guy that had a cool head all the time was Brooks."

Gene Woodling, a veteran of five championships with the Yankees, had commented to a reporter about Brooks's maturity down the stretch. "He acts like he's been through 20 pennant races. That guy must eat pressure."

While the Orioles refused to fold and fought to catch up the last two weeks, the Yankees went on to win nine in a row and pulled away. "It was just hard to beat the Yankees in September," says Pappas. "Back then every year everyone else was fighting for second place. That Broadway play summed up our feelings: Damn Yankees."

But the Orioles didn't feel too bad after it was all over. It had been a great year. They had shown themselves and the rest of baseball that they were now one of the elite teams; Paul Richards's Oriole way was proving to be a success. The club gave a party—unusual for non–pennant winners—September 30 for players, officials, and wives. Lee MacPhail told reporters, "We don't have too much to complain about. We did better than we had a right to expect when we faced the season back in spring training, and the future looks good."

The season had been fun. "Overall for being a bunch of kids mixed with a few veterans, we had a pretty good year," says Estrada. They had been playing regularly in the major leagues for the first time, having good seasons, and making a run at the pennant. It was all new. They would go on to even greater success in future seasons, but to a certain extent, it would never be as fun as it was in those crazy summer days of 1960, when they had surprised the city and the baseball world; when the city really fell in love with the Orioles for the first time. "It's good to be young and have talent," says Estrada. "That whole year was just great."

The 1960 season would turn out to be a watershed year for the

Oriole franchise. The ghosts of the Browns and the laughable chronically losing teams would become only a distant historical footnote. It would be decades before the Orioles would be viewed as anything other than perennial contenders.

It was a banner year for the three boardinghouse roommates. In addition to being All-Stars, each collected end-of-the-season hardware. Estrada won 18 games and was the Rookie Pitcher of the Year. Hansen hit 22 homers, collected 86 RBIs, and beat out Estrada for Rookie of the Year. Brooks finished at .294 with 14 homers and 88 RBIs. His batting average was good for seventh place in the American League, where the leader, Pete Runnels of Boston, hit .320 and there were only five .300 hitters (the fewest since 1945). Brooks was selected by Baltimore sportswriters and sportscasters as the Most Valuable Oriole of 1960. He finished third in the American League MVP voting, coming in behind only a couple of guys named Maris and Mantle. The voting was very close: Maris 225, Mantle 222, Robinson 211. Brooks was the only player to get votes on every ballot cast (24).

Brooks had now firmly established himself as the premier fielding third baseman in the league. The Gold Glove Award had been created by the Rawlings Sporting Goods Company in 1957. Initially, only nine professional players—one at each position—received the award. In 1958, the number increased to 18, one for each position in each league. The selection was made by a vote of managers and coaches of the major league teams near the conclusion of the regular season. Frank Malzone of the Red Sox had won the Gold Glove for third basemen in 1957 and then won it for the American League in 1958 and 1959. Brooks Robinson decisively defeated Malzone in 1960: 184 votes to 32. Brooks led A.L. third basemen with a .977 fielding percentage, in putouts (171), in assists (328), and made only 12 errors the whole season. It would be 1976 before anyone else would win an American League Gold Glove at third base.

After the 1960 season ended, Brooks drove directly to Windsor, Ontario, for a previously scheduled appointment. After his first date with Connie Butcher in Boston, Brooks's days as a carefree bachelor had been numbered. Connie had been raised in Detroit and neighboring Windsor with eight brothers and sisters in a wealthy family. Her father owned a packaging firm and also owned the hockey team and arena in Windsor. Consequently, Connie knew much more about hockey than baseball and, at the time of their first date, had no idea who Brooks Robinson of the Baltimore Orioles was. That soon changed. They remained in touch through mail and frequent phone calls the rest of the 1959 season and Brooks spent time in Chicago during the off-season, where Connie lived near Wrigley Field with two other stewardesses. Connie flew to Little Rock to spend Christmas with the Robinsons and later visited Brooks in Miami during spring training.

Brooks spent as much time as possible with Connie during the 1960 season when their schedules matched, and they burned up the phone lines. Soon, they were making plans for a wedding after the 1960 season. Connie quit her job with the airline in midsummer and returned home to get everything ready.

There had been some anxious moments late in the season as the Orioles unexpectedly charged toward a pennant. Had they won, the wedding would have had to be delayed while the team finished business in the World Series, but alas, there was no need.

Connie's parents were not immediately in favor of the wedding. Not knowing Brooks very well, they wanted the couple to wait. Also, they were not sure the life of a baseball wife was appropriate for their daughter. "I told her that if she did [marry Brooks] she'd be raising her children by herself," said Mrs. Butcher in 1984. The fact that she was Catholic and he was Methodist was a significant hurdle in those days for both families to consider. Despite these potential problems, the young couple plunged ahead and never looked back.

"Brooks and I didn't want to wait," Connie told a reporter in 1983. "We loved each other. So we got married and my dad and mom got to love him too. I can understand how they felt when they found out I was marrying a ballplayer. But this wasn't just any ballplayer. This was Brooks Robinson."

The 1960 season ended on a Sunday and Brooks and Connie were married the next Saturday, October 8, in Christ the King Roman

Catholic Church in Windsor. Connie's sister, Barbara, was the brides-
maid and her husband served as best man. A picture of the happy
couple appeared in the *Sporting News* November 9, 1960.

After the wedding, they drove west through Montana, and then
turned south, listening to the World Series on the radio, on their way
to Lake Tahoe, where Brooks had previously promised to speak at a
Little League banquet. It made a nice honeymoon trip. Their mean-
dering return trip took them through Yosemite, Las Vegas, and Little
Rock, then back to Windsor to pick up Connie's stuff.

They drove, pulling a packed U-Haul trailer, through a near-
constant driving rain and arrived in Baltimore on Halloween night,
pulling up to the house Brooks had bought from Colts halfback L. G.
"Long Gone" Dupre near the end of the season. The main attraction
of the house was that it was only 10 blocks from Memorial Stadium.
Connie got her first view in the dark of the row houses in the neighborhood—a totally foreign type of architecture to her midwestern
upbringing. All the houses shared an adjacent outside wall with the
neighbors—there were no side yards. Each house was one room and
a hallway wide and three stories high; living room, dining room,
and kitchen on the entry level, with bedrooms above and basement
below.

"Welcome home, Mrs. Robinson," Brooks announced when they
arrived at the door. He then carried his bride over the threshold into
the nearly empty house, which contained only the bed and refrigera-
tor Brooks had bought before leaving.

In Connie, Brooks had found someone who closely approximated
his easygoing, friendly personality. "Connie was kind of quiet, but
not snobbish," says Milt Pappas, "a real first-class lady. She was very
down-to-earth, just like Brooks. They were perfect for each other. I
always joked with him that I couldn't believe he got somebody that
nice: 'How'd a guy like you get somebody like that?' But they made a
great couple."

For the first time, Brooks spent the winter in Baltimore. The decision
to live in Baltimore full-time had been a sort of compromise. Brooks
didn't have a desire to live in Windsor and, similarly, Connie was not
thrilled about Little Rock. So Baltimore was a natural choice. It would
turn out to be a great choice—for the happy couple and the city itself.

Baltimore was now officially, and forever, home for the Brooks Robinsons.

The second place finish in 1960 came with the burden, never before felt by the Orioles, of high expectations. With the young aces on the pitching staff and the equally young core of infielders, there was no reason to think of them as anything other than the team of the future. The Orioles were now firmly entrenched in the city. The pennant run had helped the team show a $318,000 profit, as opposed to the $53,000 loss of 1959. Brooks showed a profit also, signing in January for $20,000, doubling his 1960 salary, and eagerly reported to Miami a week early.

Paul Richards worked hard keeping the young players from taking things for granted, which he felt was the key to avoiding the sophomore jinx. He stalked the fields in the spring, looking for signs of complacency. Nevertheless, the Orioles started slow and quickly dropped back as the Tigers and Yankees pulled away from the league. Jim Gentile had a great season, hitting 46 home runs with 141 RBIs, but several of the young Birds had a letdown, particularly on the pitching staff, which was hit by a rash of sore arms. The Orioles wrestled for third place and held on for the season. Although they won 95 games, the most in their history, in the expansion year of 162 games, they were never in serious contention as the 1961 Yankees, behind 61 home runs from Roger Maris and 54 from Mickey Mantle, proved to be one of the best teams of all time while winning 109 games.

Brooks nearly duplicated his performance of 1960. The title of an article in *Sport* early in 1961 said it all: "Brooks Takes Charge in Baltimore." His reputation as a fielder without peer continued to grow. Bob Addie of *The Washington Post* wrote, "The 'young old-timers' in the press box are beginning to compare Baltimore's Brooks Robinson with the great third basemen of the past." And, in 1961, the greatest third baseman of the past was unanimously considered to be Pie Traynor, the Hall of Fame Pirate. More and more, baseball people were linking the names Robinson and Traynor in the same sentence. There were few others to be equated with the young Oriole third baseman. The only contemporary close was Clete Boyer of the Yankees, an exceptional fielder with a great arm to whom Brooks would often give a nod as his choice for the best third baseman. The comparison between Robinson and Traynor would be repeated for several years and then, without much fanfare, the comparisons would stop—by then Traynor would no longer be considered the standard.

"Robinson is unbelievable," said Richards in early 1961. "Just when he makes a play that you blink at to believe, he comes right back with one better. And he's consistent. He makes the big play for us in almost every game." Brooks also showed that his hitting performance of 1960 was no fluke. Batting in the leadoff spot most of the season, he hit .287 and finished with 192 hits—second in the A.L. only to Norm Cash's 193—breaking his own team record of 175 set in 1960. He also set a team record with 38 doubles. He was one of only two A.L. players to appear in all their team's games.

On the home front, things were changing rapidly as Connie soon announced that she was expecting. The delivery date was projected for July and Connie flew to Detroit to be with her parents, since they had no way of knowing where Brooks would be playing at the big moment. As it turned out, Brooks David Robinson arrived on July 24, 1961, at Providence Hospital in Detroit while Brooks was with the team playing in Cooperstown in the Hall of Fame game. He was in the field when the public address announcer broke in to inform every-one that the Orioles third baseman was now a father. Brooks left the field between innings and placed a phone call to the new mother. He did not get a chance to see his son until the All-Star break, a week later, when he finished up his stint as the starting third base-man, left after the sixth inning, and raced to the airport to catch the only flight to Detroit to see them.

As the Orioles were concluding their second consecutive winning season they were stunned by the abrupt departure of Paul Richards, who announced he was leaving in early September to be the general manager of the start-up Houston Colt .45s. The man who had built the Orioles and laid the groundwork for their future success was moving on. Richards's effect on Brooks had been immense. He had recognized the potential and shown patience waiting for the hitting to develop. In 2001 Brooks said, "In all my years in baseball, I don't know anyone who knew more about the game. I respect him more than any manager I ever played for."

Billy Hitchcock was selected as the new manager of the Orioles. A former halfback at Auburn, Hitchcock had played sporadically as a utility infielder in the majors with the Senators, Browns, Red Sox, A's, and Tigers in 1942 and from 1946 to 1953. He had been a third base coach for the floundering Tigers throughout the 1950s but had been passed over four times during managerial changes before finally being fired in a general housecleaning in 1960. He came to Baltimore after being voted Pacific Coast League Manager of the Year for his work at Vancouver in 1961.

All business on the field, Hitchcock was a model of restraint, every bit a gentleman. Although he occasionally used strong language with an umpire, he was otherwise never heard to utter profanity. He was well liked by most players but it became apparent that he was just too nice to manage a baseball team. He reasoned that the players were adults and should be able to take care of themselves off the field without annoyances such as rules and curfews. The Orioles had spent years laboring under the intense, domineering leers of Paul Richards. It was natural that the new relaxed atmosphere would lead to a letdown; and it was natural that some players might take advantage of the lack of restraint. "Billy was really a nice guy," Milt Pappas recalls, "but he wasn't a very good manager. He knew baseball, but he was a tough man to get to know. He didn't communicate very well. I don't think he was very good at managing people."

The team underperformed on the field. "Billy was the nicest guy you ever wanted to meet," Brooks said later, "but we didn't play very well under him." As the team struggled to a seventh place finish in 1962, the press began hinting that the reason for the Orioles' poor play could be found in bars and nightclubs around the league. This refrain was picked up, repeated, and became common knowledge (whether correct or incorrect). Sportswriters are a funny lot. If players drink and carouse and win, they are referred to as Peter Pan–like boys who never grew up (see Mantle, M.) or a fun-loving bunch of rascals (see Mets, 1986); but if they lose, that immediately becomes the reason for the losses and something must be done about it—even though the writers are frequently spotted enjoying these same pursuits with the players.

While the team as a whole struggled, Brooks only got better. *Sports Illustrated* declared emphatically in the preseason of 1962, "Brooks Robinson (24) is the best third baseman in the league." While never becoming known as a slugger, Brooks did develop legitimate home run power and became a consistent RBI man. After flirting with the magic number for three years, he hit .300 for the first time in 1962, coming in at .303. He also hit 23 home runs and drove in 86 RBIs. In May, he clubbed grand slams in consecutive games, tying a major league record (only the sixth major leaguer to accomplish the feat).

No less an authority than Pie Traynor himself spoke glowingly about Brooks: "He has exceptional reflexes and the strongest pull hitters in the game can't seem to get the ball by him. Sure, he'll miss now and then, but it's an accident when he does."

Casey Stengel added, "I've been around a long time but I've never seen anyone make the plays he does. I saw Traynor, and he was the best, Robinson is almost up there with him."

Earlier, Stengel had said, "That Robinson feller does some things at third base that I don't believe even Traynor did. And don't forget that bat of his. . . . He hits pretty mean in the clutch. He's the feller that keeps them young Orioles going."

Near the end of the 1962 season, Angels manager Bill Rigney told a reporter, "If I had my choice of any one player in the league that I could have for this ball club, do you know who I'd take? I'd take that fellow right out there [pointing to Brooks Robinson taking infield practice]. And that includes Mr. Mantle and the rest of them. There are some good ball players in this league, but all things considered, for our ball club I'd take Robinson. What an asset he is."

Brooks responded to the praise in typical aw-shucks manner: "It's good to know that people think so highly of me, but what I have done up to now means nothing. There is room to improve and nobody knows it like I do myself."

Brooks brought a style to infield play that had rarely been seen before. He provided those indelible moments that make sports truly worth watching, plays that made fans reflexively ask, "How did he do that?" Plays that guys would rehash the next day in the clubhouse and in the workplace; plays that the box scores—those otherwise brilliant concoctions of numbers and facts—had no way of explaining; plays that you just had to see to appreciate.

He played third base like no one else. He was constantly moving, creeping forward on the pitch, unlike most third basemen at the time, who crouched motionlessly, waiting for the ball to be hit. He didn't appear to have a classically strong arm for third base—not like Yankee Clete Boyer, for example, whose throws from any spot on the left side of the infield always transcribed a geometrically perfect straight line from release to the first baseman's glove. But it didn't seem to matter. Part of this was an illusion. His release was so quick, it just didn't look like he put anything into the throw. He didn't bring the ball back and cock it before throwing—there was one seamless motion between catching the ball, transferring it from his glove to his hand, and releasing it. He usually fired from the shoulder—sometimes with only a quick flick of his elbow, sometimes almost underhanded. But the ball always got there in time.

He had the body control of a gymnast and the reflexes of a cat. Unlike pure speed, game quickness can be difficult to measure, but the results are undeniable. Balls that were singles or doubles when hit to the left side against other teams were invariably outs—double plays with men on first—against the Orioles. He made diving stops no one had seen before and was able to bounce to his feet and throw as if his stomach was made of rubber—it didn't seem as though he had even touched the ground.

His signature play—the one play he made better than anyone who ever played before, or after, the one play Brooks Robinson did with mechanical perfection—was on charging slow-hit balls or bunts. He pounced on the helpless creatures like a ravenous eagle on a field mouse. He also possessed an innate, uncanny ability to determine, on the run, in the split second of action, if a ball should be let go to roll foul, fielded with two hands or barehanded, or thrown to second or first.

John Steadman described Brooks in the *Sporting News* shortly before the All-Star Game in 1963: "Known as the Human Vacuum Cleaner, a guy who picks up everything at third base, Brooks Robinson goes on to continually surpass himself in professional perfection. He's the master gloveman at his position. There isn't any type of batted ball, line shot over the bag or swinging bunt, that he can't handle with breath-stopping dexterity. Robinson is known as 'Mr. Impossible' because of his fast hands which swallow up ground balls like he's wearing suction cups."

Steadman noted that Oriole scout Ray Scarborough said he thought Brooks should be called a Hoover Upright: "A Hoover Upright is my name for him. He's a vacuum cleaner down there at third base, so let's give him a brand name."

Teammates, who watched Brooks every day, were duly impressed. "I had come over from the Giants, and we had Jim Davenport at third, and he was a hawk," said Jackie Brandt. "I was talking to Richards before spring training, and he said, 'We got a kid over here who can really play third.' I was telling him about Davenport, and Richards said, 'Watch this kid play before you make any comparisons.' Then we got started, and shoot, Brooks didn't miss nothing. Left, right, one-handed. . . . It was just a knack he had, natural reactions to the ball coming off the bat."

"He was such a great fielder, I could have played first base sitting in a rocking chair," says Gentile. "He never gave me a bad throw. And he was so quick. The first time I played with him a ball was hit to third, I ran to first and turned around and the ball was already there. I had to tell him to give me a little time to get there. I had to start playing a few steps closer to the base. He wasn't that fast running down the line to first, but for three feet to the right or left, there was nobody faster."

"His arm didn't look as strong as some guys'," says Hansen. "But he always got the guy out. If there was a slow runner, Brooks would get him by one or two steps. If the batter was a speedster, Brooks would still get him by one or two steps. He had great instincts. He knew just how hard he needed to throw on each play. He had a knack for knowing what to do."

"At first glance, Brooks was very deceiving," says Estrada. "He didn't have a typical athletic body, he was kind of slump-shouldered, not a real muscular guy, and he didn't appear to have a strong arm.

But then watching him play, you found out that none of that mattered, because he had great hands, a quick release, and the runner was always out. He almost looked like he timed the throw, but nobody ever beat it. Some other third basemen had more natural ability, but nobody was better than Brooks. He was kind of like Arnold Palmer—he had that something that made everything he did look great. And you never wanted to miss seeing a ball hit his way to see what would happen."

"Brooks made so many great plays, he just amazed me," says Pappas. "But the ones that really stick out were with a guy on first and a bunt. He had an unbelievable ability—better than anyone I ever saw—to get the ball and throw behind to get the guy at second. And he always made the right choice."

"Before I joined the team I had heard about him," says pitcher Dick Hall, who had two tours with Baltimore, 1961–66 and 1969–71. "He had a reputation all over the league as being a great fielder. The first time I pitched, a bunt situation came up. He came over from third and said, 'You cover toward first, I got this side.'" The whole side? "I just looked at him. I had never had anybody say anything like that before. But he wasn't bragging, he really did get anything to that side. He just wanted to make sure I didn't get in his way. I learned that was the best thing to do—just get out of his way and watch him do his thing."

Brooks also earned the respect of the clubhouse with his hard-nosed play and dedication. Baseball was his job—the only job he had ever wanted—and he took it seriously. He had seen plenty of guys with more natural talent leave their careers in bars and nightclubs; there was no way that would ever happen to Brooks Robinson. He reported for his job, ready to do it, every day—a fact that did not go unnoticed by the blue-collar workers of Baltimore. He missed only three games from July 1959 to August 1963 before Hitchcock finally rested him due to a slump (after 462 consecutive games). "He never says it's too hot or too cold; that the field is too hard or too soft; that it's raining or isn't," Richards told a reporter while discussing Brooks late in the 1960 season. "He just plays."

May 28, 1963, during batting practice, Brooks had a fight with the batting cage and the cage won. "The cage in Detroit was old and not very big," says Gentile. "You almost had to move it a little bit to the right or left depending on which side you hit from so you'd have enough room to follow through after your swing. On the last pitch of batting practice we would jump in for one pitch each real quick and play for a Coke. Brooks jumped in, didn't move the cage, and on his follow-through the bat hit the pole on the cage and bounced back and hit him in the mouth really hard. He was bleeding all over the place." He lost parts of two front teeth and chipped a third. After treatment by the trainer, he came back to the dugout ready to play. "He played nine innings with cotton in his mouth. He was a gamer."

Not learning anything, September 10, 1963, he had a similar incident. Swinging through a batting practice pitch, the bat flew out of his hands, hit the cage, bounced back, and hit him in the forehead, requiring three stitches. Again he played in the game.

"Another time he was chasing a foul pop fly," Gentile recalls. "He hit a door to the clubhouse. He went in but his chin didn't. He still finished the game."

Sports fans in Baltimore were nothing if not loyal to their heroes and by 1963 Brooks was well on his way to becoming an institution in the city—not yet as popular as some of the Colts, who were certified deities, but certainly the most popular baseball player. The Orioles had possessed some good players, but they had never had an established star who had been a product of the Oriole system; one who had belonged to them from the start. Brooks was their first. Since there was no major league history before Brooks arrived, there were no expectations for him to live up to; no comparisons with an immediately departed superstar—troubles guys like Mickey Mantle and Roger Maris had to battle constantly. It was all new, this big league sports thing. Baltimore fans were happy just to be able to participate; they were still relatively optimistic, not jaded by summers of suffering and winters of discontent spent longing for next years that never came. They also remembered a time in the city's not too distant past when the best athlete was a female duckpin bowler and the biggest celebrity was a stripper, so they were very appreciative of this young star on the diamond.

The press in Baltimore was generally complimentary to players and almost gushed when reporting on Brooks. Baltimore did not have the surplus of competing papers as in other baseball cities, so there was little need to take cheap shots to make headlines and sell papers. While reporters of the time usually gave players leeway and veiled their personal lives with platitudes and discretion, Brooks did nothing that required discretion—he was as advertised. And whereas some major stars had been insulted by the media in their early years and, as a consequence, built protective barriers against outsiders and reporters, there was no need of that for Brooks. If anything the press was too nice to him. But, at the same time, he made his own luck. There were no episodes of rudeness after a bad game, no popping off or ripping teammates. He was warm and welcoming with the press and they treated him with the respect that he showed them. He became friends with most of the Baltimore writers, not for a purpose, to curry favor, but just to be friendly, like he was with everyone. The city of Baltimore was accepting, unsophisticated, and imposed much fewer demands on a celebrity than, say, Boston or New York. It was a good fit for Brooks, an easy formula: just play great baseball and be a nice guy around town. He settled into the role as easily as his game glove slipped onto his hand.

By 1963 the Orioles were in a rut with no chance of catching the Yankees. The burden of expectation weighs as heavily on fans and management as it does on players, and the euphoria of the success of 1960 came with the realization that the grace period for the new team was over. After a seventh place finish in 1962, they rebounded in 1963 to a respectable 86–76, good for fourth place, but there were many who felt that they had too much talent for fourth place finishes. Baltimore fans, used to the great success of the Colts, expected better. The citizens had become bored. Attendance dropped to an average of 10,755 per game in 1963, the lowest in team history.

The press continued to harp that the reason for the underperformance on the field was that the Oriole players were flouting the rules under Hitchcock, and, even worse, that Hitchcock did not have the respect of the team. Players openly questioned his decisions. Pitchers would talk back and argue with him on the mound while being pulled. Once, when Hitchcock informed a starting pitcher that he was being demoted to the bullpen, the pitcher told him to "Go to hell," stormed out of the room, and promptly pleaded his case to the press. Morale reached a low point when Hitchcock called a team meeting to announce a new get-tough policy that included a curfew. He was interrupted by a clear, loud voice shouting an obscenity at him from the back of the room. Changes were needed. Hitchcock was fired after the season.

8. Most Valuable

THE NEW ORIOLE MANAGER for 1964 was 41-year-old Hank Bauer. People had been saying that the Orioles needed a tough man to succeed Billy Hitchcock and there was no question that Hank Bauer was a tough man. He had joined the Marines in 1942 and had served in nearly every major Pacific invasion, including Guadalcanal, Guam, and Okinawa, coming home as a gunnery sergeant with two Bronze Stars, two Purple Hearts, and a rear end full of shrapnel. When a routine X ray during a team physical 20 years after the war found metal fragments in Bauer's back, he shrugged and casually said he thought all the stuff had been removed in surgery after the war.

Bauer's face had been described as looking like a clenched fist. It did, and the unmistakable symbolism was appropriate. With his gruff, raspy voice and intimidating mug, he commanded respect. He could be brutally frank and not particularly tactful. He didn't hesitate to show his tough side to players who didn't do their job. But Bauer was no tyrant. "He looked scary but he had a heart of gold," says Milt Pappas. "He was a great guy to play for."

Bauer was a player's manager. There was no curfew; he treated the players like men. Remembering his own baseball career in which he bent an elbow or two with his Yankee buddies Mickey, Whitey, and Billy, Bauer did not harbor any illusions about drinking and ballplayers. He didn't particularly care how late his players stayed out as long as they were able to perform on the field the next day. Baltimore writers, convinced that the team's main problem the previous two years had been lax rules—and not sore arms and an inability to beat the Yankees—were eager to hear about Bauer's plans to institute martial law. They were disappointed. At the press conference announcing his hiring, when asked if he would have any rules about drinking, Bauer replied, "Yeah, I sure do have some rules. The players aren't allowed to drink at the hotel bar. That's where I drink."

"All Bauer expected you to do was go out and play hard every day and stay in shape," says utility infielder Bob Johnson. "He was the best manager I ever played for."

Bauer's idea of managing a baseball team was to fill out the lineup card and say, "Go play, boys." And, perhaps remembering his own angst at the whims of the platoon-happy Casey Stengel, he basically wrote down the same names every day. The downside of this was that he did not use his entire roster and if a player got in the doghouse, it could be a very long time, if ever, before he got out. Bauer admitted to reporters, "I get more tired managing than I did playing. Man, I get tired thinking."

But make no mistake, Hank Bauer was in charge. No one ever talked back to Hank Bauer. The last person to tell him to "Go to hell" was a joker at New York's Copacabana Club in 1957 who woke up on the floor of the men's room with a broken jaw. Once after an early-1964 loss, someone was singing on the Oriole bus. Bauer turned around, glared, and growled, "Losers don't sing as long as I'm around." The singing immediately stopped. Bauer knew how to win; he had played in nine World Series in 14 years for the great Yankee teams of the 1940s and 1950s. He brought to the Orioles a more regimented atmosphere, founded on the Yankee tradition of acting like winners—coats and ties were worn all the time on the road. "I don't believe in sports shirts," he said. "Baseball is big business. Players are the same as salesmen and should look like salesmen."

"It was a completely different atmosphere when Bauer came in," says Pappas. "He treated you like a human. He was a good guy to play for and the guys responded accordingly."

Typical was the case of Jackie Brandt, originally touted as a cross between Mays and Mantle but who had made a habit of being more like Lewis and Martin—driving managers nuts with the perceived waste of talent. Where Richards and Hitchcock had talked themselves blue trying to get through to Brandt without success, Bauer never chewed him out. He simply made him the leadoff hitter and

left him alone. Suddenly Brandt was playing like one of the best center fielders in the league. When asked about his psychological brilliance in managing Brandt, Bauer shrugged. "Just wrote his name on
the lineup card and I said 'the hell with it.'"

Despite his self-deprecating quips to the press and disavowals of
intellectual prowess, Bauer was a very knowledgeable baseball man.
"Hank Bauer was a better manager than people gave him credit for,"
says Eddie Watt, who joined the Orioles in 1966. "He understood
the game. He just wasn't a showman who would make moves just to
be making moves, to prove what a smart manager he was, like some
guys do. He didn't care what the press or fans thought of him. All
he wanted to do was win. He treated the players very well and we
appreciated that. In 1967, I didn't throw an inning in exhibition
games—I had been hit in the mouth with a ball during a drill. A lot of
guys would have cut me, but Bauer came up to me at the end of camp
and said, 'Can you throw strikes?' and I said, 'Yes.' And he said,
'That's all I need to know. You know you can do the job'."

In the spring of 1964, Brooks spent extra time working with new hitting coach Gene Woodling. Brooks had slumped to .251 in 1963, hitting
only .219 after the All-Star break. Woodling, who had played on the
Orioles from 1958 through 1960, had an easy humor and a sharp wit,
and loved to needle teammates. He helped keep younger players
from getting overconfident—reminding them not to get too happy
with themselves just because they got a few hits. He also marveled at
Brooks's ability to remain upbeat after a bad game, once remarking
tongue-in-cheek, "Brooks, you're so dumb you go oh-for-four and
you go home and never even worry about it." Although Brooks
struck out relatively infrequently (only once in his career would he
strike out more than 70 times in a season and he had several seasons
with fewer than 40 strikeouts), he had always been somewhat of a
free swinger, happy to hack at pitches several inches off the plate. As
word got around, pitchers would try to extend that farther and farther if he obliged them. He had developed into a good curveball hitter, but in 1963 pitchers had particularly been getting him out by
making him chase a steady diet of letter-high fastballs. Woodling
stressed cutting down on swinging at bad pitches.

He also switched him from a 30–31 ounce bat to a 33–34 ounce bat with a thicker handle, modeled after one Brooks had borrowed from Dodger Tommy Davis in the preseason because he liked the way it felt. Woodling later admitted that the switch to a heavier bat may have been psychological as much as anything. He felt that rather than not being quick enough for high fastballs, Brooks was swinging through them and he didn't want him to feel that he wasn't quick enough with his swing.

It was soon evident that the 1964 edition of the Orioles was a team to be reckoned with. The Kiddie Korps of 1960, with the exception of Milt Pappas, who regularly supplied 15 or 16 wins a year, had largely flamed out due to injuries. But the Oriole system at the time had an endless supply of great young pitchers. In 1964, 19-year-old Wally Bunker burst on the scene and won 19 games.

Dave McNally, a 22-year-old left-hander from Montana, was also coming into his own. McNally, who had originally signed with the Orioles for over $70,000, their second largest bonus ever, would become a close friend of Brooks's. Quiet, rarely displaying emotion on the field, McNally did not possess the overall speed or stuff that some of the other pitchers had but he developed into a very smart pitcher—a master at altering the speed of his fastball—and he was a bulldog on the mound; one of the most competitive players in baseball.

Thirty-seven-year-old veteran pitcher Robin Roberts, finishing a Hall of Fame career, joined the Orioles and won 13 games. Brooks needled him in front of reporters: "You played with Abe Lincoln, didn't you, Robbie?" Smart, articulate, with a good sense of humor, Roberts provided a strong positive influence in the clubhouse. Known on the Orioles as "Old Man," in 1965 Roberts would room with another 19-year-old rookie pitcher, Jim Palmer. Late one night, the inquisitive Palmer kept badgering Roberts, "Tell me about pitching." The tired veteran finally answered, "Throw the hell out of the ball. Now go to sleep." Roberts later told a writer, "He said that was some of the best advice he ever got."

Ron Hansen had been unable to regain his rookie form—slowed by a stint in the Army and recurrent back problems. He had been traded after 1962 to the White Sox in a deal that brought Luis Aparicio.

The little shortstop from Venezuela was one of the best fielding shortstops of the era and was also an offensive force who regularly led the league in stolen bases. He and Brooks made an almost impenetrable wall on the left side of the infield.

"You had to be stupid to pitch high with them over there," says Pappas. "Nothing got through that side."

John Wesley Powell, who had first stirred interest after showing up in spring training of 1960 as a giant of an 18-year-old with an 18¾-inch neck, was also developing into a force. Known as Boog, he had pitched his team to the Little League World Series when he was 12. An excellent overall athlete, he had been an All-State basketball player at Key West High School in Florida, and Colts coach Don Shula routinely told reporters he would love to have Powell play tackle for him. Powell spent his first few years with Baltimore lumbering around the outfield while Jim Gentile played first, and he would stay out there in 1964 while Norm Siebern, whom the Orioles received from the A's in a trade for Gentile, played first. Boog finally moved to first base in 1965. While he was serving his tour of duty in the outfield, Powell appreciated the help he got on ground balls from the left side of the Orioles infield. "I played behind Brooks in left field," he recalled later. "I used to break on balls out there but we had Aparicio at short and Brooksie over at third, and nothing ever came through. I hardly ever got any ground balls in left field." Powell had a breakout year in 1964 with 39 home runs and 99 RBIs.

Aparicio stole a career-high 57 bases and scored 93 runs in 1964 to aid Brooks and Boog with the offense, but the Oriole forte, as was becoming tradition, was pitching and defense, which kept games close. And, just as they had in 1960, the Orioles thrived on close-game wins.

They broke from the gate quickly, winning 30 of the first 45 games, and were in first place for 22 straight days in late June and early July. Batting in the cleanup slot most of the year, Brooks had a string of late-game clutch hits that was even better than 1960. And, of course, his glove work was as good as ever. Early in the season, at Yankee Stadium, Brooks pulled off what was generally agreed to be the play of the year. Bobby Richardson stroked a hot grounder between third and short. Brooks dove to his left to stop the ball, then, from a sitting position, threw a strike to first to nip the batter. A three-picture sequence of the play was carried by wire services to papers across the country.

In the All-Star Game at new Shea Stadium in New York, Brooks hit a two-run triple off Chris Short in the sixth inning to tie the game at three. After a provisional vote in the top of the ninth, Brooks was in line to be the MVP; however the Phillies' John Callison hit a three-run homer in the bottom of the ninth to win the game for the Nationals and copped the MVP award as well.

As the Fourth of July rolled around and the city of Baltimore celebrated the 150th anniversary of "The Star-Spangled Banner," the Orioles still led the chase for the American League banner, having won 19 of 21 one-run games by then, 12 times winning in their last at bat. The late-game theatrics contributed to Hank Bauer's cigarette consumption, which reached four packs a day before he gave it up in what would become an annual midseason concession to his doctor (the continuing close games always made him take up the habit again before the end of the season).

During a mid-August series with the Yankees, the Orioles set a three-day attendance record as almost 140,000 fans packed Memorial Stadium for the three games. Brooks hit a three-run homer to beat the Yankees 5–4 in the opener of the series. It was sweet revenge as Yankee manager Yogi Berra had earlier told reporters that Brooks Robinson didn't hit in the second half.

Brooks continued to pound the ball. In one August stretch, he had five home runs and 11 RBIs in six games. And he seemed to be in the middle of every important rally. August 20, playing the White Sox, who were a half game back, Brooks homered in the fourth inning to break a scoreless tie, then singled to knock in the winning run in the ninth inning. The next day, the Orioles trailed White Sox ace Joe Horlen 2–1 with one out in the ninth when Brooks struck again—this time with a three-run job. The next day, he had three hits. In the final game of the series, Brooks singled in a run early, which Steve Barber nursed for six innings before the White Sox rallied to win 3–1.

Afterward, in the Oriole clubhouse, a reporter asked Brooks if he was "doing it for the Booger," because Powell had recently been hurt.

He had injured his wrist while plowing into the left field fence at Fenway Park the previous series. (Although newspaper accounts did not state how much damage was done to the fence, it is certain it was considerable.) "Yeah," Brooks replied, "we won the first two games of this series for Boog and the third one for Dick Brown (who got hit in the chin with a warm-up pitch), but in the fourth game we didn't have anybody to win one for. No one was hurt." He spotted the team's shortstop walking by. "Why didn't you get hurt, Aparicio?"

"Oh, no, Brooksie," Aparicio answered. "I can't afford to get hurt. At Rochester, Davey Johnson has 17 home runs and 60 runs batted in." The Orioles left Chicago with a one-and-a-half-game lead.

Then it was on to Cleveland where the Orioles were swept, prompting Bauer to remark dryly, "As Custer said, 'Where'd all them blasted Indians come from?'"

The Orioles, Yankees, and White Sox steamed into the last month all knotted up atop the American League standings. September during a pennant race is when legends are made. For the past three years, Brooks had proven to be the best third baseman in the league. Now he took his game to another level. When it mattered most, when the team was counting on him, when the whole baseball world was watching, he was brilliant. In addition to, as Frank Deford stated in *Sports Illustrated*, "averaging about one great play every series," he was carrying the team on his back at the plate. September 7, Brooks was hitting .295 and not in the top five in RBIs in the American League. Thereafter, in the heat of a pennant race, he hit .464 (39-for-84) to finish second in batting average at .317 (to Tony Oliva's .323) and had 28 RBIs, including 24 in the last 17 games, and wound up leading the league with 118 (four more than runner-up Dick Stuart).

Moreover, Brooks seemed to be single-handedly keeping the Orioles in the race as most of the team slumped at the plate. Boog Powell was injured and out from August 20 to September 5. Other than Powell, who returned to contribute mightily with a .343 average and seven homers in the final month, no other Oriole hit over .263 for the month of September.

Brooks had four hits against Washington September 10, four hits against Minnesota September 16, and four RBIs in the first game of a doubleheader against the Angels September 20, and he added another

RBI in the second game. September 23, he had three hits against the Tigers. He had one stretch of 14-for-23 and a streak of seven hits in a row that was stopped by a triple play against the Senators.

Billy Martin, then a scout for the Twins, discussed Brooks in September: "The talk about the Orioles looking for years for a team leader is a lot of stuff because they not only have a great natural leader but he's also the league's most valuable player." And that was the general thinking around the league at the time.

In Baltimore, Brooks's popularity soared as knowledgeable fans realized that without his continuous heroics the Orioles' pennant hopes wouldn't have been worth a two dollar bet on the favorite to show. Late in the season, a special day was held for Brooks at Memorial Stadium. It was organized by the Oriole Advocates, a local booster group. Bob Maisel summed up the city's feelings about Brooks in the *Baltimore Sun*: "He's the best fielding third baseman in the game today and from what I've heard some old timers say, he might just be the best of all time. He plays every inning of every game and you never hear him gripe about this hurting him, or that hurting him, or how tired he is. . . . On top of this, he is the definition of a team man. He'll give himself up, push the ball to the right side to move a runner and do anything else to help the team win, whether he increases his own average by doing so, or whether he doesn't. He manages to do these things while never once making a member of the opposition even slightly angry. In fact, I don't think I've ever seen a player so universally liked by everybody—teammates, opposing players, fans, umpires, newspaper men, etc. Besides that, he's a clean-cut, clean-living, red-blooded young man, a solid Baltimore business man and citizen, an excellent husband and father, with a beautiful wife—real All-American boy stuff."

In the pregame ceremony, Maryland governor J. Millard Tawes proclaimed the day "Brooks Robinson Day" in the state. Baltimore mayor Theodore McKeldin presented him with a key to the city. Brooks was showered with approximately 75 gifts, including a 1965 station wagon, a $600 300-pound-capacity freezer, a ton of lawn fertilizer, a mink stole for Connie, dance instructions, a quart of milk for each point of his batting average, a typewriter, a jungle gym, cookies, two Bibles, a stuffed tiger, a German shepherd puppy, and two live ducks on leashes. The ducks were from J. A. W. Iglehart, one of the larger stockholders of the club. Brooks hunted on Iglehart's farm with several other players but always got skunked. Iglehart explained that it was easier to hand Brooks the ducks rather than wait for him to shoot one. There was also a fishing outfit that had been sent anonymously from New York. Dave Barrett, president of the Oriole Advocates, told reporters that he suspected it came from the Yankees, hoping Brooks would go fishing and forget about the rest of the season.

The crowd of 35,845, which had responded to the club's urging to "come alive for No. 5," cheered enthusiastically throughout the ceremony. Brooks told the crowd, "I'm really thrilled to think that the folks of Baltimore think enough of me and my family to present us with so many wonderful gifts." He gave a special thanks to Connie and his parents, who were in attendance, and concluded, "My last thanks are reserved for you folks. Those of you who are so kind to be here tonight and those of you who have made my last five years in Baltimore the happiest of my life. . . . My only hope is that I'll be able to repay your kindness, at least in part, by helping to bring the 1964 pennant to Baltimore."

Maisel wrote, "He was nervous and there were a few tears hanging around the edges. . . . He gave as fine a summation of his gratitude as I've ever heard a man give. Robby is a sincere and humble person, and these qualities came through in his talk. As he stepped from the platform, the applause was long and well-deserved. Probably the greatest tribute paid him all night might have escaped him. That would be the tremendous ovation he received from his own dugout. It was spontaneous and it was unanimous, and it is something that isn't given lightly. It has to be earned."

It proved to be a busy weekend for Brooks's parents. His brother, Gary, was a senior wingback for the University of Arkansas team that was on its way to an undefeated, National Championship season. The Robinsons flew to Baltimore for Brooks Robinson Night, and the next day hurried home to see Gary and Arkansas take on Oklahoma State in a Saturday night game.

Trying to keep up with the Yankees in September was a difficult task in those days. They had been through so many pennant races;

they had confidence and experience; they stayed cool and other teams, full of adrenaline, inevitably made mistakes. And when the pile of money on the table was the biggest, they always raked. Although the Yankees were aging and there was a feeling that this year, finally, they could be had, they proved in 1964 that they were not quite done yet. They got hot and won the pennant after taking 13 of 14 games (including 11 in a row) from September 12 to September 26. The Yankees and Orioles were tied September 17, but, although they won seven of their last eight games, the Orioles could not keep the murderous pace and were finally eliminated October 2 and finished two games behind the Yankees and one behind the White Sox.

Brooks's charge in September of 1964 compares favorably with some of the great pennant race efforts in baseball history. Three years later, Carl Yastrzemski would be lionized for his end-of-season heroics. Over the final 23 games of the 1967 season, Yaz hit .427 (35-for-82) with 23 RBIs. Over the final 23 games of 1964, Brooks hit .446 (37-for-83) with 29 RBIs. Brooks only lacked Yaz's last weekend heroics for a team that won the pennant—admittedly not a small thing. Robin Roberts, who played 19 years in his Hall of Fame career, later called Brooks Robinson's 1964 season "the best year I've ever seen from a teammate."

Although they fell short in the pennant race, it had been a very good year for the Orioles. The 97 wins broke the Oriole team record of 95 from 1961. The team drew 1.1 million fans, the second highest in team history. Brooks played in every game and missed only two innings all year. He was named Oriole MVP for the third time in five years. An even bigger honor would follow, however. Brooks was named American League Most Valuable Player in a landslide victory. He received 269 of a possible 280 points in the voting. Mickey Mantle was second with 171. Brooks became only the third non-Yankee to win the award in 11 years.

The great season set up a busy winter as Brooks was in much demand on the knife and fork circuit. At the time, before cable television routinely brought athletes into private homes, there were an infinite number of dinners and ceremonies in towns across the country in which patrons would plunk down cash in order to see real live baseball stars in person and listen to their stories and attempts at humor. Such an affair in the 1964 off-season was the 29th annual Dapper Dan Award Dinner in Pittsburgh, where a capacity crowd of 2,000 paid $15 apiece to see the dais with 90 men, including Pie Traynor and Lefty Grove. And it wasn't just restricted to large cities. The annual Manchester (New Hampshire) baseball dinner that winter drew 2,000 fans to the state armory.

A large number of the dinners were sponsored by the local chapter of the Baseball Writers' Association of America. Before the decline of the newspaper industry and when baseball was still the national pastime, the BBWAA was a significant community in and of itself. In the early 1960s, there were 10 members of the BBWAA in Baltimore, 31 in Boston, and 76 in New York.

The players enjoyed these ceremonies, as they were usually paid between 25 and 50 bucks each and it was a sign of success just to be invited. They also got the chance to meet fellow stars and other dignitaries, such as Vice President–elect Hubert Humphrey, who attended the black-tie affair of the Washington Touchdown Club, or New York's newest senator, Robert F. Kennedy, who was the main speaker at the New York BBWAA dinner.

Brooks had some experience on the dinner circuit, especially after his 1960 season, and was becoming an accomplished public speaker. He found that his self-deprecating sense of humor went over especially well. In the winter of 1964–65, he routinely started off with, "It really pleases me that you folks are honoring me as the league's MVP. At some of the banquets I go to, they give me a comeback-of-the-year award. I appreciate the fact that you're not giving me one tonight." He frequently brought up the triple play he hit into against Washington and he usually made mention of getting two hits in his first major league game and how swelled his head got, then noted that he promptly went 0-for-18 with 10 strikeouts and learned that major league pitching was a bit tougher than it first appeared. "That cured me," he would conclude with a chuckle. "I have no illusions about myself and never will."

Another favorite Brooks banquet story was that he once made an appearance at a mental institution. As he started to talk, one of the patients shouted, "Robinson, you stink." He hesitated, then started again. Once again, the patient interrupted, "Robinson, you stink."

Brooks paused, not sure if he should continue. He looked at the head doctor, who told him, "Go ahead. That's the first sensible thing that patient has said since he's been here."

The speeches were usually supplemented with corny skits such as the one at the Baltimore Annual Tops in Sports Banquet, in which Lee MacPhail was trying to get Brooks to sign his contract in public. Brooks studied it and said he thought he might be worth a little bit more. Then a Baltimore writer introduced the year's Oriole Most Valuable Player Award (to Brooks) by praising his accomplishments. After accepting the award, Brooks turned to MacPhail and said, "Now I'll be happy to talk business with you, Lee."

Also in the postseason of 1964 there were a multitude of harmonica jokes lampooning the well-publicized fight on the Yankee bus after a frustrating loss between new manager Yogi Berra and the harmonica-playing utility infielder Phil Linz. Linz was given a free harmonica by a harmonica company, which also paid the $200 fine. At one banquet, Berra quipped that Linz should have been playing a piano. At another, he mentioned that he should have fined him $5,000 and split it with him. At one, before every musical act the emcee dourly noted that no harmonica would be allowed in the act.

Baseball humor knows no bounds (or shame). The story circulated that a group of American League hitters, tired of Brooks robbing them of certain base hits, took out a contract on him with a hit man in an effort to improve their collective batting averages. The hit man came back the next day shaking his head. "Well, did you shoot him?" they asked. "I tried to," he replied. "I shot him four times. Three of them he caught, the fourth he turned into a double play."

Another time after a batter had hit a line drive into the left field stands, an old-timer in the press box, tired of hearing about the greatness of modern-day players, snorted, "Pie Traynor would have had it." Another guy replied, "Brooks Robinson would have got two on it!"

According to Bill Valentine, a Little Rock native who umpired in the American League from 1963 to 1968, Brooks once hit a long drive to the left center field gap. Valentine was umping the bases and ran beside Brooks as he chugged for second. Brooks appeared to be in a slow home run trot. Valentine kept yelling, "Brooks run, it didn't go out, it's a tweener." Brooks continued his slow jog around the bases. Finally, after Valentine had slowed down to stay with him and continued to yell at him to run, that it was not over the fence, Brooks looked at him and said, "Damn it Valentine, I know it didn't go out, but I'm running as fast as I can."

"Brooks never argued a call," says Valentine, who was the general manager of the Little Rock Travelers for over 30 years after leaving the American League and enjoys a good story. "Once I was umpiring third base during a game with the Orioles. There were three very close plays at third, Brooks made the tags and I called all three safe. Bauer came out and argued all three calls. Brooks didn't say anything. Later, there was a long drive down the left field line which curved just past the foul pole and landed in the third row. I called it foul. As I turned, I noticed the usher was tending to a lady in the stands there who was down. I asked Brooks, 'Did that ball hit her?' He said, 'No, you finally got a call right and she fainted.'

"Another time we were on the Game of the Week and I was behind the plate. Brooks was up and Dean Chance threw one a little low and I called it a strike. Brooks didn't say anything, but you could tell he didn't agree. Chance threw another one in the exact same spot and I called it a strike too. Brooks stepped over like he was going back to the bench. I said, 'Brooks, that was only two strikes.' He said, 'I know, but I brought the wrong club. I'm going back to get my pitching wedge.'"

Coming off his best year, Brooks got a raise of $15,000, to $50,000—becoming the highest paid player in Oriole history. Besides his salary, Brooks enjoyed other financial benefits. He signed with a Baltimore radio station to conduct a program by telephone from Key Biscayne in spring training in addition to regular five-minute spots during the season. He also made a Coca-Cola commercial in Miami. While early in his career Brooks had been forced to work at various off-season jobs, usually public relations for the team, now his baseball celebrity allowed more solid opportunities.

Brooks had stakes in two businesses in Baltimore. Along with ex–Oriole coach Eddie Robinson, he was part owner of Brooks and Eddie Robinson's Gorsuch House restaurant (located on Gorsuch

Avenue) near Memorial Stadium. Eddie Robinson had been a popular player for the old International League Baltimore Orioles and made his home in Baltimore while he played in the majors for the White Sox, Yankees, and Indians. He had started the restaurant in 1952. The steak-and-seafood place had a sports-related atmosphere and Eddie displayed memorabilia he had collected over the years, such as the bat Babe Ruth had used as a cane in his farewell address at Yankee Stadium and a ball Mickey Mantle hit off the facade in Yankee Stadium. The restaurant was popular and Eddie frequently spent time there greeting customers à la Stan Musial, especially after he returned to Baltimore as a player and coach at the end of the 1957 season. It became a hangout for baseball and football players; Unitas, Ameche, Marchetti, Shula, Berry, and Donovan came in all the time.

When Eddie moved with Paul Richards to Houston in the fall of 1961, he decided that he needed local partners to watch the place. "Joe Hamper, the Orioles' accountant, was a friend of mine and was interested in the restaurant and I also asked Brooks if he was interested in investing in the place and he was," says Eddie Robinson. "I thought Brooks would be a good guy to have as a partner because he was becoming a popular name in Baltimore and that would be good for business. Also, I knew he would be an easy guy to get along with. They each bought a fourth interest and ran the place while I was in Houston. It was successful—it provided us with a nice income. That worked for three or four years and then I sold out my part because it was just too hard to keep up with it living out of town.

"I don't think Brooks really enjoyed going in there as much as I had," he continues. "I spent a lot of time there, but Brooks was young and had a family and much preferred going home to them. He spent some time there, but not near as much as I had."

In 1963 Brooks went into the sporting goods business with George Henderson, a part-time Oriole scout, and Henderson's brother, Bill, a former catcher at Baltimore University. George Henderson was a fixture in the Baltimore baseball scene, dating back to when he played on neighborhood teams with Baltimore Southern High School's Al Kaline. In the 1950s, while still in college, Henderson worked part-time selling sporting goods, in addition to being associated with the famed Baltimore 20-and-under baseball program known as Leones, which would later boast major league alumni Reggie Jackson, Phil Linz, Tom Phoebus, Ron Swoboda, and Dave Boswell.

"I had known Brooks through the Orioles, seeing him around the stadium since he came to Baltimore," says Henderson. "I had been working in the sporting goods business for years, using my contacts in Baltimore youth baseball—I knew all the teams around town and knew the business, but I had been working for someone else. I wanted to go into business myself. One night in early 1963, Brooks called me and wanted a favor—he was having a Hawaiian-themed party for Connie and needed some fins and swim gear and fishing lines; stuff like that. I asked my owner if he would let him use the stuff and he said he wouldn't charge him if he brought it back the next day. Anyway, I delivered it to Brooks at his restaurant and we were sitting there drinking a Coke and, out of the blue, I asked him if he wanted to go into the sporting goods business. He said, 'When?' and I said, 'How about right now?' So we put up the money and we were in business in a few weeks." And that's how easy it was to start up a business in 1963.

The Henderson brothers and Brooks each plunged an initial investment of $5,000 to get the store going and it became Brooks Robinson Sporting Goods. George Henderson ran things at the store and Brooks acted as public spokesman. Starting very small, they struggled initially; however, due to Brooks's name and Henderson's connections, they soon began to develop a large business, 80 percent of which was wholesale to local leagues and teams. "Of course, in 1964 Brooks won the MVP and that really made our business go," says Henderson.

In 1965 Brooks hit over .300 most of the season before fading to finish at .297. The Orioles won 94 games and stayed in a three-team race before they faded also. Minnesota won 102 games and took the pennant. Brooks finished third in the voting for American League Most Valuable Player, trailing Zoilo Versalles and Tony Oliva of the champion Twins.

In the years from 1960 through 1965, Brooks Robinson had firmly established himself as one of the best players in baseball. He had averaged .292 and 83 RBIs per season, had won six consecutive Gold

Gloves, and had played in every All-Star Game. He had finished in the top three in MVP voting three times in the six years. Although his salary was climbing and he was enjoying more money from endorsements, and increasing popularity around the league, he did not get caught up in the trappings of wealth and fame and remained the simple, easy-to-please country boy he had been when he first showed up in Baltimore 10 years earlier. He didn't like fancy clothes (in fact, one year, he was voted "worst dressed" by his teammates), he drove a family car, often a testosterone-challenged station wagon, and he behaved as he always had. He was happy to be playing baseball—fulfilling his lifelong dream; performing perhaps better than he could have ever realistically dreamed.

He didn't mind the fact that, as a player in a small market, his face was still not universally known, and he didn't mind a little humor at his own expense. His roommate at the time, Bob Johnson, recalls an incident during dinner in Cleveland that helped keep Brooks from getting a big head. Johnson, who bore a striking resemblance to former Indian slugger Rocky Colavito, noticed several guys staring at them while they ate. Finally one approached them. "You're Rocky Colavito, aren't you?" he asked. Johnson answered, "Yes, I am." The guy said, "We're big fans of yours, would you mind signing this?"

"I'll be glad to," Johnson replied. Then he whispered to Brooks, "How do you spell Colavito?" After Johnson handed over the autograph, the guy looked at Brooks and asked, "Is this one of the ballplayers too?" And Johnson replied, "He's a new guy, he just came up from the minor leagues." The fan reached over and shook Brooks's hand. "Congratulations, I hope you have a nice career, son," and he happily left with his prized Rocky Colavito signature. "To this day he probably doesn't know that he shook hands with a Hall of Famer but didn't get his autograph," says Johnson.

Brooks and Connie were a class act and became firmly ingrained in their adopted city. They were frequently spotted around town, and were perceived as down-to-earth, nice people. Although Brooks didn't spend all his time at the restaurant, he often appeared there, as well as in his sporting goods store during the off-season. Connie's good looks, sense of fashion, and status as the wife-of-the-best-player made her a frequent target for local photographers during fundraisers put on by the Oriole wives. But, by all accounts, she was as pleasant and friendly as her husband and never played the Mrs. MVP card.

As the Robinson family grew, they sold their row house to Dave McNally and moved into an impressive new ranch house in the Lutherville-Timonium area, about a 20-minute drive from Memorial Stadium. Although the neighborhood held a number of Baltimore athletes—Mr. and Mrs. Unitas lived a few blocks away, as did fellow Colt Tom Matte and several Orioles—this was far from an exclusive, gated community. Brooks and Connie fit right in with their other neighbors.

Brooks David was followed by Chris (1963), Michael (1964), and finally Diana (1968). Neighborhood kids noted that in school the Robinson kids were just like everyone else—there were no egos or problems, no sense of entitlement just because their father was a baseball star. Part of that was due to the fact that their father didn't act like a star at home. Once Brooks David (who had a large poster of his sports hero Johnny Unitas in his room) came home from elementary school and said, "Hey, Dad. Some of the kids in my class say you're really something special playing third base for Baltimore. Why didn't you tell me that you were famous?"

"He was a great family guy," says Pappas. "Their kids were really well mannered. Brooks and Connie and the kids made a perfect family."

While Connie had initially been a baseball novice, she soon became a knowledgeable fan and rarely missed an All-Star Game (she knew one of the players). She quickly adapted to the life of a baseball wife, taking care of all the family matters and handling the kids while her husband was on the road, as well as coordinating the housing and travel arrangements for spring training—an especially difficult task when the three boys were toddlers. Being a baseball player who so zealously refused to sit out a single game, Brooks sometimes missed family things he later regretted. In 1983, he spoke to a reporter about the time in spring training of 1964 in which Connie had just given birth to their third son, Michael, and was still in a Miami hospital. The next day, the team had a road exhibition and

Brooks left with the team. "That was absolutely stupid," he said, "but all I could think about was there was a game the next day and I had to play. I didn't even ask Hank Bauer if I could have the day off. She and I still talk about it once in a while and she'll say, 'How could you have left me the very next day?'"

Brooks tried to help with the kids when he was home. In the off-season, he was a regular chauffeur. "I used to see him all the time driving the kids around in the station wagon," says Frank Cashen, who was an Oriole executive in the 1960s and lived in the same neighborhood as the Robinsons. As the kids got older, Brooks, who enjoyed history, tried to do as many family activities as possible, frequently taking the crew on trips to historic sites in the Washington and Baltimore area and to Gettysburg.

As Brooks's play improved, writers continued to tell national readers what word of mouth around Baltimore had known for years—that Brooks Robinson was one of the friendliest, most approachable players in professional sports. Bob Maisel wrote in the *Sporting News* in 1962 of Brooks's nice-guy reputation, ending with, "Brooks is one of those fellows it's a pleasure to see nice things happen to. . . . There can't be many players in the game who are better liked than Robby."

John Steadman, who was occasionally given to hyperbolic prose, wrote in the *Sporting News*, "All that's recognized as class in personality and professional ability is exemplified in the characteristics of Brooks Calbert Robinson, Jr., who befits success like the glove he wears. Robinson, apart from being the American League's All-Star third baseman, carries himself in a manner that suggests he's more inclined to be a model citizen first and a baseball performer later. In both respects, he's first-rate. The image he has created for himself and the team he represents, the Orioles, brings only admiration from an adoring public which too often in the past has found its muscled heroes have clay feet."

Steadman added in 1964, "Graciousness in personality. Greatness in performance. These are the sterling qualities which set Brooks Robinson apart as a man and baseball player. . . . The men, women and children of Baltimore hold Robinson in esteem that amounts to almost fanatical fondness. . . . He admits that if he could be like any man he has ever met or heard about, it would be Musial. . . . He is friendly, but not forward. He is cooperative but not a politician. He is humble but not withdrawing. He is polite but not gushing. It's these characteristics which make him easy to like. He isn't just a good guy on the days he goes 3-for-4, nor is he selfish or desirous of attention. He has time for any sports writer, be he from Baltimore or Boston, Bangor, Butte. [He is so popular] it makes him a virtual untouchable. . . . He's one player destined to spend all his baseball days with the Orioles."

It was reported that Brooks had played 1,300 professional games without ever being tossed out by an umpire (he would keep that record intact through retirement), although admittedly he was occasionally noted to argue mildly after a particularly bad call. The notorious men in blue concurred: "If all the players were like him we'd never have to throw anyone out of a game," said Bill Valentine.

Baltimore writers called him Mr. Perfection. His wife told reporters in 1965 he was so mild-mannered that she worried one day he might just explode. When a Baltimore writer noted that Brooks had never been heckled from the stands, team president Lee MacPhail reflected on Baltimore fans' affection for him and said, "Anyone who might be tempted to boo him would be too scared to."

"People may have thought we were exaggerating but all those things we wrote about him were true," says Bob Maisel fifty years later. "He was always friendly. I never heard him say anything bad about someone else in all the time I was around him. I don't think he has it in him to get mad or say bad things about people. And he was always there for everybody, always ready to do anything you asked. He was like that right from the start. There was a reason he was so loved in Baltimore."

The stories were indeed true, and the remarkable thing is that Brooks was just as nice when no reporters or cameras were around. In April 1965, Ernie Paicopolos, a 13-year-old Red Sox fan, and a friend were waiting outside the visitor's clubhouse at Fenway Park following a game with the Orioles, hoping for some autographs. After several players had passed by, Brooks, straggling behind the others, walked out alone. "Hi Brooks," one of the kids said. "Hey, how are you guys doing?" Brooks answered, then, noticing that the bus had already left, asked, "Do you know where I can get a cab?" The kids shrugged. "Well, it's a nice day, the hotel's not that far away. You guys want to walk there with me?"

After the two kids picked up their jaws, they got the walk of their lives, chatting amiably with the reigning American League MVP. "The whole way he talked to us real casual, just like you would have a conversation with another regular guy," says Paicopolos, who now runs a popular Red Sox blog. "He talked to us about baseball. He asked if we played, what position we played and asked about our team. He talked about hitting, fielding, and life in the big leagues. He just talked like we were his peers or teammates. When we got there, he thanked us for walking with him—*he* thanked us. I had a copy of *Street and Smith's Baseball Yearbook* for 1965 that had a picture of him on the cover and he autographed it for me. It's just amazing looking back on it. He was 28 at the time. But he was just so natural and such a nice guy to us kids. I can't imagine a major star doing that now."

Bob Scherr was a batboy for the Orioles from 1964 to 1967 and witnessed Brooks's personality up close. "There were basically three types of players as far as how they treated batboys," says Scherr, who was 15 in 1964. "The first type treated you like you were invisible, just ignored you as you did your job. The second type treated you like a servant, sending you out to run personal errands and stuff like that. They were sometimes rude and belittling. The third type was friendly and talked to you. Brooks was definitely the third type. He was the greatest. The moment I got there he just went out of his way to be welcoming. He would come up and sit next to me and talk. He would joke around with me, let me know that he appreciated what I did.

"Brooks's wife was very friendly also," he continues. "She would see me coming out and say 'Hi' and remember my name. I can't remember any other wives that did that. And even years later, when I occasionally will see Brooks at various events, he is as friendly as ever. He recognizes me, acknowledges me, and remembers my name."

Brooks apparently made a habit of being nice to batboys. In 1970 a Miami 15-year-old named Roy Firestone talked his way into a job as batboy for the Orioles in spring training. "The very first player I met in the clubhouse was Brooks," he wrote in 2007. "He wasn't condescending. He didn't call me 'kid.' He looked me straight in the eyes and asked my name. 'Roy,' I said. 'And you are our new bat boy?' he asked. 'Yes, Mr. Robinson,' I stammered. 'Call me Brooks,' he replied with a smile. 'Roy, how would you like to play some pepper with me?'

"He opened every spring afternoon with a smile for me and the other clubhouse kids," Firestone continued. "He hit fungoes. He played pepper with us. He took pictures and signed autographs all day, every day. And he never ever pulled a star trip on anyone."

Firestone, who would later enjoy a long career in broadcasting, said that he never forgot the kindness of his first encounter with a sports superstar. "Knowing Brooks Robinson has spoiled me. Before I met some of today's seemingly boorish, vulgar, egocentric, rude and entitled athletes (not all by a long shot, but enough), I met this guy—the Orioles' No. 5."

Brooks's reputation progressed to the point locally that it could be used as a parody. In a commercial for a Baltimore bank, the announcer asked, "Tell me, Brooks, does anything ever get you mad?"

Brooks: "No, not me. You can't lose your temper and play in this game. No, I never get mad."

Announcer: "How about when you come to bat in the 9th inning with the bases loaded and strike out?"

Brooks: "Well, you can't get a hit every time. No, that doesn't make me mad."

Announcer: "How about when you play back for a power hitter and he lays down a bunt you can't handle?"

Brooks: "Well, that's the way the ball bounces. No, that doesn't make me mad."

Announcer: "Well, how about if you buy a home and find out you could have gotten a better rate on your mortgage with no appraisal fee and no prepayment penalties?"

Brooks (angrily): "Ooh, that makes me mad."

While virtually all Baltimore citizens at the time agreed that Johnny Unitas was the best thing to happen to their city since Francis Scott Key, Brooks Robinson was rapidly becoming a very close second in their affections. But for all of Brooks's steady hitting, his brilliant fielding, and his great character, there were some who wanted him to do more. The Orioles still could not get over the hump. There was some criticism of his leadership abilities.

One day during batting practice at the Polo Grounds before a Dodger-Giant game in 1946, Dodger manager Leo Durocher was engaged with a writer in his second favorite activity, talking about baseball (his favorite was talking about himself). The writer noted that Giant manager Mel Ott, whose team was in seventh place, had been a great player but a failure as a manager. In what would become one of the most famous discourses in baseball history, Durocher nodded out to the infield where his second baseman, Eddie Stanky, was taking grounders. "Look at him. He can't hit, he can't run, he can't throw—all he can do is beat you." Then he pointed to the Giant bench. "There's Mel Ott, take a good look at him. A nicer guy never put a pair of shoes on. Fine fellow. But he didn't come to win. That's the answer. Nice guys finish last."

Durocher couldn't have picked a better example than Stanky. Nicknamed the Brat, he was one of the most disliked players in the game by opponents. He kicked the ball out of gloves when sliding; he carried a handful of dirt on the base paths to fling into the eyes of fielders on close plays; he was a relentless, vicious bench jockey. He basically would do anything—legal or otherwise—to win a game. In other words, he was Durocher's kind of people. Durocher liked the quote "Nice guys finish last" so much he used it as the title of his 1975 autobiography. It entered into the vernacular of the game because it laid out, plain and simple, what most people felt. How can someone who is nice, and maybe even plays by the rules, defeat someone who is so driven that he will resort to any means necessary to win?

By 1965 some writers, and possibly even others in the game, were applying that logic to Brooks Robinson. Although he was acknowledged as the leader of the Orioles, they said he just stood back and refused to take command. The Orioles had never won a pennant. Some said the Orioles needed a holler guy, someone to get on teammates and kick some butt to make the team better. Brooks was too nice of a guy to win championships, they said.

Even if the criticism was misplaced or inappropriate, there was some truth to it. Brooks could not be the guy to kick butts. He was a popular teammate and well liked by virtually everyone. He simply could not bring himself to call out a teammate. It was not in his personality. He led by example, by playing hard, by playing through pain, by being on the field early fielding hundreds of balls every day, but he was not a butt kicker. "I think this take-charge business is overrated," Brooks responded to reporters. "If I'm hitting .340, fine. I hope the guys will follow me. But if I'm hitting .250, I sure don't want them to follow me."

Robin Roberts added in his defense, "If you can't run, hit or throw, then holler. That's what a holler guy is, a guy who can't do anything else."

Brooks further explained his position: "Team leaders are managers in the making and I wouldn't be a manager for any money. Managing takes a man that can crack the whip, a hard driver. I don't travel in that gear."

He also said, "You don't have to shout or shake your fist or charge umpires to be a good ball player. In fact, if you give 100% of yourself at all times, you really can't find time to be a so-called holler guy."

In December of 1965, news of a trade was announced that would change the Orioles forever—a guy was coming to the team who had no trouble hollering.

9. A Giant Leap

THE TRADE WAS OFFICIALLY CONSUMMATED December 9, 1965. In an era when major stars rarely changed teams while in the midst of their powers, the deal was big news, but no one could have predicted the effect it would ultimately have on the Orioles and the American League. While commonly remembered as Frank Robinson for Milt Pappas, it was actually a three-team, five-player transaction. As part of the arrangement, the Orioles obtained relief pitcher Jack Baldschun, whom the Reds coveted, from the Phillies for Jackie Brandt and immediately packaged him with Pappas and outfielder Dick Simpson to the Reds for Robinson. Reds owner Bill DeWitt, who would be burned in effigy in downtown Cincinnati later that summer by fans disgruntled over the trade, defended himself by emphasizing that the Reds desperately needed pitching (correct) and wanted the great speed of Simpson, who DeWitt felt would be a future star (incorrect), and that Frank Robinson was an old 30 (definitely incorrect).

Frank Robinson was not like Brooks Robinson. Actually, they were about as different as two men who were known for excellence in the same profession could be. Whereas Brooks had grown up in a small, happy, two-parent, middle-class family, Frank had barely known his father. He was the youngest of 10 kids whose father had left when he was four. He was raised by his hardworking mother in a poor section of Oakland.

Unlike the easygoing, friendly Brooks, Frank was outspoken and didn't seem to mind making enemies. Frank Robinson was never a serious candidate for any sort of nice guy award. He had few friends in the baseball world on opposing teams—and "few friends" is a polite way of saying that most players on opposing teams hated him. "I'm not out there to win friends," he had told *Sports Illustrated* in 1963, "just ball games, and I'll do that any way that I can." It was not an idle statement. Frank played the game with a zeal that bordered on fanaticism. He was the scourge of pitchers who fought him for possession of the inside half of the plate, second basemen and short-stops who risked their limbs and livelihoods while trying to turn double plays as he barreled down on them, catchers who dared to block the plate, and outfield walls that stood between him and fly balls. He was called a "black Ty Cobb."

Both Robinsons were exceptional athletes who stood out in a business of exceptional athletes, but while Brooks possessed an unimpressive physique, Frank's body belonged in marble atop Mount Olympus. Broad-shouldered with massive biceps and rippling forearms—especially impressive compared to his peers in the days before weight training—his mere presence was intimidating. Other than a chronically sore throwing shoulder, the result of a minor league injury, Frank had no discernible weakness and was one of the best all-around players of the era.

Brooks was unquestionably an organization man. He had never had a documented problem with a manager at any level; George Haynie, George Staller, Joe Schultz, Charlie Metro, Paul Richards, Billy Hitchcock, Hank Bauer—they all loved him. Similarly, there was never any trouble with the front office. His salary negotiations were routinely concluded quickly and painlessly for all concerned. While Frank had been very fond of his first Cincinnati manager, Birdie Tebbetts, he had publicly butted heads on several occasions with successors Mayo Smith and Fred Hutchinson. Frank had brawled with Bill DeWitt (whom he referred to as Bill CheapWitt) in yearly salary battles that had left both men bloody and bitter.

Despite the fact that Frank had spent a decade in Cincinnati averaging over 30 home runs and 100 RBIs a year while hitting over .300, and had been the National League's Most Valuable Player in 1961 while leading the Reds to the pennant, he had never been truly appreciated and certainly was not embraced by the city. He had been booed loudly at home throughout the 1965 season even as he hit .296 with 33 homers and 113 RBIs. While some smelled racism as a contributing factor, there had been well-chronicled unpleasant incidents, the most notorious being the gun episode before the 1961 season. Frank and some friends stopped off at a hamburger joint and an argument ensued with other customers. When a restaurant employee made a threatening gesture while brandishing a butcher knife, Frank calmly showed him the gun he was carrying. A nearby policeman arrested Frank for possession of a concealed weapon. Interestingly, Bill DeWitt refused to bail him out—a local sportswriter, Earl Lawson, freed him instead. Frank later pleaded guilty and received a fine—along with a public relations stigma that would haunt him for years.

In 1963, with the Reds underperforming, insinuations appeared in print that the team's problem was that Frank and his buddy Vada Pinson had formed a "Negro clique" that was damaging the morale of the team. While Frank and Pinson did occasionally behave as if they were stars, there were only three African Americans on the team that year—it is ludicrous to believe that three players could be called a morale-damaging clique. Some of this was most likely leaked from the Reds' front office, which resented Robinson's salary and his attitude. Later that year, rookie Pete Rose—who had been getting the silent treatment from everyone on the team except Pinson and Robinson—was called into the front office and advised to quit hanging around with the "colored players." (He refused the advice.) While virtually every young player on the Reds in 1964 and 1965 confirmed that Frank was the undisputed leader of the team and appreciated his influence, these incidents led to a mutual dislike between Frank and the front office, sullied his reputation with the city as a whole, and undoubtedly led to the team's desire to get rid of him (and his big salary).

Soon after the trade was announced, writers and baseball men, needing something to talk about during the winter months, began openly questioning how Frank and Brooks would coexist. Trouble appeared inevitable between the two men of such disparate backgrounds and personalities. Brooks, in his 11th year with the Orioles, was the elder statesman and de facto leader of the team. Now a new guy was showing up; a new guy with a reputation; a new guy who was different in almost every way; a new guy whose personality and style made him impossible to ignore. Would the vast presence of Frank Robinson, portrayed as a moody, sometimes angry superstar change Brooks Robinson? "The average ballplayer would be envious of the newcomer who has taken away so much of the spotlight," wrote one reporter. Who could blame him if he resented it? Brooks was a former MVP himself, the big bat in the lineup. He had spent over a decade working in this city, building up goodwill. He could be justified in begrudging this new guy any attention; resenting it when reporters made a big deal about needing this new bat—what was wrong with the old one?

Also, while Brooks had played with African Americans since entering professional baseball, Frank would be the first black star with whom he had needed to share the spotlight. This was 1966; American cities were aflame with racial tensions and here was a graduate of the infamous Little Rock Central High School suddenly having an outspoken, aggressive African American move in on him. Not only that, but this newcomer immediately vaulted to the top of the Oriole pay scale: Brooks signed in early March for $55,000; Frank had made $60,000 with Cincinnati in 1965 and, after a brief holdout, signed with the Orioles for $68,000. Resentment was inevitable, wasn't it?

Not exactly. For all their differences, there were two things Brooks and Frank had in common; two very important things that trumped all the rest: they both loved the game of baseball—neither had considered any other means of making a living—and they were totally committed to winning. Frank, like Brooks, not only was very talented physically, but had an extremely high baseball IQ. They both understood and appreciated all the little things that go into a winning team. They were very cognizant of the role they played and the role baseball played in their lives. Early on, each recognized this quality in the other and grew to respect it. That became their bond.

It also became apparent that much of Frank's bad boy image was unearned or, at least, exaggerated. Some of the incidents in Cincinnati had occurred when he was very young—he had since matured—and others were simply not true. Also, in the mid-1960s Frank made a conscious decision that he wanted his future to include baseball once he stopped playing and he realized that few owners would hire an angry black man as a coach or manager. He later said that when he went to the Orioles, aware of his reputation, he "made an effort to be more outgoing, to be more relaxed and to smile more."

Brooks immediately understood what the addition of Frank Robinson would mean to the Orioles and their pennant hopes. If there was any jealousy or resentment, it never showed. "Frank, you're exactly what we need," Brooks said as he approached Frank at the batting cage to shake his hand the first day. The rest of the team followed suit.

The Oriole players, most of whom had never seen the career National Leaguer play, were impressed with Frank's talent upon watching him up close. Reputation didn't do justice to the actual sight of him menacingly wielding a club in the batter's box. The first day Frank stepped into the batting cage and immediately sent a rocket down the left field line. Watching nearby, Jim Palmer turned to a teammate and said, "I think we just won the pennant."

Frank was quickly introduced to the team's sense of humor. In an early spring game, as he rounded the bases after a home run, he was confused that he didn't hear a whisper coming from the Oriole bench. When he crossed home plate, Brooks, the next batter, turned his back instead of offering the customary handshake. As Frank entered the dugout, no one looked at him—he was met with silent indifference. Finally, realizing what his new teammates were doing, Frank grinned and said, "Well, you know what you all can do." They all broke out in laughter and came up and congratulated him. He was officially a member of the team.

Frank impressed his fellow players in exhibition games by sliding headfirst, taking extra bases when most players wouldn't even try, tagging and advancing from first to second on a fly to center, throwing his body around the field—in general playing the game of baseball like a middle linebacker. And his play was contagious. The change in the team atmosphere was evident immediately.

"Frank really made a difference right from the start," says Bob Johnson. "The day he showed up in spring training, he started talking about winning the World Series, and we all thought, 'Why not?'"

After a month of spring training, the 1966 Orioles were a confident bunch. "I came over from the Cubs at the end of March," says backup catcher Vic Roznovsky. "I didn't know anything about the team because the Cubs trained in Phoenix and there was no inter-league play back then. My locker was next to Davey Johnson. The first day I asked him, 'What's this team like?' And he said, 'We're gonna win it all.'"

Brooks spoke for the entire team when he talked to a reporter about Frank near the end of training camp, "We heard stuff like that [being a troublemaker] and naturally some of us were curious. I talked to some of the Cincinnati ballplayers and asked them what kind of a ballplayer he is. They told me he was a helluva ballplayer and a helluva guy and do you know something, he's even better than they said he was in both departments."

The feeling was mutual. Like everyone else, Frank was awed by Brooks's defensive skills. "Before coming to Baltimore I had always felt that Ken Boyer and Jim Davenport were the best third basemen in baseball," he wrote in his 1968 autobiography. "I couldn't believe that Brooks Robinson could be any better. But after watching him that spring [1966] I found that he was far better than I had heard he was. He was the best I'd ever seen at that position. When the ball was hit down the third-base side of the field, I found myself in the out-field just standing there, watching him, like a fan. The plays he was making at third base amazed me.

"Brooks and I got along very well," he continued, "as well as any two ballplayers can get along. He is a friendly person and an easy person to get to know and he was very helpful to me from the time I got to spring training. He helped make it a lot easier for me to adjust to playing with Baltimore."

Frank wasn't the only one who felt that way. While Brooks may have specifically targeted Frank to greet the first day, he didn't re-serve his hospitality for fellow superstars. "Brooks was great," says Roznovsky. "My first day there he came over in the clubhouse and introduced himself and welcomed me to the team. Just casual and offhanded; you would have never known he was a star. Then he drove me home after we were finished that day. He was great in the clubhouse—always cheerful. He was friendly to everybody. He was the type of leader who would get people going and talk to you when you were down. He could be in a slump, hitting .200, and he would still be friendly and talk to you. Tomorrow was another day, he didn't let anything bother him. You got the feeling that he was just happy to be there, playing baseball, getting to do what every kid dreamed of. He knew how lucky he was to be a pro baseball player and he loved every minute. Ernie Banks had been like that with the Cubs—always happy and optimistic."

"I first came to camp in 1966," says pitcher Eddie Watt. "I had heard of him, but I was just totally impressed with how down-to-earth and humble he was. And he did a lot of things quietly that nobody knew about. That year I was married with two kids, no money, one glove to my name, just trying to make the team. One day after a game in spring training, some kids got in and stole my glove. The next day I came in and there were two brand-new gloves in my locker, the kind I used. Nobody said anything. I asked the clubhouse guy about them. He said, 'Brooks put them in there for you.'"

"Ask a young player what teammate he remembers most from his first spring with the big club and, usually, he'll say Brooks Robinson," Dick Kaegel wrote in the *Sporting News*. "He really took me under his wing for a while," Dave May, a young outfielder, told reporters the next spring. "He got me a lot of contacts for my glove and my bats and that really helped me out."

With Frank batting third and Brooks hitting cleanup, the Orioles started fast. In the first inning on Opening Day in Boston, Red Sox pitcher Earl Wilson immediately made Frank feel welcome in the American League by treating him like the pitchers in the National League had—he plunked him with a pitch. Brooks followed with a home run. Frank added a home run of his own in the fifth. The Orioles took a 5–4 lead in the top of the 13th. "Bauer brought me in to pitch the last of the 13th with a one-run lead," says Eddie Watt. "It was my first major league game. With two outs, [Rico] Petrocelli hit a bullet to third base. I was worried when I saw it come off the bat. Brooks smothered it and nonchalantly threw him out, like it was routine, and that was the game. That was my welcome to big league defense. I thought, 'I'm gonna like this.'"

The next day, Frank and Brooks hit back-to-back homers in the first inning. After 11 games Brooks was hitting .400 with 19 RBIs, prompting the Associated Press to state, "If Brooks Robinson gets any hotter at the plate, he's liable to be tagged with a good hit–no field label by a newcomer to the baseball scene." Not to be outdone, Frank hit .474 with 10 RBIs over that period. People started talking about the "Robinson boys." The Orioles won nine of their first 10 and 16 of the first 20.

After slowing down briefly, the team caught fire from May 24 to July 3, winning 36 of 47 games. They finished the streak with a five-game sweep in Minnesota of the defending champs, giving them a seven-game lead. Their lead would not drop below six the rest of the season.

The Orioles had a good mix of veterans and young players. It was a close-knit team with no cliques. Rookies Davey Johnson, at second base, and Andy Etchebarren, at catcher, stepped into the lineup and immediately made an impact. Second-year center fielder Paul Blair was now playing regularly and was rapidly becoming one of the best at his position in the game. In the clubhouse, the players had a rare closeness in which everyone could be ripped by a teammate for any perceived indiscretion—without worrying about hurt feelings. Frank Robinson had a sharp wit and he maintained a loud running commentary and a barrage of one-liners in the clubhouse and on the bus. No one escaped his wrath. But he wasn't the only smart-ass— the clubhouse was filled with them. "The whole team was made up of needlers," Frank later wrote, "and that's what kept us loose all year long . . . all that clowning and joking served a purpose, I think. The mood of a ball club is very important. If you have happy players, they're going to put out extra and do things that a discontented ballplayer won't do. And we had that good mood, that attitude. We were a young club and had the type of fellows who liked to laugh and joke a lot. These kids were subject to a lot of pressure, and the horsing around relaxed them a bit. If an individual was going through a period when he wasn't hitting or pitching well, the jokes and things served the purpose of cutting the tension a bit. But when it came time for the ball game, that was it. Then it was time to get serious, and everyone did."

Their biting sarcasm showed in their nicknames, such as Clank for outfielder Curt Blefary, known for his lead glove, Lurch for Andy

Etchebarren, whose facial features and ferocious unibrow reminded the veterans of the Addams Family butler, and Motormouth for Blair, for obvious reasons.

Aparicio enjoyed digs at his partner on the left side of the infield. He complained to reporters that he was tired of making Brooks Robinson look like a solid third baseman. When Brooks slumped badly in August and September, teammates kidded him, "Don't lose your glove." Aparicio, feeling magnanimous after a five-hit performance, offered to donate two of his hits to Brooks, "my favorite .260 hitter."

First baseman Boog Powell never let the infielders forget that they owed him. "That's forty-two," he would loudly announce in the dugout after he had snagged one of their errant throws—keeping a running total for the year. "You're just lucky you've got me over here," he frequently told Brooks. "Because you wouldn't be a Gold Glove guy unless I dug all those bad throws out of the dirt."

On a team bus in New York, Frank spotted an accident involving a truck and a car. "Looks like Etchebarren blocking the plate. Get up Andy!"

From the back of the bus, Boog cracked, "All right Robinson, stop limping," alluding to the fact that Frank had been limping for a month with a sore leg and always seemed to walk like an old man in the clubhouse due to miseries of some sort.

Frank: "Quiet Crisco."

Boog: "At least I don't have sticks for legs. If you didn't have feet, your legs would stick in the ground."

Frank: "Better than having elephant legs."

"The humor has no boundaries," wrote Doug Brown of the *Baltimore Sun*, who traveled with the team. "It can be profane. It can be irreverent. It can be about the color of a guy's skin."

In the mid-1960s, the color of a guy's skin was not often a cause for humor. Frank had initially been apprehensive about Baltimore, which was still largely segregated. Soon after arriving in Miami for spring training he had received a call from his wife, upset that she could not find suitable housing in Baltimore. Realtors had been very happy when she first called, falling all over themselves to help Mrs. Robinson whose husband played for the Orioles. Upon meeting her and discovering that she was not Mrs. *Brooks* Robinson, they had suddenly made excuses and directed her to the other side of town. Even though Oriole owner Jerry Hoffberger intervened to help, the Frank Robinsons were eventually forced to find accommodations in a black neighborhood.

While Frank had never experienced overt racial trouble with teammates in Cincinnati, the Reds, like most baseball teams in the early 1960s, did not socialize across racial lines off the field. "Under the unwritten rules of baseball in those days . . . the Negro players and the white players were friends on the field, but once the game was over, went their separate ways," he later wrote. "Vada [Pinson] and I were never really invited to go along [with the white players] so we went our own way." Frank and Vada had been embarrassed when they showed up at a Cincinnati restaurant for a team celebration of the 1961 pennant and were initially asked to leave by management. Teammates quickly intervened but the insult was plain. And as with the players, black and white wives rarely mixed.

Frank found that things were different on the Orioles. The Orioles had always maintained good race relations in the clubhouses and between their wives. "Brooks's wife, Connie, was just a beautiful person," says Fred Valentine, an African American outfielder who played for the Orioles in 1959 and 1963. "She associated with my wife and got along good with everyone, just like he did. The wives on the team did a lot of things together."

Some reporters initially had been surprised by this. There was a perception in the media that anyone from the South was a racist, summed up by this statement that appeared in the *Vancouver Sun* after one of Brooks's first games there in 1959 when he bounded out to greet teammate Joe Taylor at home plate after a game-winning home run: "Robinson is from Little Rock, which isn't exactly a city of brotherly love. Robinson, though, has the right instincts. There'd be nothing significant in him being the first to warmly greet Joe Taylor's home run, except for one thing. Taylor is a Negro."

In an interview during his breakout season of 1960, Brooks had been asked what he thought about the disturbance at his old high school due to desegregation. He had replied, "That happened after I graduated. . . . Everyone is entitled to the same kind of education. I never tried to figure where I stood before, chiefly because no one's asked me until now. But there's no color trouble in baseball, so I am against segregation."

While some in baseball might have disputed that there was no color trouble in baseball in 1960, especially players who still were not allowed to live with their teammates or eat at certain restaurants around the league because of their skin color, it was a rather bold statement by a 23-year-old southerner at a time when many southern states were voting for segregationist governors. Although the players got along, it would be 1963 before all Orioles could stay in the same hotels while in Florida for spring training.

While not making a big deal over things, Brooks quietly set the tone for integration on a more personal level. "I suspect Brooks was a key reason why, for the first time in my 14 years in professional baseball, black players and white players had drinks together and meals together when we were on the road," wrote Frank. "Not every single night but two or three times on most road trips. None of the players ever really invited me, Paul Blair and Sam Bowens [the three blacks on the Orioles at the time] to join them. But Brooks might ask me where I was going after a game, and not knowing the restaurants in most American League cities, I might say I wasn't sure. Then Brooks would say something like, 'Well Boog, Jerry [Adair], Curt [Blefary] and I are going over to this restaurant.'

"We always knew where the group was going, and we'd end up there when we wanted to sit around over a meal or a few drinks and talk baseball. We all wanted to be together on the Orioles because we enjoyed one another's company and had a lot of respect for each individual as a person and as a player. Even when the food wasn't all that good, the talk and the camaraderie made for a lot of fun." In 1966, that was a big deal.

"The shame of it," Frank continued, "was that this kind of mingling of the races had never happened before and it never happened to me again after my 6 years in Baltimore."

The familiarity inevitably led to jokes—things that in other situations might have been left unsaid to become a possible source of resentment, became fodder for wisecracks—everything was fair game. "With me being from Little Rock and having gone to Little Rock Central High School, Blair and those guys used to make comments like, 'Well, I know I'm not going through Little Rock when I'm going somewhere,'" Brooks said later. "And I'd always say, 'Just tell 'em you know me; you're in good shape.' We had good rapport. Blair always talked basketball. He knew I was an all-state player and said, 'But you didn't have to play against any black guys. That's the reason you were so good.' He's probably right. We were pretty open about things."

Once on the bus, Sam Bowens, looking at a newspaper picture of the Red Sox' George Scott, joked that Frank bore a striking resemblance to Scott. When Frank protested, Brooks backed up Bowens: "That's all right, Sam, I think he looks like Scott, too."

"That's different," said Paul Blair. "You think we all look alike."

Another time, getting on the bus and looking for a seat, Brooks placed his coat between Frank and Blair in an empty seat, but remained standing. "Look at this Frank," Blair said. "I've been telling everybody what a great guy Brooks is, and he's prejudiced, too."

During the World Series, an out-of-town photographer approached Frank: "Keep your shirt on, Brooks, I want to take a picture."

"You'd think after a whole season, people could tell us apart," Frank replied. "After all, we do wear different uniform numbers."

When Frank and Brooks stepped onto the field at Memorial Stadium before a midseason game to shoot an unpaid commercial, Brooks joked, "I don't know. He's got 24 lines and I got one. I think they're prejudiced."

In July, when the team visited Chicago, they witnessed rioters roving the city's West Side, looting businesses. On the bus, the team's white players told Frank they were going to hide behind him. "Get up in the window so they can see you," they said, reasoning that, seeing a black face, the rioters would allow the bus to pass safely. Frank insisted that he didn't want to be anywhere near his white teammates when the gunfire started—he didn't want to take a chance on being collateral damage. "Baby, you're all on your own," he told them as he ducked down under the seat.

The Orioles continued to roll over their opponents, opening the largest July lead in the American League in eight years. As opposed to their usual pitching-and-defense style, the 1966 Orioles were a dominant offensive team. They bludgeoned the rest of the league, frequently winning games by double digits. By midseason, they boasted four of the top six American League batting averages (Russ Snyder, Frank, Brooks, and Boog). A contest for the RBI title developed between Frank, Brooks, and Boog, who were the top three in the league by a comfortable margin most of the season with Brooks setting the early pace, knocking in 45 runs in the first 44 games and 70 by midseason. Brooks, at 29 years old, was at his physical peak and had never hit better, even in 1964. The ball was jumping off his bat; he was driving in runs almost every day.

While the bullpen was brilliant, the starting pitching staff was mostly young and battled injuries. A midseason report in *Sports Illustrated* stated, "The basic Orioles starters—Dave McNally, Jim Palmer and Wally Bunker—are not Koufax, Drysdale and Osteen." They didn't know it at the time, but that statement would ring true in ways they could not imagine in October.

The Orioles had barely missed out on the pennant in close finishes several times, but now there was no doubt about who had the best team in the league. When they didn't pummel teams into submission, they pulled out games with late heroics. It was one of those years when they seemed to get every break—they knew they were going to win.

Brooks was the top vote getter in either league for the All-Star team picked by the players. The game was played in new Busch Stadium in St. Louis. With the game being close to Little Rock, Brooks's parents, a few former Legion teammates, and George Haynie drove up for the game, giving Brooks a thrill to play in an All-Star Game in front of hometown friends and family. The game would be remembered for the oppressive heat, which reached 105 degrees. Hundreds of fans collapsed. Smelling salts and oxygen were used in the dugout. Brooks performed as though he didn't notice the heat, however, playing the entire 10-inning game.

In the second inning, facing Sandy Koufax, Brooks lined a fastball to left field where Hank Aaron initially broke back, lost the ball in the sun, then came in and missed a shoestring attempt. The ball went to the wall for a triple. Brooks scored moments later on a wild pitch. He singled in the seventh and 10th innings, giving him half of the American League's six hits. He also shined in the field, setting an

All-Star Game record by handling eight chances flawlessly. In the second, he snared Ron Santo's scorching liner. He ranged toward the third base bag and dug out Aaron's wicked grounder and threw him out in the sixth and topped that in the ninth by going over the bag to come up with another Santo smash and threw him out. The game gave Brooks an All-Star average of .391 over the past seven years. The N.L. won 2–1. Brooks's three hits and brilliant defense earned him the MVP award: the first time a player from a losing team had been named MVP.

A nationwide airline strike added to the hectic travel arrangements for the week. Monday, the four Oriole All-Stars took a bus from Baltimore to New York where they caught a flight to St. Louis. After the game, they flew back to Baltimore and immediately boarded a bus to Philadelphia for an exhibition game that ended up going 13 innings. Next, they took a bus to Newark, spent the night, then flew to Detroit for a game against the Tigers.

The chaotic schedule and lack of rest contributed to Brooks's rare outburst soon after the All-Star Game. When asked by a reporter if he was tired, he angrily replied, "Of course I'm tired. . . . We won't get to sleep until five o'clock in the morning when we get home from this trip, then we have to go out and play another game. This is ridiculous. . . . They don't think about the players. . . . When you go in there in the winter for a $500 raise, all they say is, 'Sorry, we can't give it to you.' It's wrong, that's all." He continued complaining of the schedule, especially having to play the last game of a series at night before taking off for another city. "Know why they schedule night games on getaway days? Money. They know they can't draw good crowds during the day, so they schedule the games at night. But do we get any of that money? No."

That night the Orioles arrived home at 4:30 A.M., got a little sleep, and reported to the baseball field. Then, as if the wise guys on the team wanted to prevent Brooks from making a point, they went out and collected 19 hits in a 13–3 demolition of the Tigers. After the game, Frank wryly told reporters, "It looks like we'd been resting for a month."

Reporters continually questioned whether Brooks was jealous of the newcomer taking away the spotlight. "Frank makes us a better offensive ball club than we've ever been before," said Brooks late in the season, not showing any sign of being annoyed by writers belaboring the point. "As far as I'm concerned, he's a better ballplayer than I am. What wrong with being number 2? According to the ads, you just try harder. Frank has been good for me and we get along fine. Actually it doesn't matter who's number one as long as we win the pennant."

Late in the season *Sport* ran a piece in which the Robinson boys discussed each other. "He's the best hitter I've ever played with," said Brooks. "With him in the lineup, our club is better offensively than it's ever been in its 13-year history. But just as important to a team involved in a pennant race are the intangibles.

"If he weren't a good guy, there might be friction between us," Brooks continued, addressing their clubhouse camaraderie. "As it is, there's merely the natural urge to outdo each other. Frank spurs me on." He concluded with, "I've never played with a better hitter, a better all-around player and a better competitor than Frank Robinson."

Not to be outdone in the mutual admiration contest, Frank said, "I sensed right away the feeling of looseness that is created when no one is allowed to take anything—the good or the bad—too seriously. Only a leader can cultivate this atmosphere. And for six years the unquestioned leader of this club has been Brooks Robinson. The leadership Brooks provides really can't be measured. He is an inspiration without trying to be.

"Until I was traded to the Orioles, I frankly had my doubts about how good Brooks was. . . . To judge a guy, you must play with him day in and day out, and I've never seen a third baseman who can compare with Brooks. . . . Thanks to Brooks, I'm not under the suffocating pressure that I was in Cincinnati. No longer does everything depend on me. . . . Neither he, nor anything he does, is bigger than the team. Thanks to Brooks, the transition was easy."

After compiling a 70–35 start and building an insurmountable lead in the standings, the Orioles went 27–28 the rest of the season. Sore arms affected the staff and several other players battled injuries as they coasted into September. Brooks slumped badly late in the season. In one 28-game stretch in August, he had one home run, three RBIs, and a .187 average. But it hardly affected the team—the only question of clinching the pennant was when.

That came on September 15 in Kansas City. After the Orioles beat the A's to officially take the pennant, the players had a raucous two-hour party in the clubhouse, drowning the ghosts of 12 years of frustration in Baltimore. Niceties and congratulations soon turned into sprays of champagne and dunks in the hot tub and showers.

When the players were completely soaked, they turned on their bosses. General manager Harry Dalton was thrown in the shower, then Bauer. Someone spotted team owner Jerry Hoffberger, who was innocently circulating through the room shaking hands, and noted that he was still dry. He was quickly carried into the shower.

The players sloshed through champagne, and when it ran out they pelted each other with pickles and ketchup. Bauer received a mustard-and-mayonnaise shampoo—after he had been thrown into the shower. So many condiments ended up on the players that they resembled, according to the *Baltimore News American*, "ambulatory sandwiches."

Someone trimmed the announcer's pants at the knees while he still had them on. Several writers had their shirts ripped off their backs, leaving them wearing nothing but a collar. Frank found Brooks in the trainer's room trying to make a phone call and noticed that he hadn't discovered that the telephone wire had been ripped from the wall. Frank picked up the broken wire, held it up to Brooks's ear, and said, "Here, try this end."

While all the players enjoyed the euphoria of the moment, it was especially sweet for Brooks. Everyone else on the team had only known quality baseball and pennant contenders in Baltimore (Steve Barber, who joined the team in 1960, was the next longest-tenured player)—only Brooks had endured the difficult building years of chronic second division teams. He was heard to announce in the locker room, "I've waited ten years for this."

And while Brooks maintained an attitude of humbleness, he clearly understood, and was proud of, his own worth. When a reporter asked him if he felt left out because of his struggles in the second half, insinuating that he was merely along for the ride, he replied, "I'll tell you what—we wouldn't be here without me."

Back in Baltimore, the mayor and the Chamber of Commerce held a luncheon the next day and hailed the Orioles. "Bomb 'Em Birds" was announced as the civic war cry and was soon found on flags, pennants, T-shirts, caps, and in store windows throughout the city.

After holding their emotions throughout the season because of so many near misses in previous years, the citizens of Baltimore gave themselves over to the team. When the tickets for Games 3–5 of the World Series became available through a mail lottery system, 84,000 requests arrived the first day.

All season, the one-two-three punch of Frank, Brooks, and Boog devastated opposing pitchers. At least two of the three were hot at any one time. All three finished the season with 100 RBIs or more. While Brooks slumped late, Frank got hot and ended with Triple Crown numbers: 49 homers, 122 RBIs, and a .316 average. Brooks would finish second to Frank in the MVP voting, with Boog third.

While the Orioles coasted through September, the winner in the National League was not decided until the Dodgers won the second game of a doubleheader the last day of the season. The World Series was nothing new to the Dodgers as they had won it in 1963 and 1965. Among the Orioles, only Frank (Cincinnati in 1961), Aparicio (Chicago in 1959), and reliever Stu Miller (San Francisco in 1962) had been to a Series before and none had played on a winner.

The Dodger pitching staff was formidable. Sandy Koufax boasted a record of 27–9 in 1966, with an ERA of 1.73 and 317 strikeouts. In addition to Koufax, there were two other future Hall of Famers, Don Drysdale and twenty-year-old Don Sutton, in the starting rotation, as well as 17-game winner Claude Osteen. At a team meeting before the Series, Oriole advance scout Jim Russo described at length the dominance of the Dodgers' pitching. Finally, Bauer growled, "If these guys are that good, we got no chance. Meeting over."

But while Russo worried over the Dodger pitchers, he had discovered a key weakness in their hitters. He had followed the Dodgers for two weeks in September and watched them struggle against hard-throwing opponents. He passed this information along to Bauer and the Oriole pitchers.

The Dodger hitters indeed did nothing to inspire fear, except among their own fans. The oft-told joke of Don Drysdale, in another city for a function, being told that his pitching mate Koufax had thrown a no-hitter for the Dodgers that night and responding, "Did we win?" painfully summed up their offense. During the 1966 season, the entire Dodger roster combined to hit only as many home runs as Brooks, Frank, and Boog. In a bit of foreshadowing to the Series, the New Hampshire Forestry Division sent a message to the Dodgers congratulating them for being the major league team "which has done the most to conserve wood—one of our most important natural resources."

The Orioles' play had been sloppy after clinching. In Los Angeles the day before the Series, Bob Maisel asked Brooks if he was concerned about whether the team would be able to regain their intensity. "Don't worry about it," Brooks answered. "We can turn it back on, no problem. . . . The only things that worry me are things we don't know about now. Like background. We've never played here in the daytime [the Orioles had played a number of games in Chavez Ravine against the Angels while awaiting the completion of the Angels' stadium in Anaheim], with the center field bleachers." He had heard that it was difficult for a batter to follow a pitch in the sea of white-shirted fans. "That might complicate things some."

Bauer tried to keep his players from being intimidated by the mystique of the Dodgers. When a reporter said that the Dodgers had never lost a Series game at Dodger Stadium, he replied, "Well we've never lost a World Series game at Memorial Stadium either." Before the Series, Bauer held one of his infrequent clubhouse meetings and told his team "to hell with the odds, because the guys that make odds don't play baseball."

Although the bookmakers had the Dodgers 8 to 5, and the Orioles couldn't escape constant reminders (the bus that carried the team to Dodger Stadium for the opening game passed a bank that flashed the message: *Would you believe four straight by the Dodgers?*), the players themselves seemed loose. They had enjoyed bringing their families to California for the opener, staying in the swank Continental Hotel, owned by Angels owner and movie cowboy Gene Autry, and basking in the pre-Series atmosphere. "There was really no pressure on us before the Series because we were big underdogs," says Bob

Johnson. "But we also knew that, although they had a good ball club and great pitching, they didn't have anybody who could hit the ball out of the park like Frank, Boog, or Brooks. We knew we had a chance."

"I was surprised at how loose the guys were on the bus going to the opening game," recalls batboy Bob Scherr. "If they were nervous, it sure didn't show. They were all joking and laughing, not talking about the game. They had a joke set up with me as the object of the joke. Eddie Watt said that he was friends with actress Ann-Margret. He said she was coming to the game and needed a date for after the game. The other guys said, 'We're all married, we can't go out with her, why don't you fix her up with Bob?'

"I thought that was the greatest idea I had ever heard," says Scherr, who was 17 at the time. "They kept talking about it all the way to the stadium. I was really looking forward to it—at that point I didn't care about the game anymore. When we got on the field, Eddie went over to the stands and was talking to a female. They were too far away, I couldn't recognize her, but she waved to me, so I waved back. Brooks walked by and said, 'See, he's fixing you up, you're all set.' They later let me in on the fact that it was all a hoax. At the 40-year reunion of the team, I reminded Watt that he still owes me a date with Ann-Margret."

Dodger Game One starter Don Drysdale was more than intimidating. A growling dog is intimidating; Drysdale was downright dangerous. Unshaven, glowering menacingly, he was 6-foot-5, with a whiplike delivery that was almost side-armed. He defended the inside half of the plate the way the Russians defended Stalingrad. Drysdale was well on his way to a Hall of Fame career and in 1966 was still the most famous member of the Van Nuys, California, class of '54 (a left-handed classmate, Robert Redford, would surpass him after appearing in *Butch Cassidy and the Sundance Kid* in 1969). The popular Drysdale's number 53 was used as the number for Herbie, Disney's Love Bug, but Drysdale was anything but lovable on the mound. He and Frank Robinson had waged epic battles when Frank was on the Reds—battles that often ended with either Frank getting a hit or being hit—neither backed down.

In the top of the first inning with one out and Russ Snyder on first,

Frank bombed a home run. Brooks stepped in. Drysdale, snarling and nasty, threw the obligatory duster high and inside. The second pitch was a fastball and Brooks turned on it and launched it seven rows deep into the left field stands, giving the Orioles a quick 3–0 lead. The Dodger Dogs were barely warm in the concession stands and the Orioles had already scored as many runs as the Yankees (one in two games) and the Twins (two in three games) had in the past two World Series in Dodger Stadium.

"Two swings and the Orioles had produced one of the dramatic innings in Series history and had taken away the go-go Dodgers' tools—the bunt, the hit-and-run and all that," wrote Jack Mann in *Sports Illustrated*.

The fast start against the defending champs changed the whole atmosphere in the Oriole dugout. Jim Palmer later said, "When Brooks and Frank hit home runs in the first inning, guys said, 'Gee, maybe we have a chance to win here.'"

After watching his lead grow to 4–0, the Oriole starter, twenty-three-year-old lefty Dave McNally, experienced control problems and was soon in deep trouble. Unable to get used to the severe slope of the mound, he was consistently wild high. He gave up a run in the second, then walked the bases loaded in the third, throwing only three strikes to his last four batters. Oriole reliever Moe Drabowsky then walked out of the bullpen and into baseball history.

Amid all the preseason hoopla regarding the Frank Robinson trade, the Orioles' acquisition of the thirty-year-old Drabowsky for the grand sum of $25,000 had been almost a whisper. Drabowsky had been a flamethrowing phenom when signed in 1956 by the Cubs, but arm trouble quickly hampered his progress. By 1966, he had bounced between four different teams and had not had a winning record since 1960.

After being converted to a full-time reliever by the Orioles, Drabowsky had turned in the best season of his career, going 6–0. In addition to being a good pitcher, Drabowsky was one of baseball's greatest pranksters and he fit right in with the fun-loving Orioles. He was a master of the hotfoot, eventually getting everybody, including owner Jerry Hoffberger and commissioner Bowie Kuhn in his time with the Orioles. He once put goldfish in the water cooler of the opposing team's bullpen. After terrorizing teammates, especially Aparicio and Blair, with rubber snakes for several weeks during the 1966 season, he made a visit to a pet store in Anaheim and purchased a real one. He casually walked into the clubhouse with the snake draped around his neck and sat down next to Aparicio. The little shortstop, determined not to be fooled again, continued dressing until the snake lifted its head right next to his face and flicked its tongue. Aparicio ran out onto the field in his underwear and refused to return to the clubhouse—forcing Bauer to have his uniform brought out to the dugout.

Drabowsky's greatest moment came when he called the A's bullpen phone during a game in Kansas City (he remembered the number from when he was on the team). Imitating A's manager Al Dark's voice, he ordered reliever Lew Krausse to get warm—even though it was early and the A's starter had a shutout going. Krausse shrugged and dutifully got up and started throwing. The real Dark, surprised to see his reliever warming up, called and ordered him to sit down. "Moe called back two more times," says Roznovsky; "each time he got Krausse up and then Dark would call back and yell at him to quit throwing. Poor Krausse didn't know what was going on. We were sitting in our bullpen just cracking up laughing."

Now in the World Series with the bases loaded, no one was laughing. Drabowsky struggled with his control initially, walking Jim Gilliam on a 3–2 count to force in a run, and going 3 and 2 on John Roseboro. The Dodger catcher then fouled off an obvious ball four and popped out on the next pitch to end the inning. Drabowsky had a good arm and, when he was right, possessed an excellent fastball that was capable of overpowering hitters. It quickly became apparent that Moe was throwing particularly hard on this day. When Dodger teammates asked Lou Johnson, who struck out leading off the next inning, what Drabowsky's pitches were doing, he replied, "They aren't hitting the bat." Drabowsky proceeded to have the best World Series game any reliever has ever had. He struck out 11 men (all swinging) over the last six and two-thirds innings (six in a row at one stretch) while limiting them to one hit. The Orioles won the game 5–2.

"The first game was the key," Brooks said years later. "Frank and

I talked about it beforehand. We needed to win the first game to show the guys that we could play with them and not be overwhelmed."

Even more important than the final score was the fact the rest of the Oriole staff, including Game Two starter Jim Palmer, noted that what Russo had told them about the Dodgers was correct—they could be beaten with high hard stuff.

On the national stage for the first time other than All-Star Games, Brooks was making a positive impression. Interviewed before Game Two, Casey Stengel, who threw out the first pitch, said in his unique version of the English language, "From Kansas City to Kankakee and back again, I ain't never seen nothing like the guy on third. And then, when you see him, you don't believe it."

Sandy Koufax took the mound for the Dodgers under the bright West Coast sun for Game Two. Koufax had just completed one of the most dominating four-year stretches in major league history, with a record of 97–27, leading the league in ERA all four years (his worst ERA of that stretch was 2.07). But, as good as Koufax was, opposing players didn't lose sleep the night before facing him, like they might with Drysdale or Bob Gibson. Koufax never threw at batters—he didn't have to. Like a kindly doctor who assures his patient before a shot, "Relax, this won't hurt a bit," Koufax merely got batters out and sent them back to the dugout—giving them a comfortable 0-for-4.

Frank Robinson, who knew Koufax well from his National League days, warned his teammates of Koufax's rising fastball: "If it starts at the belt, take it because it's going to choke you." But, in reality, advice did nothing to help a hitter against Sandy Koufax. For several years teams in the National League knew that he tipped off his curveball— they knew when it was coming—but they still couldn't touch it. When he had his best stuff, major league batters were simply overmatched.

Facing Koufax was twenty-year-old Jim Palmer. An exquisite athlete, Palmer had taken a somewhat unusual route to the major leagues. Adopted by a well-off couple, he had initially lived on Park Avenue in Manhattan—learning to throw a baseball in Central Park with the butler. The family moved first to California, where Jim starred for the Beverly Hills Little League, and then to Scottsdale,

Arizona, where he led the state in scoring in basketball in high school and turned down a scholarship from UCLA and John Wooden to sign with the Orioles. While not yet the accomplished pitcher who would win 268 games in his Hall of Fame career, young Palmer relied on his powerful arm to fog it by hitters. Nicknamed Pancake that year due to his superstition of always eating pancakes the day he pitched, he had inflamed a tendon in his right shoulder while painting the nursery in his house earlier in the season (he was making $7,500 that year and could not afford a painter). He entered the World Series concerned about his arm.

But Koufax had concerns of his own. Although he was still a young man, only 30 years old, his left arm had aged in dog-years. It was not fully known at the time of the Series, but he had been in severe pain all year. He had thrown 323 innings during the season and had started seven games in the last 26 days—the Dodgers had needed every one of them as they battled to the last game for the pennant. The World Series start was his third in eight days.

While Koufax was not overpowering in Game Two, he was still good enough. The Orioles could not manage a run through the first four innings. Then, in the fifth, they received a gift. Dodger center fielder Willie Davis lost two consecutive fly balls in the sun, allowing them to fall in safely. After the second one, he picked up the ball and made a bad throw past third for another error. When the carnage was over, Davis had a World Series record three errors in one inning and the Orioles had a 3–0 lead.

The comedians in the press box were having a good time at Davis's expense. When he was late coming out for the next inning, one of them asked, "Do you suppose he may be about to commit suicide?" Another answered, "Hope not, he might miss and kill an usher." A third pondered, "I wonder if Davis will be able to catch the plane to Baltimore."

The Dodgers were unable to score off Palmer, and the Orioles added three more runs, courtesy of a total of six Dodger errors. Palmer finished with a complete game four-hit shutout.

The Orioles returned to Friendship International Airport in Baltimore at 1:17 A.M. and found 9,000 screaming fans, led by the mayor, who bounded up the motorized stairway, snatched Bauer's hand as he exited the plane, and raised it in triumph. The team was greeted as returning conquering heroes. Writers cautioned fans, however, that the previous year the Dodgers had trailed the Twins 2–0 and had come back to win in seven. Koufax could potentially pitch two more games if needed.

In Game Three, the largest crowd in Oriole history—54,445—crammed into Memorial Stadium. The Orioles' Game Three starter, 21-year-old Wally Bunker, had been 19–5 in 1964, but had experienced arm trouble ever since. Although not technically a power pitcher, he smartly followed the recipe of Drabowsky and Palmer and fed the Dodgers fastballs. And once again the recipe produced a masterpiece. After winning 1–0, courtesy of Paul Blair's fifth-inning home run (only the third time a 1–0 World Series game was decided by a home run), Bunker sat in front of his locker, all but neglected by the press. "I guess shutting out the Dodgers isn't news anymore," he joked.

In Game Four the Dodgers came back with Drysdale, holding Koufax ready for the next game if needed. A fourth-inning one-out Frank Robinson home run gave the Orioles a 1–0 lead. After Brooks grounded out, Boog Powell hit a towering drive to deep center field that appeared to add to the lead. Willie Davis turned his back and ran to the fence, waited, took five steps to his right—just in front of the 410 sign—and jumped. With the armpit of his fully extended right arm above the fence, he caught the ball to rob Powell of a home run.

The great play in center field gave the Dodgers a spark of life as they prepared to hit. Jim Lefebvre opened the inning with a single. The next batter, Wes Parker, slapped a bouncer into the hole to Aparicio's right. Brooks ran to his left, stretched, and stabbed the ball, stumbled, took a couple of steps to regain his balance, then delivered a perfect chest-high throw to Johnson at second, who relayed it quickly to first for a double play. The Dodger momentum was over.

There were still tense moments, however. In the eighth, Lefebvre drilled a long fly to center that looked like a home run. Blair ran back, leaped at the fence, and robbed him (a spectacular play, but not quite as good as Davis's at nearly the same spot in the fourth). In the ninth inning, with one out and the Orioles clinging to their 1–0 lead and starter Dave McNally still on the mound, pinch hitter Al Ferrara singled to center and was replaced by a pinch runner. McNally walked the next batter. Willie Davis then popped out to right field, too shallow for the runners to advance. With the crowd roaring on every pitch, Lou Johnson worked the count to 2–2. Brooks walked over to the mound. McNally expected a pep talk. Brooks went for a laugh instead. "Whatever you do," he told his friend, "don't let him hit the ball to me." McNally smiled, then obliged, getting Johnson to lift a can of corn to Blair in center to end the Series. Brooks bounded in to congratulate McNally.

Watching the final out, ready with his camera, was *Baltimore Sun* photographer Paul Hutchins. "When the last ball was hit to the out-field, I thought, 'This is gonna be a big deal,'" he said in 2012. "So I watched the pitcher [McNally] and, as he came off the mound, I snapped his grin. . . . I remember looking at McNally in the view-finder, and seeing something coming from the left. I didn't know it was Brooks, in midair, until I got back to the *Sun* and developed it." After turning in the photo, Hutchins was walking downtown, enjoy-ing the celebration, when he spotted a newspaper box with the early edition of the *Sun*—the picture was plastered on the front page, above the fold, under the headline "Would You Believe It? Four Straight!"

The picture, showing the unadulterated joy of winning the Series, featured Brooks suspended in air, seemingly flying. While winning the Series was more than a small step for the team, the picture showed what was definitely one giant leap for a third baseman. "My kids still think it was trick photography," Brooks said forty years later. "They tell me, 'Dad, you never jumped that high in your life.'"

After the Series, teens were noted to be doing a new dance called "The Brooks," patterned after his steps as he raced across the infield and jumped up and down with McNally.

Throwing mostly high fastballs, the Oriole pitchers had blanked the Dodgers for the final 33 innings of the Series—giving them no runs after the third inning bases-loaded walk in Game One. The Dodgers advanced only one runner to third base over the final 25 innings. Palmer, Bunker, and McNally threw consecutive shutouts. The Series set a record for low batting averages: .142 for the Dodgers and .200 for the winning Orioles.

It had been tight and hard fought the whole way—the kind of low-scoring, close games that could turn on one hit, one error, one pitch. Yet it was not the inexperienced Orioles who made the mistakes. The Orioles did not commit an error in the four games. Bauer, playing the hot hand, used only 13 men the whole Series.

Although he got only three hits in 14 at bats, Brooks had a significant impact on the outcome. His reputation affected the Dodgers' game plan. William Leggett wrote in his Series postmortem in *Sports Illustrated*, "One of the reasons why the Dodgers could not get men around to third was their abandonment of the bunt, normally one of their strongest weapons. . . . The Dodgers were really intimidated by the presence of Brooks Robinson at third base and seemed afraid to bunt against him. Thus they psyched themselves into hitting at an infield only three quarters its normal size, as though a new foul line ran from home plate to shortstop."

The Orioles had become the first non-Yankee American League World Champions since 1948. The city of Baltimore exploded in celebration. Thousands of people swarmed downtown. A sea of torn paper was thrown from hotel windows, horns blared, and pennants were waved from car windows. The party in the streets was called "the zaniest celebration that Baltimore has seen since the U.S. defeated Japan in World War II" by the *Baltimore Sun*. That night they rang the bell at City Hall 66 times in celebration. "It was great," recalled moviemaker Barry Levinson. "Not only did we win, but we totally humiliated an LA team. That was the beginning of Oriole Pride. We had arrived."

Brooks visited Little Rock in late October for Brooks Robinson Week, returning as the local boy who made good. "We're all so proud of him," his mother told the *Arkansas Democrat*. His father added that they were "pretty proud" of his reputation off the field as well. The paper had a large pullout section dedicated to Brooks, with his athletic history in Little Rock, his professional highlights, and interviews with several ex-Doughboy teammates and coach George Haynie. Brooks was the guest of honor at a morning assembly at Little Rock Central High School, a party for the Boys Club at Lamar Porter Field, and several banquets. There was also a parade. Brooks later wrote about the honor, "It was a wonderful thing for the boy who'd grown up there with dreams of a baseball career to come home and be so well received by all the folks he'd known over the years—and a lot he didn't too, like the mayor and the governor."

In 2006, Brooks still maintained that nothing ever topped that first championship. "It was the first time around, just like the 1958 Colts. You don't realize what a championship means to a town unless you live through it. Even now, anytime I think about a guy on that team, I get a smile on my face."

10. "He Does That All the Time"

ONCE THE EUPHORIA of the World Series wore off, there was some serious business to attend to. Along with Joe Torre, Hank Aaron, Harmon Killebrew, Stan Musial, and announcer Mel Allen, Brooks left San Francisco on November 1, 1966, headed for Vietnam. The purpose of the trip, cosponsored by the baseball commissioner's office and the Department of Defense, was to conduct clinics and boost morale—a goodwill tour. The war had turned difficult and the American troops desperately needed a morale boost. The commissioner of baseball, retired Air Force Lieutenant General William Eckert, had eagerly offered his assistance and asked the stars, who were glad to participate.

Whatever was originally planned for the trip, it turned out to be a much more harrowing experience than anyone could have imagined—it was definitely not a casual sightseeing tour behind the lines in secure camps. This was readily apparent soon after the group's arrival as they made their way through the crowded, trash-littered streets of Saigon to their hotel, which featured armed MPs behind sandbags and barbed wire.

As the baseball personnel were given ID cards that identified them as noncombatants, they silently hoped that the bad guys could read English. The group was informed of the difficulty of identifying Vietcong and warned never to accept anything from strangers. To tell friend from foe when approached there was this rule of thumb: "If a guy walks up and says 'Hi,' then he's a friend. If he walks up and shoots you, then he's an enemy."

They were up every day at six o'clock, meeting troops, posing for pictures, signing autographs, shaking hands, and then, at night Mel Allen would show that year's official All-Star Game film. They traveled mostly in helicopters and loud, smelly C-130s, moving from place to place on the ground only by day because, as the soldiers told them, the United States rules the day, "but at night, it belongs to Charlie."

Joe Torre, in 2009, still recalled the experience and noted that while he was not especially frightened ("I was just young and stupid"), Aaron, Allen, and Musial had the good sense to be uncomfortable. "You saw tracer bullets every night. We were in that outpost and every night you could hear that harassment fire going off."

On one of their early hops, the men noticed bullet holes in their helicopter when it arrived to pick them up—it had taken fire from the brush on the way. They usually cruised at 3,000 feet and never came in for a landing at a gradual descent—instead they dropped straight down in a screaming corkscrew spiral to avoid snipers. Once they watched from their transport as an American helicopter gunship sank two Vietcong boats. As the players whisked through the air in a helicopter with no doors, watching live combat up close, reality set in.

In Da Nang, they had lunch with General William Westmoreland, the commander of the U.S. operation in Vietnam, and dinner with Lieutenant General Lewis Walt, the commanding general of the III Marine Amphibious Force. Shortly thereafter, the general's quarters were bombed. A reporter later described Musial as "shaking like a leaf" as he described the adventure upon returning to the States.

During a similar trip by football players that year, when asked by General Westmoreland if there was anything he could do for them, Green Bay Packer Willie Davis answered, "Yeah, get us a gun."

It was the first group of baseball players to tour Vietnam and the visits were a highlight for the soldiers. Jim Lucas, a Pulitzer Prize–winning war correspondent based in Vietnam, reported that the group accomplished its mission. "Wherever I've gone, I've heard nothing but raves," he said. "They did a lot for baseball as an entity with the top brass, from General Westmoreland on down and they did a lot for the morale of the troops."

"We didn't sit back at the bases," Aaron told a reporter after returning. "We went right to the troops in the field and visited the men in the hospitals. That's what made the trip so good. They were anxious to see us. We created a crowd wherever we went."

"Baseball Stars Give Fighting Men a Lift," proclaimed armed forces newspaper *Stars and Stripes*. "Six famous men of baseball are batting 1.000 in morale boosting as they tour the four corps area of the Republic of Vietnam."

The group spent 17 days there, visiting firebases, MASH units, and hospitals from the Mekong Delta to Da Nang, and all were moved by what they witnessed. Brooks was particularly impressed by the courage of the soldiers, but distressed by the carnage he saw. He later wrote, "I met a lot of brave American kids who were badly shot up. It shook me to see them—arms and legs missing, faces shattered, blind."

At one hospital they met a young soldier who had recently been brought in after stepping on a mine. One of his legs was gone and the other was badly mangled. As the boy tried to raise a glass of water to his mouth, he couldn't do it and Aaron helped him. An attending doctor asked the soldier if he knew who the visitors were. When he replied no, the doctor introduced each of the players in turn. The soldier started apologizing for not recognizing them. The players were overwhelmed with emotion. Brooks later wrote, "Imagine—here was this boy with one leg gone and the other perhaps about to be amputated, and he was concerned about our feelings at not being recognized. I don't know about the others, but I had to fight against tears."

"Those kids over there are just unbelievable," Brooks said when he returned. "I came home feeling a great deal of respect for our boys. I just couldn't believe they could be there, do the job they have to do and keep such a high morale going."

When it had been announced that he was going to Vietnam, several Baltimore fans had asked Brooks to visit their sons over there. One soldier was on a night mission when Brooks arrived at Da Nang. The group stayed overnight so he could greet him when he returned the next morning. Later, the mother of the soldier called the *Baltimore Sun* "to say for all the rest of her life she would be on her knees nightly, before going to bed, and in her prayers ask for blessings on behalf of Brooks for what he had done."

The baseball group made no political statements, either for or against the war, but rather maintained their respect for Americans in harm's way. An editorial in the *Sporting News* stated, "These men are members of baseball's elite. All have been well-rewarded for their accomplishments in money, prestige, applause and publicity. They have captured no headlines in Vietnam nor will they gain financially. Their trip might not be necessary either, but it surely is worthwhile." After returning, the group was invited to the White House to meet President Lyndon Johnson in a private reception.

The Orioles showed up in spring training in 1967 as the world champs, with little expectation of anything other than continued success. Great hitting and young pitching provided boundless optimism. Along with optimism, there were more tangible signs of good feelings. Brooks signed in early February for $75,000, a raise of $20,000—his biggest ever. Frank, fresh off a Triple Crown–MVP season, signed for $100,000.

When camp opened, the Orioles discovered that their uniforms hadn't made it to Miami yet. Once delivered, the lettering on the front was the wrong color. Brooks was beaned by a Phil Niekro fastball in an early exhibition game against the Braves and sustained a mild concussion. They didn't know it at the time, but these were merely signs of things to come for the 1967 Baltimore Orioles.

Brooks started the regular season with three spectacular plays in the opener, but he slumped at the plate early, along with the rest of the team. The Orioles lost nine of 10 in mid-May and dropped to last place. The young pitchers were either ineffective, injured, or both. Every cab driver in Baltimore became an expert on tendinitis. Jim Palmer couldn't get rid of the pain in his shoulder and, after several ineffective starts, was sent to Rochester. He failed to improve and was put on the disabled list—he would not pitch in Baltimore again for almost two years. Wally Bunker had recurrent elbow problems, was relegated to the bullpen, and crawled to a 3–7 season. Dave McNally missed a large part of the season with an injury. Steve Barber, who had won 18 games in 1961 and 20 in 1963, continued to have arm trouble and was finally traded.

Frank alone was duplicating his 1966 success; however, he would not be spared from the bad luck. June 27, while he appeared to be on his way to another Triple Crown, hitting .337 with 21 home runs and 59 RBIs, he barreled into second base to break up a double play against the White Sox, and rammed his head into the knee of second baseman Al Weis. When he awoke, he discovered that he had double vision—an intracranial nerve (called the fourth nerve) responsible for the movement of one of his eyes had been damaged. Frank would miss 28 games, and when he returned, the residual effects of the fourth nerve palsy made him tuck his chin into his chest and cock his head at a peculiar angle to avoid seeing two baseballs. Not surprisingly, he was ineffective the rest of the season.

After Frank went down, Brooks broke out of a slump, going on a 10-game tear of 17-for-39, while hitting five home runs. One reporter looking for an angle suggested that Brooks had slumped because he couldn't keep up with Frank and, freed from the shadow of Frank after the injury, had blossomed. "Ridiculous," said Brooks. "A month ago when I started swinging the bat better, I had a hunch somebody would come up with reasoning like that. All I can say is that it's ridiculous. Frank Robinson is just a better hitter than I am, that's all."

Once again, Brooks made his presence felt in the All-Star Game, tying it 1–1 with a home run in the bottom of the sixth inning. The National League won 2–1 on a 15th-inning home run by Cincinnati's Tony Perez. After the All-Star break, Brooks continued his hot hitting, but the Orioles never could mount a run. Late in the season, he endured a 2-for-51 nightmare of a slump and ended the year hitting .269—identical to his 1966 average but with only 77 RBIs compared to 100 in 1966. The Orioles finished in sixth place.

Misfortune continued to haunt the Orioles in 1968. Brooks was beaned on the ear flap by Steve Blass in spring training. Frank Robinson got the mumps April 20 and spent a week in the hospital, then hurt his arm in May.

There were bright spots, however. Tom Phoebus pitched a no-hitter April 26 against the Red Sox, winning 6–0. In the eighth inning Rico Petrocelli of the Sox hit a sinking line drive over third base. Brooks dove to his right and backhanded the ball shoelaces-high to save the no-hitter.

But, as in 1967, the Orioles could not get going. The Tigers ran out to a huge lead behind Denny McLain, Mickey Lolich, Al Kaline, and Norm Cash. Frank was still bothered intermittently with double vision. The pitching staff remained a mass of sore arms. Hank Bauer's laissez-faire attitude toward the veterans had worked well when the team was winning. He remained loyal to the players who had helped him win the pennant, but as their performance fell off, many came to view that loyalty as a liability. Though he retained the respect of both Robinson boys, there were whispers (very loud whispers) that Bauer, who had vowed to get tougher after 1967, was losing the team.

Major league managers can get away with losing games (as long as it is not too many). They can get away with losing their temper. They can even get away with losing their minds (many are suspected of doing just that). But the one unforgivable sin for a manager is to lose his team. Once that specter is raised, the manager's days are numbered. In midseason, Bauer called a meeting after a particularly bad series and chewed out players for their lackadaisical play. He snapped at them, "I'll be here when a lot of you guys are gone." The statement would turn out to be a gross misjudgment on baseball club politics.

As the team continued to founder, management became convinced things needed to be shaken up. And they had just the guy in mind to shake them up—he was as close as the first base coach's box. Earl Weaver grew up in a tough section of St. Louis, playing baseball and dreaming of the big leagues. A scrappy second baseman long on guts and short on talent, he was buried in the Cardinal organization and never got above Triple A. He came to realize that, whereas he would never make the majors with his body, he might with his brain. The Orioles gave him a chance at managing as a 26-year-old player-manager at Knoxville in 1956. Weaver was so dedicated to winning that when he took over as a player-manager, one of his first acts was to bench himself. He proceeded to manage 10 straight winning seasons in the minors. He worked all the small towns in the system, slowly climbed the ladder of the Oriole organization, and impressed at every level. By the time he won the pennant at AAA Rochester in 1966, he was viewed as the best manager in the system. He was brought to Baltimore for the 1968 season, against Bauer's wishes, ostensibly to be first base coach, but most suspected that the first base coaching box was merely a way station for Weaver.

At the All-Star break, with the Orioles in third place, 10½ games back, Bauer was fired and Earl Weaver took over, getting a one-year contract for a whopping $28,000. At 37, he was the youngest manager in the league. Early in the season, Weaver had kept quiet, almost ignored by Bauer, content to hit grounders and offer advice only when asked. Once in charge, however, he immediately took command. Weaver had endless energy and an intense desire to win that he passed on to his players. He was shrewd and innovative, and knew how to motivate players.

He also knew how to infuriate umpires. With his Mickey Rooney build, feisty demeanor, and sharp wit, he possessed a singular talent for finding an umpire's raw nerve and then stomping on it with his spikes. Consequently, he was thrown out of more than a few games. Some of his debates with umpires became legendary. One of his best lines had occurred in the minors when he had been given the heave-ho after an umpire offered to show him a rule book to interpret a play. Weaver retorted, "Not your rule book because it's written in Braille."

Weaver immediately put switch-hitting Don Buford in the lineup regularly in the leadoff slot. Buford, a former Southern Cal halfback obtained from the White Sox in a preseason trade for Luis Aparicio, had the kind of speed the Orioles needed at the top of the order, but had played sparingly under Bauer. Weaver alternated Buford between center field and left field for Paul Blair and Curt Blefary, sitting them against righties and lefties, respectively. Buford quickly jump-started the offense.

Weaver had been instrumental in bringing in catcher Elrod Hendricks, who had spent years in the Mexican League and had played for Weaver in Puerto Rico. The left-handed-hitting Hendricks was installed in a platoon with Andy Etchebarren, whose average had fallen to .215 in 1967. The Etchebarren-Hendricks platoon would provide the Orioles with as much production behind the plate as any team in the league over the next several years. The outgoing, good-natured Hendricks talked nonstop and had a great sense of humor.

He would eventually become one of the most beloved Orioles over the next 30 years as a player and coach. Hendricks would long remember his first "Brooks moment." It occurred in the 1968 season opener in Oakland. Early in the game, with one out and a runner on first, the A's speedy Bert Campaneris pushed a bunt between the mound and third. "Where I'd come from, that was a hit," Hendricks later recalled. "Brooks was on it instantly, and never even looked at second base, just threw the ball across his body [to second] as his momentum took him all the way across home plate." A quick relay to first completed the double play and ended the inning. "I was sitting in the bullpen and my mouth fell open. I went, 'You've got to be kidding me. I don't believe what I just saw.'" The veterans in the bullpen were unimpressed. "They said, 'Oh, he does that all the time.' By the next year I knew they were right. All the time."

Hendricks's experience was not unusual for new teammates. Oriole coach Billy Hunter told a reporter, "Kids come up at the end of the year and sit on the bench and in the course of one week they'll say half-a-dozen times: 'Holy cow, that's the best play I've ever seen.'"

"We all knew his reputation when we joined the team," says relief pitcher Pete Richert, who was obtained from Washington in 1967, "but you just can't appreciate it until you see it every day. The first few great plays you're just amazed, but after a few weeks of watching him, it becomes routine. It's like, 'Oh, there he is, he did it again.' You just expect it after a while. It was just the standard for him to be that good."

"He never ceased to amaze me with the things he did," says Eddie Watt. "Everybody knew that Brooks was the best. The first time I realized how good he was, we were playing the Yankees and Richardson laid down an absolutely perfect drag bunt. It was a hit all the way. I was watching from the mound and I thought there is no way he can make the play. And Brooks came in on a dead run, barehanded it, and threw in one motion and got him. And kind of nonchalantly went back to his position like it was a routine play. I thought, 'This guy's good.'"

"The bullpen in Memorial Stadium was out in left field behind the fence," says Dick Hall. "We would be out there and new guys would see him make a great play and say, 'Holy cow, he really is as good as they say.' It was always fun to see someone's reaction the first time they saw him do something great up close. From where we sat, we looked over his shoulder at the batter and we would tell new guys, 'Watch him every pitch, how he gets ready.' Every pitch was like it was the seventh game of the World Series in the bottom of the ninth inning. He was on his toes and ready to field the ball every single pitch, every single inning, every single game. I never saw anybody who was so keyed up every pitch, ready to make a play. And they would realize, maybe that's why he's so good."

Of course, nobody is perfect and Brooks made so many good plays that the bad plays sometimes are the only ones that stick out in memory. "One play I'll never forget," says Watt, "we were in Yankee Stadium, tied in the ninth with a man on third and there was a routine grounder to Brooks. And it went right between his legs and dribbled out into the grass. Game over. As we were going into the dugout, he said, 'Did you see that? Well, we won't worry about that, we'll get them tomorrow.' Just like that. No throwing the glove or anything. It was more like he was just amazed that it happened. It did prove that he was human, though."

The Orioles were soon playing exciting baseball under Earl Weaver. The whole bearing of the team changed. They won 11 of the first 15 games under the new manager and 22 of 32, climbing into second place. It was too late to seriously threaten the Tigers in 1968 but it was a sign of good times ahead.

11. "The Best Team Doesn't Always Win"

IN THE SPRING OF 1969 it quickly became evident that the impressive finish to the previous season by the Orioles had been no fluke. After tearing through the preseason with the best record in baseball, they started the regular season at the top of the standings, challenged only by the equally fast-starting Red Sox. The Orioles exploded in May and over a period of one month the pennant race was essentially over.

The 1969 Orioles were a team without a weakness. The pitching staff, with the emergence of ace Dave McNally, who was 22–10 in 1968, was already expected to be good. Then they received a huge lift from two unforeseen sources: Jim Palmer and Mike Cuellar. Palmer's two-year battle with arm trouble had progressed to the point that many doubted that he would ever make it back to Baltimore. He had been left unprotected in the early rounds of the expansion draft but neither the Royals nor the Pilots felt him worthy of selection. While in Puerto Rico in the winter of 1968, however, he made a miraculous recovery. He was soon throwing better than ever before.

Cuellar was obtained from Houston for Curt Blefary. A 32-year-old lefty from Cuba, Cuellar had been in the majors regularly since 1964, but while showing flashes of brilliance, he had won more than 12 games in a season only once. He had a deceptive motion and was a magician with change-ups and screwballs, possessing the ability to fool hitters into some of the most pathetic, off-balance swings ever seen. Despite the obvious skill, he had never been able to put together any form of consistency in the majors. Bothered by financial and personal problems, he had struggled badly during 1968, going 8–11. Once he was in Baltimore, Oriole management helped him get out of debt and he benefited from the presence of catcher Elrod Hendricks, who spoke fluent Spanish. Comfortable in his new environment, with a clear head, he would turn out to be one of the best pitchers in the big leagues for the next five years.

The starting rotation became the best in the majors. Cuellar won 23 games, McNally 20; Palmer was 16–4 and Tom Phoebus was 14–7. McNally opened the season with a 15-game winning streak and Palmer later had a streak of 11 straight wins.

The hitting was almost as good. Paul Blair, recovered from the ankle injury that had hobbled him much of 1968, was back to full speed and playing every day after Blefary was traded. He hit 26 home runs. Buford hit .291 and scored 99 runs for the first of three consecutive seasons. Frank Robinson, seeing the ball clearly for the first time in almost two years, once again terrorized pitchers, hitting 32 homers with 100 RBIs and an average of .308. His fire on the bases and in the field once again inspired the team as he plowed over catchers and crashed into right field walls around the league. Boog Powell recovered from the injuries that had plagued him the previous two seasons and had a great year with 37 home runs, 121 RBIs, and a .304 average. Brooks contributed 23 home runs and 84 RBIs.

Defensively, Orioles won Gold Gloves at second (Davey Johnson), third, short (Mark Belanger), and center field (Paul Blair). Blair played the shallowest center field in the league, taking away certain hits on line drives up the middle. His great speed and ability to get a jump on the ball prevented him from getting burned deep. The sure-handed Belanger, who had taken over at short after Aparicio was traded, proved to be as good as or better than his Hall of Fame–bound predecessor. Boog Powell never got the acclaim he deserved as a first baseman, but he had surprisingly good footwork around the bag and was peerless at digging balls out of the dirt. The defense was so good, it intimidated other teams. Tiger manager Mayo Smith said, "Trying to hit a ball through the Baltimore infield is like trying to throw a hamburger through a brick wall."

"Where were you going to hit it?" Brooks said later. "Davey was a shortstop coming up and outstanding at second. I don't see how you can be any better than Belanger. . . . And Blair in center. How can it get any better than that?"

The defense was not an accident. While they had great fielders to begin with, Weaver prepared the team in the field like no manager ever had. They worked on defensive fundamentals and team defense all spring.

The groundskeeper even got in on the act. "Nobody had paid much attention to the infield grass," says Dick Hall. "but they used to let it grow to help the pitchers so the ball wouldn't get through so easily. Then they realized that with Brooks and Belanger and Davey Johnson that our infielders were better than anyone else's, so they changed it."

Pat Santarone, the Memorial Stadium groundskeeper, later said, "Earl asked me if I could speed it [the infield] up. Of course I could, and I did with shorter grass, de-thatching that grass, top-dressing it to get more bounce, keeping the infield dirt a little firmer by watering it and letting the sun bake it a little." Balls hit by Oriole batters shot through the infield, but opponents' hits were still smothered by the superior Oriole defense.

The glove work behind them gave Oriole pitchers a huge edge in confidence. "The pitchers would give up rockets, and we'd go back to the dugout, and [pitching coach George] Bamberger says, 'Nice pitch,'" said Hendricks. "And I'm saying 'Nice pitch? He almost got Brooks killed—took it off his chest and threw the guy out—and he said nice pitch?' But the other pitchers listened, and they realized, 'Well, OK, I can afford to make a mistake, I don't have to be perfect with that defense.'"

By the 1969 season, Earl Weaver was, as noted by Jim Palmer, "in charge, charged up, and charging, like a rhino in cleats. . . . He was a possessed, obsessed, driven man." Chain-smoking, constantly riding umpires, Weaver was always in the game, pulling strings and playing the odds—he was the first manager to fully exploit statistics based on individual matchups, not just righty-lefty stats. At one point or another, he had managed almost two-thirds of the Orioles in the minors, so they were familiar with each other, for better or for worse. Weaver could be difficult with everyone and was particularly caustic and demanding with his players, constantly pushing their buttons, looking for an edge. He liked players who would stand up for themselves—he would push and push until they erupted and a screaming match ensued. Weaver didn't mind the yelling—he could always yell louder and shout them down. But the arguments never resulted in a lineup change. The next day, the batting order would be the same—the screaming insults of the previous day were forgotten—the only thing that mattered was to get the best team on the field ready to win each day.

While players were frequently annoyed by Weaver's act, they usually responded and all agreed that he knew how to manage a major league baseball team. He was a baseball man through and through and he gave his team every chance to win. He didn't hesitate to take the heat for his men. "Weaver really stood up for his players," says Hall. "A lot of times he got thrown out to save one of us. We knew he always had our backs."

Although they were not entirely immune from Weaver's barbs, the two Robinsons were left alone for the most part as Weaver was confident in what they could do. "You never had trouble with the superstars," Weaver said in 2012. "Those guys knew how to play. What could you say to Brooks or Frank? Brooks was an easy guy to manage. You didn't need to teach him anything. He knew when to hit the ball to right and when to give himself up for the team. You didn't have to motivate him; you just left him alone."

"Brooks just loved the game so much he was always in it," Weaver wrote in 1982, discussing the remarkable ability to concentrate throughout an entire season—an ability he said only Brooks and Frank had. "There would be days in August when we either had a big lead or were out of it and the game didn't mean anything. I'd tell myself to rest him. But by the time Brooks got his uniform on he was like a sixteen-year-old who couldn't wait to get on the field. There was no way you could keep him out."

Frank Robinson was the unquestioned holler guy on the team. He was usually the last player out of the clubhouse before and after a game, dressing slowly, calling out to everyone. His constant chatter, sharp wit, and barbs dominated the bus and the clubhouse. His smile could light up a room, but occasionally he turned cold and moody. And a Frank Robinson glare could slice through leather. Frank was sometimes demanding to batboys and brutal to official scorers he disagreed with or writers who asked the wrong question. He was hard on teammates when he thought they didn't hustle, and he didn't hesitate to let them know. Above all, Frank did not let anything interfere with winning.

Brooks was also a leader, just not in the same manner. He was much more low-key, still always pleasant to everyone, from the lowliest person on the payroll to the club's owner—his leadership, perhaps, formed a perfect symbiosis with Frank's. Brooks would dress quickly and be out on the field early. Over and over he demonstrated that after a game he was remarkably the same—good game or bad game, his attitude never changed; he was always ready with a relaxed comment or an easy laugh. While he didn't make the most noise, his presence in the clubhouse was unmistakable—take him away and the volume may not have changed but everyone would immediately realize that something was missing. There was respect from his teammates for his résumé—the accumulation of numbers on the back of his baseball card—but also an inherent, unspoken respect for his persona; an admiration not easily accorded by strong men to another.

"Brooks was our quiet leader," says Richert. "Frank was much more vocal, but Brooks was just as important of a leader in his own way. He had his fun, he was one of the guys, laughing and kidding, but he was kind of quiet in general. He did a lot for the team without making himself conspicuous."

"Brooks and Frank had lockers side by side," says Watt. "They got along but were completely different. Frank was the most intense competitor I ever saw. Brooks was a tremendous competitor but much more laid-back. Frank could be ruthless in his competitiveness. Brooks was not a rah-rah guy, he was not particularly outgoing or boisterous; he was just himself. He had a quiet confidence in his own ability. You could never get him to speak about himself. He would always defer the topic to somebody or something else. If a stranger walked into our clubhouse and didn't know who anybody was, and just watched for a while, he would think Brooks was just a backup or something. That was just his nature."

Once he walked out of the clubhouse onto the field, however, there was no doubt that Brooks was much more than just a backup or something. "Brooks led by example, by the way he played and prepared for the game," says Richert.

And there was no mistaking the example Brooks Robinson set for teammates in that respect. "Brooks would work," said Hendricks. "I made it my business to watch him take ground balls because I never knew what he was going to come up with. He'd take 150 ground balls a day and work on everything. He'd work on short hops, backhands, the slow jumpers, the things he would do in the game. Billy Hunter would hit him ground balls, and instead of coming in and making the play, he'd back up and try to get it on the in-between hop."

He would also frequently field his position during batting practice to see the ball coming off a live bat, to get a better feel of real game situations and the concentration involved. In a trick learned years earlier from Willie Miranda, he would sometimes boot balls on purpose in practice—to work on recovering the ball quickly and making a snap throw.

Davey Johnson recalled, "Brooks took a bunch of ground balls every day, getting his uniform dirty and I went to him and said, 'Brooks, why do you take so many grounders when you already have [all those] Gold Gloves?' He said, 'Because I want to get another, and the only way to do it is work at it.'"

Pitchers particularly appreciated and admired Brooks's training habits. "Looking back, you really understand and realize how much he prepared," says Richert. "It wasn't an accident or just natural. Nothing was left to chance, he worked on everything. In the spring, he would take Billy Hunter and have him roll balls down the line and he would do it over and over—a good half hour or hour before the rest of us started practice. And he worked on making sure he picked up the ball on the correct foot so he could immediately make a good accurate throw. If you pick it up on the wrong foot, you either throw off balance or have to take another step and it costs you time. He did it so many times that in games he always had his feet where they should be, and he did it so smooth and quick by then that fans wouldn't even notice."

"He practiced all the time," says Dick Hall. "In the spring in Miami, there was an infield down behind the left field line and he would go down there and practice, even after he had been in the league 15 years. Also when we took infield, he worked on leaning forward at the right angle so that if he got a bad hop, it would hit him and bounce straight down so he could pick it up and still make the play; those little things that look like they just happen naturally in a game. He made it look so easy that you didn't realize all the footwork and stuff that went into it. There were other guys who were actually quicker but they didn't get their feet right on those tough-to-handle balls and maybe the throw would be good and maybe it wouldn't. With Brooks, the throw was always right there."

His preparation extended to the way he selected, cared for, and maintained his gloves. These were the tools of his profession; he viewed his game glove the way a master violinist would his Stradivarius. He would often try 10 to 15 gloves until he found one that was worthy, and he was constantly on the prowl for the next replacement. He would walk through the clubhouse and try on other players' gloves, frequently trading several of his for one if he liked the way it felt. His game glove of 1969, which he would also use the next two years, had been obtained in a three-for-one trade with young reserve outfielder Dave May. He scratched out May's name on the leather and wrote his name over it with a marker.

Once he had found a suitable glove, he would work on it—often it would take as much as a year to get it fully prepared for game use. First, he would tighten the laces to his liking. Then he would take out some of the padding on the heel and at the base of the thumb because that made for a flatter pocket and prevented balls from bouncing off a thick heel. He would continually flex the fingers to give them a slight inward curve. He frequently restrung his gloves to keep the feel just right. He always took pregame warm-ups with the backup gloves to get them ready for their time in the spotlight a few years down the road. He would carefully wrap his glove in his uniform before putting it in his road bag for trips. Nothing was left to chance.

As in 1966, the Orioles had a very good clubhouse atmosphere. Weaver had defined roles for everyone on the team—he used all 25 guys, which helped keep them happy. Everyone on the team knew his job. The team atmosphere was further helped when the Orioles instituted a kangaroo court. The judge of the court, naturally, was Frank Robinson, who conducted his cases using a Louisville Slugger as a gavel and wore a mop on his head as a judicial wig, for dignity. The court met after every victory and meted out punishment for offenses committed by team members. The idea had been used before by other teams, but the unique personalities of the Orioles raised it to an art form.

There were several recurrent awards that came with a one dollar fine and the stigma of a memento that had to be kept by the offending player until someone else claimed the prize. An old spiked shoe painted red was given for the John Mason Memorial Baserunning Award, named for a player once in the Baltimore organization who was notorious for his gaffes on the base paths. A cheap silver-painted glove was called the Chico Salmon No-Touch Award, named after the Orioles' utility man, and was given to the player who looked the worst on defense during the day's game. A scuffed-up baseball with the stuffing leaking out was named the John O'Donoghue Line Drive Award in memory of the pitcher who in 1968 had an ERA of 6.14 and was given to the pitcher who most endangered baseballs in the game.

Other fines were incurred for various infractions, such as when Paul Blair mounted a large poster above his locker that read, "World's Greatest Centerfielder," signed by an artist named Evelyn Blair. Coach Charlie Lau and Boog Powell were nailed for cleaning fish in the shower; reliever Dave Leonhard for arriving several times to the ballpark without socks; and utility man Bobby Floyd for wearing Popsicle-colored pants.

A team member who committed a grievous sin would be brought before the court by another player. The accuser had to have at least one witness to the crime. The (presumed) guilty party was allowed to plead his case, albeit often amid catcalls and insults. The entire team then rendered the verdict (invariably guilty as charged) with a thumbs-up or thumbs-down. In the name of fairness, a player had the right to appeal a negative decision, but a losing appeal cost two dollars, and appeals were notoriously difficult to win.

Brooks was fined a dollar when he was caught yawning on the bench during a game. Reserve outfielder Merv Rettenmund, greatly disappointed by the behavior, beseeched the court, "Your honor, a major league dugout, I submit, was not made for sleeping. Players should get their sleep in bed. Yet, I saw Brooks yawning on the bench and I have Dave Johnson as a witness."

"Did you see Brooks yawn on the bench?" Frank asked gravely.

"I did, your honor, and it was a huge yawn," Johnson concurred.

"Brooks, do you have anything to say in your defense," Frank asked. The accused didn't answer—he had his eyes closed, feigning sleep. "I guess he's guilty then," pronounced the judge.

Earl Weaver incurred the wrath of the court for inserting Belanger into a game in the late innings for defensive purposes, only to have Belanger make two errors. "Your honor," said shocked and much aggrieved coach Hunter, "I have to charge Earl Weaver with mismanagement for sending in a defender who did not defend."

Don Buford was once fined for talking to female fans in the crowd, a fine of one dollar per lady, and was assessed a total of three dollars. He loudly objected—not to the offense or fine, but said that he had actually talked to five ladies.

Players told reporters that Brooks probably contributed more money to the kangaroo court than anyone else. "Every day Brooks would make the first motion to adjourn the court so he could go home," McNally said, "and right off the judge would fine him for contempt of court."

No one was immune. The court even fined 15-year-old batboy Jay Mazzone. Mazzone had lost both hands in a childhood fire and had only hooks. He was fined by Frank for failure to vote with a proper thumbs-down gesture.

A record of the awards and fines was kept by Charlie Lau, who had suggested the idea of fines after witnessing a player walk to the food table in the clubhouse after a game with no clothes on. "That started it," Lau explained to a reporter later. "Frank took charge of it and made it go. The thing that was good about it was that it brought everyone on the team closer together. A baseball team lives together for a long period of time and has to have things to keep it loose and lift the tensions."

Since the court was only conducted after a victory, that gave players extra incentive to win. "You'd have something good on someone, and you'd go, 'Man we gotta go on and win, because we gotta nail him on this,'" said Dick Hall. "Because things never carried over to the next day."

While the court built camaraderie and provided laughs, it also was instructional for the younger players on the team—a way of pointing out serious errors such as throwing to the wrong base, missing a cutoff man, or failing to move a runner over—without causing hard feelings. "It made you pay attention," said Paul Blair, "and you learned from mistakes. Guys didn't make those same mistakes again. That helped us tremendously. And it brought the club closer together, made us more of a family, to the point where we could laugh at our mistakes."

While the team was having a great year, Brooks struggled through several hitting slumps. He started slow at the plate, was hitting .216 at the end of May, and never got over .250. "The problem with his batting average stemmed partly from his lack of foot speed, which prevented him from beating out infield rollers and high bouncers," Weaver later wrote. "But the main problem was that whenever Brooks started slumping he would forget about his strike zone and swing at bad pitches. I mean everything from fastballs at the shoulders to curveballs that broke outside in the dirt. The harder he struggled, the further his average would plummet."

As Brooks battled slump after slump, Weaver's barbs finally got under his skin, festered, and came to a head. Weaver later told a reporter, "I was on Brooksie a little. He was too anxious to raise his average. He'd get a count of 2–0 and reach for pitches he should have been letting alone. Naturally Brooks didn't like me jabbing at him. He was mad at himself anyway. Well, this night the count goes 3-and-1 and here comes a pitch that's maybe an inch from the ground. I say to myself, 'Don't do it Brooksie. Take the walk.' But he swings and grounds out. Now here he comes back to the dugout, straight to me before I can say a word. 'That pitch,' Brooksie snapped, 'was right on the black.' I had to laugh."

But Earl Weaver thoroughly appreciated the magnificent player he had inherited in Brooks. "He was just such a great guy to have on a team," he said. "A complete ballplayer. He made my job so much easier." He also respected the diverse skills Brooks brought to the game, in addition to his Gold Glove. "Brooks almost never got thrown out stretching a single into a double or a double into a triple. He was an excellent base runner once he got rolling, and he had a keen sense of exactly where a batted ball would land." He was always aware if a fielder got to a ball with his momentum going the wrong direction, which would prevent a good throw. "Brooks was also a tremendous clutch hitter, a guy who batted over .400 through most of his career from the seventh inning on. Nobody was better at driving in a man from second base with two outs. With Frank or Boog coming up behind him, pitchers always challenged Brooks, which amazed me, because he would get his bat on the ball and just stroke it over the infield for the run."

Brooks finished the 1969 season with a .234 batting average. While he did hit 23 homers and 84 RBIs, the four-year trend in his average was a concern: back-to-back .269 seasons followed by .253 and .234. He was 32 years old, hitting a lot of harmless fly balls, and there were whispers that his bat had slowed down. Also, some questioned if maybe he shouldn't take a day off every now and then. From 1960 to 1969, there were only 35 games in which he did not play and 18 of those were in 1965 when he was shelved with a shoulder injury. He finally sat out a game August 20—after 282 straight, going back to 1967.

Still peerless in the field, Brooks tied Washington's Ken McMullen with a fielding percentage of .9761, becoming the only man in either league to lead his position eight times. And he won another Gold Glove—this one was his 10th in a row. By this time, the bulky things were starting to be a bother. To save room in his den he had begun to give some of them away. He had given one to his parents, one to his brother, another to coach Billy Hunter as thanks for all the hours hitting ground balls, and another to the Little Rock Boys Club.

In 1969, for the first time, the team with the best record in the league did not proceed directly to the World Series. The leagues had been split into divisions and the divisional winners met in a best-of-five playoff series. The Orioles took the East by 19 games. The Minnesota Twins won the American League West. In reply to the uncertainty of how he should celebrate the Western Division title in the new format, Twins first-year manager Billy Martin said, "You split a bottle of champagne and drink the western half."

On paper the Twins appeared to be the Orioles' equal in every department except fielding. Most Valuable Player Harmon Killebrew hit 49 home runs and 140 RBIs. Second baseman Rod Carew hit a league-leading .332, and Tony Oliva had 101 RBIs while hitting .309. The Twins' pitching staff boasted 20-game winners Dave Boswell and Jim Perry along with the always tough Jim Kaat, and Ron Perranoski was one of the best relievers in the game.

The playoff series promised to be close and Game One was about as close as a game could get. Cuellar started for the Orioles and was lifted after eight innings, trailing 3–2. Boog Powell tied the game with a dramatic home run leading off the bottom of the ninth. Brooks followed by stroking a single to left (the third of four singles on the day for him), and took second when the left fielder misplayed the ball. With two outs, Brooks on third and Belanger on first, Weaver reached into his bag and tried to pull out a win, but it backfired. He signaled for both runners to break on a 2-and-2 pitch. The pitch from Perranoski was so wide it looked like a pitchout. Catcher George Mitterwald snagged it, ignored Belanger off first, and Brooks was trapped between home and third for the final out of the inning. The exact intent of the plan remained a secret as Weaver refused to comment on the tactic to writers after the game, claiming he might want to use it again.

Fortunately for the Orioles, four different pitchers from the Baltimore bullpen were perfect and kept the score tied until the 12th when Perranoski, still on the mound for the Twins, lost the game without a ball leaving the infield. Belanger opened the 12th by singling off Killebrew's glove at third. He moved to second on a sacrifice, and to third on a groundout, bringing up Paul Blair. Blair, mired in a 3-for-42 slump, dropped a two-out bunt down the third-base line. No one could make a play and Belanger crossed the plate standing up with the winning run. The bunt had been a complete surprise to everyone in the stadium, including Oriole coaches and players.

Dave McNally was brilliant on the mound for the Orioles in Game Two. Typical of most frontline pitchers of the era who wanted to finish what they started, he battled the whole way and threw a complete game, 11-inning, three-hit shutout. The Twins' Dave Boswell matched him for 10 innings. Boog Powell led off the 11th with a walk, Brooks bunted him to second, and pinch hitter Curt Motton won it with a line single to right to knock in the only run of the game.

In the first inning of Game Three, Rod Carew hit a smash toward left field off Jim Palmer that Brooks speared and threw to first. The Orioles then proceeded to batter seven Twin pitchers for 18 hits and won the game 11–2 to take the series. Brooks ended the playoffs 7-for-14 for a .500 average.

Although the Orioles had won 109 games during the regular season (only the 1954 Indians with 111 and the 1927 Yankees with 110 had ever won more in the American League), swept the playoffs, and were 8–5 favorites, they were treated like uninvited wedding guests in the buildup to the Series. The Mets were the media darlings; an irresistible story of rags to riches. For seven seasons the Mets had been nothing more than perennial punch lines. In winning 100 games in 1969, the Mets had experienced not only their first pennant, but the first winning season in their existence.

The Mets had a lineup that consisted of platoon players with names like Ed Kranepool, Ken Boswell, Al Weis, Wayne Garrett, Ron Swoboda, Art Shamsky, and Rod Gaspar. It was not the kind of lineup that made a pitcher quiver with fear—more often it made the pitcher ask "Who?" During the Orioles' postgame celebration after beating the Twins, Frank Robinson stepped onto a folding chair, squirted a spray of champagne to attract attention, and announced to the team, "Ron [sic] Gaspar just said on television that the Mets will sweep the Birds in four games. Bring on Ron Gaspar, whoever the hell he is." Unfortunately, the Orioles would soon learn who the hell he was, along with a bunch of other no-name Mets who were playing the best baseball of their lives.

The Mets were deceptive. There was much more to them than just the unknown names on their roster. The platoon players filled in capably around three offensive stars who were having career years—Cleon Jones, who hit .340, Tommie Agee, and Donn Clendenon—along with feisty shortstop Bud Harrelson. The pitching staff, led by 25-game winner Tom Seaver, was formidable. And they were peaking at the right time; everything was going for them. They had won 39 of the last 50 games of the regular season—needing them all as they rallied to beat out the Cubs, who had seemed to be in control in August. The last month of the season had been played out under such intensity and media spotlight in New York that they approached the World Series as battle-hardened veterans, immune to pressure.

In Game One of the World Series, in Baltimore, Mike Cuellar beat Tom Seaver 4–1. In the top of the seventh, with the Orioles leading 4–0, the Mets scored a run with a bases-loaded sacrifice fly and had men on first and second with two outs, threatening to get back into the game. Pinch hitter Rod Gaspar topped a slow bouncer toward third. Cuellar, tired after throwing more than 100 pitches, took one look at the kind of bad-luck, seeing-eye infield bleeder that can change history and bring down strong men and knew he had no chance. Gaspar, heading for first base, knew he had a hit. Brooks charged the ball, reached down and bare-handed it as it took a small hop—picking it up with his left foot forward just as he had practiced over and over. In one motion, without fully straightening up, he fired a nearly underhanded strike to first. As *Sports Illustrated* noted, "The play, amazingly, was not even close. Gaspar, who is not all that slow, was out by two steps."

After the game Met first baseman Donn Clendenon, talking about the play, said, "That wouldn't have happened to me. I'm not hitting the ball to Robinson in this series. He's the vacuum cleaner, don't you know that? . . . You don't get any hits going toward third base."

A grateful Cuellar said, "I never give up on Brooksie. I thought he could make the play." Gaspar added, "I was surprised he got me so easily."

Earl Weaver told reporters, "I don't believe any other third baseman could have made that play." It had been a spectacular play; a Brooks Robinson special. And it would have been long remembered except for some unusually great plays turned in on the other side in the days to come.

In Game Two, Brooks once more had a magnificent day at third. He made another charging-bare-handed-grab-and-quick-throw, nearly identical to the play on Gaspar, to get Jerry Grote. But the Orioles could do nothing with Mets left-hander Jerry Koosman. The best left-hander in the National League in 1969, Koosman had gone 17–9 with a 2.28 ERA and had finished the season by winning his last six starts with three shutouts and only eight earned runs in that period. Continuing his hot hand against the Orioles, he threw a no-hitter for six innings. Clendenon (staying true to his vow to keep the ball away from third) hit a lead-off homer in the fourth for the first run. Blair broke the no-hitter with a single leading off the seventh and promptly stole second. Brooks, who had seen Koosman in the All-Star Game (striking out on three pitches), then brought Blair home with a single up the middle, making the score 1–1. Neither team scored in the eighth.

In 1967, Frank Robinson had crashed into White Sox second baseman Al Weis breaking up a double play. The play, which gave Frank double vision and essentially ended his and the Orioles' season, also tore up Weis's knee, knocking him out for the year. As so often happens in baseball, the incident had long-reaching implications that would prove fateful. The injury caused the White Sox to dump Weis to the Mets the next year—a move Weis was not happy about. He had struggled in 1969, hitting only .215 as a platoon player. Now in Game Two of the World Series, Al Weis came to the plate in the top of the ninth with two outs, runners on first and third, and the score tied 1–1. He lined McNally's first pitch into left center to drive in the go-ahead run.

The Orioles battled in their half of the ninth. After Koosman retired the first two batters, Frank and Boog both walked, bringing up Brooks. Relief pitcher Ron Taylor came in and Brooks ran the count to 3–2. Then he hit a hot grounder to third to end the game and the Series was tied at one game apiece.

After losing Game Two, the Orioles were a relaxed bunch, laughing and enjoying themselves on the train to New York, unable to fathom losing three straight. They had already faced the Mets' two bright young aces and played evenly. Now it was time for the vaunted Oriole offense to break out. New York, and destiny, had a surprise waiting for them, however.

The Mets' starter for Game Three, Gary Gentry, was a hard thrower. In 1969, he was somewhat overshadowed by the great seasons Seaver and Koosman had turned in, but there were those who thought that, on a given day, Gentry had just as much stuff. The Orioles had a scouting report, however, that said Gentry possessed only an average fastball. In those days before radar guns, a scout's estimate and word of mouth were all they had to go on. Apparently, the scout had seen Gentry on a bad day. Less than a week earlier, he had been battered by the Braves in the playoffs—lasting less than three innings. While the Orioles were not expecting much from him, unfortunately Game Three of the 1969 World Series turned out to be one of those given days for Gentry. He plowed through the Oriole lineup, striking out batters and sawing off their bats. There were four weak infield pop-ups in the first three innings. The Orioles did not get a hit until the fourth inning and would get only four all day.

Meanwhile, Tommie Agee led off the Met first with a home run off Jim Palmer. Gentry added a two-run double in the second. Then the Mets began pulling rabbits, and great plays, out of their hats. In the fourth, after Frank and Boog hit back-to-back singles and Brooks struck out, Elrod Hendricks, who almost never hit the ball to left field, came to the plate. Center fielder Agee was playing him almost in right center. Hendricks smoked a ball deep in the gap to left center. The right-handed Agee raced over, wavered a bit near the warning track as he was running full speed, then lunged and backhanded the ball two steps from the fence. The white of the ball showed prominently in the top of his glove as his momentum carried him into the wall directly under the 396 marker, but it remained in his grasp and the inning was over.

Gentry tired in the seventh with two outs and walked the bases loaded. A young, wild fireballer named Nolan Ryan came out of the bullpen for the Mets. Paul Blair greeted him with a shot deep to right center. Agee sprinted to his left and made a diving two-handed grab on the warning track—sliding on his belly before rolling over and showing everyone the ball. The two plays by Agee saved five runs.

Ryan shut the Orioles down the rest of the way, buckling the last batter's knee with a devastating curve that dropped in for a called third
strike, and the Mets won 5–0. Game Three was the turning point in
the Series; the unexpected dominance of the Mets' third starter, Gentry, combined with the miraculous plays in the outfield left the Orioles staggered.

Before Game Four, Vietnam War protesters demonstrated outside Shea Stadium and distributed pamphlets for Moratorium Day.
Some carried signs that said, "Bomb the Orioles, Not the Peasants."
The Mets tried to oblige the protesters as best as they could but
Mike Cuellar had other ideas. After Clendenon homered in the second inning, Cuellar was unhittable. In the sixth inning umpire Shag
Crawford, tired of what he considered to be annoying comments
from the Oriole dugout, walked over and, with dramatic effect, told
the entire dugout to shut up. As he turned back to the field, Weaver
popped out and followed him to the plate, continuing the discussion. Crawford turned and tossed him, the first time since 1935 a
manager had been thrown out of a World Series game, and only the
third time in history.

Once more the game was a pitchers' duel as the Orioles could mus-
ter only three hits in eight innings off Seaver. In the ninth, trailing
1–0, Frank Robinson singled with one out. Boog Powell followed
with a single and Frank hustled to third. Brooks approached the
plate—another rally, another chance. This time Brooks stroked what
looked like a sure hit to right field. Ron Swoboda charged in and
speared it with a diving one-handed catch barely off the ground.
Frank scored after the catch, tying the score, but the rally was dead.

The catch by Swoboda was devastating to the Orioles. The catch
itself, especially in view of the situation, is one of the all-time great
plays in World Series history. Swoboda, who incidentally had played
amateur baseball for the Leones team in Baltimore under Brooks's
business partner, still can get a free drink anywhere in New York
when recognized on the basis of that one play.

The Mets got two on in the ninth, but pinch hitter Art Shamsky
grounded out to end the threat. In the 10th, Jerry Grote led off against
Dick Hall. Hall sawed him off with a 3–2 slider on the fists, and
Grote hit a bloop into shallow left field. Again, fate intervened. It was

a bright October day with a tough sky and Don Buford in left had trouble picking the ball up off the bat in the dark background and shadows of Shea Stadium. Frozen by the hard swing of Grote, not realizing that the bat had been broken, Buford was late coming in and the ball fell between him and Belanger as Grote raced to second.

After an intentional walk, J. C. Martin laid down a bunt in front of the mound. New reliever Pete Richert fielded it quickly and threw to first. Martin was running inside the baseline and the throw hit him on the wrist and bounced toward second. The winning run scored. Umpire Crawford ignored the Orioles' protests that Martin had been inside the base path when the ball hit him—an obvious case of interference. "There were three umpires looking at it but none of them called it," says Richert. "That's just what happens sometimes in baseball. There's nothing you can do about it."

"The television showed that play over and over that night," says Hall. "And it was the same every time." It was another excruciating loss for the Orioles.

The fifth game, the Orioles took a 3–0 lead in the third inning, thanks to home runs by McNally and Frank Robinson. Koosman cruised the rest of the way as the Mets countered with homers from Clendenon in the sixth and Weis in the seventh. The Mets took the lead in the eighth, 5–3, and Koosman shut down the Orioles in the ninth. The Series was over.

Whenever a great team crashes and burns, the stat sheet is the black box for investigators. For the 1969 World Series the debris is particularly disturbing to pick through and starts with hitting, or lack thereof. The Orioles were held to the lowest five-game Series hit total ever, 23. Boog Powell, with a .263 average, was the only regular to hit over .200. Frank hit .188, Blair and Buford hit .100, Johnson .063, Brooks .053 (1-for-19).

Nine months earlier New Yorkers had ripped the hearts out of Baltimore fans when the Jets of Joe Namath dismantled a great Colts team in Super Bowl III. Now the sonsabitches had done it again. The shocked and weary Orioles were amazed when they returned to Baltimore to find 5,000 fans at the airport to greet them. Some of the players and their wives had tears in their eyes as they witnessed the show of affection and support for the losing team. According to team vice president Harry Dalton, the fans' demonstration gave the players a great lift. "They became more determined than ever to win it all this year," he said the next season.

The loss in the Series was tough to take and the passage of time has not eased the pain. Years later, many Orioles believe the 1969 team was the best they ever played on. But they ran into a hot team, with extremely hot pitching, who got every break and made every play at the right time.

"Our problem was not unusual for hitters in playoffs and World Series games," wrote Weaver later. "They often become overanxious at the plate. They swing at pitchers' pitches instead of waiting for their pitches. Overanxiousness was to plague us through the series."

"The Mets played super," says Richert. "We hit balls and they made plays. There's nothing you can do about that. You take away the two catches by Agee, the catch by Swoboda, the interference play on Martin, and it's a whole different Series."

Brooks later said, "My thought during the winter was, you got Tom Seaver, you got a Jerrry Koosman, you got a Gary Gentry, hey, these guys are big-time pitchers. It was just one of those things. I don't know how you can explain it. When something gets started like that, it's hard to turn it off. The thing that affected us most was that we had never had our backs to the wall like that, and we started trying to do things we were not capable of doing. . . . It was a little embarrassing, I think, because that was one of the biggest upsets in the history of the game."

"That was a lesson for us, the best team doesn't always win," said Frank years later.

"The Mets won 100 games," said Palmer in 2005. "If you do that, you have a good ball club. And they had a good ball club because they had good pitching. . . . When they run it on ESPN Classic, I walk out of the room. . . . Game Three was the only time in my career I gave up a leadoff home run. . . . I got in touch with how easy it was to lose a World Series, how fast it could go and how little it took, because you're in the games, and they're close, and then it's over."

12. The Vacuum Cleaner

THE SERIES DEFEAT APPEARED to have no lasting effect on the Orioles' psyches as they prepared for the 1970 season. "I didn't see a whole lot of difference in our attitude in spring training," Brooks said later. "We knew we had a good ball club." So confident was Brooks that he put the following identification on his suitcase at the beginning of the season: "Brooks Robinson, Baltimore Orioles, 1970 World Champions."

"We knew we were going to win again," said Weaver. "You kept the team together in those days. We had everybody coming back, at the right age, even more mature and better."

The Orioles did do it again. They opened the season with five straight wins and never looked back—winning 108 games this time—behind three 20-game winners, Palmer, Cuellar, and McNally. While McNally was the intense competitor, battling no matter what kind of stuff he had on a given day, refusing to lose, and Cuellar was the master of deception, torturing hitters with an array of vertigo-inducing pitches, Palmer was the gifted athlete with overpowering ability and by 1970 he had fully established himself as a great pitcher. Never at a loss for confidence, Palmer developed a habit of positioning his fielders from the mound, waving at them like a conductor—a habit that, not surprisingly, annoyed more than a few. But he rarely bothered with Brooks. "I never told him [Brooks] where to play," he later wrote. "If he thought he should be in the second stall of the bathroom in the locker room, I'd just pitch, and he'd kick open the door and catch the ball."

Unlike 1969, in which he got off to a 2-for-17 start and never recovered, Brooks came out smoking in 1970 with eight hits and six RBIs in the first six games. He hit .311 for April and his average would not dip below .273 the entire season. Baseball streaks and slumps often come and go without rational explanation but Brooks, continuing his career-long practice of constantly trying new lumber, attributed the improvement to switching to a heavier bat.

He was now at the point in his career where he began reaching milestones. He hit his 200th career home run May 9. This extended the record he had set in 1969 when he had passed Al Rosen for the most career home runs by an American League third baseman. He collected his 2,000th career hit with a game-winning three-run homer against the Senators, June 20.

September 4, against the Red Sox, he went 5-for-5 with two home runs and 4 RBIs, his first 5-for-5 day since 1960. He finished the season with a .276 average, 18 home runs, and 94 RBIs. It was his best batting average and most RBIs since 1966.

The Orioles beat out the second-place Yankees by 15 games, then faced the Twins again in the playoffs. In Game One, the Orioles were losing 1–0 to Cy Young Award winner Jim Perry when Brooks singled with one out and Hendricks on first. Davey Johnson was hit by a pitch, loading the bases. Belanger then bounced to short in what appeared to be an inning-ending double play. Johnson went in hard to second, however, and the relay throw to first was low and wide, allowing both Hendricks and Brooks to score.

In the fourth inning, Brooks hit a sacrifice fly to score Frank and break a 2–2 tie. The Orioles then loaded the bases and Mike Cuellar, a .089 hitter during the season, popped the ball into right. A tremendous blast of wind carried the ball just over the fence in the right field corner for a grand slam. Brooks added a double and a single for a 3-for-3 day and the Orioles went on to win 10–6.

The Orioles pounded the Twins 11–3 the next day. In Game Three, the Orioles were up 2–0 in the third inning when Brooks led off with a double into the left field corner off Jim Kaat. He moved to third when Johnson followed with a line drive off the second baseman's glove. Etchebarren then hit a bouncer to short and Brooks broke for home. The throw from Leo Cardenas appeared to be in time but the catcher couldn't come up with it and Brooks slid in for the third run. That was more than Jim Palmer would need as he overpowered the Twins with 12 strikeouts in a complete game 6–1 victory. Brooks was 7-for-12 for the three games, the second straight year of .500 or better in the playoffs.

As the Orioles prepared for the 1970 World Series, Brooks Robinson was 33 years old. He had established his defensive brilliance by leading the league in fielding percentage at his position a record nine times and winning 11 straight Gold Gloves. And he had been remarkably consistent—from 1959 through 1970, he never had more than 17 errors in a season and twice had as few as 11. He had made the past 14 All-Star teams (two games were held in 1960–62), fielding 34 chances without an error in those games, and held a reputation as a solid clutch hitter and a leader on a great team.

He had also firmly established a reputation as one of the game's leading good guys; a solid citizen active in community affairs, always friendly to fans. He was vocal about his feeling that athletes should be role models and, unlike some athletes who maintain carefully cultivated public appearances while leading much different private lives, he was as advertised—there was no secret life of Brooks Robinson. He was chairman of the Baltimore County Cancer Crusade and director of the Maryland Chamber of the National Multiple Sclerosis Society. He actively supported area Boy Scouts and Little Leagues. Along with Johnny Unitas, he was one of the guiding forces of a group called America's Sports Stars for POW-MIAs that helped communicate with POWs in Southeast Asia and offered support for their families and those of MIAs.

For several years Brooks had been winning national nice guy awards, such as the Lou Gehrig Award in 1966, when he was honored for his "personal qualities that make him an exceptional credit to his team and the game of baseball," and the Ken Hubbs Memorial Award in Chicago in 1967 for "exemplary conduct on and off the playing field."

John Steadman voiced what many writers around the league felt in a *Sporting News* article entitled "Brooks Robinson—As Gracious off Field as He's Graceful on It" in August of 1967. "That Brooks

Robinson is a gentleman personified, thoughtful of others, and a model individual comes as no striking disclosure. It's like saying it gets hot near the Equator or cold at the North Pole. Belaboring the obvious. . . . But incidents are constantly occurring which increase the awareness that Brooks Robinson has a character commensurate with his ability. . . . He's not ready for sainthood, not yet, but in a world that is replete with crass commercialism, individual selfishness and greed, Brooks comes through like a beacon in a sea of fog." Steadman quoted Ed Hurley, the retired umpire, who had recently watched Brooks and said, "The worst thing you can say about that fellow is that he's a great guy.

"Nothing is ever too much trouble for Robinson," Steadman continued. "He takes the bitter with the sweet, the good days with the bad, the success with the failures. . . . He is everything everybody says he is. . . . The success of Brooks Robinson as the premier third baseman in baseball history—a belief that even an old-timer with the longevity of Casey Stengel admits to—proves that an athlete can be gracious, decent and considerate without taking anything away from his professional standing. Too often, Brooks Robinson is taken for granted. He shouldn't be. As a man and performer, by viewing the record, he's in a special category."

Over the years, the stories about the thoughtfulness and saintly acts of Brooks had grown so much that Steadman once felt the need to tell his managing editor at the *Baltimore News American*, "I know you read what we write about Brooks Robinson and you think that either we're exaggerating or he's a phony. Just to set the record straight, neither is true."

But for all the devotion by local fans, writers, and teammates, Brooks was somewhat underappreciated nationally. Great play and great character did not necessarily translate into great fame. This was 1970, the time of social upheaval and the antihero; nonconformists were celebrated, authority figures doubted, traditionalists ridiculed. Humbleness was no longer a virtue. The nation had changed drastically over the course of the decade; attitudes, music, hairstyles, everything had changed; except Brooks Robinson. He remained so unchanged that he had become decidedly square. Brooks was on the wrong side of the culture gap. Writers and the public had found much more colorful players, with more charisma, who beat their chests and tooted their own horns, dated starlets and closed down nightclubs all over the country and, in general, made better copy.

Some reporters even began expressing annoyance at the fact that Brooks seemed too good, that he only recounted happy memories of an idyllic childhood. He was derided for his bland, blissful up-bringing. They wanted tales of hardship and maybe defiance. They wanted rebels. Mark Kram wrote about Brooks in *Sports Illustrated* before the World Series: "He never slips a question and he always manages to be earnestly dull. . . . He belongs, of course, in some boy-hood novel now lost in the mustiness of a church rummage sale. John R. Tunis, the boys' author, would have loved him, but Tunis would have added some conflict. As it is, even in adolescence, there hardly seems to have been even the smallest crisis. It was all shade and warmly American anecdotes."

And warmly American anecdotes were most definitely out of style by 1970. Brooks had become relegated to the status of the reliable old truck in the garage—the one that always works, but nobody wants to be seen driving. Fielding had rarely been a top priority among base-ball mythmakers. That was about to change.

The Orioles' opponents in the 1970 World Series were the Cincinnati Reds. The powerful Big Red Machine was led by Johnny Bench's 45 home runs and 148 RBIs. Tony Perez chipped in with 40 homers and 129 RBIs and Lee May had 34 and 94. Pete Rose and Bobby Tolan each hit .316. The Reds had spent a total of one day out of first place all season, leaving a trail of wrecked pitchers in their wake. Las Vegas oddsmakers rated the Reds as 11–10 favorites going into the Series.

In 1970, the World Series still held the undivided attention of the nation for a week. The games were all played during the day. School kids across the country smuggled transistor radios into their class-rooms or conned their teachers into letting them watch on television. American sentiment for the Series was summed up by Jack Nichol-son's character, R. P. McMurphy, in *One Flew over the Cuckoo's Nest* when he told Nurse Ratched: "I'm talking about the World Series Nurse Ratched. . . . I haven't missed the Series in years. Even in the cooler. When I'm in the cooler they run it there or they'll have a riot."

And that was about right. Everybody watched the Series in those days. It was sport's biggest stage—the place where legends were made.

Before leaving Baltimore for the opening game, the Orioles appeared loose as they went through a simulated game for the benefit of pitchers Cuellar and McNally, to prevent rust caused by the layoff after the playoff sweep. When Paul Blair, who had slumped in the playoffs, made an out, McNally said, "This is like a regular game. Blair walking back to the dugout."

The diminutive Earl Weaver inserted himself as a pinch hitter in the seventh inning and Brooks yelled from third base, "Bill Veeck got into trouble putting a midget up there."

Cincinnati's Riverfront Stadium had opened in midseason, just before the All-Star Game had been played there. It was at the forefront of the wave of multipurpose, bland, round, artificial turf stadiums— later derisively referred to as cookie-cutters as players couldn't tell if they were in Cincinnati, Philadelphia, Pittsburgh, or St. Louis. The field was entirely covered with synthetic grass except for cutouts around the bases, home plate, and the pitcher's mound. The 1970 World Series would be the first played on an artificial surface. Since there were no similar fields in the American League yet, there were some questions of how the Orioles' vaunted infield would perform on the lightning-quick turf and the players were not even sure which type of shoes to wear until the day before the opening game. Only Brooks, Davey Johnson, and Frank Robinson had played there during the All-Star Game. In response to a pregame question regarding how different it would be, Brooks answered, "I'm a major league third baseman. If they ask me to play on a parking lot, I'm supposed to stop the ball."

Some criticized Earl Weaver for not bringing the Orioles into Cincinnati until Friday, feeling that the players needed more of a chance to practice on the infield. Reds manager Sparky Anderson defended Weaver, however, stating, "There is nothing to adjust to on Astro-Turf." And in a bit of foreshadowing, he added, "Those guys already have hands like vacuum cleaners. I think if Brooks Robinson played in this park his whole career, he would have set fielding records that would never be broken."

Warming up on the turf for the first time, Brooks noticed something—he liked the way the ball behaved on the carpet. Although it reached fielders quicker, it was remarkably predictable—there was no worry about a bad hop. The surface was perfectly made for a man with quick reflexes. Ten to fifteen minutes of ground balls was all he needed to feel ready for anything.

Rain fell in Cincinnati on Friday night and the forecast called for a chance of a dreary weekend. Although the skies would be crystal clear by game time, the Reds didn't realize how dreary the weekend would still turn out to be. After the Jackson 5 sang the National Anthem, 18-game-winner Gary Nolan took the mound for the Reds in front of a Riverfront crowd of 51,531 and set the Orioles down in order with two pop-outs and a strikeout. The Big Red Machine appeared in full gear as it manufactured a run in the first off Jim Palmer and threatened to score more. With two outs, Lee May on first and Johnny Bench on second, left-handed batter Bernie Carbo sliced a line drive toward left. Brooks took a step to his right and caught the ball with two hands over his head to end the inning. Anderson later would call the play a turning point: "If that ball doesn't go right at Robinson, we have at least one more run and maybe two." It was a nice play, but a play any other major league third baseman would likely have made; nothing spectacular. There would be more to come, however.

The Reds scored two more runs in the third to take a 3–0 lead. Baltimore fought back with a two-run homer from Powell and a solo shot by Hendricks and the score was tied at three after five innings. Then things got interesting.

Lee May led off the sixth with a smash down the line on which Brooks made his signature play, backhanding the ball and throwing May out from the third base coaching box. The events that followed made the play even more important. Bernie Carbo walked and took third on a single. Pinch hitter Ty Cline followed by chopping a high bouncer almost directly in front of home plate. The pre-Series scouting report had noted that Carbo was something of an aggressive base runner, sometimes even overaggressive, but no one expected him to try to come home on this—especially not umpire Ken Burkhart.

Burkhart leaped from behind the plate, straddled the third base line facing home plate, and signaled that it was a fair ball. Catcher Elrod Hendricks quickly jumped in front of the plate and waited for the ball to come down. Carbo took off from third. As Hendricks reached up for the ball, planning on throwing to first, Palmer, running in from the mound, screamed, "Tag him, tag him, he's coming!" Hendricks grabbed the ball, turned, and ran into Burkhart, who was lurching forward from a collision with Carbo, who, trying to reach the plate and avoid the tag with a slide, plowed into the umpire's back. Hendricks, holding the ball in his right hand, swiped Carbo with his glove.

It all happened in an instant and then there was a tangled mass of the two players and the umpire on the ground, surrounded by a cloud of dust. With his back to the play, Burkhart did not see that Hendricks did not tag Carbo with the ball. He also did not see that Carbo never touched home plate. Finally turning, sitting on his rump, Burkhart jerked his right fist into the air, calling Carbo out. Carbo, Sparky Anderson, and the entire state of Ohio disagreed with the call. The play would be rehashed far into the future, with none of the participants changing their opinions. When the dust settled— literally and figuratively—and the Reds jogged out of their dugout for the next inning, it was apparent that had May's ball gone through for a double leading off the inning, the Reds could have had a big lead.

Brooks wasn't finished. In the seventh inning he came to bat against Nolan. He swung at an 0–1 change-up and lifted it high in the air to left field. Bernie Carbo ran to the warning track and stood as the ball disappeared over the fence to break the tie and provide the winning margin in a 4–3 win. After the game, no one seemed to notice that Brooks had hit the home run, however. All they wanted to talk about was the play on May. In the Reds' clubhouse, Pete Rose told reporters that Robinson should be declared illegal. He added, "I never saw a play like that. I couldn't believe it."

"He was going toward the bullpen when he threw to first," said Reds reliever Clay Carroll. "His arm went one way, his body another, and his shoes another."

"When you play with Brooks, you just go to the bag and hold the glove out," Powell nonchalantly told reporters in the Oriole clubhouse. "He'll get the ball there, you always know that."

"So Brooks Robinson made another great play," quipped Weaver. "So what? Watch him day in and day out and he'll do something unbelievable around every third day. No, the amazing is nothing new when it comes to Brooksie." Those who didn't follow the Orioles thought Weaver was trying to be funny. They didn't know he was telling the truth.

Oriole general manager Harry Dalton told Weaver, "That's got to be one of the ten best plays Brooks ever made." Weaver disagreed. "I'd put it in his top 100 plays." Then he added, "Those hundred are only since I've been here."

Brooks struggled to explain the play to reporters. "It was one of my better ones," he conceded. "He hit a nice—"

"A nice double?" interjected a reporter.

Years later, Brooks said, "I can never remember making a play like that. Usually on that play you stop, plant your foot, and throw. It might have been because of the AstroTurf. . . . What you had to remember was that when you go after balls [on AstroTurf] you really have to pick up your feet. You can't drag them across the AstroTurf because they just stop. So when I got the ball, I might have been worried about that and just whirled and threw it to Boog."

"Only Brooks could have gotten to that ball and made the play," Richert says. It was destined to go down as one of the best plays in Series history. But it was only the beginning.

In Game Two, Brooks and his magic glove were at it again, only this time the great plays came more frequently. In the opening inning, with Rose on first base, left-handed Bobby Tolan swung at a Mike Cuellar curveball and hit a nubber off the handle that softly bounced to the left side of the infield in no-man's-land. Shortstop Belanger, playing back, had no play on the ball. Brooks charged to his left, cut across in front of Belanger, reached down, fielded the ball with two hands, and snapped a quick sidearm throw to second to barely get the hard-sliding Rose for the force-out.

The Reds led 4–0 after three but it could have been worse. In the third, after Tolan's one-out home run, Bench walked and Cuellar was done for the day. May then greeted reliever Tom Phoebus by smoking one between Brooks and third base. Brooks only had time for one quick movement—a turning lunge back and to his right. He backhanded the ball in what appeared to be a self-protective motion. The force of the movement (and the ball) spun him in a complete clockwise turn, his back to the infield. He bounced up, planted his right foot, and quickly threw sidearm to second just in time to get Bench. Johnson's relay to first nipped May. The you've-gotta-be-freaking-kidding-me play turned a sure double into an inning-ending double play in the blink of an eye. When viewed in slow motion, the play was perhaps more impressive than the one the day before. This ball had been hit much harder, leaving no time for even one step. It was a pure reflex play in which each out had been made by less than a foot: the catch, the recovery, the throw—and Johnson's pivot—each had to be perfect. Few men could have made it.

The Orioles then mounted their comeback. Boog Powell blasted a monster home run to the upper deck in center to lead off the fourth. The next inning, after two more runs had scored, Brooks grounded a two-out single into right for an RBI to tie the game, then, running on a 3–2 pitch, followed Powell across the plate and scored the final run of the five-run rally on a Hendricks double down the line.

In the seventh, with Oriole reliever Dick Hall nursing a one-run lead, the Reds had runners on first and second with two outs. Tony Perez grounded sharply to Brooks, who snagged it and threw to Johnson at second for the force-out. The Orioles held on for a 6–5 win.

Brooks had made three great plays to contribute to the two victories, any of which would have been talked about for years, but when combined in a single work of art, they were unimaginable. After the first two games, Anderson told reporters, "The way I see it, he's [Brooks] the difference between the two clubs in this series. That guy ought to be in another league. He's unbelievable. I know he's the best third baseman I've ever seen. I don't see how anybody could do what this guy does."

"I never saw a third baseman like that," said May, who had been robbed two straight days. "Every time you look up, there he is. I was sure that ball was already by his glove."

Reds third baseman Tony Perez said, "He has to be the greatest third baseman of all time. I just enjoy watching him play. He's in the right place every time."

Anderson added the classic line: "I'm beginning to see him in my sleep. If I dropped this paper plate, he'd pick it up on one hop and throw me out."

In the Oriole clubhouse, Harry Dalton deadpanned, "Why are all the writers crowded around Brooks? Did he do something unusual?"

"Not unusual Harry, just the routine spectacular," Bob Maisel wrote. "You can look at scouting reports and hear people talk about him, but until you see Brooks Robinson with your own eyes, you can't possibly realize what he can do with that piece of leather he wears on his left hand."

Over 10,000 delirious fans greeted the returning Orioles at the airport as the Series shifted to Baltimore. Cincinnati had lost two straight one-run games. Both games had been well played and exciting—the Reds could only wonder what might have been without the series of plays made down at third.

In Game Three, unbelievably, Brooks did it again. This time he made outstanding plays in the first, second, and sixth innings. In the first, the Reds got two runners on, then Tony Perez hit a high bouncer to Brooks, who jumped to catch the ball over his head with two hands. He turned and outraced Rose to third, stepped on the base with his right foot, pivoted, and unleashed a strong throw to first for a double play. With a runner on second, the next batter, Bench, sent a wicked liner directly at Brooks, who barely had time to get his glove up to catch it while dropping straight down to his knees. He casually rolled the ball toward the mound and jogged into the dugout with his head down—another Reds rally snuffed out.

At the plate, Brooks continued to contribute also. In the bottom of the first, with the bases loaded, he faced Tony Cloninger. On a 1–2 pitch he got a fastball up and in; the pitch cracked the bat but the ball was lined into left center for a double that scored the first two Baltimore runs. While Brooks was standing on second, Reds second baseman Tommy Helms walked over to the bag. "What kind of juice you been taking, Robbie?" he asked.

The next inning, Helms found out that Brooks had plenty more juice left. He hit a slow roller just inside the third base line. Brooks raced in, circled the ball slightly to give him a better angle, scooped it, planted his foot, and threw. Boog Powell stretched and caught it to get Helms by a foot.

In the sixth, with two outs and the Orioles leading 4–1, Johnny Bench stepped to the plate again. Bench ripped a low line shot in the hole. Brooks dove to his left and stabbed it. As he hit the ground, the ball briefly snow-coned in his glove, then snugged back in the pocket. Brooks remained belly-down on the ground, and raised his left hand, showing the umpire that the ball was still there, posing for the picture that became the most well known of his work from that week. He then scrambled to his feet, underhanded the ball toward the mound, and, with his head down, amid furious cheers, hurried to the dugout. The *Sporting News*'s managing editor, Lowell Reiden-baugh, wrote, "Bench drove a savage liner into the hole. There was no way anyone could prevent the ball from going into left field for a single. Nobody, that is, except the fellow the Reds refer to as 'Hoover' (the vacuum cleaner)."

Watching in the crowd, Dick Moss, assistant to Marvin Miller of the Major League Baseball Players Association, turned to Miller and said, "Brooks is so good it's unfair to the rest of the players."

When Brooks came to bat in the last of the sixth, as the Reds were making a pitching change, he was greeted with a prolonged standing ovation from the hometown 50,000-plus crowd. As they waited for the relief pitcher to make his way to the mound, Bench looked at his tormentor and muttered, "Next time I'll hit it over your head."

Brooks promptly laced the ball to the wall in the left field corner for his second double of the game, putting men on second and third. After a walk and a strikeout, pitcher Dave McNally put the game out of reach with a two-out, two-strike grand slam. The Orioles won 9–3.

By now even those who hadn't been paying close attention realized that something special and spectacular was going on at third base for the Orioles. Media members and players couldn't come up with enough adjectives to describe it. "He's unreal," said broadcaster Joe Garagiola.

"I don't believe it," said Dave Grote, longtime publicity director of the National League.

"This guy is playing as though his car has been repossessed," said

Tommy Helms in the Reds clubhouse, alluding to the sports car that went to the Series MVP.

"If we'd known he wanted a car so badly, we'd have chipped in and bought him one," said Bench.

"I've never seen anything like him in my life," added Rose.

"I know it's starting to sound corny," said Anderson, "but I've still got to talk about that guy. You would think one of our shots would get through—and we've stung the ball pretty hard—but, no, he keeps coming up with the ball and choking off our opportunities. . . . He's taken us out of three ball games."

Over in the Oriole clubhouse, Baltimore PA announcer Rex Barney got off the best line, telling reporters looking for Brooks, "He's not at his locker yet, but four guys are over there interviewing his glove."

Earl Weaver told them, "Come back tomorrow, and he'll do it again."

Brooks later admitted that even he felt like things were getting out of hand. "After the third game, I went in the clubhouse and thought, 'This is unbelievable. Let's hurry and get this thing over. I can't keep this up.'"

Trailing three games to none, the Reds refused to go quietly into the night. This was a team of great hitters and they scored first for the third time in four games. In the bottom of the second inning, trailing 1–0, Brooks led off against Gary Nolan. On a 3–2 pitch, Nolan came in high and inside. Brooks turned on it and sent a line drive to left field that carried four rows deep in the bleachers.

The Reds took a 2–1 lead in the third, but once again the Orioles absorbed the early haymakers and began counterpunching. Palmer singled leading off the bottom of the third. Two outs later Powell walked, then Frank singled in Palmer. Brooks followed with a single up the middle to score Powell, a line shot that almost hit umpire Emmett Ashford. Brooks and Frank both moved up when center fielder Bobby Tolan mishandled the ball. Hendricks then singled to right scoring Frank but Brooks was nailed at the plate by a perfect throw from the charging Pete Rose, giving Bench a chance to finally inflict some pain of his own.

With one out in the sixth, after the Reds had cut the lead to 4–3, Brooks singled and Hendricks followed with another hit to right field. This time when Rose tried to get Brooks as he chugged toward third, the throw skipped past Tony Perez and went into the dugout and Brooks trotted home to make it 5–3.

In the Reds' eighth, Lee May hit a three-run homer to put the Reds up 6–5. The lead held. May happily told reporters after the game, "I finally found a way to get it past that Hoover. I hit it over him." The win for the Reds broke a streak of 17 consecutive victories for the Orioles going back to the last week of the regular season. The champagne was packed away for another night.

Brooks had a 4-for-4 day, which gave him a .536 average (15-for-28) for the 1970 postseason up to that point. Baltimore fans were getting the feeling he could do anything. When the Reds put two men on base with nobody out during the fourth game, someone in the stands yelled, "Get three Brooks."

October 15 began with heavy rain and it was still overcast and gloomy with intermittent showers just before game time. Andy Etchebarren, sitting in the Baltimore dugout watching the rain fall on the tarp covering the infield, looked at the team's miracle worker. "Brooksie," he said, "make it stop raining."

"Thanks," replied Brooks, "but I'm not going that good."

Although no meteorological evidence points to the efforts of the Oriole third baseman, the rain stopped and it cleared enough to play the game. Once again, the Reds rabidly assaulted Oriole pitching and jumped out on top, scoring three times in the first inning. Jim Merritt, who had won 20 games for the Reds before September 8, but had pitched little since due to elbow tendinitis, tried to gut it out in his Series start, but gave up a two-run homer to Frank in the first, making it 3–2. Oriole starter Mike Cuellar then settled down and shut the Reds out the rest of the way. Meanwhile, the Orioles hammered the Reds' beleaguered pitching staff and scored seven unanswered runs.

With the Orioles up 9–3, the Memorial Stadium crowd showed their appreciation with sustained applause for Brooks when he walked to the plate in the eighth inning. After he took a called third strike and made his way back to the dugout, they gave him another standing ovation. A standing ovation after a strikeout? "It's the most touching thing that has ever happened to me on a baseball diamond," Brooks wrote later.

There was one more inning to play. Bench led off the ninth and hit a liner down the third base line. Brooks caught it with a diving backhanded stab in which he landed sprawled across the foul line—the third time in two days he had robbed Bench. It was an exclamation point for the whole week of plays at third. "For years people have asked me, 'How could you be there?'" Brooks said in 1990. "It was no big deal. Mike Cuellar was pitching. I knew a big curve was coming and Bench figured to be out in front with the bat."

Fittingly, the final batter of the Series, pinch hitter Pat Corrales, grounded a slow hopper to Brooks, who scooped it and threw to first. Brooks had fielded 23 chances during the World Series, converting two into double plays. He ended up 9-for-21 (.429) at the plate and set a record with 17 total bases on two home runs, two doubles, and five singles. The nine hits equaled the record for a five-game Series. He also set a record for the most one-liners inspired by the opposing team. The Series MVP voting was a mere formality.

Afterward, Anderson said, "Those plays Robinson made during the Series weren't luck. That was skill you saw out there at third base. Really I'm eager to see the World Series films so that I can fully appreciate the plays he made."

When he had been told after one of the games that he should have seen Robinson five years ago, Anderson replied, "If he was any better five years ago, Baltimore wouldn't have needed a shortstop."

Johnny Bench told reporters, "I hope we can come back and play the Orioles next year. I also hope Brooks Robinson has retired by then."

Brooks's teammates refused to let him bask in adulation. In the clubhouse, in front of reporters, Elrod Hendricks carefully handed Brooks a bottle of champagne. "Don't drop it," he said. At the victory party, a buffet dinner and dance at the Tail of the Fox in nearby Timonium, in front of the players, families, and friends, Frank Robinson convened the kangaroo court one last time and assessed a fine of one dollar on Brooks for "showboating it during the entire series."

Brooks protested, "If you fine me a buck I won't give you a ride in my new car."

"Case dismissed," the judge replied.

The lack of respect continued at home. After Brooks drove home from the final game, he received the kind of ego-deflating come-down only a child can give. When he entered the house after becoming the toast of the athletic world, six-year-old Mike asked, "Hi, Dad, who won?"

But there was plenty of praise from everywhere else. In his Series wrap-up, Bob Maisel wrote, "In retrospect, one of the best things about the World Series was that people all over the country found out what we've known in Baltimore for years, that Brooks Robinson is one of the best fielding third basemen of all time. . . . The Reds hit balls in exactly the right places to show Brooks at his best, and television and the instant replay carried his skills all over the country."

Jim Murray of the *Los Angeles Times* wrote, "If there's ever a call-back and they suspect industrial sabotage on the Big Red Machine, they might check a white male Caucasian American who was seen leaving the scene of the accident with a baseball in his glove. Brooks Robinson kept reaching in and removing vital parts of the Big Red Machine. He systematically dismantled it. Every time it seemed to spark up, he would reach down and take another coil out of it. You couldn't have shot a bullet down third base in this Series. At third, Brooks Robinson is the athletic equivalent of a 20-foot wall."

Time did nothing to diminish the effect of Brooks's performance on those who watched it. Thirty years later Sparky Anderson said, "He took us out of the games himself. . . . Every time we got it going, bam, he made a play. . . . I asked Earl Weaver. And Earl said, 'You know something, everybody is saying how wonderful he is. We see this day in and day out.' And I said, 'Earl, you mean to tell me he plays like this?' And he said, 'Sparky, there's nobody that can play third base like he plays it.' Then I realized, this guy wasn't making no great plays against us. This was what he always did.

"I got to know him that winter because we were at a lot of things together," Anderson added, "and I realized this guy couldn't only do that, he did the off-field stuff just as well. And I said, 'My God, this guy's got the whole package.'"

"The amazing thing was the chances he got," said Weaver. "The plays he made we had seen throughout the course of the season. . . .

Brooks as he appeared in his junior high school newspaper, October, 1951. (*Little Rock School District*)

The 1953 Little Rock Doughboys. They won their second consecutive Arkansas American Legion state championship. Brooks is on the back row, third from the right. Coach George Haynie is on the back row, far right. (*Robert Nosari*)

Brooks and friends enjoying a day with the family car, circa 1954. Little Rock Central High School is in the background. Brooks is in the front at the bottom on the upper picture and in back with his arms around his friends in the lower picture. (*Buddy Rotenberry*)

Senior picture from the school yearbook, 1955. Optimism and clean-faced good looks. Brooks was voted Best All-around in the senior class. (*Little Rock School District*)

Young Orioles infielder, circa 1957–1958.
(*National Baseball Hall of Fame Library, Cooperstown, NY*)

Brooks leaps for joy as he rushes to celebrate the last out of the 1966 World
Series with catcher Andy Etchebarren and pitcher Dave McNally. (*AP Images*)

Brooks makes the catch in front of the Orioles' dugout as the umpire and fans look on, July 5, 1968. (*Reprinted with permission of The Baltimore Sun Media Group*)

Brooks and Connie having fun before the Orioles lost to their wives in the annual softball game, August 5, 1970. Most observers felt that C. Robinson looked better in her uniform than B. Robinson did. (*Reprinted with permission of The Baltimore Sun Media Group*)

Armed with cameras, (from left to right) Joe Torre, Hank Aaron, Harmon Killebrew, Brooks Robinson, and Stan Musial tour Vietnam, November 1966. Someone forgot to tell Brooks that white clothes make an easier target. (*Photo by Ray Belford. Used with permission from the* Stars and Stripes)

Brooks lands on his stomach but hangs on to the ball to rob Johnny Bench in the third game of the 1970 World Series. (*National Baseball Hall of Fame Library, Cooperstown, NY*)

He also did some damage during the 1970 World Series with his bat.
(National Baseball Hall of Fame Library, Cooperstown, NY)

Brooks makes a diving stop off a Gene Tenace smash, July 6, 1974.
He got to his feet and threw Tenace out at first. *(AP Images)*

Brooks Robinson, 1975.
(National Baseball Hall of Fame Library, Cooperstown, NY)

Brooks shows off his Gold Glove, circa 1974–1975.
(National Baseball Hall of Fame Library, Cooperstown, NY)

Brooks Robinson shakes hands with Brooks Rogers, 2011. The Orioles held a promotion in 2012 for a drawing for free tickets for anyone with a first or middle name of Brooks. There were 493 entrants. (*Greg Rogers*)

The Oriole Hall of Famers pose in front of the Brooks Robinson statue at Camden Yards, September 29, 2012. Left to right: Cal Ripken Jr., Eddie Murray, Earl Weaver, Brooks Robinson, Frank Robinson, and Jim Palmer. (*Reprinted with permission of The Baltimore Sun Media Group*)

You might see one of those spectaculars—and he made them all through the season—but they're not that frequent. . . . Third basemen just don't get that many chances."

"He made those kinds of plays every day," Powell said in 2004. "I mean what he did in the 1970 World Series was just normal kinds of plays for him. Of course, we kidded all the time about what a great half a play that was. Every one of those plays was a ball [thrown to first] in the dirt, and if I missed it, it was just E-5. . . . So he ends up getting the car from *Sport* magazine. . . . And I just told him, 'If I don't catch those balls, I probably win it. So I want half that car."

"I think it was neat that Brooks got a chance to show what he could do," says Dick Hall. "He got a lot of chances and it just happened to be in the World Series and millions of people all of the sudden noticed what he could do."

Discussing it later, Brooks said, "I went into that Series thinking, 'Boy, we're gonna get a lot of work,' because they had guys like Perez and Bench and Lee May, and they got one thing on their mind and that's to hit it as far as they can. I remember telling Belanger, 'We're gonna get a lot of ground balls, a lot of work in this Series.' When it was all said and done, I told people I played 23 years professionally, that's 162 games a year, and I don't ever remember having five games in a row like that."

Brooks added, "As an infielder, you can play for a week and never get a chance to do anything spectacular. In this particular series, every game I got a chance to do something; make an outstanding play. I was hitting well too. It was a once-in-a-lifetime five-game series and it just happened to be the World Series."

While baseball is foremost a game and the routine stats of wins and losses matter, it is also entertainment; theater. The most memorable players have the ability, that showman's gift of timing, to raise their level of play when the stakes are the highest and the lights the brightest; the diva's theatrical flair—through luck or talent or a combination of both—in which they transcend mere statistics to create the special moments never to be forgotten by the audience.

The 1970 World Series was Brooks Robinson's magnum opus, his greatest work; a singular show of genius on sport's biggest stage.

Unlike those who are remembered for one at bat or one catch, Brooks did it repeatedly in varying degrees of artistry over five games. Had he gone 1-for-19 at the plate, instead of providing a game-winning home run, a two-double game, and a 4-for-4 game, it still would have been a magnificent performance. He made four legitimate great plays: the one over third base on May, the dive to the left on Bench, the dive to the right on Bench, and the spinning double play on May. He added more than a few other excellent plays on an assortment of drives, hot smashes, choppers, and balls that needed to be charged—he exhibited his entire repertoire.

It was one of those performances that every legend needs to be truly complete, to unquestionably have his ticket punched for the Hall of Fame. Brooks had been great in 1964, it was his masterpiece season, but it had ultimately ended in defeat and lots of guys have an MVP award—they give out two every year. To be truly certified as an immortal of the game, to reside in the rarefied air of the pantheon, there needs to be something else. There have been great players in baseball who never reached that upper level of fans' consciousness because, through chance or circumstance, they never had that signature moment on the big stage. Ernie Banks, Eddie Mathews, Harmon Killebrew, Ken Griffey, Jr., Greg Maddux, Don Sutton—the list goes on of 500-home-run guys and 300-game winners who never had that moment. Even though they may have played in World Series, they did nothing memorable. Now Brooks Robinson had his moment. With the 1970 Series, he crossed the one-way threshold from great player to legend. For five games he held the nation's attention; he amazed and astounded; and he dominated the Series as few men ever have.

And the way he did it captured the imagination of the country. Like a singular warrior, standing with remarkable coolness a mere 90 feet away from club-wielding Philistines, with only his wits and a small leather glove to defend himself; fielding projectiles that most sane men would have tried to dodge. A lot of players had turned in great hitting or pitching performances in the World Series, but no one had ever come close to the fielding brilliance he exhibited over and over. He was a true one-of-a-kind artist, at the top of his game, at just the right time. The grace and nonchalant humbleness combined to form the perfect ingredients for mythology.

Brooks Robinson became a household name after that week. He would be forever linked to the 1970 Series—it would be impossible to think of one without the other. And it solidified one of the great nicknames in baseball history. Brooks had been called a vacuum cleaner in word and print at least since 1958, but other fielders occasionally had been said to have vacuum-cleaning tendencies. Now, and forever, Brooks would be *the* vacuum cleaner. Say Vacuum Cleaner on a baseball field and everyone knows who you are talking about. Say 1970 World Series, and everyone thinks of one player.

13. End of the Era

SUDDENLY IT SEEMED as though Brooks Robinson had just been discovered—a Rembrandt found under another painting, tucked away in an attic. He was the toast of the nation; everyone wanted a piece of him. He appeared on television with Ed Sullivan, with Dick Cavett, and on a show called *Man-to-Man* with Los Angeles Rams Roman Gabriel and Merlin Olsen. Brooks and Connie were guest cohost and hostess of *The Mike Douglas Show*. Douglas quipped that with Connie and singer Jeannie C. Riley both on the stage, the boys in the band watched the show for the first time since he could remember.

The shows were only a prelude to the busiest winter of Brooks's life. He flew to Buffalo, then to Oswego and Glen Falls. Then it was off to the West Coast for other television appearances. There were trips to Charlotte; Dallas; Stevens, Iowa (to judge a beauty contest); Chicago; Houston; Phoenix; Washington; New York; Hanover, Pennsylvania; and South Bend (to attend a Boy Scout jamboree).

In between there was a week in Hawaii for the player reps meeting. He squeezed in tapes for the March of Dimes, Multiple Sclerosis, and Goodwill Industries and visits to several area hospitals. There was also the annual trip he took with Connie after the baseball season as a reward for her hard work on the home front all year—this time to St. Croix.

Brooks traveled to Rochester to receive the Hickok Professional Athlete of the Year Award. Given at an annual dinner, the Hickock Award was a big deal in 1970, a major prize in the sporting world. Named for the founder of the Hickok Manufacturing Company of Rochester, the award was presented from 1950 to 1977. The prize was an alligator-skin belt with a solid gold buckle, encrusted with a four-carat diamond and 26 gem chips, valued at over $10,000.

Then it was off to the corporate headquarters of the A-T-O company, the conglomerate that owned Rawlings Sporting Goods, where he was given 975 shares of their stock as thanks for the fine work he had performed in the public's eye with their product over the years. The number 975 (worth $8,500) was equal to his career fielding percentage.

Brooks accepted the busy schedule as a trade-off for his phenomenal Series success. "I figure I have to. I owe it to people, to baseball, to the writers, to the fans if they want me." And after the 1970 World Series, everybody wanted Brooks Robinson.

In his talks at dinners and award ceremonies, Brooks usually shrugged off his Series heroics with some version of "I was just lucky to be in the right place at the right time," as if anyone who happened to be standing there, and happened to have a glove on his hand, could have done the same—similar to his comments after his great plays in the 1969 Series when he said, "I always keep my glove open. You never know when the ball is liable to jump in there."

And, in a self-deprecating refrain he would continue for the next 40 years whenever asked about the 1970 Series, he always led off explaining how he had made an error on the first ball hit to him, "a little 24 hopper, and I picked it up and threw it over the first baseman's head."

At many of the banquets, Johnny Bench was also a speaker. Bench frequently dropped the line about the car Brooks won as World Series MVP: "The rumor is that the car has an oversized glove compartment." Brooks, Bench, and Sparky Anderson attended so many banquets together and heard each other's talk so often that they joked about switching speeches for some of them.

Brooks signed with the Orioles in early February for a $20,000 hike to the magical number of $100,000. This put him in select company as he joined a group of only 12 men who were paid $100,000 or more for playing baseball in 1971. A look at the list of top-paid players provides a stark contrast to modern baseball economics. Willie Mays and Carl Yastrzemski topped the list at $150,000, followed by Bob

Gibson at $135,000, Frank Robinson at $130,000, and Hank Aaron at $125,000. Frank Howard, Juan Marichal, Roberto Clemente, Pete Rose, Harmon Killebrew, and Billy Williams rounded out the list. The fact that 10 of the 12 eventually made the Hall of Fame (Rose, of course, is ineligible and Howard's career ended too soon to put up the final numbers required, but he had hit 44, 48, and 44 home runs in the preceding three years), most on the first ballot, shows that the owners were getting their money's worth and did not frivolously throw big bucks at mediocre players.

Earlier Brooks had remarked to writers that he was only paid for what he did with his bat, that fielding was never mentioned in contract talks. Harry Dalton disagreed. "Perhaps his glove wasn't brought up by me because I think you can understand that I would have everything to lose by bringing up his defense [during negotiations]. How could I bring up defense? How could I debate perfection?"

The Orioles, and Brooks Robinson, picked up where they left off as the 1971 season began. Brooks had a streak of 50 errorless games, his second such streak in four years. The team raced to the front of the standings and pulled away from the pack.

Brooks was the top American League vote getter for the All-Star Game in Detroit. The American public was dying to see him do it again, and again. And, on the national stage once more, he did what everyone expected—he made the defensive play of the game—spearing a vicious Johnny Bench line drive. Bench barely had time to drop his bat on his follow-through before seeing that the ball was secure in Brooks's omnipresent glove. He took one step and threw his hands over his head, as if to say, "You again?" In the ninth inning, Brooks squeezed a pop-up from Johnny Bench (who else?) to end the game for a 6–4 American League victory. This broke a streak of eight straight All-Star losses for the A.L. Of the 1971 All-Star squad, only Brooks, Aparicio (then with the Red Sox), and Al Kaline had played the last time the American League had won—back in 1962 at Wrigley Field.

Brooks made headlines against the A's in Baltimore on July 28— the kind of headlines that made readers think they had woken up in Bizarro World. "Brooks Robinson Makes 3 Errors," screamed the *Milwaukee Journal*; "Brooks Robinson Is Human," read another headline; "Bad Night for Brooks: 3 Errors in One Inning," said *The New York Times*. In the fifth inning of a scoreless game, Brooks threw wildly on Bert Campaneris's bunt, allowing Campy to take second. Then he fumbled a grounder, recovered, and threw it over the first baseman's head. Two unearned runs scored in the inning—after two were out—courtesy of the Oriole third baseman. The fact that Frank hit a dramatic three-run homer in the ninth to win the game 3–2 made little difference to the writers—Frank had hit ninth inning home runs before, but men had literally walked on the moon before Brooks Robinson had made three errors in a game. "It just wasn't my night," Brooks told reporters after the game. In the seventh inning shortstop Belanger was hit in the face by a bad hop. "I went over and told him, 'I think that ball was meant for me.'"

The 1971 Oriole pitching staff produced four 20-game winners: Cuellar, McNally, Palmer, and Pat Dobson. The team once again proved to be the best in the league as they topped 100 wins for the third consecutive season, winning 101, and took the Eastern Division by 12 games. Brooks hit .272 with 20 home runs and 92 RBIs and finished fourth in the league MVP voting, behind Vida Blue, Sal Bando, and Frank Robinson. At 34 years old, he was not showing any signs of slowing down.

The Orioles swept the playoffs for the third straight year—this time the victims from the A.L. West were the up-and-coming Oakland A's. The sweep gave the Orioles 14 straight wins heading into the World Series. It also gave them a 9–0 record the past three years against the Western Division champs in the playoffs. Brooks finished the series with a .486 average (18-for-37) in three years of playoffs.

The Orioles faced the Pittsburgh Pirates of Roberto Clemente and Willie Stargell in the World Series. The Orioles won the opener in Baltimore 5–3. In Game Two, Brooks had three run-scoring singles, scored two runs, and had a pair of walks to tie Babe Ruth and Lou Brock as the only players to reach base safely five times in a World Series game. He also made a sensational play in the eighth inning, diving to his left to stop a bouncing ball hit by Manny Sanguillen. After the stop, he landed hard on his chest, then recovered to throw a bullet to Powell in time for the out. The Orioles took the game 11–3.

Afterward, Pirate manager Danny Murtaugh, discussing the play with resignation, told reporters, "You just expect Brooks to play the way he does."

As the Series moved to Pittsburgh, it appeared to be a mismatch. Oriole pitching was having little trouble with Pittsburgh's sluggers and the offense was unloading against the Pirates' lightly regarded pitching staff. Frank Robinson had a .625 average after the first two games, Brooks .571. The players didn't realize it at the time, however, but they had just about reached the high-water point for the Oriole dynasty.

In Game Three, Brooks turned in another fielding gem in the first inning. With one out, the normally slow-starting Cuellar appeared to be in trouble. With Clemente on second and Stargell on first, big Bob Robertson lashed a wicked liner that Brooks snagged and quickly threw to second for a double play. Pirate pitcher Steve Blass came up with the game of his life, however. The Orioles did not get a hit until Brooks singled with one out in the fifth. Other than a Frank Robinson home run, Blass was brilliant as he pitched a complete game three-hitter to give the Pirates a 5–1 victory and turn the tide in the Series.

Pittsburgh won the next two games, their pitchers suddenly unbeatable. Game Four was memorable as the first World Series game to be played at night. Although major league baseball games had been played under lights since the 1930s, daytime had remained the exclusive domain of the Fall Classic. With the visible pot of gold to be had from a prime-time television slot, however, the tradition suddenly seemed antiquated.

Back in Memorial Stadium for the sixth game, facing elimination, the Orioles trailed 2–0 after five innings but gamely clawed back to tie it with runs in the sixth and seventh. The two teams carried their fight into extra innings. In the 10th, with one out, Frank walked. Merv Rettenmund then bounced a single up the middle. Frank, running on two sore Achilles tendons, hustled around to third, arriving in a cloud of dust. Brooks came to the plate with a chance to once more be the hero. He worked a 1–2 count on Bob Miller, fouled one back, then hit a fly to center field that brought Frank sliding home with the winning run and the Series was tied at three games each.

In Game Seven, Blass once again shut the Orioles down, giving up only two hits through the first seven innings while the Pirates built a 2–0 lead. In the Orioles' half of the eighth, the team tried for one last rally. Singles by Hendricks and Belanger and a sacrifice bunt put runners on second and third with one out. Buford grounded to first, scoring a run, but Johnson ended the threat by grounding to short. In the ninth, the Orioles went down in order, Brooks watching helplessly from the on-deck circle as Rettenmund grounded out to end the Series. Brooks had hit .318 (7-for-22) and tied for the lead for both teams with five RBIs, but the Orioles hit only .205 as a team.

The 1969–71 Orioles were a special team. They had a unique blend of talent and personalities, got along well, and had fun together. These were indeed the glory years of Baltimore baseball, never to be replicated. The community loved the players—there were no problem guys; they were all good citizens. Remarkably when viewed from the state of teams in present-day baseball, the lineup was nearly identical all three seasons: Hendricks and Etchebarren platooning behind the plate, Powell, Johnson, Belanger, and Robinson in the infield, and Robinson, Blair, and Buford in the outfield (with the exception of Merv Rettenmund getting more playing time in 1970 and 1971). The only difference to the starting rotation of McNally, Cuellar, and Palmer was the trade of Tom Phoebus for Pat Dobson after the 1970 season. Watt, Hall, and Richert anchored the bullpen.

"The biggest thing I remember about the Orioles from then is the players, not so much the games," said Eddie Watt, a team member from 1966 to 1973. "Life was different then than it is now. . . . The most important thing was the day-to-day interactions, the friendships, knowing and being able to rely on each other for everything and anything that came up. I think that was the most outstanding thing about the Orioles back then. It was just a feeling. I always felt if I truly needed something, there was any number of people I could ask for help."

He adds, "Everyone meshed well together in talent and personality. Weaver didn't always keep the 25 best players in camp—he kept the 25 who best filled all the roles; everybody had a role and he used the entire roster."

"The key to those great Oriole teams was that the stars were all good team players," says Dick Hall. "On some teams, the stars are only out for themselves and their own stats. Depending on the situation, the guys on the Orioles did whatever was needed to win. When your stars are team players, then all the other guys are going to adopt the same attitude. That helps a lot. We had 25 guys all playing for the team. There was never any rivalry like 'I'm number one' or 'it's my team,' like you hear sometimes. There was none of that on the Orioles. There was never any trouble between Brooks and Frank. They were the two leaders and they got along great. And sometimes that's not an easy thing to happen with two stars of that magnitude on the same team."

The Orioles had the best record of any team in baseball from 1965 to 1968. Then they started playing well. The Orioles played in four World Series in six years, the last three in a row. The 1969–71 team won 318 games and was the first American League team since the Philadelphia A's of 1929–31 to win over 100 games a year three consecutive years. The closest any team finished to them in the Eastern Division in the three years was 12 games. It is unfortunate that the losses in the 1969 and 1971 World Series dampened their legacy. "One thing that always bothers me is that the '69 to '71 team doesn't get mentioned when they talk about great teams," says Richert. "That was a truly great team. There were no weaknesses. And what a lot of people forget is that we were 9–0 in the three divisional playoffs those years—and the Twins and A's weren't pushovers."

It was a great team and a great era for Baltimore baseball. Two days after the 1971 World Series, the Orioles left for Japan for a 31-day, 18-game tour. They didn't know it while they were touring Japan, but big changes were in store when they got back. The era was coming to an end.

14. Good-bye Frank

THE ORIOLES TRADED FRANK ROBINSON, along with Pete Richert, to the Los Angeles Dodgers for Doyle Alexander, Sergio Robles, Bob O'Brien, and Royle Stillman on December 2, 1971. While some were shocked, a trade had been hinted—even by Frank himself—several times during the 1971 season. He obviously had fuel left in the tank, but the combination of his age and all-out style of play was making it harder for Frank to keep his body intact 162 games a year. Oriole management didn't want to make the mistake of waiting too long to reload the aging team. With Paul Blair, Don Buford, and Merv Rettenmund—all much younger—Weaver had juggled four outfielders the past two seasons, with Rettenmund hitting over .300 in his limited playing time. Added to this mix was Don Baylor, a future star who had been named the Minor League Player of the Year in 1970 after hitting .326 with 107 RBIs at Rochester.

Also, there was the fact that Frank was pulling down $140,000—by far the most on the team. Although the Orioles had a loyal fan base, the team was hampered geographically by the closeness of major league teams in Washington and Philadelphia, along with the summertime lure of the Atlantic Ocean. They also had to compete with the multitude of horse racing options in the area. As a result, they had trouble drawing more than a million fans, even as they won the pennant year after year. This affected their ability to meet ever-increasing payroll demands. Along with Frank and Brooks, now McNally, Cuellar, Palmer, and Powell all approached the $100,000 level. Someone had to go.

The one detail that did not show up on stat sheets and actuarial tables, however, was Frank's ability as a winner; the ability to rally the entire team. Billy Martin, who had managed the Tigers to second place in 1971, clearly understood this. "When I heard about that deal," he told reporters, "all I could think of was that I'd won the pennant and I hadn't done a single thing."

Some in the press suggested that the shadow of Frank Robinson had hung over Brooks Robinson the past six years. Writers pointed out that the Orioles had never won a pennant until Frank arrived and never failed to win it when he was healthy. They questioned whether the Orioles could continue to win without his clubhouse presence. While these comments could have been construed as backhanded slaps at Brooks, he handled them with class and with deference to Frank. He told John Steadman that he believed Frank was responsible for turning the Orioles from contender to champion. "We couldn't have won it without him. . . . His ability put us over the top. He had ability that everyone could see and he also had intangibles that meant a lot to us." Brooks said that, as far as he could recall, there was never a cross word between them. "The more I was with him on the team, the more I admired him."

Another time in the spring, Brooks said, "Frank was just fantastically unselfish. I mean whatever was for the good of the ball club as far as moving a runner to position or breaking up the double play. Whatever the situation called for, this is what he did and whatever he did, he did 100 percent. He played when he was hurt, when he shouldn't have played. He never saved himself, and I think these things rubbed off. He was able to show them [teammates] a lot of things including knowing how to win."

While Brooks signed in February for $110,000, a lot of Orioles held out. Frank Cashen, the new general manager, channeling his best Winston Churchill, stated, "Never in the history of baseball have so many refused to play for so much." But holdouts were the least of the labor headaches for owners in the spring of 1972. Big trouble was coming and Brooks Robinson would be in the middle of it.

The problem had been festering for years. While at first glance Brooks appeared to be the ultimate company man—contented playing the game every day, rarely speaking out in defiance or making trouble and continually voicing how lucky he felt to be able to make a living as a baseball player—he was a staunch supporter of players' rights and maintained a leadership role in the Players Association. He had been either the team player rep or alternate rep on and off since the early 1960s. Being a player rep, a nonpaying position that was elected by team members, had historically involved attending two meetings a year, one at the All-Star break and the other after the season, presiding over team meetings, keeping the players informed of health care and pension plans, and occasionally carrying player gripes to management. After the Players Association hired lawyer Marvin Miller in the late 1960s, became more organized, and began challenging the owners, the position took on a more important role. Although Brooks was now well paid he realized that it was important for the upper crust, men like Willie Mays, Hank Aaron, and Brooks Robinson, not to relax and be happy with their lot and forget about the other players and those to come later. To Brooks, they were all members of the same club, the same lucky club, from the superstar to the guy who got called up for a week at the end of the season.

At this point in his career, Brooks had signed 16 consecutive one-year contracts. He remembered how difficult it had always been to get even a token raise. General managers and team vice presidents who discussed contracts with the players were professional negotiators—the players were hopelessly outmatched. And, under the reserve system, there really was nothing to negotiate. The players knew it, and more importantly, the owners knew it. The only negotiating option for players was to go home and get a different job.

Progress in contract talks was especially difficult for players like Brooks who did not enjoy confrontations. He was often one of the first players to sign each year. When he wanted more, his experience of 1963 was typical. Coming off his 1962 season in which he had played every game, hit .303 with 86 RBIs, made the All-Star team and won a Gold Glove, Brooks decided that he deserved $500 more than the club's offer. Harry Dalton, the general manager, let him stew for a few days, then called him in. Dalton gave him the usual sob story about how bad the team had done at the gate the previous year and how tight the budget was—the extra $500 was such an enormous demand that it might just break the team. Unfazed, Brooks doggedly said he wanted the money or he wouldn't sign. Realizing the determination of his normally agreeable player, Dalton got up and dramatically told Brooks he was going out in the hall to give him ten minutes to search his soul, to decide how much the game of baseball meant to him. When Dalton returned, he was surprised to find that Brooks had not budged on his demand. With great reluctance, as if he was giving Alaska back to the Russians, Dalton agreed, but added, "Just remember when we negotiate next year, you took advantage of me." And that's what it took for a .300-hitting All-Star Gold Glover to get an extra $500.

The players and owners had waged public battles for several years, narrowly avoiding a threatened strike in 1969. This time, the owners vowed to hold the line; negotiations were at a standstill. Brooks and assistant player rep Mark Belanger flew to Dallas for a meeting during spring training with the reps from every team and the executive board of the negotiating committee. A strike was authorized by a vote of 47–0 with one abstention (Wes Parker of the Dodgers). It would be the first players' strike in baseball history. Brooks returned to the team and informed them of the decision.

As the March 31 deadline loomed, Brooks continually stressed to reporters that the players' main objective was to improve health care and the pension plan and that it was vital that the players stick together. "I want to play," he said. "All players do. It all boils down to whether the owners are willing to make some concessions. I think our fellows are willing to make some, too, and that seems to be the best chance."

The players were disappointed to find that most fans and sportswriters blamed them for the strike and agreed with Tiger general manager Jim Campbell when he called them "damn greedy" and said, "I'm disgusted with the whole lot of them. This game has been pretty good to them."

As the team's spokesman, Brooks was singled out and bore the brunt of the fans' frustration, which grew as the strike caused the cancellation of regular season games. Baltimore was a conservative city and citizens, with the local sportswriters fanning the flames, erupted. In their view, strikes by sanitation workers, teachers, even air traffic controllers were only a regrettable nuisance, but this was baseball dammit—a baseball strike was catastrophic. The average fan didn't care about pension plans or health care. Working stiffs making $10,000 a year looked at players pulling down six figures for playing a game and blamed them. In the opinion of fans, the major issue, pure and simple, was greed—these guys were making good money doing something every guy in the country would gladly do for free and they weren't happy; they wanted more.

Hell certainly hath no fury like that of a baseball fan scorned. Brooks Robinson's popularity was affected negatively for the first time in his career. Scorching letters to the editor condemned him:

"Brooks Robinson, the fair hairless boy, turns wolf. Put this in your headlines."

"As I understand it, Mr. Brooks Robinson, Baltimore's hallowed third baseman, owns a sporting goods store and a restaurant. I wonder if he gives his employees as good a pension plan and fringe benefits as he demands for himself from his employer."

"All my autographed baseballs, along with my prize picture of my favorite Oriole, Brooks Robinson, will be thrown in the trash. This is one fan who is finished with baseball."

"That guy Brooks Robinson is nothing but a hypocrite. When the baseball players went on strike, Robinson was quoted as saying this is a terrible thing. Didn't he vote for the strike? Wise up, Robinson. You can't fool all the people all the time. Some people can see right through you."

There were many others.

In spite of the public disapproval, Brooks held firm. He told reporters that he bore no malice due to the attacks and expressed genuine concern for the fans and the damage to the game's image. "I realized that this [fan backlash] could happen," he said. "When you think you are right, though, then you do what you think is right. I can think of a lot of other places I would prefer to be. But the longer it goes, the less concerned I am about this kind of feeling. The good thing about our country is that a man can have his own ideas."

April 5, with tensions running high, Marvin Miller and 18 Baltimore players met at Brooks's house. Afterward, Miller spoke to the press and accused Earl Weaver and owner Jerry Hoffberger of coercing the players. Brooks told reporters that the players were more unified than ever before. Hoffberger, who had always been on good terms with Brooks, viewed this as a betrayal and it would not be forgotten soon.

The strike was finally settled but wiped out the first ten days of the season, along with wiping out a great deal of the affection between fans and players. The owners' proposal for the settlement included a payment of $500,000 to the players' pension fund and $490,000 to the health care fund along with the stipulation that players would not be paid for the games missed due to the strike and the games would not be made up. Miller proclaimed the settlement a triumph for the players, if for no other reason than the fact that they had stood together and forced the owners to deal with them as a group. *The New York Times* agreed: "The compromise agreement between the club owners and the players is important not for who won and who lost in money terms, but for the implicit decision by management to accept players as grown-up men entitled to a collective voice in the determination of their own destinies." Most media personnel and fans were less than magnanimous in their view of the striking players, however. April 16, as he approached the plate for his first at bat of the year, Brooks was booed at home for the only time anyone could remember. Outwardly, he appeared to take the boos calmly and singled on the first pitch to drive in a run. He added another RBI single later, turning the boos into cheers, as the Orioles won 3–1.

Brooks would remember the strike as one of the worst periods of his baseball career, a time when a wedge was driven between him and his fans, a time when the game he loved was threatened. The players had won needed concessions in their battle with management—future generations of players would reap the benefits, but that didn't help the feeling of frustration. "When I look back on it, it was a terrible ordeal," he later said. "The worst ten days of my life."

As the strike receded in the rearview mirror and the baseball season progressed, transgressions were quickly forgotten. Brooks Robinson's popularity returned as great as ever. He was one of the most universally liked players in the major leagues. His consistent play had something to do with it, but there was much more.

Early in 1972, Brooks had received a special honor from Commissioner Bowie Kuhn at a luncheon in New York as the player who best typified the game of baseball on and off the field—an accolade Kuhn called baseball's most distinguished award. The winner of the award, which would be renamed the Roberto Clemente Award the next year, was selected by a special committee of sportswriters, sportscasters, and baseball executives. Others in the final field in 1972 were Ernie Banks, Al Kaline, and Harmon Killebrew. Brooks was cited because, "as flawless as his work is on the field, it is matched by his actions, behavior and manners off the field. No request is too big, no demands placed upon him are too great." His many civic activities, including involvement in drug abuse education and prevention programs, visits to hospitals, and work with youngsters in underprivileged neighborhoods, were noted. In accepting the award Brooks said, "The award means so much because it recognizes you as a person, not just for what you do on the field." He reiterated his sense of duty to set an example for youth. "I feel I have an obligation to kids—to the younger generation. Some guys don't feel they have to do anything to represent baseball off the field. But I do feel players have an obligation to the kids. . . . I want them to see sports as a great thing, the race relations, how Frank Robinson, Don Buford, Paul Blair and Brooks Robinson get along—that it is a common denominator. I like to show that."

Washington sportswriter Ed Linn (who ironically would be Leo Durocher's coauthor in 1975 on the book *Nice Guys Finish Last*) addressed Brooks's popularity in a cover article for *Sport* in June of 1972 entitled "Why Everyone Loves Brooks Robinson." He wrote, "He's a phenomenon in this age, combining extraordinary skills on the field with an endearing humanity off the field. And, at age 35, neither his skills nor his humanity seem to be diminishing." In addition to listing all his well-known qualities, Linn mentioned that after winning the Hickok Belt, Brooks had called the Little Rock Boys Club and asked if they might want to put it on display (with fake jewels substituted of course) "so that some other kid might come in off the street some day and say to himself, 'Well, one of our boys made it. Maybe I can make it too.'"

Linn told the story of the time Brooks had committed to a joint fund-raising banquet that was being held in Baltimore for a Vietnam vet who had lost both legs and was trying to swim the English

Channel and a Baltimore lady who had been single-handedly running baseball and basketball teams for handicapped kids. The event was being held on the Sunday after Thanksgiving in 1970—previously scheduled without the knowledge that Brooks would turn out to be in great demand in the months following the World Series. After making the endless appearances his newfound celebrity demanded, he was planning to spend the holiday weekend with family in Little Rock. Even though he would have to contend with the fact that there were no flights from Little Rock to Baltimore, he assured the organizers of the fund-raising event that he would be there. He ended up flying to Washington from Little Rock, renting a car to drive to Baltimore, and then flying back to Little Rock for the rest of the holiday. He later refused to accept any expenses.

"If he's wanted for any kind of a sports or civic affair, he'll not only be there to grace the dais, he'll be hanging around long after the affair is over exchanging pleasantries with all comers," wrote Linn. "Invite him to present the trophy to the winner of a wheelchair bowling tournament and he'll not only arrive early, he'll probably know most of the guys in the wheelchairs personally." Linn addressed the Frank Robinson trade: "The Baltimore Orioles would never dream of trading Brooks. Despite everything F. Robinson did for the ball club, F. Robinson was a disposable item. B. Robinson isn't. Baltimore saw Brooks grow up. The feeling the city has about Brooks goes beyond his ability and into his personality. From the early years, Brooks has made his home in Baltimore, and the people of Baltimore have come to know him as the most decent, obliging and available of men.

"We of a certain age do have a picture of what a big-league ballplayer is supposed to represent," continued Linn, summing up Brooks's beliefs in the obligations of his celebrity. "If it is composed in part of boyhood dreams and old newspaper copy, it also has a solid component of truth. As the man who has made it to the top of that mountain which every boy dreams of climbing, the big-league ballplayer does represent something having to do with both the rounding of third base on that last triumphant leg of the grand slam home run and the gracious signing of autographs for raggedy little boys and girls afterwards."

The eight-page article was flattering, but it only scratched the surface for answering the question of why everyone loved Brooks Robinson. While he had remained popular across the country since the 1970 World Series, around Baltimore he was ready for canonization. By 1972 Brooks Robinson was as much a part of the Baltimore landscape as crab cakes and horse racing. He had been appearing in an Oriole uniform for seventeen years. A generation of Baltimore kids had grown up being Brooks Robinson in backyard games and arguing over who got to be number five when Little League uniforms were passed out.

Fans loved watching the routine before he hit: grabbing the top of his helmet, waving his bat with his left hand, digging in, and rocking back and forth; the way he crouched on the balls of his feet and leaned forward in the field on every pitch—like he couldn't wait for it to be hit; the way he ran all out on the base paths, frantically swinging his arms; the way he scurried around the bases with his head down, like a kid getting away with something, after he hit a home run. Even the funny-looking sawed-off brim of his batting helmet—the fans loved it all—the little quirky-familiar mannerisms a man comes to love about his wife after fifty years of a good marriage.

Fans close to the field could see how much he enjoyed the game and he cut them in on the action, frequently shaking hands and striking up conversations along the rail before and after games. These were his fans; he appreciated them and he never let them forget it. "The box at Memorial Stadium for my family was right over the third base dugout," says Frank Cashen. "Brooks used to throw gum over to kids. My kids always remembered that—he was their favorite."

"One thing that made Brooks such a fan favorite was the way Chuck Thompson [Oriole radio and television sportscaster] always referred to him as Brooksie," says Tom Blazucki, a longtime Oriole fan who came of age in the 1960s. "It just made him feel like a buddy. He never threw a helmet or bat, he always acted like it was still a game—he never forgot that he was playing a game and having fun. And he always came through when we needed it. I can't tell you how many times the game would be close in the ninth and Thompson would say, 'And here comes Brooksie to the plate.' You just knew we were going to win."

"It was obvious that he cared about fans when you would see him around town," says Patricia Ranocchia, who grew up in Baltimore in the 1950s and remained a lifelong Oriole fan. "He would make eye contact with you and act like you were an old friend, even if you only talked to him for a minute. He was a kind, loving human being and a role model who loved baseball and Baltimore and always did whatever he could to help out. As a parent you appreciated those things more than what he did on the field. He quickly became a fan favorite when he was young. He was always doing things in the community. And he was a regular guy. A lot of times big stars act too important to interact with normal people. He acted just like one of your neighbors."

"I started following baseball as a four-year-old in 1963 when my dad took me to games," says Terri Hett. "Everybody in the stands loved Brooks. Your dad tells you, 'That's Brooks Robinson, he's great,' and you hear everyone cheering when he makes a great play—it just made it something special you shared with your dad, and made your dad seem like a genius. Then when you got older, you found out that he's an even nicer guy. He showed up for my nine-ten-year-old softball league all-star event in 1968. As a nine-year-old, it was amazing to see him there. He just walked around like a regular guy. He talked to every single kid and shook our hands."

"Brooks Robinson was the greatest gentleman I've ever met," says Bruce Genther, who worked at the Brooks Robinson Sporting Goods store for almost a decade. "He was only in sporadically during baseball season, but he was there a lot in the off-season. He would talk to the customers and sign autographs. Sometimes, he would be in his office and hear a kid come in to buy a glove and he would come out and say, 'What kind of glove are you looking for?' And then he would help them pick one out. It blew them away—can you imagine you're a kid and here's Brooks Robinson helping you pick out a glove? He was very down-to-earth. He understood who he was and would go out of his way to be nice. But he had no concept of the aura that surrounded him."

Having no concept of the aura that surrounded him, Brooks had always, whether through design or simply by being himself, been accessible and generous to his fans. How generous was he? He would give them the shirt off his back. Literally. Stephanie Vardos was a sophomore at Yale who needed something special to wear for a Halloween party one year. She decided to go as Brooks Robinson since he was her favorite player. She wrote to him, "Dear Mr. Robinson: If your uniform isn't doing anything near the end of October would you consider letting me borrow it for Halloween? I promise I'll take really good care of it and send it right back."

A few weeks later, she received a handwritten reply saying that he thought it was a great idea and would be pleased if his uniform was worn to the party but technically the uniform didn't belong to him, it belonged to the Orioles. He suggested that she write to Jack Dunn III, the appropriate Oriole official, and tell him that Brooks said it was okay. She showed the letter to a friend, who exclaimed, "Wow! That's like getting a letter from God!" While John Updike had famously written after Ted Williams had refused to tip his hat to fans after his last home run, "Gods do not answer letters," apparently Brooks didn't get the memo.

After writing to Jack Dunn, Vardos received a package in a plain brown wrapper with Memorial Stadium, Baltimore, as the return address. It contained Brooks's home uniform, cap, socks, and stirrups. "You could tell it was real because there was a button missing and the leg was worn from sliding," she said. "I had it for about a week before Halloween and every night after dinner I would lay it out on my bed and people would come over and just view it." She sent it back after Halloween, happy that she became the only other person since 1955 to wear number five for the Orioles.

The sentiment about Brooks was not just restricted to fans—players felt the same way. He was popular with teammates and opponents alike. He was never known to be involved in a fight—on the field or in the clubhouse. He had no enemies in baseball. What made the guy tick? How could someone play such a demanding game, such a frustrating game, as baseball, and play it with such obvious passion and determination, without ever losing his cool? To get to the top level in any sport requires a strong personality; mice don't make it. It's inevitable that bad things will happen. Even that paragon of virtue John

Wooden was known to let fly with a "goodness-gracious-sakes-alive" when things didn't go his way. Baseball fights, between opponents, umpires, and teammates, are part of the lore of the game and the most competitive players are at the forefront. Their drive and unwillingness to settle for anything less than the best is often the very thing that separates the elite players from similarly talented, less achieving peers. How could Brooks Robinson play so hard, stay afloat in that pool of testosterone, and remain in such control of his emotions? There should have been at least one angry outburst, one incident of spiking a player on the other team, one episode of making gestures at the opposing dugout or unruly fans. Maybe a furious bat-wielding charge of the mound after one of his beanings. At least a broken water cooler. Something. Anything. But there never was. About the only such occurrence anyone could remember was once in the early 1970s when Brooks flied out in a close game with runners on second and third and one out and, although the ball appeared to be deep enough to score the runner on a tag, a surprisingly strong throw went to third and got the trailing runner before the run scored—double play, end of inning, no run, no sacrifice fly. Disgusted, Brooks threw his helmet down in anger. But even then, he couldn't pull it off. It was such a laughable sight that for days thereafter, Oriole players jokingly imitated him, throwing their helmets every chance they got.

Possibly due to the interruption of organized batting practice in the spring, hitting was down all over the majors in 1972. Only Dick Allen (37) and Bobby Murcer (33) hit more than 26 home runs in the American League and Rod Carew led the league with a .318 average. The Orioles' entire team struggled early and they fell behind. Brooks slumped to .250 with only eight home runs. Boog Powell missed the first two months with an injury. Buford dropped from 19 to five home runs and hit .206. Merv Rettenmund didn't contribute as expected. The Orioles clawed back into contention late in the year, but couldn't catch up. Billy Martin had been wrong; he didn't win the pennant—he only won the division, then fell to the Oakland A's in the playoffs. Frank Robinson had a very difficult season in Los Angeles, butting heads with manager Walter Alston, having his worst season to date with a .251 average, 19 home runs, and 59 RBIs, and was traded to the Angels after the season. Although it was a subpar season for Frank, the Orioles certainly could have used his 19 homers, as only one Oriole hit more than 12 for the season.

It would be a mistake to assume that Frank Robinson was the only reason for the Orioles' fantastic run from 1966 to 1971. He was a major ingredient—perhaps the most important, providing a needed spark—but only an ingredient. Frank and Brooks seemed to bring out the best in each other and they had a lot of help from teammates. Together they won four pennants in six years. While Brooks never won a pennant without Frank, it is a fact that Frank only won one pennant in 10 years in Cincinnati and never won another with three different teams after leaving Baltimore.

Brooks's drop in production cost him; his pay was cut $5,000 to $105,000 for 1973. When asked by reporters if he thought he was slowing down, he laughed. "I only have one speed and it's never changed. That speed is slow." But it was no laughing matter. He was now 36 years old, the age when a big drop in hitting, such as the one he had experienced, raises the specter of the beginning of the end.

Besides the decrease in home runs and batting average, there were also other, less obvious signs that age was catching up with Brooks. He was mistaken for the maître d' at the Pfister Hotel while the team was in Milwaukee. On a team flight he asked the flight attendant if he could have dinner and she replied, "Yes, after I've served the ball players." And there was trouble at a commercial shoot for Vitalis, the hair tonic, when the ad executives got a good look at Brooks's head when he showed up—not exactly the luxurious mane needed to sell hair products. "We had seen a picture of Brooks in his cap, with hair peeking out around the edges, and everything looked perfect," said Martin Blackman, the lawyer who had set up the commercial. It was shot anyway, but with careful camera angles that masked his follicular liabilities.

After years of roster stability, the Orioles were a changing team. For 1973, only 12 of the 25 Orioles who lost to the Pirates in the 1971 World Series were still around. Brooks's clubhouse role shifted somewhat. Much older than most of the other players now, he sometimes went his own way, often dressing and getting home as soon as possible after home games. He had never been the kind of guy to get up in a clubhouse and make speeches, but he still had an unmistakable presence and was very much appreciated by the younger players. His attitude helped pass along the Oriole way of life. "Brooks was a class act," says pitcher Don Hood, who played for the Orioles in 1973 and 1974. "He was one of the best guys I ever played with. He was one of the few guys, being a veteran, who always took time and talked to rookies and new guys. He just went out of his way to be nice and welcome you to the team.

"He had a great sense of humor and was easy to talk to," continues Hood. "One of the best things of my career was meeting and getting to know Brooks Robinson. My first major league win came in Oakland. Brooks hit a three-run homer to win it. After the game, he came up to me and gave me the bat. He was such a nice guy; sometimes that's unusual from a superstar. When I first got to the big leagues, my friends would come up to the games and they all wanted to meet Brooks Robinson. I would go up to him and say, 'There's some friends here who want to meet you,' and he would say, 'Sure, no problem.' And he would always take his time and talk to them and sign autographs. It always made me feel great that he was so nice to my friends and they always left thinking, 'What a great guy to meet.'"

After hitting two home runs on Opening Day in 1973, Brooks only got one in the next eight weeks and he was hitting less than .200 by mid-June. When he was selected to the All-Star team by the fans, writers harped upon the obvious—that he was only picked because of sentiment—a popularity vote; a lifetime achievement award. An article in the *Sporting News* pointed out that 10 American League third basemen were outhitting him at the time.

The Oriole team as a whole rebounded from 1972 and was back on top. The heart of the pitching staff was still present. In mid-August, with Brooks finally hitting, the Orioles won 18 of 23, including 14 in a row, and pulled away to win the division handily.

Brooks hit at close to a .300 clip the final two and a half months to finish at .257. He passed Pie Traynor as the all-time major league leader for hits by a third baseman with his 2,417th early in the season. August 18, he got hit number 2,500. Brooks and teammates celebrated afterward by eating a watermelon the clubhouse boy had brought emblazoned with "2500" on its side. "You can go 0-for-600 now and still wind up hitting .250," joked Paul Blair (actually the number was 781).

Waiting for the Orioles in the playoffs were the defending World Champion A's. Jim Palmer staked the Orioles to a one-game lead with a complete game shutout. Catfish Hunter evened the series up the next day, getting late-inning help from Rollie Fingers, who gave up an RBI single to Brooks in the eighth, then shut the door to preserve the 6–3 win.

The series shifted to Oakland where the A's won Game Three in dramatic fashion. Both Mike Cuellar and Ken Holtzman threw complete games. Oakland shortstop Bert Campaneris ended the game when he led off the 11th inning with a home run to break the 1–1 tie. The Orioles bounced back to stave off elimination in Game Four. Trailing 4–0 in the seventh inning with men on first and second, Brooks got Baltimore on the board with a single to center field off Vida Blue. Andy Etchebarren followed with a three-run homer. Bobby Grich provided the winning run with a home run for the Orioles in the eighth. Catfish Hunter then slammed the door on the Orioles with a complete game, five-hit shutout, winning 3–0. Brooks had a single in the seventh and a double in the ninth, but the Orioles could not score against the A's Hall of Fame–bound pitcher. The A's went on to win their second consecutive World Series, supplanting the Orioles as the American League dynasty team.

Brooks started the 1974 season well and was hitting .311 at the All-Star break when he was once again voted in as starter—this time with no controversy—and played in a record 14th losing All-Star game. While he was hitting well, he had a few more errors than usual, mostly on bad throws. In May, Palmer asked, in front of writers, "Which is higher Brooks, your batting average or your fielding average?"

The Orioles struggled to stay in contention, however, fighting a multitude of slumps and injuries. They sank to eight games out by August 29, were barely playing .500 ball, and appeared to have little chance of repeating as division winners. In late August, the remaining veterans of the World Series years decided to revive the kangaroo court. Hendricks assumed the bench as judge. Just to prove that he was impartial, he quickly fined Brooks for undressing too soon after a game and Blair for trotting onto the field with a chocolate bar in his pocket.

While the kangaroo court helped loosen things up, the Orioles still needed help on the field. The players realized that they no longer had the overall power to supply the regular three-run home runs that Earl Weaver coveted and grew frustrated at Weaver's insistence on maintaining the same offensive approach. A players-only meeting was held at Paul Blair's house, and they agreed to begin squeezing every base out of every hit. They began stealing, bunting, running, and manufacturing runs one at a time—regardless of what sign the manager gave. "It took Earl about three or four games to finally figure out what the heck we were doing in that situation," Brooks later said. "And I think he ended up saying, 'Well, you'd better be right.' That was one of the times that, I think, the guys got a little upset at Earl. But it worked out well. And Earl loved us all anyway."

Earl certainly loved the results. The Orioles were suddenly a team on fire. Jim Palmer returned from the disabled list and Boog Powell began hitting home runs like it was 1970. By mid-September, it was anybody's race. The previous Oriole division winners had won by at least eight games—this was their first nail-biter. The pressure and emotional strain were exhausting. Every game in September held a playoff atmosphere. The Orioles were winning almost every day; and winning almost every day, it seemed, by one run.

With a week to go, the Orioles, Yankees, and Red Sox were neck and neck and neck. The Orioles won games the last week on an Etchebarren suicide-squeeze bunt, a Tommy Davis two-run hit that squirted off the end of his bat, a 17th-inning topped roller, and a bases loaded walk.

On October 1 against the Tigers, Brooks chugged all the way from first on Etchebarren's pinch-hit double to left center in the ninth inning to give the Orioles a 7–6 win. It was their eighth straight win, 15th in the last 17, and 28th in their last 34 games. They had won 15 one-run games in that stretch, and in the tight race where one error could mean the difference between winning the division or not, they did not commit a single error between September 22 and October 1.

After the Tiger game, the Yankees were playing in Milwaukee—a Brewer win would give the Orioles the division title. Brooks, Etchebarren, and McNally retreated to Weaver's hotel room at the Sheraton-Cadillac Hotel in Detroit at 11 P.M. with several coaches and writers. For three hours they listened to a phone—Weaver had asked Brewer president Bud Selig to place a phone next to a radio at County Stadium in Milwaukee—and Weaver relayed the play-by-play. Weaver grew hoarse as the game went into extra innings and Etchebarren took over. The room erupted when George Scott got a base hit in the 10th with the bases loaded to win the game for the Brewers and the division title for the Orioles.

Once again, the Orioles met the A's in the playoffs. In the opener, the Orioles won 6–3 over Hunter. Brooks hit a solo homer and made a diving stop behind third and a long throw to get Dick Green. The A's were too strong, however, and rebounded to win the playoffs, then won their third consecutive World Series. It would be the last hurrah for the old Orioles. Cuellar was 22–10, McNally won 16, and Blair had a solid year with 17 homers and a .261 average. Brooks hit .288, his best average since 1965. He finished the season with 2,698 career hits. Easy math showed that two decent years of 151 hits each would give him the magic number of 3,000. The way he finished the 1974 season, it did not seem out of reach.

Brooks's autobiography, *Third Base Is My Home*, was published in 1974. While it had become popular for many athletes to brag about their sexual exploits in books at the time (Joe Pepitone, Johnny Bench, Joe Namath . . .), Brooks's book, coauthored by writer Jack Tobin, was often found on the shelf in church libraries. In addition to recounting his childhood and baseball career, he voiced his view of his obligation to the community: "I feel strongly that public sports figures must not only support our own area of interest but provide a helping hand to the many others less fortunate than we. We really receive much more than we give when we share something of ourselves with organizations like Little League, churches, hospitals and the many charitable groups that call on us from time to time."

He devoted an entire chapter to his religious beliefs, stating, "I believe in Jesus Christ, and Christianity, thanks to my parents, has been a part of my life as long as I can remember." He gave advice to young athletes: "Take the time to thank everyone who has helped you in any way down the avenue of success in your particular endeavor. . . . Learn to appreciate what God has given you. . . . Trial and tribulation will be with us along much of the way we must walk through life, and it will be impossible to take a single step forward without strong, deep-seated faith."

It was somewhat unusual for a major sports star to take up valuable pages with messages of a religious nature, but Brooks had never been shy about sharing the fact that religion played a major role in his life. In a 1972 article in *Guideposts*, he wrote, "As you move through life, winning some, losing some, you begin to see that what really counts is your consistency, your overall performance. . . . There is no substitute for work. . . . So many times I've seen good come out of what seemed a setback. The Bible explains it this way: All things work together for good to them that love God. I don't pretend to understand all the deep truth behind this, but the way I've seen it work is that when you begin to love God more, you love self less. This makes you more tolerant, more grateful; it makes you less subject to stresses, and—almost incidentally—less inclined to make mistakes. . . . A large part of success is simply good timing."

Brooks had been a member of the Fellowship of Christian Athletes since his early days in the majors. He had been particularly impressed watching his mentor George Kell address a full house at Emmanuel Baptist Church in Little Rock in the late 1950s, and while he did not make ostentatious displays on the field, he didn't hesitate to offer his beliefs when asked. Brooks was quoted in the *Sporting News* as saying, "I believe that anything worthwhile we may accomplish, we accomplish because of God's strength and under his direction. And it should be for his glory and not our own."

Brooks had regularly attended a Methodist church in Baltimore throughout his baseball career, when his schedule allowed, while Connie and the kids had attended mass at a Catholic church. "I recognized the need to share religion with my family," he said in a 1977 article, "How Famous Parents Pass on Their Religious Values." "I began to realize that something was left out of our family life when the kids went off to church with Connie: they wanted to know why their dad wasn't going with them." Brooks felt that the kids had a point and that it was important for the family to worship together. He began studying the Catholic faith with Oriole chaplain (and tennis partner) Monsignor Martin A. Schwalenberg, Jr. He was received into the Catholic faith in the late 1960s at the Church of the Nativity in Timonium. "On Sundays, when we sit together and pray together, we have something special to share. These sessions make us a stronger family."

As the 1975 season progressed, it appeared that Brooks Robinson suddenly needed help from a higher power while on the baseball field. He had only one extra base hit through early May and that was a routine fly ball that fell for a triple when two outfielders backed off at the same time. He was bothered by a bad thumb, could no longer drive the ball, and had trouble getting around on a fastball. He had fought slumps periodically throughout his career and they always eventually cleared. But now, as he turned 38 years old, he experienced the slump-that-never-clears, the one every aging player knows is out there. His average dropped as low as .159 in midseason. July 7, Brooks suffered another of the indignities that all veterans dread: mired in a 3-for-25 nosedive, he was removed for a pinch hitter (Tom Shopay) in the ninth inning of a game against the Yankees. It was the first time he had been pinch-hit for since 1958. His 15-year streak of All-Star Games came to an end—the first one he had missed since 1960. His average never got higher than .210 after the beginning of May and he finished the season at .201.

15. Poor Brooks

IN THE SPRING OF 1976, there were questions at third base for the Orioles for the first time since 1959. Brooks Robinson, preparing to turn 39, was coming off a season in which he had led American League third basemen in fielding percentage for the record 11th time. He had committed only nine errors—the fewest of any season since he became a starter—and won his 16th consecutive Gold Glove. The soft hands and reflexes were still there in the field. Any quickness he may have lost was offset by knowledge achieved through years of experience in positioning and knowing how to charge balls and how to make the split-second decisions of where to throw. He was still a much better than average major league third baseman.

At the plate, however, it was a different matter. Brooks had hit better than .260 only once (1974) in the past four seasons. In the days before the benefits of weight training for baseball players were appreciated, his power had experienced a tremendous drop—he hadn't hit double digits in home runs since 1971. Many were questioning openly if it wasn't time for Brooks to hang it up, to stop before he tarnished his image.

Cognizant of the effects of age, Brooks had worked hard at conditioning over the winter and showed up in Miami at 188 pounds—well under his usual reporting weight of 198. Reporters gathered in the spring, like circling buzzards, waiting for the carcass of another old-timer to finally lie down and give up. Brooks told anyone who would listen that all he wanted was a chance, but he knew he wouldn't have all season this time. "I figure I've got about 35 or 40 games to show Earl that I can still hit," he said. "If I can't do it anymore, I'll just quit."

Weaver outwardly gave Brooks support. "He probably can't hit with the power he had when he was younger. Other than that, we're expecting Brooksie to do everything he's always done. You never know when a guy has reached the end of his career. The only way to find out is to let him go out there and play. . . . In 1974 he was the second-best among our regulars with a .288 average. That was only the season before last, and I can't believe Brooksie has lost his hitting that quick." Weaver had privately told Brooks at the end of the 1975 season that the third base job was his and he wouldn't lose it in spring training—he would give him time, but they both knew he would have to hit better than .201.

Brooks dodged questions from reporters who asked about retirement. "I'm going to play this year, and then sit down and decide what I'm going to do next year," he told them. "I may play one or two or three or four or five more seasons. I don't have any set timetable. If I don't hit and somebody else plays, I'm still going to be here for at least the rest of this year trying to help them with what I can do.

"I just don't think you go from .290 to .201 without some explanation other than just losing it. I got into some bad habits last year and never got straightened out. Now I've put a lot of pressure on myself because I know I've got to come back and hit much better if I'm going to continue to play."

It was obvious that he was not ready to consider giving up the game. "I still love to play baseball. It's easy for somebody else to sit on the outside and tell you to quit but nobody ever wants to quit. I'm gonna play forever. I know a lot of people say athletes should quit while they are on top, but I don't necessarily agree with that. If a man can contribute something, why shouldn't he continue if that's what he wants to do?" Brooks startled many by adding that if the Orioles did not feel he could help them, he would be open to a trade to someone willing to play him regularly. "I'd like to retire in a Baltimore uniform, but if I can't make it here, and somebody else wants me, I'll go. I would never want to embarrass the club, and I wouldn't want the Orioles to feel they had an obligation to me."

One man, particularly, hoped Brooks would hurry up and go: 25-year-old Doug DeCinces, the Orioles' third base heir apparent. While DeCinces was a solid player who had a lot of power at the plate, he was only fair defensively. He was not particularly smooth in the field—and comparisons with the man he hoped to replace did nothing to make him look smoother. He had hit .251 in 61 games as a rookie in 1975, filling in around the infield as a utility man. Initially, DeCinces was appropriately deferential, but as reporters continued to prod him, he became more vocal about being ready for his chance. A major league baseball player has only a brief window of opportunity for a career. DeCinces's own clock was ticking; he had put in several good seasons in the minors and was now ready.

In March, DeCinces voiced his frustration to the media over Brooks hanging around so long. "If something doesn't happen this year, I'll have to force a trade." He added, "The only thing that makes it easier is that I'm sitting behind a Brooks Robinson. I have a lot of respect for him. Fact is, we're very good friends. But I'm twenty-five. These are my peak years. I've waited too long already."

The 1976 Orioles were essentially a new team. Other than Brooks, only Belanger, Blair, Hendricks, Cuellar, and Palmer remained from the glory years and only Palmer was still effective. Cuellar was 39 years old, headed for a 4–13 season, and would be released at the end of the season. Blair would hit .197, Hendricks .139—they would both be gone before the year was over.

The Orioles had a new general manager, Hank Peters, who was committed to rebuilding the team. In addition to the six holdovers, the Oriole clubhouse contained a bunch of youngsters and a few new players obtained in trades. Just before the season, the Orioles traded happy and productive players, Don Baylor and 20-game-winner Mike Torrez, to the A's for disgruntled Ken Holtzman and Reggie Jackson. Both were unsigned at the time. Jackson, eyeing a fortune the next year on the free agent market, promptly held out for more money while Holtzman sulked. As compared to the camaraderie of the past 15 years, there was an emptiness in the clubhouse, especially for the older players who remembered the good years but were no longer able to perform as they had in the past.

As the season began, Brooks did nothing to silence his detractors, getting only one hit in the first six games. The team got off to a slow start as well and the others were not hitting enough to take up the slack. Brooks was 1-for-19 by April 18. He struggled on, convinced that he only needed to make some adjustments or get some extra batting practice; convinced that he would come out of it. The aging athlete reaches a time when he realizes that the small aches and pains that years earlier only took a day or two to resolve now linger for weeks. There is always something—a sore heel, a stiff back, a tender elbow, a tight hamstring—that prevents him from performing at maximum level. He longs for a day, just one day, when everything feels good again; when there is no soreness, no stiffness; when the muscles feel loose and strong, just like when he was young. But those days become harder to find. While people in everyday life can kid themselves, or even temporarily fool others, into believing that age is not catching up to them, it is hard for a professional baseball player. The daily box score and the Sunday averages give a black-and-white picture that is unavoidable.

On defense, he was still Brooks Robinson. "I saw him make great plays when I played [1976 and 1977]," said pitcher Tippy Martinez, "but older players would say, 'You should have seen him in the 1960s and early '70s.'" At the plate, it was becoming painfully clear that Brooks Robinson could no longer hit major league pitching.

The situation weighed heavily on Earl Weaver, who appreciated all they had been through together. "He won a lot of games for me," said Weaver in 2012, "and he was the best person I ever met in baseball. But it became obvious we were going to have to do something. It was really hurtful to have to sit him down. I worried about that for over a month. How could I sit down a guy who had done as much for me as Brooks? I talked myself into waiting, I kept hoping he would turn things around and come back. I was hoping something else would happen that I wouldn't have to make the decision."

But the decision was inevitable. In mid-May, DeCinces had been in the lineup for 10 straight games, subbing at second for the injured Grich, and was hitting well. With Grich ready to return and Brooks sitting on a .165 average, Weaver decided to keep DeCinces in the lineup. "When Grich got healthy, both he and DeCinces were hitting and we needed both bats in the lineup," Weaver said. "Brooks was still below .200. I finally made the decision that the time had come—it was best for the organization and the team. I called Brooks in and told him." It was May 17, the day before Brooks's 39th birthday. "He took it well—he could have really made it hard for me. But he just said, 'Skip, do what you have to do. I'll be here if you need me.'"

Speaking of the anguish that went into the moment, Weaver said in 2005, "Those are heartbreaking things that eat at you forever and ever and ever. You just don't forget those kinds of things. Telling Brooks 'I've got to take you out of the line-up,' that still eats at me."

Brooks refused to show a bitter side to the press and was noted to demonstrate good spirits and humor on the bench. He called to coach Billy Hunter, "Are we using the same signs tonight?"

"What do you want to know for Brooksie?" asked Belanger.

"I might have to come off the bench," he replied with a wink.

"It's no big deal. If my name's in the lineup, it is. If it isn't, it isn't," Brooks told reporters after watching DeCinces play an errorless game at third with a single and a double at the plate. "Doug has been swinging the bat real good, and he deserves the chance to play. It wouldn't be fair to him to stick him in there for a few games and then jerk him out if he doesn't hit. That's part of baseball."

It's never easy to replace a legend and it was especially hard for DeCinces, as he had to replace a man who was not only a legend on the field, but one of the most popular men in baseball. Reporters would seek out DeCinces in every city and ask him some variation of the same questions about whether he thought he could replace Brooks. Every missed play was an opportunity for the fans to rub it in. He received hate mail. He heard boos, at home and on the road, when the lineup was announced with DeCinces playing third base.

The worst came in Baltimore against the Twins June 6, 1976. With DeCinces's parents, wife, and son in the stands, along with his grandmother, who was seeing him play for the first time, fans began chanting, "We want Brooks!" when DeCinces took the field at third base. Cuellar started on the mound and was being hit hard. With the bases loaded, Larry Hisle hit one down the third base line, DeCinces dove and knocked it down, but the ball trickled over by the tarp, and two runs came in. The fans started the "We want Brooks!" chant again. The next batter hit a sharp bouncer that DeCinces took off the chest and everyone was safe. The chants grew louder. The next inning, DeCinces fielded a grounder and threw it over the first baseman's head for another error, and the fans loudly voiced their displeasure. When he came up to bat, he was met with boos and more chants and promptly struck out. He came back in the game to have three hits, including a home run and a triple, but nothing seemed to quiet the fans' protest.

And it wasn't just the fans who had problems. The pitchers also missed Brooks. Palmer and DeCinces had a public press-fueled spat a couple of years later after Palmer felt that DeCinces should have made a difficult play on a crucial batter late in a game. Palmer later wrote that the feud wasn't his fault or DeCinces's fault, "It was Brooks Robinson's fault. Even though Brooks wasn't playing that day . . . it was definitely his fault. If Brooks hadn't been the best third baseman of all time, the rest of the Orioles wouldn't have taken it for granted that any ball hit anywhere within the same county as Brooks would be judged perfectly, fielded perfectly, and thrown perfectly, nailing (perfectly) what seemed like every single opposing batter. And then we wouldn't have been disappointed in any other third baseman who judged, fielded, threw, or nailed any less than perfectly . . . which means basically, all other third basemen ever, including Doug DeCinces. We were spoiled. Especially me."

There was no friction between the two third basemen, however. "Brooks did everything to make it easier for me," DeCinces said in 1977, but it was something that would take time for everyone else to accept. DeCinces hit .259 in 1977, and when he got off to an even worse start in 1978, his agent suggested that he undergo psychotherapy. His psychiatrist, Skip Connor, who specialized in counseling athletes and executives, later explained to *Sports Illustrated*, "Here's a guy who has all the ingredients—size, speed, ability, good looks, education—and he comes into a situation that may preclude greatness. How many guys who have replaced legends have turned out to be outstanding in their own right? Historically it's almost a no-win situation. And because Brooks was hero-worshiped in Baltimore, whatever Doug did was viewed by fans, if not management and maybe even his teammates, as inherently inferior. Doug brought with him a personal sensitivity that made it impossible for him to ignore these circumstances. . . . Our conclusion was: let his subconscious do his thinking . . . taking his mind off details, letting his body do the work." DeCinces let his body do the work and eventually recovered from the psycho-trauma to have a 15-year career with the Orioles and Angels in which he hit 20 home runs or more five times and became the second best Oriole third baseman ever.

At Brooks's request, the Orioles began quietly looking for a team that might want him to play regularly and brokered a deal that would have sent him to the White Sox just before the June 15 trading deadline. Brooks nixed the deal, however, because White Sox owner Bill Veeck would not give him a contract through 1978. In late June, with DeCinces in a slump himself, Brooks returned to the starting lineup and went on an eight-game hitting streak (13-for-28), but it was much too little to boost his average up to respectability. He would end the season at .211 with three home runs in 71 games.

Brooks continued to say he wanted a chance to play somewhere in 1977 and both he and the team made a conscious effort to avoid any note of finality as the end of the 1976 season approached. Oriole fans wanted to have a special day, however. An unofficial farewell was planned by the volunteer groups the Oriole Advocates and the Waverly Improvement Association, which represented the neighborhood where Memorial Stadium was located.

Perhaps since it wasn't officially announced as Brooks's final game, only 8,119 fans showed up for the meaningless game on the last day of the season. Before the game, with reporters hovering around Brooks, Jim Palmer asked, "Brooks, who's giving the eulogy?" When the Orioles gathered on the dugout step before the game, Belanger urged Brooks to "lead us out for the last time." Brooks ran out to a standing ovation, then discovered after a few steps that he was the only player on the field—the rest of the team remained in the dugout howling with laughter.

Five times Brooks got standing ovations during the game. He was hitless the first three times up to bat, then hit a soft liner into center field for a single. The ball was retrieved and given to Brooks. As he left the field for a pinch runner, the applause continued and rose to a crescendo. He stopped at the dugout, took off his helmet, and waved. Fans, not satisfied, stopped the action on the field, chanting "We want Brooks." At the urging of teammates, Brooks stepped out again and saluted the fans once more. After retreating to the clubhouse, alone, Brooks sobbed. After the game he gave the ball to his daughter, Diana, with the inscription "Last hit, Memorial Stadium, 1976."

But Brooks wasn't quite ready to retire from baseball. The Orioles told him after the 1976 season that DeCinces would be the regular third baseman for 1977. Thinking he could still play, Brooks worked with coach Cal Ripken, Sr., over the winter to make adjustments on his hitting stroke. But there was no way to adjust the ticking clock.

The reserve clause had been struck down before the 1976 season and everybody was thinking about money now. Jackson, Grich, and pitcher Wayne Garland played out their options and signed huge contracts. But it was too late for Brooks Robinson. He would not get a huge contract. Actually, he was just hoping to get any kind of a contract. He communicated with both expansion teams, the Mariners and Blue Jays, inquiring about their interest. In November of 1976, he was left unprotected for the expansion draft but neither team selected him. He then requested that general manager Hank Peters shop him around to other teams that were in need of a regular third baseman—he wanted a two-year contract and assurance he would play every day—but there was little enthusiasm for committing to a 40-year-old infielder coming off a .211 season.

Looking back, Brooks later wrote, "Just about every player played too long. Everyone thinks that they can still do it. Everyone thinks that they've found the fountain of youth. . . . But I loved it, and never wanted to do anything else. The best thing that happened to me was to get no response from those two teams [Blue Jays and Mariners], and come back to Baltimore and finish up my career."

While he was worrying about his future in baseball, Brooks Robinson's name appeared prominently in the news in the fall of 1976. And for once, it was not in a good way. Baltimore residents were surprised to learn that Brooks was in serious financial trouble. August 12, Baltimore County Circuit Court Judge Edward A. DeWaters,

Jr., ruled that Brooks's house would be auctioned off due to a bad bank debt owed by the Brooks Robinson Sporting Goods Company.

The revelation was surprising because there had been few signs of trouble. After its humble conception over a couple of Cokes, the sporting goods company had grown consistently. Brooks had regularly contacted local schools, leagues, and semipro teams plugging the business. High school varsity jackets and uniforms throughout the area soon bore the distinctive little cloth patch of a cartoon figure in an Oriole uniform batting, wearing number five, with the words "Brooks Robinson Sporting Goods Company." By 1969, the business had added additional employees and they were doing $8,000 worth of business a year with Little Leagues alone. In an interview that year, Brooks and partner George Henderson estimated the worth of the original investment to be around $80,000.

They also began to make inroads with area professional teams. A short-lived Baltimore ABA team called the Claws wore Brooks Robinson Sporting Goods Company–supplied uniforms. In 1971, Brooks sold the Orioles on a double-knit uniform of solid bright orange. The Orioles soon dropped the hideous uniforms, rumor has it, because Boog Powell objected to looking like the world's largest pumpkin.

In the early 1970s, through hard work, the business experienced tremendous growth. They merged with a larger store and eventually had several locations, including the original one downtown on Howard Street, about a block from where Camden Yards is located now, and were also in a large department store. Quite a few local athletes, such as Orioles Don Baylor and Tom Shopay, worked there, further increasing the draw for local fans. By all appearances, the business was thriving. Brooks admittedly had little to do with the day-to-day operations, later explaining, "I'd usually be away from home, playing ball, from the time spring training began in March until the season ended in October, and then, when the season finally was over, I didn't want to spend my time in the store, I wanted to stay home and be with Connie and the kids. That was basically the agreement with George. He operated the business. I provided some of the capital. I trusted him and gave him complete control."

"We became the number one sporting goods store in Baltimore," says Bruce Genther, who worked there as a graphic artist from 1971 until it closed. "We did all the uniforms and lettering in-house, which no one else in the area was able to do back then."

"We were ahead of our time," adds Henderson. "We were drilling our own bowling balls, stringing our own rackets."

"If a pro team had a trade and needed a uniform in a pinch, they were referred to us," says Genther. "We did the nameplates for the back of the jerseys for the Orioles, the Colts, lettering for the Bullets, and sold a lot of equipment and uniforms to colleges and high school teams. We did a lot of special things for pro players. Some guys would come in for certain types of shoes and equipment."

George Henderson and Brooks Robinson were friends as well as co-owners; close enough that when Brooks converted to Catholicism in 1969, Henderson became his godfather. Brooks later became god-father to Henderson's son. The store was a success and a great place to work. "He [Brooks] was very interested in all his employees," says Bruce Genther. "He would go through and talk to everybody, secre-taries, art guys, salesmen—he would go in and visit. He genuinely wanted to know about us and our lives, honestly meaning it. He made us feel like superstars just for working there."

With the business going well, they decided to expand further by adding a satellite store in another city in 1974. They settled on York, Pennsylvania, in part because Brooks still had some ties to the com-munity in which he had begun his professional career. The Orioles had always drawn well from the area and Brooks's name was well known and popular there—it seemed like a good fit. The store was planned to be located in a soon to be built strip mall. A loan was taken out with the National Central Bank and Trust Company of York to help launch the new store. "This was 1974, the worst reces-sion since the Depression," says Henderson. "It was hard to get a loan then, even at double-digit interest rates. We felt fortunate to get the loan."

Trouble arose, through no fault of Henderson's or Robinson's, when the strip mall was held up by rival merchants whose lawyers forced a block to the construction. The steam shovels and grading equip-ment sat idle in the snow, waiting for the legal process to work. Meanwhile, interest on the loan accumulated. The new store never materialized. With no structure in place for the store, they had no place to go and the bank sued to recover the unpaid balance on the loan, $288,000.

"We had never missed a payment," says Henderson. "We had been in the sporting goods business 15 years—that's no fly-by-night thing."

It was in response to the foreclosure suit brought by the bank that the judge ordered the sale of both Brooks Robinson's and George Henderson's houses to pay off the debt as the men and their wives had personally guaranteed the loan. It progressed to the point that announcements were placed in the *Baltimore Sun* advertising the auction on September 7, posting that conditions of the sale required deposits by cash or certified check of $10,000 on each home at the time of sale.

The story went national. Rumors of the impending financial doom of Brooks Robinson flourished. Everyone was shocked at the news— Brooks had never been extravagant with his spending; he drove conservative cars, lived in a modest house, famously wore plain clothes, and spent his time with family. "Brooks Robinson has the best pair of hands in baseball," Milton Richman of United Press International wrote. "They're so good, they've earned him 16 straight 'Gold Glove' awards and nearly $2 million, yet they've also fumbled away all his finances. . . . How could it possibly happen to somebody like upstanding, clean-living Brooks Robinson, baseball's All-American boy?"

New York writer Phil Pepe noted, "Brooks Robinson says he's not ready to quit and others say he can't afford to quit and maybe they are all right. . . . If he must keep playing because he needs the money, that's sad. It boggles the mind to think of a great baseball star, of Brooks Robinson, being in such desperate financial shape that his home is in danger of being auctioned."

"He's very naive when it comes to business," an unnamed Oriole official was quoted by Pepe. "He's a wonderful guy and he's so trusting that if somebody comes to him and tells him to sign on the dotted line, he signs. Baseball is his whole life. It's the only thing he cares about and that's why he's in the financial shape he's in."

Pepe concluded, "To talk to him, to watch him, you would never think Brooks Robinson has financial problems or that he is at a serious crossroads in his life. He is still as pleasantly good-humored as ever, still as bubbly as a teenager."

Both Brooks and Connie obviously preferred not to have the entire country discussing their personal financial problems. Phrases like *fumbled away all his finances* and *can't afford to quit* were both hyperbolic and insulting, and for the first time in his career, he grew guarded around reporters. When asked in the clubhouse, Brooks only volunteered, "It's a temporary thing. We'll be all right in the long run."

Richman called the Robinson house and, catching Connie in a vulnerable state, was able to pry loose some statements that she later regretted. He quoted her as saying, "Poor Brooks, now we all know why he hasn't been able to play ball the past two years. I told him he worked 22 years playing ball, saving his money and now he has to start all over again. If he lives 500 years, he'll never get back all that he put into his business.

"You just don't know how something like that happens," she continued. "Brooks couldn't be at his sporting goods business all the time because he had to play ball. You have to put your trust and confidence in someone else in a case like that and suddenly you're told all the money is gone. Brooks isn't down or depressed at all though. He must keep everything inside him. He's unreal. He looks at me every five minutes and says, 'Are you all right?' I tell him, 'Yes, until I start thinking about what happened.'"

Richman also wrote that a neighborhood kid teased Diana, the Robinsons' eight-year-old daughter, saying "Ha ha, your father is going to the poor house," and she ran home and asked her father, "Daddy, they aren't going to take our house away are they?"

Fortunately, the answer to Diana's question was no. Gordon C. Murray, attorney for Robinson and Henderson, filed papers for an injunction to stop the sale. He soon announced that a compromise agreement had been reached with the bank.

But the trouble was only beginning. Brooks and George Henderson knew baseball very well, but neither had any formal business training. This lack of training may have contributed to the domino effect that ensued in the scramble to clear up the debt from the bank. Other suits were soon filed and made public. Uniroyal, Inc., of New Haven, Connecticut, sued for $5,131. The Albin Sales Company of

Baltimore sued for $4,700. Holloway Sportswear, Inc., of Jackson Center, Ohio, sued for $8,406. Baltimore County sued for back corporate taxes totaling a little over $7,200. In all, 10 claims amounting to nearly $30,000 were filed against the store in November and December. Before these suits could be addressed, Continental Corporation, a Baltimore real estate and mortgage holding company, filed suit claiming they were owed $43,400 in principal, interest, and commissions on a $35,000 promissory note signed in 1975. Not long after that, the Brooks Robinson Sporting Goods Company closed its doors for good.

"One of the saddest days of my life was when the business closed," says Genther. "But I got a wonderful letter saying, 'Dear Bruce, Thanks for all you did. Sorry it couldn't last. Signed, Brooks Robinson.' I've still got that letter framed, hanging in my den. It's one of my prized possessions. With everything that was going on—the troubles of the business, his baseball career coming to an end—he still took the time to personally write a note to his employees. That just shows you what kind of a guy he is."

The financial troubles didn't end with the closing of the store, however. There was still the little matter of paying off the bills. Brooks withdrew money from his personal savings and paid off the loans. The amount was later revealed by lawyer Ron Shapiro to be $179,500, with Brooks paying most of it.

Brooks refused to publicly blame anyone else, maintaining that he wasn't swindled by fast talkers as had been speculated. "It was just a bad move by me and my partners," he told Jim Murray of the *Los Angeles Times* in May 1977. He added that rumors of his financial demise were greatly exaggerated by the press. "I am by no means broke. It's all behind me now. I've gotten it all straightened out." He noted that his income as an executive with Crown Central Petroleum and as a representative for a toy and games company helped supplement his baseball income nicely.

That month, Brooks and Connie allowed Frederic Kelly of the *Baltimore Sun* to visit them in their house for an article on the whole affair. "It was just something that happened," Brooks told him. "I was never active in the business. I lent my name to it and I put some of my money into it, but I was never involved in the day-to-day operation of the business. I probably should have been, but I trusted other people to handle it." Brooks added that he had known for quite a while that something was wrong with the business but he thought Henderson could handle it. "I figured he knew what he was doing." He never really became alarmed until sometime in 1976 when "I realized things were not going to get any better." Although Brooks had to dip into his own funds to pay off the debt, he maintained that he "was never in any real danger" of personal bankruptcy.

An unidentified friend was quoted by Kelly, saying Brooks was not disillusioned or bitter from the affair. "He's not the type. He's more hurt than angry. But you'll never hear him say anything. He's totally incapable of uttering an unkind word about any human being."

Connie said that one good aspect of the whole business was the response of people who wanted to help. As with George Bailey in *It's a Wonderful Life*, people heard Brooks Robinson was in trouble and flocked to help. "We heard from people all over the country who wanted to help Brooks. They called or wrote and some of them even sent money in the mail. We sent it all back, of course, but the point is people cared enough to offer him what they had. One person offered him $10,000. It was absolutely incredible."

Connie, who had become much more cautious around the press after the initial ambush interview by Richman, concluded, "It's over and done with as far as we're concerned. It was an unfortunate thing. It had a great impact on us. Brooks was too trusting and he got hurt. But what's past is past and it doesn't do anyone any good to bring it up again."

"Connie's right, the less said the better," added Brooks. "I want to forget that part of my life and get on with something new." He said that the episode was "a learning experience" and there were no hard feelings with anyone.

"The press made me take the rap," says Henderson, summarizing the matter. "But there were a lot of other things involved that never came out. It hurt because some people would say, 'How could you do that to Brooks?' But the people who know, know what the real story is. It caused some strain between us initially, but me and Brooks are still friends. He's still my godson, my son is still his godson."

It was a sad chapter in the life of Brooks Robinson. But it was also an opportunity to display remarkable grace under pressure; character-revealing self-control. Brooks did not give in to the temptation to publicly berate his partners or air dirty laundry. He paid the debts and moved on. The troubles would soon be a mere footnote in the history of Brooks Robinson.

Still hoping to continue to play baseball, in December of 1976 Brooks told a reporter, "I hope to work out a long-term agreement with the Orioles to work in some capacity with them when my playing days are over, although this has not been discussed yet with Jerry Hoffberger or Hank Peters." He soon announced that he would return to the Orioles as a player-coach for the 1977 season, intimating that he would like to do more playing than coaching. The salary was not divulged, but it appeared he took a sizable pay cut to stay with the team as the Orioles officially asked the league and Players Association to waive the requirement that a player sit out the first 60 days for a contract having a cut of greater than 20 percent.

As spring training progressed, Brooks appeared to finally accept what most baseball people felt and told reporters that this would be his last year. Opening Day 1977 was the first since 1957 that Brooks did not start at third base for the Orioles. He played very little once the season began.

April 19, on a damp, foggy night in front of a small (4,826) Memorial Stadium crowd, the Orioles were trailing the Indians, led by their manager, Frank Robinson, 5–2 in the bottom of the 10th. With one out and Lee May at the plate, Brooks Robinson appeared in the on deck circle to pinch-hit for Larry Harlow. The crowd, which had thinned after the Indians scored three in the top of the inning, broke into warm applause when Brooks stepped out of the dugout. May singled to make the score 5–3 with two men on base.

Manager Frank Robinson conferred with pitcher Dave LaRoche on the mound. After the game, Brooks joked to reporters, "Frank probably looked up and said, 'Here comes old Brooksie. It's a tailor-made double play.'" He also admitted that he didn't expect much from the at bat himself. "It's tough when you go up and pinch hit. It takes a special kind of guy, and I don't think I'm that guy."

In what was only Brooks's third plate appearance in nine games on the season, he worked a full count, then fouled off a number of pitches, several of which barely made it into the stands to avoid being caught. LaRoche, perhaps on the scouting report that the old man couldn't get around on a fastball anymore, kept throwing heaters and Brooks kept getting a piece of them, staying alive. Finally, LaRoche came in with a curve and Brooks launched it into the left field seats for a three-run homer to give the Orioles a 6–5 win. The press box—normally not a place for cheers—went crazy.

Afterward, an emotional Weaver told reporters, "Outside of our World Series wins, seeing Brooks fighting off those pitches to run the count to 3-and-2 and finally hitting a home run was one of my biggest thrills." The home run, number 268, would be the last major league home run for Brooks Robinson.

In midseason, Oriole third base coach Billy Hunter left to manage the Rangers. Cal Ripken, Sr., moved from bullpen coach to third base coach and Brooks took his place, doing little more than answering the bullpen phone.

Brooks refused to sulk, however. In July, he told reporters that he was enjoying his final season even though he was not playing and was no longer an integral part of the team. "The kids are doing a good job. They have a lot of enthusiasm and they believe they can win."

"Brooks could have caused a lot of problems for me the last couple of years," Weaver told a reporter later in the year. "He carries a lot of weight in this town. But because he's the kind of person he is, he made the end easier for everybody." It was a struggle to show up and watch every day, though. He was dying to get out there and play.

No matter his station on the team, Brooks's attitude toward his fellow players never changed. Dave Criscione was a career minor league catcher who was called up to the Orioles for two weeks at the end of July. He would endear himself to Baltimore fans forever by hitting .333 (3-for-9), including an 11th-inning walk-off homer against the Brewers, before being sent back down. "My locker for those two weeks was right next to Brooks's locker," says Criscione. "That was great. You don't meet too many people nicer than Brooks. Even though he wasn't playing much, you could tell that he loved being with the guys; the camaraderie. He was real friendly to all the young guys. He looked after the younger players. He would sort of give you that wink and let you know, 'Don't worry about it, you belong here.' He would call you by your name or nickname and immediately made you feel like part of the team. That was important because initially you're worried about these guys, they're idols, untouchable, but he just acted like a regular guy.

"When I hit the walk-off home run, my brother was at the game and he came down to the clubhouse afterward. There was a bunch of reporters there asking me questions and Brooks just sat there and talked to my brother while he was waiting—just like I had been with the team for years. Brooks finally pointed to the crowd around me and said, 'He's been here for 10 days and he's already got more reporters than I've had in 20 years.'"

While not playing, Brooks managed to find ways to have fun and pass the time. He worked part-time in public relations for a toy company and brought one of their remote-controlled cars to the stadium. The players, and Earl Weaver, set up an elaborate race course in the clubhouse and those who arrived early every day would take turns timing their runs through the course. They decided to take it on the road and try it on the artificial turf in Kansas City. During pregame warm-ups, Brooks sent the car out and circled the Royals coach's feet while he was hitting fungoes. Then Weaver stuck a note on the car and sent it over to Royals manager Whitey Herzog.

August 21, Brooks went on the voluntarily retired list, announcing that he would remain with the team as a coach for the rest of the season. He was hitting .149 (7-for-47) for the season and had been to the plate only six times since June 5. He was given a standing ovation in Minnesota following the news of his retirement before the game. He appeared somewhat apprehensive and embarrassed by the attention. After he disappeared into the dugout runway, the Twins personnel in the dugout and players on the field joined in warm applause that would not stop until, coaxed by Belanger, he stuck his head out for a curtain call. "He's such a humble guy," said Belanger, "that you can't help but be affected by something like that. Seeing him stand out there, I was a little choked up. I think he was, too."

The move to retire early was made necessary by the return of catcher Rick Dempsey from the disabled list. The Orioles still had a shot at catching the Yankees and needed active players who could contribute. Team management had been agonizing over the decision for several days. Hank Peters told reporters that he would not have made the move if Brooks had balked. "It's the logical thing to do," Brooks told reporters. "The kids have done the job all year, and they deserve the chance to finish it."

Brooks said that leaving early was "no big deal. I was going to retire at the end of the year anyhow. All I'm doing is retiring six weeks earlier."

Dempsey, discussing the night later, said, "I struck out my first three at bats, and he [Brooks] said, 'They retired me for that?'"

The Orioles held a Thanks Brooks Robinson Day September 18, 1977. This time a Memorial Stadium regular season record crowd of 51,789 showed up to pay tribute. Brooks rode into and around the stadium in a 1955 Cadillac. Brooks's entire family and Connie's family were on hand and sat in the infield while dignitaries and friends spoke during the hour-long ceremony before the game. Paul Richards came from Texas to be part of the proceedings and was introduced on the field along with Willie Miranda, Ron Hansen, Dick Hall, and George Staller. Associated Press sportswriter Gordon Beard, a Baltimore native, emceed the event and reminded the crowd of Reggie Jackson's famous remark that if he played in New York, they'd name a candy bar after him. Beard added, "Nobody's ever named a candy bar for Brooks. Around here, we name our children after him." Although Brooks had requested no gifts, stating that any gift should go to the Johns Hopkins Hospital Children's Center, owner Jerry Hoffberger presented him with a sports car. Hoffberger said, "The piece of life-saving equipment you were interested in for the Johns Hopkins Hospital Children's Center will be provided in your name, but we wanted you to have something for yourself." The Rawlings Sporting Goods Company surprised him with replicas of 14 of his 16 Gold Glove awards he had earned over the years but had given away. There was a congratulatory letter from President Jimmy Carter. Among other gifts was a used vacuum cleaner from teammate Lee May, who had been obtained by the Orioles in 1975. After May lugged the ancient appliance out on the field, he said, "I hope that Connie makes you put it to use in your retirement. If you look close, you'll see that this vacuum cleaner has a lot in common with you, Brooks—it has a lot of miles on it."

Earl Weaver had spent hours writing his speech, trying to express his feelings for Brooks. But when it came time for him to take the microphone, he became choked up and his eyes were so watery that he couldn't read what he had written. He threw away the sheet and spoke from the heart. He talked about the generosity of Brooks Robinson "to a manager nobody knew who had been a bush leaguer all his life until he arrived in Baltimore." He spoke about how he had wondered the first time he gave Brooks the take sign if he would obey it and how, when he did so, Weaver never had to worry about Brooks from that time on "because he was a ballplayer who always tried to do the right thing and almost always managed to." He thanked Brooks "for saving my job several times over the years." Weaver concluded with, "Thanks, Brooks. Thanks one million times."

Brooks took the microphone and told the crowd, "Never in my wildest dreams did I think that 23 years later I'd be standing here saying goodbye to so many people. I don't think I would want one day to change." He thanked Connie, "the most important person in my life," and his parents: "I don't know how anybody could be more wonderful." He concluded, "It's been a wonderful 23 years."

Doug DeCinces pulled third base out of the ground and presented it to Brooks, with the crowd cheering wildly. Chuck Thompson called it "the single most effective and moving gesture I'd ever seen by one player to another."

Weaver later wrote, "I don't think I've ever heard a louder explosion of noise from Baltimore fans. Standing there looking at Brooks holding the base with that wonderful smile on his face and the crowd going wild in the background and all of the love and warmth permeating the stadium I thought, 'I'd like to be like Brooks Robinson. The guys who never said no to anybody, the ones that everybody loves because they deserve to be loved, those are my heroes." Brooks left the field for the last time to "Auld Lang Syne" and a multitude of tears.

16. Cooperstown

THE DRUDGERY OF THE LAST TWO SEASONS made it easier for Brooks to walk away from playing baseball without looking back. Brooks had consistently stated over the years that he had no interest in coaching or managing after his playing days were over and he remained true to his word in spite of several offers. In 1978 he turned down a chance to be head baseball coach at the University of Southwest Louisiana, where a longtime friend was athletic director. There were feelers from a number of major league teams, most enthusiastically from the White Sox, but he was not swayed. He knew the demands of coaching and had no particular desire to spend so much time away from home now that he was no longer playing.

Although the sporting goods store had closed and he had gotten out of the restaurant business as well, Brooks had plenty of business opportunities. In addition to the toy and games company, Avalon Hill Games, he continued his relationship with Crown Central Petroleum. He had been associated with them since 1968 as a spokesman, making numerous appearances all across the region on their behalf. He maintained an office with the company and would eventually work for them for over 30 years.

There were also speaking engagements, frequent local commercials, and a few national ones, such as the one he shared with Frank Robinson for Lite Beer from Miller in 1980. It concluded with Brooks saying, "Now I know we're incredibly alike, but don't be confused. We are not identical twins."

Frank: "I'm at least two inches taller than he is."

In the aftermath of the financial troubles with the sporting goods store, Brooks began a business association with Ron Shapiro, a Baltimore attorney and Oriole season ticket holder, who had been brought together with Brooks by Orioles owner Jerry Hoffberger. Together, they formed Personal Management Associates, a company that helped athletes manage their money with Shapiro acting as a player's agent. They soon brought in Mark Belanger. With Robinson and Belanger helping to recruit players, the firm quickly became a success. When the Orioles won the World Series in 1983, PMA represented 20 members of the team. Eventually, they worked with over 40 American League baseball players, including Eddie Murray, Cal Ripken, Jr., and Kirby Puckett.

Shapiro's son, Mark, would become general manager of the Cleveland Indians in 2001. "I remember Brooks Robinson wanted to give my dad his 15th Gold Glove (as a thank you for his assistance)," he told MLB.com in 2009. "And my dad wouldn't take it. [Robinson] rang our doorbell and ran away, and there was a Rawlings Gold Glove at our front door."

The honors soon began to roll in. Brooks was inducted into the new Orioles Hall of Fame (he and Frank were appropriately the first two members in 1977). He was inducted into the Arkansas Hall of Fame in January 1978. The Orioles retired his number April 14, 1978. Fans voted him to the Orioles Silver Anniversary team, honored before a Baltimore game on June 24, 1979. Brooks led all players with 50,295 votes; Frank was second with 45,142.

Soon after retiring, Brooks began working as a television commentator for Oriole games. Although there was an occasional complaint from an uptight purist about Brooks's homer attitude, constantly referring to the Orioles as "we," most fans enjoyed his fun, down-home demeanor and relaxed comments; it was like listening to your uncle call a baseball game. Referred to as "Old number five" by partner Jon Miller, Brooks occasionally mixed in a surprisingly biting remark. He didn't whitewash anything when the Orioles blew games or the team's play was substandard. Once after the Orioles lost a close game in the ninth, he said, "Good teams put those games out of their minds. At the same time, good teams win those games." Another time he characterized the team's play as "an embarrassment, going through the motions" and, disappointed with their effort, added, "With all the money these guys are making, let them take a little abuse now and then."

His other booth partner, longtime Oriole broadcaster Chuck Thompson, later wrote, "On the air, Brooks enjoyed what he was doing, but I got the feeling that he was thinking, 'Doggone it, I wish I was out there doing it instead of sitting here watching.'"

Working about 50 road games and 10 home games a year, the television job gave Brooks a chance to do something connected with baseball without playing. He told a writer in 1982, "When you retire, what you miss most is the camaraderie. The best thing was always putting on your uniform to play, but at least now I'm still in the game. It wouldn't be the same without baseball."

In 1985 he added, "I really think the TV thing is what helped me not miss baseball like some other players do." The only part of the job Brooks didn't enjoy was the travel. Thompson advised him to take Connie with him whenever possible and he followed that advice, especially once the kids were grown. Brooks would end up working on television until 1993 when, after his last child had gotten married, he decided it was time to slow down and work more on his other business pursuits.

There were still opportunities to suit up and take the field. Brooks played in the First Annual Cracker Jack Old Timers Baseball Classic at Robert F. Kennedy Stadium in Washington in 1982. The game was broadcast by ESPN and featured DiMaggio, Banks, Koufax, Mathews, Spahn, Mays, Musial, and Aaron among the 50 former greats in the lineup. Proceeds went to the Association of Professional Ball Players of America—a nonprofit organization that aided ill and indigent former players and coaches. The event was repeated the next year with Brooks homering off Carl Erskine in front of 31,000 fans.

Old-timers games became popular in the 1980s and Brooks participated in many of them, enjoying the chance to get together with former teammates and opponents. He also became a regular at the Orioles' fantasy camp during the winter in Florida. Brooks and other former players coached and played with the middle-aged men who paid large amounts of money for the chance to spend time on the field with their idols. "We played together at the Orioles fantasy camps for 24 years," says Jim Gentile. "That was always great fun. It was good to get together and see all the guys. When we started we were in our forties and fifties and we could still play a little when we played against the campers' teams. Brooks could still amaze everybody with his glove. It was a good time. And it was fun to get to become friends with guys from other generations."

Cooperstown is a small, pleasant town of about 2,000 in central New York. The town derives its name from Judge William Cooper, father of author James Fenimore Cooper (*Last of the Mohicans*), who once owned most of the land in the area. The town sits on the banks of Otsego Lake, which is the source of the Susquehanna River. Cooperstown itself is the source of dreams for every boy who grows up throwing a ball against the side of the house and checking box scores daily—every boy like Brooks Robinson. They all have the dream to one day be included with the immortals in the National Baseball Hall of Fame. The Hall of Fame was established in Cooperstown in 1939 by a wealthy resident, Stephen Carlton Clark, whose family fortune originated with half ownership of the patent for the Singer sewing machine. Clark was a philanthropist with eclectic interests in both arts and sports and the owner of the majestic Otesaga Hotel and Resort. He capitalized on the (erroneous) conclusion of a 1907 commission that ascribed the birth of baseball to Abner Doubleday in Cooperstown. Set up with the approval and encouragement of the baseball commissioner's office, the Hall originally contained only a few artifacts that Clark had purchased himself. Once established, the museum became quite popular.

Brooks received the call every baseball player longs for on January 10, 1983. On the line was Jack Lang, secretary-treasurer of the Baseball Writers' Association of America, who had counted the votes. Brooks got 344 votes of 374 (92 percent), well more than the 281 (75 percent) needed for election. At the time, selection in the first year of eligibility was the ultimate honor, reserved only for the upper crust of players. Brooks was the 14th player (not including the original five) to get in on the first ballot.

That he was selected to the Hall of Fame was hardly a surprise; a mere formality, but he still reacted with emotions and humility. "I'm a little overwhelmed," he told reporters upon hearing the news.

"When you start playing, you hope to get to the major leagues, but the Hall of Fame—it seemed something unattainable."

Brooks was inducted on July 31, 1983, along with Juan Marichal, George Kell, and Walter Alston (Kell and Alston were selected by the Veterans Committee). Brooks and Kell were just the sixth and seventh third basemen to be inducted in the Hall, after Jimmy Collins, Home Run Baker, Pie Traynor, Fred Lindstrom, and Eddie Mathews. It was a special treat to go in with the good-natured Arkansas native Kell, who had been a mentor in Brooks's early days in Baltimore and remained a friend throughout the years. "We grew up 60 miles apart," Kell told reporters at the ceremony. "We wanted the same thing and we made it."

Baltimore fans converged on Cooperstown to show their love; 56 buses, 14 planes, and countless individual cars made the 250-mile "trip of pride" sponsored by the business community of Baltimore. Police estimated the total crowd at 12,000, at least 4,000 more than any previous induction ceremony. "When Brooks went in [to the Hall of Fame], it was like a member of your family going in," said Bill Tanton, sports editor of the *Baltimore Sun*.

"There was no way we would miss that," says Ron Meyers, who grew up in Baltimore watching Brooks's career, still has the autograph Brooks gave him at a Little League All-Star Game when he was 12, and drove to Cooperstown with a group of buddies for the induction. "He was Baltimore for our generation. It was incredible how many Oriole fans were there."

Brooks confessed that he was completely overwhelmed by the affection shown for him. "I can't believe it," he said. "It's just unbelievable for all these people to make this hike up from Baltimore to see me go into the Hall of Fame. If I'm making them happy in any way, then that makes me happy. That was all I ever really wanted to do when I was playing ball—make people happy. I loved baseball the way most people love life. I feel my love for the game overrode everything else."

Fans started gathering on the grass surrounding the Hall of Fame Library more than an hour before the ceremony started. Bathed in a sea of orange and black, they chanted "Brooks, Brooks, Brooks," displayed banners, launched dozens of orange balloons into the sky, and interrupted Commissioner Bowie Kuhn 11 times during his brief introductory remarks. "I never saw a man who so dominated a baseball event as Brooks Robinson dominated the 1970 World Series," Kuhn said. "A truly great Cincinnati team, the Big Red Machine, drove into a concrete wall at third base." Brooks received a 90-second ovation as he approached the microphone.

Wearing a strawberry-colored sports jacket, Brooks looked almost sheepish as he smiled during the cheers. "I keep asking myself, how could any one man be so fortunate?" he told the crowd. "One thing I am grateful for, and it may not happen much in the future because of the changing nature of baseball, and that is I played in one city: Baltimore, my adopted hometown. They cheered me on my good days, and on my bad days." As the cheers erupted again, from the back of the crowd, a voice called out, "There were no bad days, Brooks."

"Throughout my career, I was committed to the goodness of this game," Brooks added. "To be recognized at the Hall of Fame is more than any one human being can expect."

His plaque states: "Established modern standard of excellence for third basemen, setting major league records at his position for seasons (23), fielding pct. (.971), games (2,870), putouts (2,697), assists (6,205), and double plays (618). Hit 268 career home runs, named to 18 consecutive All Star teams. MVP of 1970 World Series. American League MVP in 1964." The crowd included former Orioles Paul Richards, Dave McNally, Mark Belanger, and Dick Hall, along with George Haynie and a mass of friends from Arkansas. Also attending were Baltimore mayor William Donald Schaefer, former Oriole owner Jerry Hoffberger, current owner Edward Bennett Williams, and Maryland senator Paul Sarbanes. Connie, the Robinson children, and Brooks's mother were also present.

A tragic note to the Hall of Fame induction was that Brooks's father, the man who, above all others, had been responsible for molding his career, did not live to see it. Brooks Robinson, Sr., had been stricken with a sudden illness and died a few years earlier. At the Hall of Fame ceremony, John Steadman spoke with Brooks's mother and mentioned that it was sad that Brooks Sr. wasn't there. "I have great faith," she answered. "I believe his dad is in heaven and knows about this." When Steadman added, "Well, you and his father made him the kind of man he is by the direction you provided as he grew up," she refused the flattery. "No," she answered, "we can't take credit. Where we lived in Little Rock was a block from the School for the Blind and a block from the School for the Deaf. Brooks grew up playing and having fun with those children, and I believe the experience gave him his deep sensitivity for others."

Once inducted, Brooks embraced membership in the Hall of Fame like the most enthusiastic new member of the local Rotary Club. He began the tradition that continues today of returning to Cooperstown each year for induction weekend and seeing the Hall of Fame family, thoroughly enjoying himself. By 2012, 50-plus of the 65 living Hall of Famers made the trip annually, participating in a parade, a breakfast, a private dinner, and other activities throughout the weekend—a chance to be seen by fans and meet with other Hall of Famers. "It would be an unusual Induction Weekend without Brooks," says Jeff Idelson, president of the Hall of Fame. "Every year he's a fan favorite. He's beloved.

"As far as people go, there is nobody finer than him," Idelson continues. "He has a unique and uncanny ability to connect with people. He is able to turn the conversation around—you're excited that you're meeting your hero and next thing you know, he's got you talking about yourself. He makes other people seem more important than himself. He can relate to anyone at any level. That's why he is universally revered."

Brooks served on several Hall of Fame committees, was a spokesman for the Hall, and was appointed to the board of directors in 1995, a post he has held since. He also participated in the Hall of Fame Golden Era Committee and in 2011 was instrumental in the election of fellow 1960s third baseman Ron Santo—Brooks had been adamant for years that Santo deserved the honor. "He is very active in the Hall of Fame," says Idelson. "He has a connection and a dedication to the Hall. He has served on so many committees over the years. He's always ready to help—he never says no. I can't think of too many people who do as much as he does. He cares so deeply about the game."

Because he cared so deeply about the game, Brooks was always ready to help promote baseball and help former players. The Major

League Baseball Players Alumni Association became the perfect venue for him, and once again, he was in the right place at the right time. In 1982 Chuck Hinton, a former major league outfielder with the Indians and Senators, played in a Super Bowl golf tournament sponsored by the NFL Alumni Association, an organization of former football players that hosted fund-raising events and worked for benefits for retired players. A ringer, Hinton was brought in by someone from the Redskins chapter and he won the tournament. Hinton enjoyed the whole thing so much he wondered why baseball didn't have such a group. He checked around and found out that, despite the fact that professional baseball was over 100 years old, there indeed was no professional baseball alumni association. He talked to former Senators teammate Jim Hannan, who still lived in the Washington, D.C., area, about the possibility of starting one.

Hannan turned out to be a good guy to talk to. Before starting his baseball career with the Senators, he had graduated from Notre Dame and had later earned a master's degree in finance. His master's thesis was on the Major League Baseball pension plan. The thesis was so good that Marvin Miller used it to get up to date on the issue when he became the head of the Players Association in the 1960s. Hannan had been a longtime player rep for the Senators; he knew the issues players faced and how to get things done. He thought Hinton had a good idea. "We attended a few NFL meetings to see how they ran and decided 'we could do this,'" says Hannan.

They gathered all the baseball alumni they could find in the Washington area to pitch the idea. "By then there hadn't been a team in Washington for over 10 years," says Hannan, "so there really weren't a lot of guys." After a few small meetings, mostly with Hannan, Hinton, Fred Valentine, Dick Bosman, Jim Lemon, Frank Kreutzer, and Walt Masterson, they decided they needed more people.

Fred Valentine and Chuck Hinton had played briefly with the Orioles in the early 1960s. "We thought about bringing in the Baltimore guys because they were close," Valentine says. "Naturally we went through Brooks. He immediately liked the idea and offered to help. That really got things rolling." Brooks called his buddy Ron Hansen and they got several other Baltimore alumni including Dick Hall,

Billy Hunter, Joe Durham, and Oriole announcer and former Brooklyn Dodger Rex Barney.

Initially, they had no money, only big ideas. "We didn't have anything to go on," says Valentine. "A hotel in Washington let us use a room for our meetings. The original guys sacrificed a lot of their own money and time to get it started."

The group met several times and eventually expanded to 17 founding members. They formed a board with Hannan as the president, then set down some ideas of what they wanted the organization to be, deciding on goals of promoting baseball, reinvolving players in the community, raising money for worthy charities, and developing programs for former players. "Obviously we wanted to help out guys who were down and out, but we also wanted something for guys who weren't down and out, to give back to the game and community," says Hannan. Brooks was instrumental in formulating the goals, which were essentially what he had been doing the past several decades on his own. They wrote bylaws and retained a lawyer for guidance through the legal process. The lawyer, Sam Moore of Washington, was a big baseball fan and had done work with one of the former Senators. He offered his services gratis until they got enough money to get going. They opened a small office in Virginia and hired someone to run the association full-time since they all had other jobs.

"We needed seed money to really get things going," says Hannan. Where to get the money was the problem. "We went to Edward Bennett Williams, who owned the Orioles at the time. A group of us, Brooks, Valentine, Hinton, Kreutzer, and me, met with Williams. He said, 'You're coming to the wrong place.' We all thought, 'Uh, oh.' Then he said, 'You want to go to the commissioner's office—they have the money.' He arranged the meeting for us." The group traveled to New York to present the plan to Bowie Kuhn and the league presidents. The baseball executives were receptive and gave them $30,000. Getting the approval of Major League Baseball was the final hurdle.

The local group went national. They each passed the word to former teammates and friends around the country. It was a slow, piecemeal process at first. Hannan's former teammate Rick Reichardt lived in Florida and was friends with Roger Maris, who had a Busch distributorship in Gainesville. Maris helped start Alumni Association golf tournaments for charity and got Anheuser-Busch to sponsor them. Ex-Twins Harmon Killebrew, who had been friends with Brooks since the Vietnam trip, Bob Allison, and Jim Kaat came in. From the humble beginnings, the association took off. They eventually moved the headquarters to Florida, then to the present location of Colorado Springs to assure West Coast players that it was not merely an East Coast club.

Hannan was simultaneously starting a career as a stockbroker and soon became too busy to be president, so Kaat became the second president. About a year later, Kaat got a broadcasting job and the travel became a burden. "Brooks said he'd gladly be president in the late 1980s and he's been president ever since," says Hannan. No one would consider running against him.

"The thing really took off and became huge," says Hannan, reflecting on the small group's handiwork. "This year there will be 122 events, including 82 free youth clinics, bowling and golf outings, and dinners. From the initial staff of one or two, now we have 23 or 24." The association has nearly 6,000 members, including almost all current players and the vast majority of alumni, and is involved in charity and community causes nationwide. The Swing with the Legends golf series, in which donors are matched with former players for a round of golf, has raised over $21 million for charities such as Children's Hospital, the American Diabetes Association, Boys and Girls Clubs, Cystic Fibrosis, and Special Olympics. They also have added other causes, such as pension and health benefits for players who played before the current agreements took place. In 1999, they started the Legends for Youth Dinner, which is held annually in New York and is the primary fund-raiser for their youth programs. At the dinner, which also serves as an annual gathering point for members, former and current major leaguers are recognized for their accomplishments. The association's community service award, given annually at the banquet, is named for Brooks Robinson.

"It's the number one sports alumni association in the country now," says Alumni Association CEO Dan Foster, who has worked with the association in various capacities since 1986. "In my opinion, in running the day-to-day operations, having Brooks's name on the letterhead, with his reputation and integrity, really helped get it going and made it take off. He's one of the nicest guys I've ever met—probably the nicest guy. He's a great ambassador for the game. He's what baseball is all about."

The players soon discovered a side benefit of Alumni Association events: they provided a way for former and current players to form friendships that were not possible before. "When we played there really was no fraternization between teams," says Hannan. "Opponents were the enemy. Also back then guys didn't change teams as much. The only way you got to know other guys was if you played with them or met them after the season, like at banquets. Now we got to know each other and became friends. We discovered that guys from other teams were great guys and we all had fun together."

Brooks had known that all along. He had always viewed professional baseball as a club and all players, even rivals, as club members. As a player he had gone out of his way to form friendships with opposing players, chatting up rival first basemen every time he got on, calling out to enemy players around the batting cage, and being cordial on the dinner circuit.

In 1971 Brooks had traveled to the studio of Norman Rockwell to pose for a painting. Harry Figgie, owner of a conglomerate that included Rawlings Sporting Goods, had commissioned Rockwell to do a number of paintings over the years, and after the 1970 World Series he ordered one of Brooks. The painting, which Rockwell called *Gee Thanks Brooks*, depicts a young Brooks Robinson, glove tucked under his right arm, standing near stands full of fans, their happy faces beaming at him, as he signs an autograph—left-handed of course—for an eager freckle-faced kid in a crumpled Oriole cap leaning over the rail. Rockwell, unknown to Brooks until much later, snuck himself into the painting, as he sometimes did, being in the right-hand corner with a cigar.

Rockwell was a big baseball fan and he and Robinson became friends during the sessions. They made a great pair. Roy Firestone later said that the painting "reveals many attributes about both men. Both represented a time in America when institutions were revered and innocence wasn't considered corny or out of style."

Brooks was impressed with the inference in the painting. "That's what baseball is all about," he later said. "Your father . . . that little boy. . . . And I'm signing an autograph. . . . To me, that's what baseball is all about, connecting generations."

Later, when Figgie retired, he put all his Rockwells up for auction. Brooks heard about it and wanted to get his painting. The day of the auction, which was held at Sotheby's in New York, Brooks was in Puerto Rico playing in a charity golf tournament. He sent his son to the auction with instructions that he could go as high as $175,000. While Brooks was on the golf course, a lady from Sotheby's gave Connie a running account of the bidding—125, 135, 145. It eventually hit 195. The lady said, "Mrs. Robinson, the bidding has stopped." Connie answered, "Tell him to go one more."

"I went $200,000," said Brooks in 2007. "I got the painting. I got the original and when I came home from the golf course, I looked at Connie and said, 'Am I poor again?' She said, 'Yeah, you're poor.' "

October 6, 1991, the Orioles said farewell to Memorial Stadium. Brooks and Johnny Unitas were chosen to throw out the ceremonial first balls (Unitas tossed a football). After the game, in what Chuck Thompson called "the most magnificent pageant I've ever seen in a ballpark," over 100 former Orioles walked onto the field, one by one, wearing the type of uniform of the era in which they played, to man their old positions. Their names were not announced; the fans knew who they were. Brooks was the first player to come out, Cal Ripken, Jr., was the last—appropriately, two respected men whose single-team careers bookended the Orioles' history at Memorial Stadium. As Brooks stood at third base, he bowed his head and scratched the dirt with his feet as he had between thousands of pitches when he played. The theme from *Field of Dreams* hung in the air. There were tears throughout the field, stands, and press box. The players shook hands and hugged their old teammates. Then the players waved good-bye to the fans. Home plate was dug up by members of the grounds crew, who were wearing white tuxedos with orange bow ties and cummerbunds, and transported to Camden Yards. The funeral for the field of their youth was complete.

Brooks never forgot his Arkansas roots or the people and places that had been so helpful in his formative years. "Over the years Brooks came back to Little Rock quite a bit, especially when his parents were still alive," says Bill Valentine. "He also did a lot of things with the Boys Club and Lamar Porter Field. He came for a lot of local causes. They would always sell out when he came and he hated to turn anybody down."

Brooks returned for events such as the Doughboy reunion and tribute to Coach Haynie in 1988, in which he was the featured speaker. He participated in numerous local charity golf tournaments—chaired some and lent his name to others—such as the Brooks Robinson Celebrity Classic in Hot Springs in 2005 to benefit the Arkansas Sports Hall of Fame. He rarely missed a high school reunion.

To Brooks, Lamar Porter Field was a priceless memory of his childhood—the many hours he had spent there and the special role it played in his development would always be remembered. By 1980, the field needed care. It had fallen into disrepair as the Legion teams and youth leagues had gradually moved to other parts of town. Brooks's friend Lee Rogers headed a renovation committee for the field and Brooks became the honorary chairman. Through their efforts and those of many other former players, the field was restored to its original splendor and once again used by high schools and adult leagues. Brooks returned to help Lamar Porter Field once again in 2006. The field had been added to the National Historic Register to help preserve it by this time. Brooks's input helped land an $85,000 grant to fix the field for RBI (Reviving Baseball in the Inner Cities).

In 2005 Brooks became involved in baseball in a formal way for the first time since retiring when he became part owner of Opening Day Partners, a group that owns and operates minor league franchises. Appearing at news conferences, opening day ceremonies, and fundraisers, he enthusiastically talked up the teams and their league. Before becoming a part owner, Brooks had spent several years as a special assistant. He told reporters that part of the stipulation when he accepted the responsibility of joining the ownership group was that he could work when he wanted to. "I don't want to do something that's going to take up all of my time because I'm doing other things, too," he said. "I play in a lot of golf tournaments, I'm making a lot of speeches, I'm on the go a lot. I'm 70 years old now and I'm having a ball, just doing the things I want to do."

"He appreciates minor league baseball and what it represents to these communities," said Opening Day Partners president Jon Danos in 2007. "He loves the game at this level, loves the people. He just flat out enjoys this. And on the non-baseball side, he has a great influence on the community. We're just thrilled to have him. . . . He has a personal touch that you need in this industry." Typical was the reaction when Brooks spoke in Leesburg, Virginia, addressing the Board of Supervisors before a crucial vote concerning the establishment of a new team. He talked about the community feel such a gathering place promotes, the baseball legacy of families, the park's effect on local livability, and the joy of a father bringing a son out to the American game of baseball. Not surprisingly, the vote passed by a landslide.

Brooks was instrumental in establishing a new team in York, Pennsylvania. The city was a natural fit for Brooks as it was the site of the start of his professional career and he had maintained friends and sentiment there. The city of York had been out of baseball since 1969. The new franchise, named the Revolution, was a quick success. The 2011 season was their fifth and they set an attendance record with 301,740—a little over 4,000 fans per game. They play in new Sovereign Bank Stadium, which is located at 5 Brooks Robinson Way (the street name was officially changed in 2006). Fans enter the stadium by way of Brooks Robinson Plaza. A special page on the team's Web site is dedicated to Brooks and his baseball history.

ODP currently owns four teams: the Lancaster Barnstormers, the Camden, New Jersey, Riversharks, the York Revolution, and the Southern Maryland Blue Crabs. The teams play in the Atlantic League, an eight-team minor league with no affiliations with the major leagues, situated in Maryland, New York, and New Jersey.

In July 2008, Brooks received the Rawlings All-Time Gold Glove for third base in a pregame ceremony in York. Rawlings awarded it for each position based on voting by fans. Brooks finished with more votes than any other player at any position. All living recipients were presented in the major league city where they started, except for Brooks, who moved his presentation to York.

Fame—to be known, to evoke emotions in strangers, to be loved merely for deeds performed on a field—is a double-edged sword for many athletes. They like the money and idolization and other spoils, but not the bother of being pawed over and talked to by strangers. And not the constant requests and demands for their name scribbled on a ball or a program or a napkin every time they leave the house. They come to hate this and oblige only when trapped or paid, often behaving rudely while doing so. Not so with Brooks Robinson.

Brooks never minded the attention; he always took it in stride, even appeared to enjoy it. "Of all the game's greats, perhaps Robinson has been least cursed by his own fame," Thomas Boswell wrote in *Baseball Digest* in 1977. "He had great talent and never abused it. He received adulation and reciprocated with common decency. While other players dressed like kings and acted like royalty, Robinson arrived at the park dressed like a cab driver. Other stars had fans. Robinson made friends." Brooks's graciousness with fans became legendary.

Chuck Thompson noted that in 1983, in the lead-up to the Hall of Fame induction, "there were TV and radio interviews in every city on the road and I never heard him complain. He never once found fault with the incessant requests or said he would be glad when it was over. One thing I learned from Brooks was his understanding and compassion for people. [Once] with the game in progress, a little boy stood up on the ground level behind the box seats and held up a program to indicate he would like to have an autograph. Brooks held up one finger as if to say, 'wait a minute.' As soon as the inning ended and we started to roll a commercial, Brooks left the booth, ran downstairs, signed the autograph and returned without missing a play.

"I've been present when fans asked for autographs and Brooks would engage them in conversation. He'd ask where they were from, where they went to school, and why they were fans of the Orioles.

The fans could feel he was genuine in his concern and were honored by such attention. His wife, Connie . . . acts the same way with strangers."

When asked about his fame in 1983, Brooks said, "It wasn't a bother, it was an honor. Being a hero, if that's what I really turned out to be, is something you dream about when you're a kid, and I got to live my dream. I came here a couple of years after the team moved from St. Louis and I kind of grew up with the Orioles—lived through the bad years and played in four World Series. I signed autographs and I went everywhere the people wanted me. I worked at being Brooks Robinson, but I loved it. It's just the way I was."

In the 1980s, baseball players realized that their signatures had value. The memorabilia market exploded as baby boomers turned nostalgic and gladly paid big bucks for anything associated with memories of their heroes. There had always been a market for appearances, but it had been largely for the most famous players and had been relatively low-paying. Now players were able to make more money signing their name than they did playing baseball; and players with "Hall of Fame" after their name were set for life.

In this newly minted industry some players became infamous for being rude—the only thing people saw was the top of their heads as they wordlessly signed, allowing no verbal exchanges and certainly no touching. Some of the biggest stars became well known among organizers for acting like divas with outrageous lists of demands—everything down to how they were addressed.

Brooks had always enjoyed interacting with the public, whether at organized events or informally when spotted around town. He was no different now. He became universally recognized as one of the most friendly, accommodating ex-stars on the autograph and memorabilia circuit; smiling and warmly talking to each fan, standing up to shake their hands, gladly walking around the table to pose for pictures, staying until the last fan had an autograph.

If the basic economic law of supply and demand were in force in regards to professional athletes' autographs, a Brooks Robinson would be worth about 10 cents because there are so many of them out there. "My wife says, 'I know you signed autographs for everyone in this country,'" Brooks said in 2007. "And I'd say, 'I think you're probably right.' I enjoy people. I enjoy talking to the kids. . . . If I walk downtown with my hat off down on Baltimore and Charles Street, I guarantee you four or five people will hang out the car window: 'Hey Brooks, you gave me my autograph back in Highlandtown or Trappe, Maryland.' "

"Everywhere I go, it seems I signed something for someone," he added. "And most people have stories, which is nice."

George Trout, who, in addition to being the longtime public address announcer for York baseball games, was also a sports memorabilia show organizer, witnessed Brooks's behavior around fans many times, starting when he played his first professional game. It never changed. "Over the years, Brooks has been to York for many appearances," he says. "He is just always so accommodating. He loves kids. He likes the fact that people pay attention to him and respect him, but he doesn't carry it like a star. He will do anything he can to accommodate people within reason. I've seen so many great players change over the years. Once they got to be big stars, it just changed their whole attitude. I've seen some who were really rude to fans or would leave as soon as their contracted time was up, but Brooks was one guy who never changed from the night he first showed up here. He behaves just like a guy who might deliver the mail or work at a bank. He has a great sense of responsibility to the people he feels made him so popular, the fans. I never saw Brooks turn his back on anybody under any circumstances."

Longtime fan Terri Hett agrees. "I've been around the park and met a lot of players at signings and things over the years. There has never been anyone close to Brooks as far as being nice and a classy guy. He looks you in the face and shakes your hand. He makes you feel like you're the only person standing in line—the only person in the world. He's patient with fans and takes time with each one, even when he's being mobbed. I've never seen him be rude or grumpy or even hurried with fans. He's so humble, he acts embarrassed when you compliment him."

Rick Hubata has had a close working relationship with Brooks since 1995. Brooks frequently appears at Hubata's store, the Dugout Zone, in Ellicott City near Baltimore, and Hubata also has maintained Brooks's fan Web site since 2000. "I don't think I have ever met anyone quite like him," Hubata says. "His fans are very important to him. He remembers names, shakes hands, takes pictures. He sincerely feels bad if he makes a mistake signing something or forgets someone's name. The energy he puts into public appearances is incredible. He really tries to make sure everything is perfect and everyone is happy.

"The result is that a lot of people come back and want to spend time with him. Some people go to every appearance he makes, not because they need another autograph, but just to spend a minute or two in his presence. He makes people feel so good that they came to see him. He makes people feel like they're talking to an old friend, not a Hall of Fame player. He's just incredible. I've dealt with a lot of great athletes and we're lucky to have a lot of really good guys in Baltimore—the old-timers, football and baseball players from the 1950s and 1960s—but nobody's like Brooks. He's special."

It's not just that he writes his name down for fans, gives them something that may be of value later. It's the way he does it; the personalized attention. It's the feeling they get standing in the presence of their childhood hero; the emotions when they introduce their son or daughter or grandkids to him—to the greatest role model a kid ever had. Brooks makes it seem as though he is genuinely happy fans come to see him, that the fan is the special person, not vice versa. He frequently carries on long conversations with people lucky enough to catch him at the end of an event. Never heard to utter a negative word about anyone, even off the record, he always seems more happy to talk about others from his playing days. He takes his time to insure that his autograph is legible. Each letter is recognizable—nothing worse than an autograph from a player that later looks like an indecipherable scribbled line. "We've got all the time in the world," he is heard to say, telling staff at a charity event to wait until he has finished with the last fan. He has a special awareness of people, frequently coming around the table to better assist and talk to someone in a wheelchair or an elderly fan. And if someone is spotted communicating to a deaf person in sign language, you can be sure Brooks will soon be in the middle of a sign language gabfest, dusting off the skill he learned years ago playing at the Arkansas School for the Deaf.

"I've met Brooks numerous times over the years at signings," says Tom Blazucki. "People always ask him for something, so I started giving him things. I would take him nachos because he always joked about eating nachos when he was on TV, or I would bring him coffee. He's a big history enthusiast, so I started bringing him books about World War II or the Civil War. He was always so gracious. He would say, 'Thanks,' and 'You don't have to do that.' Over the years we have exchanged notes and letters. When I had bypass surgery a few years ago, he sent me a card and wrote a nice note."

"I met Brooks when I was a little girl, about 10," says Roberta Thornton. "My dad was an associate manager of a store outside Annapolis and one day Brooks was there to sign autographs. Before it got started, my dad sent one of the employees out to get me. When I went inside, there was my dad and another man sitting at a table having coffee and talking to Brooks Robinson. He looked right at me with his big blue eyes and asked, 'So what would you like to drink?' and got me a Coke and told me to pull up a chair. He turned his attention away from the adults and talked directly to me as if I was one of them. He asked about school and talked about his son who was about my age. I was smitten—he became my biggest hero after that.

"Years later, I had the opportunity to take my own daughter to meet him," she continues. "He was appearing at a car dealership. On the way I told her the story of when I had met him years earlier. She was only about five or six, young enough to be optimistic, and she said, 'I'll bet he still remembers you,' even though I knew that he had met thousands and thousands of fans since then. When we got there and got through the line, he looked at my daughter and talked to her just like he had talked to me and signed a ball for her. Then she said, 'Mr. Brooks, my mommy met you when she was 10 years old. Do you remember her?' And he looked at me and said, 'You know what, I do remember that.' She just beamed. It made her day. She said, 'See Mommy, I told you he would remember you.' He made my day years ago and darned if he didn't do the same thing for my daughter."

"I took my son, Brooks, to see Brooks Robinson last year at a show in Towson," says Greg Rogers. "It was all about my son, introducing him to my hero, the guy he was named after. He had heard the stories but was too young to see him play. Brooks was very nice to everyone. He talked to my son for several minutes. I got to shake his hand. We got a picture. It was great. My brother-in-law lives in Boston. Once he said, 'I've never seen anybody up there named Brooks, but there are Brookses all over the place down here.' "

Brooks has been humbled and honored by the number of Brookses. "I try to keep a list of people [who are named after him,]" he said in 2007. "I mean I still get films every year. Little videos of, 'This is Brooks now. He's twelve years old and he's playing here.' I was down at this steakhouse the other day and a lady said she named her son Brooks. That's unbelievable. You know I always try to write them a little note: 'I'm honored to know you.' " In 2012 the Orioles ran a local promotion in which fans with a first or middle name of Brooks were entered for a chance to win free tickets to a game honoring their Hall of Fame third baseman—there were 493 entrants.

As he entered his seventies, Brooks remained active and in the public eye. His popularity, especially in the Baltimore area, grew with the years and approached the level of unreserved love usually only proffered to royalty or popes. Baltimore fans realized they were lucky. They had a guy who had spent his whole career in the organization, who remained in the city, never tired of interacting with the public, and never let them down—few major league cities were so fortunate. He was the old standby; the hero who had never done anything to disappoint his followers, who always came through, who always remained in character. As stories multiplied of modern athletes who were involved in scandals and exhibited boorish behavior, the appreciation for Brooks became more passionate. Michael Olesker wrote in the *Baltimore Sun*, "He was a man who transcended our declining ability to believe unquestionably in heroes."

John Steadman, in summing up Brooks Robinson's popularity, had stated in 2000, "Why? The public is smart and observant. It isn't duped or dumb; it realizes the special qualities of an extraordinary individual, a man of good taste and purpose. Worthy of emulation."

Once, after Brooks had long been retired, he was extolled during a sports banquet at Towson University. John Steadman walked out with Cal Ripken, Jr. Ripken observed to Steadman, "Those things about Brooks were beautiful. Stop to think how much time and effort it takes to do all that. It just doesn't happen. Brooks had to want to do it."

Brooks remained in love with the game of baseball, continuing as an ardent fan and ambassador, and didn't hesitate to wax nostalgic when asked. "I consider myself fortunate," he said in 2009. "The longer I'm out of the game, the more I appreciate playing for one team. I know almost every player who has ever played for the Orioles, except for a few guys from the first year."

He also said, "It passed so fast that sometimes it feels like I didn't play at all. Now I'll be watching on TV and someone will make a nice play at third, and I'll go, 'Did I really used to do that?' Then the announcer will say, 'That was a Brooks Robinson play,' and I'll go, 'Well, I guess I did.'"

In 2009 he recounted, "Someone asked me if I enjoyed hearing on TV when someone makes a great, great play and they'll say, 'That's a Brooks Robinson play,' and I said, 'You bet I love it. I tell them I can still dive and catch it, but I can't get up anymore."

Brooks retained his love for the Orioles and referred to them as "we," but it had been hinted in the papers that a rift, or at least an uncomfortable relationship, existed between the present Oriole management and Brooks because he made few appearances at Camden Yards or on the Orioles' behalf. Receiving the Gold Glove Award in York rather than Baltimore further stirred the speculation. Oriole team director of communications Greg Bader told reporters, "People are going to draw their own conclusions, but the club has a very strong relationship with Brooks. He is always welcome as our guest at the ballpark, and he has an open invitation to come down to the clubhouse to visit the team at any time."

Brooks refused to say anything bad about the team, frequently doing a quick dance step to slide into another topic when asked by reporters. "I have a wonderful relationship with the Orioles," he said in 2008. "I've talked to [owner] Peter [Angelos] a few times, and they want someone who can work for them 24/7. I don't have time to do that."

Brooks still does some appearances and autograph shows, though not as many as in the past. "The hardest thing for everybody close to him now is to get him to say no," says Hubata. "People ask and he always says yes. He's slowed down some the past year due to the medical problems he's had. I think he finally realizes that he can't do everything for everybody."

The effects of time eventually slow everyone down. In 2009 Brooks underwent successful treatment for prostate cancer. It was diagnosed early and he was treated with radiation. He chose a Baltimore luncheon for the American Cancer Society to reveal the illness publicly for the first time. "I've been very fortunate to have an incredible wife and family to support me, the finances to get medical care and the good fortune to be in my adopted hometown of Baltimore, which boasts the best medical care you can get anywhere in the world," he said. He underwent a very large abdominal operation in 2010 that was complicated by a serious infection, causing hospitalization for almost a month at the Greater Baltimore Medical Center. The condition and further related surgery plagued him the rest of the year.

In January 2012, as he was regaining his strength from the medical problems of the past year, he had a near-catastrophic fall at a charity banquet in Florida. "He shouldn't have even been there," says a close associate. "He was still too weak from his other problems, but that's Brooks, he didn't want to turn anybody down." He and other baseball stars were sitting on an elevated platform that had a curtain behind it. There were three levels of chairs and Brooks was on the third level. Brooks leaned back, thinking there was a support behind the curtain; his chair slipped and he fell backward off the platform. He dropped four feet and landed on his back and neck on the hard surface of the auditorium. The horrified audience and other players could only watch.

Former New York Yankee Fritz Peterson later wrote about the accident: "It was sickening, but even worse when we found out it was Brooks, the nicest but most frail player among us that night. . . . I was looking at Brooks, that sweet, wonderful man lying on the floor all sprawled out with his grey hair all disheveled. I just wanted first to throw up and then, more importantly, just go down and hug him and fix him. I wish I could have taken the fall for him. Seeing my buddy on the floor made me cry."

Following the accident, Brooks remained in a Miami area hospital for almost a month, then flew home to Baltimore for more rehab. He did not make a public appearance until June. That came when he showed up for the dinner before the dedication of the Earl Weaver statue at Camden Yards on June 30, 2012. Weaver was moved that, although Brooks was still visibly weak, he made a special effort to be there for his former manager. "He came to the dinner for my statue dedication," Weaver said shortly thereafter, emotion obvious in his voice. "That was a special thing that he came out. Only Brooksie would do that."

17. Statues

IT CAN BE SAID ABOUT SPORTS IDOLS that memories fade and records are eventually broken, but bronze lasts forever. Only a few of the true unforgettables are honored with statues. Usually a single statue is a sign of someone's place in history. Brooks Robinson has three. The first was dedicated in York in 2008. It was based on the Norman Rockwell painting. There is a likeness of Brooks in a York White Roses uniform, with his glove tucked under his arm, signing a baseball for two young fans. The statue sits in Brooks Robinson Plaza at the entrance to the stadium.

For years, Baltimore fans had lamented the lack of a statue of Brooks in their city. As the baseball icon of the franchise, he deserved one, similar to those of Stan Musial in St. Louis, Ernie Banks at Wrigley Field, and Ted Williams in Boston. In 2009, plans were made public for a nine-foot-tall bronze statue near Camden Yards on a city-owned plaza just west of Oriole Park. The statue was not commissioned by the Orioles, however. Baltimore businessman Henry A. Rosenberg, former chairman of Crown Central Petroleum, for which Brooks worked from 1968 to 2003, headed a group that had worked for six years to erect the statue. Brooks was depicted in his Orioles uniform, gripping a ball in his right hand, getting ready to throw a runner out at first.

Public donations eventually paid for one-third of the $700,000 venture; the rest came from the 81-year-old Rosenberg's pocket. The statue was dedicated in October of 2011. Maryland governor Martin O'Malley proclaimed Brooks "first in the hearts of the people of Baltimore." Longtime Maryland U.S. senator Barbara Mikulski said,

"It's not about the Golden Gloves. It's about the golden heart that Brooks had."

Brooks, looking weak from his medical troubles, was clearly emotional, choking back tears as his wife stood behind him. He said, "To all my friends out there, you've always been good to me. I just want you to know I have never considered you fans. I've always considered you my friends. Thank you for the way you've treated me over the years. Never did I expect to have a statue, let alone a statue 300 yards from a statue of the greatest player in major league history, Babe Ruth. And another 300 or 400 yards is the statue of the greatest quarterback in NFL history, Johnny Unitas, a dear friend of mine that I miss very much.

"Of all the decisions I've had to make throughout my lifetime, the two most important ones I got right, electing to sign with the Baltimore Orioles over all the other teams. . . . My greatest achievement and happiness was not in baseball, it was marrying Connie. I knew the instant I saw her. She has been the love of my life for fifty-one years. . . . She has been the wind beneath my wings and the one constant rock of my life. Always happy to be in the background enduring my lengthy absences, sacrificing her own life with complete unselfishness and devotion. Assuming all responsibility for our home and our children. She has not only been the best wife in the world but also the very best mother. Connie, you'll never know how grateful I am of you darling."

In 2011, the Orioles announced plans to honor their six Hall of Famers—Brooks, Frank, Earl Weaver, Jim Palmer, Eddie Murray, and Cal Ripken, Jr.—with bronze statues in a picnic grove beyond the center field wall at Camden Yards. Originally the dedications, which were made throughout the 2012 season, were planned to be chronologically in the order the players were inducted, making Frank first and Brooks second. Because Brooks was still recovering from the fall his dedication was moved to the end, to be conducted on the last weekend of the season. It turned out to be a fitting move as spirits were high, with the Orioles finishing their first playoff season in a decade, when the final statue was dedicated in front of a full house on September 28, 2012. This time, becoming accustomed to seeing himself in bronze, Brooks was much less emotional and spent most of his speech joking and calling out to former teammates in the crowd.

In the movie *Sleepless in Seattle*, Meg Ryan's character writes, "Brooks Robinson was the best third baseman ever. It's important that you agree with me on that because I'm from Baltimore."

Tom Hanks's character replies, as if annoyed at having to state an obvious fact, "Everyone thinks Brooks Robinson is the greatest."

As with any "greatest ever" discussion, however, there are always divergent opinions. There have been other third basemen who were better hitters, but a strong argument can be made for Brooks as the best all-around third baseman or as the best fielder. Offensively, although he was no slouch, Brooks's statistics pale in comparison with those put up in the steroid era. But they weren't bad: 2,848 career hits, 1,357 RBIs, 268 home runs (he was all-time leader for third basemen until Graig Nettles passed him in 1980). In four World Series, he hit .263 with 14 RBIs in 21 games; in five playoff series he hit .348. It should be remembered when viewing Brooks Robinson's career batting average that he played in the toughest decade for hitters, often referred to as the second dead ball era. From 1962 through 1968, the highest batting average in the American League was .326 (Pete Runnels in 1962). Often only a few men hit over .300 in a season, and in 1968 Carl Yastrzemski memorably led the league with a .301 average. In his prime Brooks was routinely in the top 10 in the league in batting average.

How do you define the best fielder? It's difficult to measure a baseball player like Brooks Robinson with numbers alone. There are some numbers, however. Brooks's career fielding percentage of .971 was the highest by a third baseman in history at the time he retired. This number—which eclipses that of other notable slick fielders such as Graig Nettles (.961), Mike Schmidt (.955), Clete Boyer (.965), and Ron Santo (.954)—attests to the fact that he made relatively few errors among the chances he got. But numbers can be second-guessed; maybe he didn't get to as many balls as others? He led the league in assists for third basemen eight times, six in a row from 1963 to 1969—so he must have been getting to quite a few balls. He fares well sabermetrically. Wins Against Replacement (WAR) gives an indication of how many wins a player would give his team as opposed to a "replacement level" player at that position. According to baseball-reference.com, Brooks's defensive WAR of 38.8 ranks third all time among all position players, trailing only Ozzie Smith (43.4) and Mark Belanger (39.4). Buddy Bell is the next closest third baseman with 23.0 (25th place).

There are a few other numbers: 18 straight All-Star teams, a record 11 years leading the league in fielding percentage (nine times from 1960 to 1969) and the career records for third basemen in assists, chances, put-outs, and double plays. Also there are the 16 Gold Gloves. Mike Schmidt won the next most Gold Gloves for third basemen with 10. Buddy Bell and Eric Chavez are second in the American League with six each.

Brooks's artistry with the glove was about much more than numbers, though. The numbers only certify what the old-timers saw and back their opinions. Forty years ago, Jim Murray of the *Los Angeles Times* wrote, "In the future, Brooks Robinson will be the standard every third baseman will be measured by." That statement has withstood the test of time. Today when people want to conjure up the most gaudy superlative for third base play, they invariably arrive at the same phrase. Consider a small sample of comments in the media the past year:

Tiger manager Jim Leyland, talking about the progress of Miguel Cabrera's switch to third base: "He's doing great at third base. Is he going to make plays like Brooks Robinson?"

A manager talking about a Cleveland Indian minor league third baseman: "He's not Brooks Robinson over there."

A reporter talking about Brandon Inge: "In other words, he's no Brooks Robinson."

A writer talking about a prospect: "Lonnie Chisenhall doesn't have to be another Brooks Robinson at third base."

And it's not just in the media. In a July 2012 game in the over-40s softball league in Columbus, Indiana, a third baseman made a falling-down stop, scrambled to his feet, and threw to second in time to nail a waddling codger for a force-out. Someone on the opposing bench yelled, "Brooks Robinson." He didn't yell Alex Rodriguez. He didn't yell Mike Schmidt. He didn't yell Graig Nettles, Clete Boyer,

Eddie Mathews, or Pie Traynor. He yelled Brooks Robinson, and, 35 years after Brooks had played his last game, everyone in the park knew what he meant.

Reading the remarks of longtime sportswriters about Brooks Robinson, one could come to the conclusion that they were all maudlin schlepps; emotionally immature softies who cry at the sight of a limping puppy or a dead bug. But then you read their other columns and find out that these were hardboiled curmudgeons who often enjoyed ripping their subjects to shreds. What was it about Brooks that reduced these men to sappy sentimentalists? Certainly, it was more than just his making himself available and being polite to them.

"The baseball park was no place for his performances," wrote Atlanta's Furman Bisher. "He should have played at Carnegie Hall."

Jim Murray once wrote, "When they talk about Brooks Robinson, Jr. around baseball, you feel like taking your hat off and bowing your head. You're sure they're talking about someone who passed away years ago, somebody from the Golden Age of Baseball. You'd expect him to be on a stained-glass window instead of a bubblegum card."

Joe Falls of Detroit once said, "How many interviews, how many questions, how many times have you approached him and got only courtesy and decency in return? A true gentleman who never took himself seriously. I always had the idea that he didn't know he was Brooks Robinson."

Washington columnist Bob Addie wrote in 1976, "All major leaguers should pattern themselves after Robinson, unfailingly courteous to the press and fans alike. He was in the nice-guy mold of Stan Musial."

C. C. Johnson Spink, editor and publisher of the *Sporting News*, wrote upon Brooks's retirement: "Robinson's character is commensurate with the great ability that he had shown as a player. In a sports world that is replete with commercialism, selfishness and greed, Brooks stands out as a gentleman personified."

Talk to guys who played with Brooks Robinson and invariably they will say he was the best teammate they ever had. Not just a lot of them. Not just most of them. Every single one; without exception.

Usually, they will throw in that he was the nicest guy they ever met, in or out of baseball. They have as much respect for him as a person as they do for his fielding ability, which is not a small statement.

"Brooks Robinson is one of the greatest people I have ever met," said Earl Weaver, summing up for everyone. "He gets along with people better than anyone I've ever known. The whole room brightens when he walks in. He goes out of his way to do things for people. I don't believe I ever saw him mad and we were together on the field for almost 10 years. He never had trouble with a teammate. How can you have trouble with Brooks?"

Brooks Robinson is a man who made a habit of being in the right place at the right time throughout his baseball career and his life. He never lost sight of that fact and considered himself to be lucky, even though luck had little to do with it. "It's fantastic to be able to do what you do best and love most," he said in 1972. "If that isn't what happiness is, then, I don't know."

"I try to be kind to the world because the world has been extremely kind to me," he wrote in his 1974 autobiography.

"I've been blessed, I can tell you that," he said in 2007. "There's not a day that goes by where someone doesn't say, 'Thanks, Brooks.' And I just say, 'The thanks should go to all the fans.' I played in the best time, with the best players and had the most fun. And they're thanking me?"

In 2008, summing up his career, Brooks wrote, "I'd like to be remembered as someone who had a dream and never wanted to do anything in his whole life except be a professional baseball player, someone who loved the game with all his heart." He will certainly be remembered as that. But he will also be remembered for much more. Unlike many sports heroes, he is not defined by his athletic exploits; they are only a small component of the man. His most unique feature is the way he has carried himself off the field for the past 75 years. The class, humbleness, ability to make friends, and thoughtfulness of others have eclipsed anything he did on the field.

His friend since childhood, Buddy Rotenberry, says, "Brooks Robinson's personality and character are such that I would be proud to say he is my friend even if he had never played a game of baseball."

That's true of everyone who ever met him. In talking to people who played with him and knew him over the years it becomes apparent that there *is* a secret to Brooks Robinson; something a father can pass on to his kid. The secret is how he treats people. The best that's ever been? *Everyone thinks Brooks Robinson is the greatest.* And it has very little to do with how he handled a baseball glove.

Acknowledgments

As always, any work of nonfiction is only as good as the people who volunteer their memories to the author. I am indebted to a number of people who helped with this book. It is perhaps a sad state of modern journalism that prompts many people to assume that a writer is initially looking for dirt on his subject. One of the first people I talked to cautioned me, "If you're digging for bad things to write about Brooks Robinson it's going to be the shortest book in history—there isn't anything. Also, more than a few good ole boys from Arkansas might come looking for you." I found that he was right on both counts. The reverence and loyalty that Brooks has inspired over his life from friends and fans is indeed impressive.

I was lucky enough to be able to talk to a number of former professional baseball players. It is always a treat to hear their stories. I would like to thank the following people who were kind enough to talk to me: Robert Baird, Larry Barnett, Tom Blazucki, Wally Bunker, Frank Cashen, Wayne Causey, Dave Criscione, Harold Ellingson, Chuck Estrada, Eddie Fisher, Dan Foster, Glenda Gazette, Marshall Gazette, Jim Gentile, Bruce Genther, Dick Hall, Jim Hannan, Ron Hansen, George Henderson, Terri Hett, Don Hood, Rick Hubata, Jeff Idelson, Bob Johnson, Mrs. Ronald LaMartina, Tommy Lauderdale, Bob Maisel, Charles Metro, Jr., Elena Moreskoni Metro, Ron Meyers, Robert Nosari, Ernest Paicopolos, Milt Pappas, Art Quirk, Patricia Ranocchia, Jim Rasco, Bobby Richardson, Pete Richert, Eddie Robinson, Gary Robinson, Greg Rogers, Jay Rogers, Ted Rogers, Buddy Rotenberry, Vic Roznovsky, Bob Scherr, Bill Short, Wes Stock, Roberta

Thornton, Gus Triandos, George Trout, Bill Valentine, Fred Valentine, Jerry Walker, Eddie Watt, Earl Weaver, and Pat Wilson.

I feel fortunate to have been able to talk with Hall of Fame manager Earl Weaver shortly after he returned from Baltimore for the dedication of his statue at Camden Yards. Although busy, he took the time to talk with me, mainly because he wanted to add his admiration and thanks to Brooks Robinson. I was greatly saddened to learn of Mr. Weaver's death later in the year.

I would like to especially thank fellow Society for American Baseball Research member Jim Rasco for helping get me started on my search for Brooks Robinson's Arkansas roots and for showing me through his museum-quality memorabilia collection. Jim is also a board member of the Arkansas Hall of Fame and knows everyone who ever had anything to do with sports in the state and was of great assistance in putting me in touch with the right people.

Thanks to Buddy Rotenberry for giving up an entire day to personally take me on a tour of Little Rock, past and present, and for patiently answering my calls and e-mails to further fact-check their childhood and teen years.

Special thanks to Robert Nosari, Buddy Rotenberry, George Trout, Harold Ellingson, and Greg Rogers for contributing pictures. Although there wasn't room to use them all, they are greatly appreciated. Thanks to Beverly Griffin of the Little Rock Public School District, John Horne of the National Baseball Hall of Fame, Kevin O'Sullivan of AP Images, Zach Dixon of the *Baltimore Sun*, and Jenifer Stepp of *Stars and Stripes* for assistance with photos.

Thanks to the folks at Baseball Almanac for the use of tables and stats.

I would like to thank the staff of the Bartholomew County Library and the Little Rock Public Library for their help with research materials.

This book would not have seen the light of day were it not for the efforts of my agent, John Talbot, editor Rob Kirkpatrick, and assistant editor Nicole Sohl. They are all a pleasure to work with and help keep me on the right path.

Thanks to Teresa, Kim, and T.J. in my office for cheerfully and patiently fielding baseball calls in addition to taking care of ophthal-mology business.

Thanks to my kids, Ben, Matt, and Stephanie, for listening to my ideas and stories about baseball players.

Last, thanks once again to my wife and best friend, Kathy, for her patience and support.

Appendix: Brooks Robinson's Career Statistics

HITTING

Yr	G	AB	R	H	2B	3B	HR	RBI	BB	SO	SH	SF	HBP	AVG	OBP	SLG
1955	6	22	0	2	0	0	0	1	0	10	0	0	0	.091	.091	.091
1956	15	44	5	10	4	0	1	1	1	5	0	0	0	.227	.244	.386
1957	50	117	13	28	6	1	2	14	7	10	0	1	1	.239	.286	.359
1958	145	463	31	110	16	3	3	32	31	51	7	1	5	.238	.292	.305
1959	88	313	29	89	15	2	4	24	17	37	1	0	2	.284	.325	.383
1960	152	595	74	175	27	9	14	88	35	49	13	8	0	.294	.329	.440
1961	163	668	89	192	38	7	7	61	47	57	8	9	4	.287	.334	.397
1962	162	634	77	192	29	9	23	86	42	70	10	10	1	.303	.342	.486
1963	161	589	67	148	26	4	11	67	46	84	8	4	1	.251	.305	.365
1964	163	612	82	194	35	3	28	118	51	64	8	10	4	.317	.368	.521
1965	144	559	81	166	25	2	18	80	47	47	4	4	2	.297	.351	.445
1966	157	620	91	167	35	2	23	100	56	36	1	4	5	.269	.333	.444
1967	158	610	88	164	25	5	22	77	54	54	5	8	4	.269	.328	.434
1968	162	608	65	154	36	6	17	75	44	55	3	8	4	.253	.304	.416
1969	156	598	73	140	21	3	23	84	56	55	3	10	3	.234	.298	.395
1970	158	608	84	168	31	4	18	94	53	53	1	7	4	.276	.335	.429
1971	156	589	67	160	21	1	20	92	63	50	1	7	3	.272	.341	.413
1972	153	556	48	139	23	2	8	64	43	45	4	7	2	.250	.303	.342
1973	155	549	53	141	17	2	9	72	55	50	8	4	3	.257	.326	.344
1974	153	553	46	159	27	0	7	59	56	47	5	5	3	.288	.353	.374
1975	144	482	50	97	15	1	6	53	44	33	8	4	1	.201	.267	.274
1976	71	218	16	46	8	2	3	11	8	24	3	2	1	.211	.240	.307
1977	24	47	3	7	2	0	1	4	4	4	0	1	0	.149	.212	.255

G	AB	R	H	2B	3B	HR	RBI	BB	SO	HBP	AVG	OBP
2,896	10,654	1,232	2,848	482	68	268	1,357	860	990	53	.267	.322

FIELDING

Team	POS	G	GS	TC	CH	PO	A	E	DP	FLD%
1955 Orioles	3B	6	6	12	10	2	8	2	1	.833
1956 Orioles	2B	1	0	0	0	0	0	0	0	.000
1956 Orioles	3B	14	9	36	34	9	25	2	3	.944
1957 Orioles	3B	47	32	103	100	34	66	3	5	.971
1958 Orioles	2B	16	0	15	14	6	8	1	2	.933
1958 Orioles	3B	140	126	447	426	151	275	21	30	.953
1959 Orioles	2B	1	0	0	0	0	0	0	0	.000
1959 Orioles	3B	87	80	292	279	92	187	13	25	.955
1960 Orioles	2B	3	0	5	5	3	2	0	1	1.000
1960 Orioles	3B	152	152	511	499	171	328	12	34	.977
1961 Orioles	2B	2	0	1	1	0	1	0	0	1.000
1961 Orioles	3B	163	162	496	482	151	331	14	34	.972
1961 Orioles	SS	1	0	6	6	4	2	0	0	1.000
1962 Orioles	2B	2	0	2	2	1	1	0	0	1.000
1962 Orioles	3B	162	162	513	502	163	339	11	32	.979
1962 Orioles	SS	3	0	1	1	1	0	0	0	1.000
1963 Orioles	3B	160	158	495	483	153	330	12	43	.976
1963 Orioles	SS	1	0	1	1	0	1	0	0	1.000

CONTINUES.

Team	POS	G	GS	TC	CH	PO	A	E	DP	FLD%
1964 Orioles	3B	163	163	494	480	153	327	14	40	.972
1965 Orioles	3B	143	143	455	440	144	296	15	36	.967
1966 Orioles	3B	157	157	499	487	174	313	12	26	.976
1967 Orioles	3B	158	158	447	552	147	405	11	37	.980
1968 Orioles	3B	162	161	537	521	168	353	16	31	.970
1969 Orioles	3B	156	156	546	533	163	370	13	37	.976
1970 Orioles	3B	156	156	495	478	157	321	17	30	.966
1971 Orioles	3B	156	155	501	485	131	354	16	35	.968
1972 Orioles	3B	152	149	473	462	129	333	11	27	.977
1973 Orioles	3B	154	151	498	483	129	354	15	25	.970
1974 Orioles	3B	153	151	543	525	115	410	18	44	.967
1975 Orioles	3B	143	134	431	422	96	326	9	30	.979
1976 Orioles	3B	71	59	191	185	59	126	6	11	.969
1977 Orioles	3B	15	10	34	34	6	0	0	2	1.000
Career	POS	G	GS	TC	CH	PO	A	E	DP	FLD%
3B Totals		2,870	2,790	9,165	8,902	2,697	6,205	263	618	.971
2B Totals		25	0	23	22	10	12	1	3	.957
SS Totals		5	0	8	8	5	3	0	0	1.000
23 Years		2,900	2,790	9,196	8,932	2,712	6,220	264	621	.971

ALL-STAR GAMES

Yr	Team	G	AB	R	H	2B	3B	HR	RBI	BB	SO	SH	SF	HBP	AVG	OBP	SLG
1960	AL	2	3	0	0	0	0	0	0	0	0	0	0	0	.000	.000	.000
1961	AL	2	5	0	1	0	0	0	0	0	1	0	0	0	.200	.200	.200
1962	AL	2	1	1	0	0	0	0	0	1	0	0	0	1	.000	.667	.000
1963	AL	1	2	0	2	0	0	0	0	0	0	0	0	0	1.000	1.000	1.000
1964	AL	1	4	0	2	0	1	0	2	0	0	0	0	0	.500	.500	1.000
1965	AL	1	4	1	1	0	0	0	0	0	1	0	0	0	.250	.250	.250
1966	AL	1	4	1	3	0	1	0	0	0	0	0	0	0	.750	.750	1.250
1967	AL	1	6	1	1	0	0	1	1	0	1	0	0	0	.167	.167	.667
1968	AL	1	2	0	0	0	0	0	0	0	0	0	0	0	.000	.000	.000
1969	AL	1	1	0	0	0	0	0	0	0	1	0	0	0	.000	.000	.000
1970	AL	1	3	1	2	0	1	0	2	0	0	0	0	0	.667	.667	1.333
1971	AL	1	3	0	1	0	0	0	0	0	0	0	0	0	.333	.333	.333
1972	AL	1	2	0	0	0	0	0	0	0	0	0	0	0	.000	.000	.000
1973	AL	1	2	0	0	0	0	0	0	0	0	0	0	0	.000	.000	.000
1974	AL	1	3	0	0	0	0	0	0	0	0	0	0	0	.000	.000	.000
Career		G	AB	R	H	2B	3B	HR	RBI	BB	SO	SH	SF	HBP	AVG	OBP	SLG
15 Years		18	45	5	13	0	3	1	5	1	4	0	0	1	.289	.319	.489

ALL-STAR GAMES: FIELDING

Team	POS	G	GS	TC	CH	PO	A	E	DP	FLD%
1960 AL	3B	2	0	0	0	0	0	0	0	.000
1961 AL	3B	2	2	5	5	0	5	0	0	1.000
1962 AL	3B	2	0	2	2	0	2	0	0	1.000
1963 AL	3B	1	0	2	2	1	1	0	0	1.000
1964 AL	3B	1	1	3	3	1	2	0	0	1.000
1965 AL	3B	1	1	3	3	1	2	0	1	1.000
1966 AL	3B	1	1	8	8	4	4	0	0	1.000
1967 AL	3B	1	1	6	6	0	6	0	1	1.000
1968 AL	3B	1	1	1	1	0	1	0	0	1.000
1969 AL	3B	1	0	2	2	1	1	0	0	1.000
1970 AL	3B	1	0	2	2	1	1	0	0	1.000
1971 AL	3B	1	1	4	4	1	3	0	1	1.000
1972 AL	3B	1	1	1	1	0	1	0	0	1.000
1973 AL	3B	1	1	4	4	1	3	0	0	1.000
1974 AL	3B	1	1	0	0	0	0	0	0	.000
Career	POS	G	GS	TC	CH	PO	A	E	DP	FLD%
3B Totals		18	11	43	43	11	32	0	3	1.000
15 Years		18	11	43	43	11	32	0	3	1.000

LEAGUE CHAMPIONSHIP SERIES

Yr	Team	G	AB	R	H	2B	3B	HR	RBI	BB	SO	SH	SF	HBP	AVG	OBP	SLG
1969	Orioles	3	14	1	7	1	0	0	0	0	0	1	0	0	.500	.500	.571
1970	Orioles	3	12	3	7	2	0	0	2	0	1	0	1	0	.583	.538	.750
1971	Orioles	3	11	2	4	1	0	1	3	0	1	0	0	0	.364	.364	.727
1973	Orioles	5	20	1	5	2	0	0	2	1	1	0	0	0	.250	.286	.350
1974	Orioles	4	12	1	1	0	0	1	1	1	0	0	0	0	.083	.154	.333
Career		G	AB	R	H	2B	3B	HR	RBI	BB	SO	SH	SF	HBP	AVG	OBP	SLG
5 Years		18	69	8	24	6	0	2	8	2	3	1	1	0	.348	.361	.522

Team	POS	G	TC	CH	PO	A	E	DP	FLD%
1969 Orioles	3B	3	16	16	6	10	0	0	1.000
1970 Orioles	3B	3	8	8	3	5	0	0	1.000
1971 Orioles	3B	3	11	11	4	7	0	0	1.000
1973 Orioles	3B	5	17	16	2	14	1	0	.941
1974 Orioles	3B	4	17	17	4	13	0	1	1.000
Career	POS	G	TC	CH	PO	A	E	DP	FLD%
5 Years		18	69	68	19	49	1	1	.986

WORLD SERIES

Yr	Team	G	AB	R	H	2B	3B	HR	RBI	BB	SO	SH	SF	HBP	AVG	OBP	SLG
1966	Orioles	4	14	2	3	0	0	1	1	1	0	0	0	0	.214	.267	.429
1969	Orioles	5	19	0	1	0	0	0	2	0	3	0	1	0	.053	.050	.053
1970	Orioles	5	21	5	9	2	0	2	6	0	2	0	0	0	.429	.429	.810
1971	Orioles	7	22	2	7	0	0	0	5	3	1	0	2	0	.318	.370	.318
Career		G	AB	R	H	2B	3B	HR	RBI	BB	SO	SH	SF	HBP	AVG	OBP	SLG
4 Years		21	76	9	20	2	0	3	14	4	6	0	3	0	.263	.289	.408

Team	POS	G	TC	CH	PO	A	E	DP	FLD%
1966 Orioles	3B	4	10	10	4	6	0	1	1.000
1969 Orioles	3B	5	17	17	1	16	0	0	1.000
1970 Orioles	3B	5	24	23	9	14	1	2	.958
1971 Orioles	3B	7	25	23	6	17	2	1	.920
Career	POS	G	TC	CH	PO	A	E	DP	FLD%
4 Years		21	76	73	20	53	3	4	.961

Statistics courtesy of Baseball Almanac, www.baseball-almanac.com.

Notes

All quotes in the text are from personal interviews with the author unless otherwise noted below.

Prologue

4. "Nobody's ever named . . ." Michael Olesker, "Robinson's Image Springs Eternal," Baltimore Sun, January 13, 1983.

1. Little Rock

5. "I can't recall . . ." Personal interview with George Trout (who was sitting next to Smith in press row at the game).

6. Robinsons had farmed . . . "Pope County, Arkansas Geneology," www.argenweb .net; *Goodspeed's Biographical and Historical Memoirs of Western Arkansas* (Goodspeed Publishers, 1891), www.argenweb.net; www.couchgenweb.com/arkansas /pope/popeco3.htm; Gene Boyett, *Hardscrabble Frontier: Pope County, Arkansas in the 1850s* (University Press of America, 1990); 1850, 1880, and 1920 U.S. Census.

7. The previous winter . . . Nancy Hendricks, Arkansas State University, "Flood of 1927," www.encyclopediaofarkansas.net.

7. "America's greatest peacetime disaster" Ibid.

7. By 1930 . . . 1930 U.S. Census.

10. "Find your own . . ." Brooks Robinson and Fred Bauer, *Putting It All Together* (New York: Hawthorn, 1971).

11. "He was always . . ." John Steadman, "Brooks, at 13, Charted His Course to Majors," *Sporting News*, November 28, 1964.

11. "He'd wake up . . ." Rodney Lorenzen, "Robinson's Rise to Fame Was Only Expected," *Arkansas Democrat*, October 16, 1970.

12. "My dad had . . ." Brooks Robinson, "Big Talent from Little Rock," in *Before the Glory: 20 Baseball Heroes Talk About Growing Up and Turning Hard Times into Home Runs*, edited by Billy Staples and Rich Herschlag (Deerfield Beach, Florida: Health Communication, 2007).

12. "He's the one . . ." Brooks Robinson and Jack Tobin. *Third Base Is My Home* (Waco, Texas: Word, 1974).

13. "Some parents get . . ." Brooks Robinson and Fred Bauer, *Putting It All Together.*

16. "I've never seen . . ." Ibid.

17. "He was smart . . ." Kim Brazzel, "Brooks' Enthusiasm Brought Success Even in Basketball," *Arkansas Gazette,* January 7, 1978.

17. The first issue . . . *Pulaski Heights Tip Top Times,* October 1951.

2. "Everyone Liked Brooks"

22. "You two in particular . . ." Brooks Robinson and Fred Bauer, *Putting It All Together.*

23. Like the rest of the South . . . A. Cleveland Harrison, *A Little Rock Boyhood: Growing Up in the Great Depression* (Little Rock: Butler Center for Arkansas Studies, 2010); Carlotta Walls LaNier, *A Mighty Long Way: My Journey to Justice at Little Rock Central High School* (New York: Random House, 2009); Norris Guinn and Willis Callaway, *Lamar Porter Field and Memories of Sports in Little Rock During the 1950s* (Little Rock: Self-published, 2009); "Civil Rights and Social Change," www.encyclopediaofarkansas.net.

26. "I've just never believed" Brooks Robinson and Fred Bauer, *Putting It All Together.*

27. "Our B-team . . ." Kim Brazzel, "Brooks' Enthusiasm Brought Success Even in Basketball," *Arkansas Gazette,* January 7, 1978.

27. "He wasn't big . . ." Ibid.

28. "Brooks, remember that . . ." Brooks Robinson, "When Your Best Doesn't Win," Lenten Guideposts, in *Observer-Reporter,* March 16, 1972.

28. "On the bus . . ." Kim Brazzel, "Brooks' Enthusiasm Brought Success Even in Basketball," *Arkansas Gazette,* January 7, 1978.

28. In the Dell . . . *Dell Basketball—1955* (New York: Dell, 1955).

28. "[Wilson and Robinson] are among . . ." *Arkansas Gazette,* February 10, 1955.

28. "The thing that . . ." Kim Brazzel, "Brooks' Enthusiasm Brought Success Even in Basketball," *Arkansas Gazette,* January 7, 1978.

28. "I know he . . ." Ibid.

29. "Why I Want . . ." John Steadman, "Brooks, at 13, Charted His Course to Majors," *Sporting News,* November 28, 1964.

3. The Doughboys

32. "It meant something . . ." Kane Webb, "Haynie's Doughboys Back After 35 Years," *Arkansas Democrat,* August 19, 1988.

32. "We picked him . . ." Ibid.

33. "Brooks was as good . . ." " 'Fish' Remembers Brooks as MVP in Legion Rank," *Sporting News,* June 10, 1967.

34. "hard-throwing righthander . . ." *Arkansas Gazette,* July 2, 1954.

34. "Robinson Dazzles Altus . . ." "Robinson Dazzles Altus with Slants, Slugging in 18–6 Win," *Arkansas Gazette*, July 6, 1954.

35. "Of course, times . . ." Kane Webb, "Haynie's Doughboys Back After 35 Years," *Arkansas Democrat*, August 19, 1988.

36. "a gentle giant . . ." Norris Guinn and Willis Callaway, *Lamar Porter Field and Memories of Sports in Little Rock During the 1950s*.

36. On the air . . . A. Cleveland Harrison, *A Little Rock Boyhood*; Jim Davidson, "Repaying a Debt," www.thecabin.net, September 26, 2003.

38. In February of 1955 . . . John Steadman, "How Baltimore Orioles Signed Brooks Robinson," *Baseball Digest*, February 1971.

39. "A boy like Robinson . . ." John Steadman, "Robinson Covers Post like Vacuum Cleaner," *Sporting News*, June 15, 1963.

40. "The lower half . . ." John Eisenberg, "Scouts of Merit Lay Dynasty's Foundation," *Baltimore Sun*, February 9, 2004.

4. Welcome to the Baltimore Orioles

45. "Keep it" Robert Boyle, "Cincinnati's Brain-Picker," *Sports Illustrated*, June 13, 1966.

46. "It was a major . . ." John Eisenberg, "Back in the Bigs," *Baltimore Sun*, September 28, 2003.

46. "the most thrilling day . . ." Mike Klingaman, "Opening Act: On April 15, 1954, the Orioles' First Game in Baltimore Featured 46,354 Fans, 22 Bands, 33 Floats and a 3–1 Win over the White Sox," *Baltimore Sun*, April 15, 2004.

47. "Brecheen, is that . . ." Personal interview with Milt Pappas.

47. "No manager ever . . ." Lou Hatter, "Thoughts of Paul Richards," *Baseball Digest*, January 1961.

48. "No one ever . . ." Barney Kremenko, "Paul Richards Takes a Desk," *Baseball Digest*, March 1962.

48. "He thinks . . ." Danny Peary, *We Played the Game: Memories of Baseball's Greatest Era* (New York: Black Dog and Leventhal, 1994).

50. "If he's got ability . . ." Lou Hatter, "Thoughts of Paul Richards," *Baseball Digest*, January 1961.

51. "Son, go see . . ." personal interview with Bob Maisel.

54. "Just try Bob . . ." Jim McClure, "Brooks Robinson's Debut: 'Just Try Bob, Almost Everybody's Named Bob,'" www.yorkblog.com, June 16, 2007.

54. "Rookie Bob Robinson . . ." "White Roses Lace Lynchburg Cards, 14 to 5," *York Gazette and Daily*, June 4, 1955.

55. "Bob Robinson homered . . ." "White Roses Drop Twin Bill to Lynchburg, 3–2 and 3–1," *York Gazette and Daily*, June 10, 1955.

55. "he started two . . ." "White Roses Beat Norfolk Twice by 4–2 and 13 to 0," *York Gazette and Daily*, June 20, 1955.

57. Richards touted . . . "Orioles Will Accent Youth, Richards Says," AP in *Schenectady Gazette*, August 30, 1955.

58. "Nice hit, kid . . ." Brooks Robinson and Fred Bauer, *Putting It All Together.*

58. "I went two-for-four . . ." Brooks Robinson, as told to George Vass, "The Game I'll Never Forget," *Baseball Digest*, October 1972.

58. "He plays third base . . ." Ed Linn, "Why Everyone Loves Brooks Robinson," *Sport*, June 1972.

59. "Brooks was a nice . . ." John Eisenberg, *From 33rd Street to Camden Yards: An Oral History of the Baltimore Orioles* (New York: McGraw-Hill, 2001).

59. "He [Brooks] couldn't . . ." Ibid.

60. "He was sort of . . ." Ibid.

62. "Birds May Be O.K. . . ." Bob Maisel, "Birds May Be O.K. at Third," *Baltimore Sun*, December 16, 1955.

5. Glove Wizard

65. "while uncorking . . ." Jim Ellis, "Jim Dyck Cracks Orioles' Barrier on Old Brownies," *Sporting News*, March 21, 1956.

65. "Brooks Robinson's sure handed . . ." *Baltimore Sun*, February 23, 1956.

65. "He'll be back . . ." "Robinson, Bird Third Base Prospect, Sent to Santone," *Sporting News*, March 28, 1956.

65. "Let's kick their tails . . ." Brooks Robinson and Fred Bauer, *Putting It All Together.*

65. "Arky, you're playing . . ." Brooks Robinson and Jack Tobin, *Third Base Is My Home.*

66. "third base phenom . . ." *Baltimore Sun*, September 3, 1956.

68. "because I thought . . ." George Kell and Dan Ewald, *Hello Everybody, I'm George Kell* (Champaign, Illinois: Sports Publishing, 1998).

68. "Sure he's trying . . ." Bill McFarland, "Kell Tutors Probable Successor," *Times-News*, March 12, 1957.

68. "There never was . . ." George Kell and Dan Ewald, *Hello Everybody, I'm George Kell.*

68. "We do something . . ." Jerry Liska, "Kell Giving Lots of Help to 'Successor,'" AP in *Milwaukee Sentinel*, March 9, 1957.

69. "When I first saw . . ." John Eisenberg, "Cornerstone at Third Base," *South Florida Sun-Sentinel*, May 7, 2004.

69. "Brooks was impressive . . ." Jesse Linthicum, "40 Fill Oriole Cage, but Paul Has Door Open for Backstop," *Sporting News*, January 2, 1957.

69. "a finished fielder . . ." "Baltimore Orioles," *Sports Illustrated*, April 15, 1957.

69. "That Robinson sure . . ." Frank Litsky, "Robinson, Flashy Oriole Rookie, Knows 'It's All Up to My Hitting,'" *Sporting News*, May 1, 1957.

69. "Defensively he looks . . ." Jim Ellis, "Hot-Corner Kid Robinson Blazes as Oriole Rookie," *Sporting News*, April 3, 1957.

69. "the best pair . . ." Bill McFarland, "Kell Tutors Probable Successor," *Times-News*, March 12, 1985.

69. "finest pair of hands . . ." Jim Ellis, "Richards Crowing over Birds' Young Flock as 'Best Yet,'" *Sporting News*, March 13, 1957.

69. "turning in a thrill . . ." Jim Ellis, "Dick Williams Takes Aim at Orioles' Jinx," *Sporting News*, April 10, 1957.

70. "Okay, Arky . . ." Brooks Robinson and Jack Tobin, *Third Base Is My Home*.

70. "But it made me . . ." Bill Tanton, *Baseball Digest*, September 1958.

70. "I don't want you . . ." Ibid.

71. "probably would not . . ." "Plastic Helmet Saved a Player," AP in *St. Petersburg Times*, August 4, 1957.

71. "I feel very bad . . ." Ibid.

73. "He made fantastic . . ." Ed Linn, "Why Everyone Loves Brooks Robinson," *Sport*, June 1972.

74. "He'll be a great one" Jim Ellis, "Former Boo-Birds Sing New Tune for Woodling as Oriole," *Sporting News*, May 14, 1958.

75. "Both of your hands . . ." Peter Schmuck, "An Evening with Brooks," letter, October 26, 2009, www.weblogs.baltimoresun.com.

75. "If you're looking . . ." Brooks Robinson and Jack Tobin, *Third Base Is My Home*.

76. "That kid's got . . ." "Yankee Scouts Ignored Oriole," *Miami News*, April 28, 1958.

76. "Everybody who sees . . ." Bob Addie, "Addie's Atoms," *Sporting News*, May 14, 1958.

76. "So dependably was . . ." Jim Ellis, "Young Robinson, Glove-Whiz, Also Shows Bat Magic," *Sporting News*, June 11, 1958.

77. "As a third baseman . . ." Bill Tanton, "Baltimore's Future All-Star at Third," *Baseball Digest*, September 1958.

77. "I think he's . . ." Ibid.

6. Back to the Minors

79. "We want you . . ." Brooks Robinson and Fred Bauer, *Putting It All Together*.

80. Charlie Metro would later tell . . . Jim Hunt, "The Nice Guy Who Finishes First," *Montreal Gazette*, May 1, 1965.

80. "Well, your wife'll . . ." Charlie Metro and Thomas Altherr, *Safe by a Mile* (Lincoln: University of Nebraska Press, 2002).

81. "Robinson is a sparkling . . ." *Vancouver Sun*, May 5, 1959.

81. The field was wet . . . Brooks Robinson and Fred Bauer, *Putting It All Together*; Brooks Robinson and Jack Tobin, *Third Base Is My Home*; Len Corben, "Instant Replay: Doc and the Vacuum Cleaner," northshoreoutlook.com, May 18, 2011; Tom Hawthorn, "A Tip of the Cap to Charlie Metro," www.thetyee.ca, April 6, 2011; Kevin Glew, "Brooks Robinson's Career Almost Ended in Vancouver," Keven Glew's Canadian Baseball History Blog, www.kevinglew.wordpress.com, September 21, 2010.

82. "I've never had . . ." Len Corben, "Instant Replay: Doc and the Vacuum Cleaner," Northshoreoutlook.com, May 18, 2011.

83. "He didn't even . . ." Tom Hawthorn, "A Tip of the Cap to Charlie Metro," www .thetyee.ca, April 6, 2011.

83. "But this is serious . . ." Jim Hunt, "The Nice Guy Who Finishes First," *Montreal Gazette,* May 1, 1965.

83. "Nothing goes through . . ." Charlie Metro and Thomas Altherr, *Safe by a Mile.*

84. "I'd try to finesse . . ." Ibid.

84. "I'll never forget . . ." Ibid.

85. "as did all . . ." Tom Hawthorn, "A Tip of the Cap to Charlie Metro," www.thetyee .ca, April 6, 2011.

85. "He might have become . . ." Charlie Metro and Thomas Altherr, *Safe by a Mile.*

86. "Bird Bobbles Bring . . ." Jim Ellis, "Bird Bobbles Bring Recall of Robinson," *Sporting News,* July 15, 1959.

86. "displaying his old . . ." Doug Brown, "Knuck's Little Bit of Luck Helps Bust Bird's Buckle," *Sporting News,* July 22, 1959.

86. "He only threw . . ." Doug Brown, "Hats Off . . . Jerry Walker," *Sporting News,* September 23, 1959.

87. "the best player . . ." Doug Brown, "Orioles Hand Swifty Brandt Full-Time Job," *Sporting News,* December 9, 1959.

87. "There are many advantages . . ." Jesse Linthicum, "Flock to Take Wing in '59, Make Most Long Hops by Plane," *Sporting News,* February 4, 1959.

88. As he stepped onto . . . Brooks Robinson and Fred Bauer, *Putting It All Together;* Brooks Robinson and Jack Tobin, *Third Base Is My Home.*

7. Baby Birds

90. "We have . . ." Larry Klein, "Gentile Just Wanted a Chance," *Sport,* November 1960.

90. "This gang before me . . ." Charles Dexter, "Wing Man of the Orioles," *Baseball Digest,* October 1960.

90. "That kind of talk . . ." Ibid.

91. "The large, noisy crowd . . ." Roy Terrell, "Eager Young Birds," *Sports Illustrated,* June 13, 1960.

91. "I guess it will . . ." John Steadman, "Third Sacker Robinson, 23, Old Pro of Orioles' Infield," *Sporting News,* June 1, 1960.

91. "good raise" Ibid.

91. "There is no question . . ." Doug Brown, "Tigers Stalk Orioles for Prize Prey—Power Hitter Triandos," *Sporting News,* February 10, 1960.

91. "Third base has been . . ." "Baltimore Orioles," *Sports Illustrated,* April 11, 1960.

91. "Improved tremendously . . ." Milton Richman, "The American League Managers' Private Player Ratings," *Sport,* July 1960.

94. "This year I'm going . . ." "Baltimore Orioles," *Sports Illustrated,* April 9, 1962.

94. Brandt seemed to have . . . Mike Klingaman, "In Nest of Zanies, 3 Stood Out," baltimoresun.com, August 31, 2004.

94. "I lost it . . ." Ibid.

94. "What time is this . . ." "Orioles' Courtney Distrusts Plane, Heads for Bus Station," *Sporting News*, June 14, 1961.

95. "pink-cheeked players . . ." Walter Bingham, "The Hungry Young Birds," *Sports Illustrated*, September 19, 1960.

99. "quiet, good-natured . . ." Larry Williams, "Brooks Takes Charge in Baltimore," *Sport*, March 1961.

99. "In temperament . . ." Bill Furlong, "Baltimore's Youth Movement Is Paying Off," *Sport*, October 1960.

99. "clean-cut, good-looking . . ." Charles Dexter, "Wing Man of the Orioles," *Baseball Digest*, October 1960.

100. "Hey, it's air-conditioned" "Events and Discoveries of the Week," *Sports Illustrated*, July 25, 1960.

101. "It's difficult . . ." Bob Maisel, "The Morning After," *Baltimore Sun*, September 3, 1960.

102. "Don't be fooled . . ." Brooks Robinson and Fred Bauer, *Putting It All Together.*

102. "The man at third base . . ." *Baltimore Sun*, September 4, 1960.

102. "We just stared . . ." Doug Brown, "Sweep over Yankees Fires Orioles' Hopes," *Sporting News*, September 14, 1960.

102. "I believe this club . . ." *Baltimore Sun*, September 5, 1960.

102. "no tension whatsoever . . ." Bob Maisel, "The Morning After," *Baltimore Sun*, September 5, 1960.

102. "Robinson in Hospital . . ." *Baltimore Sun*, September 5, 1960.

103. "great leaping backhand . . ." *Baltimore Sun*, September 15, 1960.

104. "the gateway . . ." *Baltimore Sun*, September 16, 1960.

105. "I don't think . . ." John Eisenberg, *From 33rd Street to Camden Yards.*

105. "He acts like . . ." Larry Williams, "Brooks Takes Charge in Baltimore," *Sport*, March 1961.

105. "We don't have . . ." *Baltimore Sun*, September 30, 1960.

107. "I told her . . ." Marjorie North, "After the Golf, Before the Game; An All-Star Party," *Sarasota Herald-Tribune*, February 21, 1984.

107. "Brooks and I . . ." Milt Richman, "Brooks Is Full of Love, You Just Gotta Love the Guy," UPI in *St. Petersburg Times*, August 1, 1983.

108. "Welcome home . . ." Brooks Robinson and Fred Bauer, *Putting It All Together.*

109. "Brooks Takes Charge . . ." Larry Williams, "Brooks Takes Charge in Baltimore," *Sport*, March 1961.

109. "The 'young old-timers' . . ." Bob Addie, "Bob Addie's Atoms," *Sporting News*, May 10, 1961.

110. "Robinson is unbelievable . . ." Larry Williams, "Brooks Takes Charge in Baltimore," *Sport*, March 1961.

111. "In all my years . . ." John Eisenberg, *From 33rd Street to Camden Yards.*

111. "Billy was the nicest . . ." Danny Peary, *We Played the Game.*

112. "Brooks Robinson (24) is . . ." "Baltimore Orioles," *Sports Illustrated*, April 9, 1962.

112. "He has exceptional . . ." John Steadman, "Like He Came Down from a Higher League," *Baseball Digest*, January 1962.

112. "That Robinson feller . . ." Larry Williams, "Brooks Takes Charge in Baltimore," *Sport,* March 1961.

112. "If I had my . . ." Bob Maisel, "Brooks Robinson—First-Class Guy on and off Field," *Sporting News*, November 10, 1962.

112. "It's good to know . . ." John Steadman, "Like He Came Down from a Higher League," *Baseball Digest*, January 1962.

113. "Known as the Human Vacuum Cleaner . . ." John Steadman, "Robinson Covers Post like Vacuum Cleaner," *Sporting News*, June 15, 1963.

114. "I had come over . . ." John Eisenberg, *From 33rd Street to Camden Yards.*

115. "He never says . . ." Dick Young, "Young Ideas," *Sporting News*, September 28, 1960.

117. Players openly questioned . . . "Baltimore Orioles: The Bright Young Men Must Come of Age," *Sports Illustrated*, April 8, 1963.

8. Most Valuable

120. "Yeah, I sure do . . ." John Eisenberg, *From 33rd Street to Camden Yards.*

120. "I get more tired . . ." Doug Brown, "Bullpen Gives Orioles a Little Extra to Toss at Berra Bullies," *Sporting News,* August 29, 1964.

120. "Losers don't sing . . ." William Leggett, "They Went and Got 'Em," *Sports Illustrated*, August 31, 1964.

120. "I don't believe . . ." Barney Kremenko, "Hank Bauer Says He Isn't Tough, Merely 'Stern,' " *Baseball Digest*, May 1964.

121. "Just wrote his name . . ." Jerry Izenberg, "Behind the Jackie Brandt Image," *Sport,* November 1964.

121. "Brooks, you're so dumb . . ." Jim Palmer, television interview, October 2009, uploaded on YouTube December 7, 2009.

122. "You played with . . ." Doug Brown, "Orioles Take Bow for Red-Hot Raps of Young Bowens," *Sporting News*, August 1, 1964.

122. "Tell me about . . ." Louis Berney, *Tales from the Orioles Dugout* (Champaign, Illinois: Sports Publishing, 2004).

123. "I played behind . . ." Ibid.

124. "doing it for . . ." Doug Brown, "AL Rivals Babbling over Brooks, Oriole Toughie with Willow," *Sporting News,* September 5, 1964.

125. "As Custer said . . ." Doug Brown, "Like Custer, Bauer Bugged by Redskins," *Sporting News*, September 12, 1964.

125. "averaging about one . . ." Frank Deford, "Baltimore's Two Flags," *Sports Illustrated*, July 13, 1964.

126. "The talk about . . ." Jim Elliot, *Baltimore Sun*, September 4, 1964.

126. "He's the best . . ." Bob Maisel, "The Morning After," *Baltimore Sun*, September 18, 1964.

127. "I'm really thrilled . . ." *Baltimore Sun*, September 19, 1964.

127. "He was nervous . . ." Bob Maisel,"The Morning After," *Baltimore Sun*, September 19, 1964.

128. "the best year . . ." Louis Berney, *Tales from the Orioles Dugout*.

129. "It really pleases . . ." Doug Brown, "Who's Idol of Banquet Circuit? This Year It's MVP Robinson," *Sporting News*, January 16, 1965.

129. "That cured me . . ." "Sock Famine After Sparkling Bow Shrunk Brooks' Hat Size," *Sporting News*, June 15, 1963.

129. "Robinson, you stink . . ." "Robby's Joke on Himself Makes Hit with Audience," *Sporting News*, November 6, 1965.

130. "Now I'll be . . ." "MacPhail and Robinson Hold Pay Debate on Banquet Dais," *Sporting News*, January 26, 1963.

130. "Well, did you . . ." Jim Murray, "Brooks Robinson, Was That Really an Error?," syndicated, *Lakeland Ledger*, July 25, 1975.

130. According to Bill Valentine . . . Norris Guinn and Willis Callaway, *Lamar Porter Field and Memories of Sports in Little Rock During the 1950s*.

135. "Hey Dad. Some . . ." Brooks Robinson and Jack Tobin, *Third Base Is My Home*.

136. "That was absolutely . . ." Milt Richman, "Brooks Is So Full of Love, You Just Gotta Love the Guy," UPI in *St. Petersburg Times*, August 1, 1983.

136. "Brooks is one . . ." Bob Maisel, "Brooks Robinson—First-Class Guy on and off Field," *Sporting News*, November 10, 1962.

136. "All that's recognized . . ." John Steadman, "Diamond Whiz, Model Citizen: That's Brooks," *Sporting News*, November 10, 1962.

136. "Graciousness in personality . . ." John Steadman, "Gentleman Brooks—Hero in Baltimore," *Sporting News*, September 19, 1964.

137. "If all the players . . ." Jerry Rush, "The Great Robinson," *Arkansas! The Democrat Sunday Magazine*, December 4, 1966.

137. "Anyone who might . . ." Frank Deford, "Baltimore's Two Flags," *Sports Illustrated*, July 13, 1964.

138. "The very first player . . ." Roy Firestone, "The Kid Who Never Forgot," www.royfirestone.com, accessed June 4, 2012.

139. Brooks's reputation progressed . . . Jim Hunt, "The Nice Guy Who Finishes First," *Montreal Gazette*, May 1, 1965.

140. Dodger manager Leo Durocher . . . Robert Shaplan, "The Nine Lives of Leo Durocher," *Sports Illustrated*, May 30, 1955.

141. "I think this . . ." Doug Brown, "Orioles' Stars Agree: 'We'll Do Just Great Without Holler Guy,'" *Sporting News*, February 8, 1964.

141. "Team leaders are . . ." Jim Hunt, "The Nice Guy Who Finishes First," *Montreal Gazette*, May 1, 1965.

141. "You don't have to . . ." Oscar Kahan, "Robinson, Boyer Win Player-of-Year Laurels," *Sporting News*, October 17, 1964.

9. A Giant Leap

143. "I'm not out there . . ." Morton Sharnik, "The Moody Tiger of the Reds," *Sports Illustrated*, June 17, 1963.

144. While virtually every young player on the Reds . . . Doug Wilson, *Fred Hutchinson and the 1964 Cincinnati Reds* (Jefferson, North Carolina: McFarland, 2010).

145. "The average ballplayer . . ." Louis Chestnut, "That Other Robinson," *News and Courier*, October 5, 1966.

146. "made an effort . . ." Frank Robinson and Berry Stainback, *Extra Innings* (New York: McGraw-Hill, 1988).

146. "Frank, you're exactly . . ." Tom Adelman, *Black and Blue: The Golden Arm, the Robinson Boys, and the 1966 World Series That Stunned America* (New York: Little, Brown, 2006).

146. "I think we just . . ." John Eisenberg, *From 33rd Street to Camden Yards*.

146. In an early spring game . . . Frank Robinson and Al Silverman, *My Life Is Baseball*.

147. "We heard stuff . . ." Milton Richman, "Is Robbie for Real?," UPI in *Beaver County Times*, April 1, 1966.

147. "Before coming to Baltimore . . ." Frank Robinson and Al Silverman, *My Life Is Baseball*.

148. "Ask a young player . . ." Dick Kaegel, "An Oriole by Day," *Sporting News*, April 1, 1967.

148. "He really took me . . ." Ibid.

149. "If Brooks Robinson gets . . ." AP in *The Morning Record*, April 28, 1966.

149. "The whole team . . ." Frank Robinson and Al Silverman, *My Life Is Baseball*.

150. "my favorite .260 hitter" Gordon Beard, *Birds on the Wing* (New York: Doubleday, 1967).

150. First baseman Boog Powell . . . Brooks Robinson and Jack Tobin, *Third Base Is My Home*.

150. "Looks like Etchebarren . . ." Brooks Robinson and Frank Robinson, "Brooks and Frank Robinson Talk About Each Other," *Sport*, October 1966.

150. "The humor has no . . ." Doug Brown, "F. Robby's Fast-Flying Needle Helps Keep Orioles in Stitches," *Sporting News*, July 9, 1966.

151. "Under the unwritten rules . . ." Frank Robinson and Al Silverman, *My Life Is Baseball*.

151. "Robinson is from . . ." Dick Beddoes, *Vancouver Sun*, May 5, 1959.

151. "That happened after . . ." Charles Dexter, "Wing Man of the Orioles," *Baseball Digest*, October 1960.

152. "I suspect Brooks . . ." Frank Robinson and Berry Stainback, *Extra Innings*.

152. "With me being . . ." John Eisenberg, *From 33rd Street to Camden Yards*.

153. Once on the bus . . . Gordon Beard, *Birds on the Wing.*

153. "Look at this . . ." Ibid.

153. "I don't know . . ." Joe Donnelly, "Frank Robinson's Crusade," *Sport,* August 1966.

153. "Get up in . . ." Frank Robinson and Al Silverman, *My Life Is Baseball.*

154. "The basic Orioles starters . . ." Mark Mulvoy, "The Batmen Strike," *Sports Illustrated,* August 1, 1966.

155. "Of course I'm tired . . ." "Robinson Levels Blast at Owners over Scheduling," AP in *Herald Journal,* July 19, 1966.

155. "It looks like . . ." Gordon Beard, *Birds on the Wing.*

155. "Frank makes us . . ." Louis Chestnut, "That Other Robinson," *News and Courier,* October 5, 1966.

156. Late in the season *Sport* ran a piece . . . Brooks Robinson and Frank Robinson, "Brooks and Frank Robinson Talk About Each Other," *Sport,* October 1966.

157. That came on . . . Gordon Beard, *Birds on the Wing.*

157. "I'll tell you what . . ." Jim Henneman, "Thanks for a Precious Past," pressbox online.com, May 24, 2007.

158. "If these guys . . ." Jane Leavy, *Sandy Koufax: A Lefty's Legacy* (New York: HarperCollins, 2002).

159. "which has done . . ." "Forestry Service Lauds Dodgers: Conserve Wood," *Los Angeles Times,* October 5, 1966.

159. "Don't worry about it . . ." Bob Maisel, "The Morning After," *Baltimore Sun,* October 4, 1966.

159. "Well we've never . . ." Gordon Beard, *Birds on the Wing.*

161. "Two swings . . ." Jack Mann, "Those Happy Birds," *Sports Illustrated,* October 17, 1966.

161. "When Brooks and Frank . . ." Louis Berney, *Tales from the Orioles Dugout.*

162. "They aren't hitting . . ." Paul Zimmerman, "Alston's Faith in Big D Unshaken Despite Bad Start," *Los Angeles Times,* October 6, 1966.

162. "The first game . . ." John Eisenberg, *From 33rd Street to Camden Yards.*

163. "From Kansas City . . ." Sid Ziff, "Series Fever," *Los Angeles Times,* October 4, 1966.

163. "If it starts . . ." Jane Leavy, *Sandy Koufax.*

164. "Do you suppose . . ." Sid Ziff, "Sad Day for Willie," *Los Angeles Times,* October 7, 1966.

165. "I guess shutting out . . ." Jack Mann, "Those Happy Birds," *Sports Illustrated,* October 17, 1966.

166. "Whatever you do . . ." Brooks Robinson and Fred Bauer, *Putting It All Together.*

166. "When the last ball . . ." Mike Kingaman, "Brooks Robinson, Etchebarren and Boog Powell Recall Iconic Image of Orioles' Title," www.kansascity.com, September 19, 2012.

167. "One of the reasons . . ." William Leggett, "The Reasons Why the Orioles Won," *Sports Illustrated,* October 24, 1966.

167. "the zaniest celebration . . ." Mike Klingaman, "O's Took Memorable Route to Bring First World Series Title to Baltimore," www.baltimoresun.com, September 24, 2006.

167. "It was great . . ." Tom Adelman, *Black and Blue.*

167. "We're all so proud . . ." Jerry Rush, "The Great Robinson," *Arkansas! The Democrat Sunday Magazine*, December 4, 1966.

167. "It was a wonderful . . ." Brooks Robinson and Jack Tobin, *Third Base Is My Home.*

000. "It was the first . . ." Mike Klingaman, "O's Took Memorable Route to Bring First World Series Title to Baltimore," www.baltimoresun.com, September 24, 2006.

10. "He Does That All the Time"

169. "If a guy walks . . ." Sam Huff, "Vietnam Diary," *Sport*, May 1966.

170. "but at night . . ." Ibid.

170. "I was just young . . ." George Vecsey, *Stan Musial: An American Life* (New York: Ballantine, 2011).

170. "shaking like a leaf" Ibid.

170. "Yeah, get us . . ." Tom Callahan, *Johnny U: The Life and Times of John Unitas* (New York: Crown, 2006).

170. "Wherever I've gone . . ." "Stan Musial, Harmon Killebrew Visit Vietnam," www.retrosimba.com, May 15, 2011.

170. "We didn't sit back . . ." "Braves' Aaron on Go; At Bat in Vietnam," AP in *Daytona Beach Morning Journal*, April 4, 1967.

171. "Baseball Stars Give . . ." Ray Belford, "Baseball Stars Give Fighting Men a Lift," *Stars and Stripes*, November 11, 1966.

171. "I met a lot . . ." Brooks Robinson and Fred Bauer, *Putting It All Together.*

171. "Imagine—here was . . ." Brooks Robinson and Jack Tobin, *Third Base Is My Home.*

171. "Those kids over there . . ." Dave Klein, *Great Infielders of the Major Leagues* (New York: Random House, 1972).

171. "to say for all . . ." John Steadman, *Days in the Sun* (Baltimore: Baltimore Sun, 2000).

172. "These men are . . ." C. C. Johnson Spink, "We Believe," *Sporting News*, November 19, 1966.

173. "A month ago . . ." Doug Brown, "Brooks' Bat Babbles with '63 Vigor," *Sporting News*, August 5, 1967.

174. "I'll be here . . ." Frank Robinson and Berry Stainback, *Extra Innings.*

175. "Not your rule book . . ." Alfred Wright, "The Birds Hop for a Lively Bantam," *Sports Illustrated*, April 13, 1970.

176. "Where I'd come from . . ." John Eisenberg, "Cornerstone at Third Base," baltimoresun.com, May 7, 2004; John Eisenberg, *From 33rd Street to Camden Yards;* John Eisenberg, "Baseball's Greatest—Brooks Robinson: The Game's Best Defensive Third Baseman," *Baseball Digest*, September 2004.

176. "Kids come up . . ." Ed Linn, "Why Everyone Loves Brooks Robinson," *Sport*, June 1972.

11. "The Best Team Doesn't Always Win"

179. "Trying to hit . . ." Dick Couch, "Palmer Tries for Oriole Sweep," AP in *Rock Hill Herald*, October 14, 1970.

179. "Where were you . . ." John Eisenberg, *From 33rd Street to Camden Yards*.

180. "Earl asked me . . ." Mike Bryan, *Baseball Lives* (New York: Pantheon 1989).

180. "The pitchers would . . ." John Eisenberg, *From 33rd Street to Camden Yards*.

180. "in charge . . ." Jim Palmer and Jim Dale, *Palmer and Weaver: Together We Were Eleven Foot Nine* (Kansas City, Missouri: Andrews & McMeel, 1996).

181. "Brooks just loved . . ." Earl Weaver with Berry Stainback, *It's What You Learn After You Know It All That Counts* (Garden City, New York: Doubleday, 1982).

183. "Brooks would work . . ." John Eisenberg, *From 33rd Street to Camden Yards*.

183. "Brooks took a bunch . . ." Ibid.

185. The team atmosphere . . . Earl Weaver with Berry Stainback, *It's What You Learn After You Know It All That Counts*; Frank Robinson and Berry Stainback, *Extra Innings*; Mark Mulvoy, "Just Call Them Plain Folk Heroes," *Sports Illustrated*, October 20, 1969; John Eisenberg, *From 33rd Street to Camden Yards*.

187. "The problem with . . ." Earl Weaver with Berry Stainback, *It's What You Learn After You Know It All That Counts*.

187. "I was on Brooksie . . ." Bill Braucher, "Brooks Robinson, Still the Vacuum Cleaner," *Baseball Digest*, July 1974.

188. "Brooks almost never . . ." Earl Weaver with Berry Stainback, *It's What You Learn After You Know It All That Counts*.

189. "You split a bottle . . ." "They Said It," *Sports Illustrated*, October 6, 1969.

190. "Ron [*sic*] Gaspar just said . . ." Mark Mulvoy, "Just Call Them Plain Folk Heroes," *Sports Illustrated*, October 20, 1969.

191. "The play, amazingly . . ." Ibid.

191. "That wouldn't have . . ." Ibid.

191. "I never give up . . ." AP in *Herald-Journal*, October 12, 1969.

191. "I don't believe . . ." Lowell Reidenbaugh, "Brooks' Fielding Gem Decides Opener," *Sporting News*, October 25, 1969.

196. "They became more . . ." Lowell Reidenbaugh, "Oh, What a Year for Beautiful Birds," *Sports Illustrated*, October 31, 1970.

196. "Our problem was . . ." Earl Weaver with Berry Stainback, *It's What You Learn After You Know It All That Counts*.

196. "That was a lesson . . ." Phil Pepe, *Catfish, Yaz, and Hammerin' Hank: The Unforgettable Era That Transformed Baseball* (Chicago: Triumph, 2005).

196. "The Mets won 100 . . ." Ibid.

12. The Vacuum Cleaner

197. "I didn't see . . ." Phil Pepe, *Catfish, Yaz, and Hammerin' Hank*.

197. "We knew we . . ." Ibid.

197. "I never told him . . ." Jim Palmer and Jim Dale, *Palmer and Weaver*.

199. "personal qualities that . . ." "B. Robinson Wins Award," AP in *Evening Independent*, December 19, 1966.

199. "exemplary conduct . . ." "Awards Planned for Robinson," AP in *Free Lance-Star*, December 24, 1966.

199. John Steadman voiced . . . John Steadman, "Brooks Robinson—As Gracious off Field as He's Graceful on It," *Sporting News*, August 19, 1967.

200. "I know you read . . ." Ed Linn, "Why Everyone Loves Brooks Robinson," *Sport*, June 1972.

201. "He never slips . . ." Mark Kram, "Discord Defied and Deified," *Sports Illustrated*, October 5, 1970.

201. "I'm talking about . . ." *One Flew over the Cuckoo's Nest*, dir. Milos Forman, United Artists, 1975.

202. Before leaving Baltimore . . . *Baltimore Sun*, October 9, 1970.

202. "I'm a major league . . ." Hal McCoy, "Boys in the Hall: Brooks Robinson," www .foxsportsohio.com, July 15, 2011.

202. "There is nothing . . ." Ken Nigro, "AstroTurf Won't Bother Birds," *Baltimore Sun*, October 8, 1970.

203. "If that ball . . ." Bob Maisel, "The Morning After," *Baltimore Sun*, October 11, 1970.

204. Pete Rose told reporters . . . Ibid.

204. "I never saw . . ." Tom Loomis, *Toledo Blade*, October 12, 1970.

204. "He was going toward . . ." Ira Berkow, "The Two Baseball Gloves," *New York Times*, December 26, 1988.

204. "When you play . . ." William Leggett, "Flying Start for the Big Bad Birds," *Sports Illustrated*, October 19, 1970.

205. "So Brooks Robinson . . ." Ira Berkow, NEA, *Meriden Journal*, October 16, 1970.

205. "That's got to be . . ." William Leggett, "Flying Start for the Big Bad Birds," *Sports Illustrated*, October 19, 1970.

205. "It was one . . ." Ira Berkow, "Brooks Robinson—Super Playmaker," NEA in *Meriden Journal*, October 16, 1970.

205. "I can never remember . . ." *Baseball Comes of Age*, video produced for Triumph Books by Frederick Koster, Kosterfilms, 2006.

206. "The way I see it . . ." Bob Maisel, "The Morning After," *Baltimore Sun*, October 12, 1970.

206. "I never saw . . ." Ibid.

206. "He has to be . . ." AP in *Gettysburg Times*, October 14, 1970.

207. "I'm beginning to see . . ." Ibid.

207. "Why are all . . ." Bob Maisel, "The Morning After," *Baltimore Sun*, October 12, 1970.

207. "What kind of juice . . ." Brooks Robinson and Fred Bauer, *Putting It All Together*.

208. "Bench drove a savage . . ." Lowell Reidenbaugh, "Reds Beaten, Robbed by Brooks the Bandit," *Sporting News*, October 31, 1970.

208. "Brooks is so good . . ." Jerome Holtzman, *Sporting News*, October 31, 1970.

208. "Next time I'll . . ." Roy McHugh, "The Third Base Magnet," *Pittsburgh Press*, October 14, 1970.

208. "He's unreal . . ." Lowell Reidenbaugh, "Reds Beaten, Robbed by Brooks the Bandit," *Sporting News*, October 31, 1970.

208. "I don't believe . . ." Ibid.

208. "This guy is playing . . ." Bob Maisel, "The Morning After," *Baltimore Sun*, October 14, 1970.

209. "I've never seen . . ." Lowell Reidenbaugh, "Reds Beaten, Robbed by Brooks the Bandit," *Sporting News*, October 31, 1970.

209. "I know it's starting . . ." Seymour Smith, "B. Robby's Play Baffles Skipper," *Baltimore Sun*, October 14, 1970.

209. "He's not at his . . ." Fay Vincent, *We Would Have Played for Nothing: Baseball Stars of the 1950s and 1960s Talk About the Game They Loved* (New York: Simon & Schuster, 2008).

209. "Come back tomorrow . . ." Lowell Reidenbaugh, "Reds Beaten, Robbed by Brooks the Bandit," *Sporting News*, October 31, 1970.

209. "After the third game . . ." *Baseball Comes of Age*, video produced for Triumph Books by Frederick Koster, Kosterfilms, 2006.

210. "I finally found . . ." *Baltimore Sun*, October 15, 1970.

210. "Get three Brooks . . ." *Arkansas Democrat*, October 16, 1970.

210. "Brooksie, make it . . ." William Leggett, "That Black and Orange Magic," *Sports Illustrated*, October 26, 1970.

210. "It's the most touching . . ." Brooks Robinson and Fred Bauer, *Putting It All Together*.

211. "For years people . . ." Phil Jackman, "Top Series Belonged to Brooks," www.sun-sentinel.com, October 15, 1990.

211. "Those plays Robinson . . ." Earl Lawson, "Skipper Sparky Proud of Losing Reds," *Sporting News*, October 31, 1970.

211. "If he was . . ." "Insiders Say," *Sporting News*, October 31, 1970.

211. "I hope we can . . ." William Leggett, "That Black and Orange Magic," *Sports Illustrated*, October 26, 1970.

211. "Don't drop it . . ." Hal Bock, "Brooks Just Bubbles Over," AP in *Baltimore Sun*, October 16, 1970.

211. At the victory party Lou Hatter "Showboat Brooks Eludes Fine," *Baltimore Sun*, October 17, 1970.

212. "Hi, Dad . . ." Brooks Robinson and Fred Bauer, *Putting It All Together*.

212. "In retrospect . . ." Bob Maisel, "The Morning After," *Baltimore Sun*, October 18, 1970.

212. "If there's ever . . ." Jim Murray, "Best of Murray," *Sporting News*, October 31, 1970.

212. "He took us out . . ." Phil Pepe, *Catfish, Yaz, and Hammerin' Hank*.

212. "The amazing thing . . ." Ibid.

213. "He made those . . ." Louis Berney, *Tales from the Orioles Dugout*.

213. "I went into . . ." Phil Pepe, *Catfish, Yaz, and Hammerin' Hank*.

213. "As an infielder . . ." *Baseball Comes of Age*, video produced for Triumph Books by Frederick Koster, Kosterfilms, 2006.

13. End of the Era

217. "I figure . . ." Phil Jackman, "Airline Working Overtime to Keep Brooks on Move," *Sporting News*, December 5, 1970.

217. "I always keep . . ." "Orioles Third Sacker Relies on Reflexes," UPI in *Sarasota Journal*, October 14, 1969.

217. "a little 24 hopper . . ." Phil Jackman, "Top Series Belonged to Brooks," www .sun-sentinel.com, October 15, 1990; *Baseball Comes of Age*, video produced for Triumph Books by Frederick Koster, Kosterfilms, 2006.

217. "The rumor is . . ." Brooks Robinson and Jack Tobin, *Third Base Is My Home*.

218. "Perhaps his glove . . ." Jim Elliot, "Dalton and MacPhail Say Defense Does Count," *Baltimore Sun*, October 21, 1970.

218. "Brooks Robinson Makes 3 Errors," *Milwaukee Journal*, July 29, 1971; "Brooks Robinson Is Human," *St. Joseph News-Press*, July 29, 1971; "Bad Night for Brooks: 3 Errors in One Inning," *New York Times*, July 28, 1971.

219. "It just wasn't . . ." "Brooks Robinson Is Human," *St. Joseph News-Press*, July 29, 1971.

220. "You just expect . . ." "Superman Does It Again for O's," AP in *Lakeland Ledger*, October 11, 1971.

221. "The biggest thing . . ." Louis Berney, *Tales from the Orioles Dugout*.

14. Good-bye Frank

224. "When I heard . . ." Peter Siversein, ed., "So Long Robby, We Love/Hate to See You Go," *1972 Baseball Guidebook* (New York: Mace, 1972).

224. "We couldn't have won . . ." John Steadman, "Frank Robinson Meant the Difference," *Baseball Digest*, March 1972.

224. "Frank was just . . ." Ed Linn, "Why Everyone Loves Brooks Robinson," *Sport*, June 1972.

224. "Never in the history . . ." "Orioles Sign Brooks but Five Still Absent," AP in *Leader-Post*, March 2, 1972.

225. Brooks decided that he deserved $500 . . . *Baseball Comes of Age*, video produced for Triumph Books by Frederick Koster, Kosterfilms, 2006.

226. "I want to play . . ." Oscar Kahan, "Players Walk Out on April Fool's Day," *Sporting News*, April 15, 1972.

226. "damn greedy" Ibid.

227. "Brooks Robinson, the fair . . ." Lou Hatter, "Some Stones Churn Brooks' Placid Waters," *Sporting News*, April 29, 1972.

227. "I realized that this . . ." Ibid.

228. "The compromise agreement . . ." *New York Times*, April 14, 1972.

228. "When I look back . . ." John Eisenberg, *From 33rd Street to Camden Yards*.

228. "The worst ten . . ." Brooks Robinson and Jack Tobin, *Third Base Is My Home*.

229. "as flawless as . . ." AP, February 11, 1972.

229. Washington sportswriter Ed Linn . . . Ed Linn, "Why Everyone Loves Brooks Robinson," *Sport*, June 1972.

233. Stephanie Vardos was . . . Mike Bryan, *Baseball Lives*.

233. "Gods do not . . ." John Updike, "Hub Fans Bid Kid Adieu," *New Yorker*, October 22, 1960.

235. "I only have . . ." "Reserve Clause Key Issue," AP in *Herald-Journal*, February 6, 1973.

235. "Yes, after I've . . ." Brooks Robinson and Jack Tobin, *Third Base Is My Home*.

235. "We had seen . . ." Judy Klemes, "Hero Hucksters: Athletes Lured by Madison Ave.," *New York Times*, May 9, 1973.

237. "You can go . . ." AP in *Lakeland Ledger*, August 21, 1973.

237. "Which is higher . . ." Doug Brown, "A New Brooks: Hot Bat, Cold Glove," May 25, 1974.

238. "It took Earl . . ." Fay Vincent, *We Would Have Played for Nothing*.

239. Brooks's autobiography . . . Brooks Robinson and Jack Tobin, *Third Base Is My Home*.

240. "As you move . . ." Brooks Robinson, "When Your Best Doesn't Win," Guideposts, in *Observer-Reporter*, March 16, 1972.

240. "I believe that . . ." Gary Warner, "Everyone Winner Under FCA Rules," September 2, 1967.

240. "I recognized the need . . ." Monica Surfaro, "How Famous Parents Pass On Their Religious Values," *Herald-Journal*, April 10, 1977.

15. Poor Brooks

242. "I figure I've got . . ." Ron Reid, "Good Field, No More Hit," *Sports Illustrated*, April 26, 1976.

243. "He probably can't . . ." Ibid.

243. "I'm going to play . . ." Ibid.

243. "I still love . . ." Milton Richman, "Orioles' Brooks Just Won't Quit," UPI in *Ellensburg Daily Record*, May 2, 1976.

244. "If something doesn't . . ." Gene Williams, "Waiting to Play Behind Brooks Has DeCinces Checking Options," *Miami News*, March 23, 1976.

245. "I saw him . . ." Doug Brown, "In '77 Brooks Offered Final Thrill," *Baltimore Sun*, May 18, 1995.

246. "Those are heartbreaking . . ." Louis Berney, *Tales from the Orioles Dugout*.

246. "Are we using . . ." Gordon Beard, "Oriole Brooks Robinson Goes to Bench," AP in *Free Lance-Star*, May 18, 1976.

246. "It's no big . . ." Ibid.

247. "It was Brooks Robinson's fault . . ." Jim Palmer and Jim Dale, *Palmer and Weaver*.

247. "Brooks did everything . . ." Thomas Boswell, "Brooks Robinson: A Man of Class Bows Out," *Baseball Digest*, December 1977.

247. "Here's a guy . . ." Jim Kaplan, "He's Out from Under the Shadow," *Sports Illustrated*, April 23, 1979.

248. "Brooks, who's giving . . ." "Brooks Robinson Honored at What Is Expected to Be Last Game with Orioles," AP in *Gettysburg Times*, September 30, 1976.

249. "Just about every . . ." Fay Vincent, *We Would Have Played for Nothing*.

249. While he was worrying . . . Milton Richman, "Brooks Robinson Saves Home but Business Wipes Out Savings," UPI in *Telegraph Herald*, September 2, 1976; Phil Pepe, "Bird's Robinson at Crossroads," Knight News Service in *Toledo Blade*, September 8, 1976; Frederic Kelly, "I Want to Forget That Part of My Life," *Baltimore Sun*, May 1, 1977.

253. "It's a temporary . . ." Allen Lewis, "Ripple Still in Brooks," Knight Newspapers in *St. Petersburg Independent*, September 25, 1976.

254. "It was just a bad . . ." Jim Murray, "Can They Do That to Brooks Robinson," *Los Angeles Times*, in *Lewiston Morning Tribune*, May 18, 1977.

256. "I hope to work . . ." Jim Henneman, "Robby Will Serve O's as Player-Coach," January 8, 1977.

256. "Frank probably looked up . . ." Matthew Taylor, "Brooks Robinson's Memorable Final Homer Embodied Orioles Magic," www.masnsports.com, April 15, 2011.

257. "Outside of our . . ." Doug Brown, "In '77, Brooks Offered Final Thrill," *Baltimore Sun*, May 18, 1995.

257. "The kids are doing . . ." Jim Henneman, "'No-No' Orioles Have 'Yes-Yes' in Their Eyes," July 30, 1977.

257. "Brooks could have . . ." Thomas Boswell, "Brooks Robinson: A Man of Class Bows Out," *Baseball Digest*, December 1977.

258. "He's such a humble . . ." Jim Henneman, "Brooks Bows Out as He Played—With Class," *Sporting News*, September 17, 1977.

259. "It's the logical . . ." Ibid.

259. "no big deal . . ." Ibid.

259. "I struck out . . ." "Baseball Legend Brooks Robinson Buoyed by Faith, Family, Friends," www.catholicstandard.org, June 15, 2010.

259. "Nobody's ever named . . ." Michael Olesker, "Robinson's Image Springs Eternal," *Baltimore Sun*, January 13, 1983.

259. "The piece of life-saving . . ." Jim Henneman, "Praises Flow in Auld Lang Syne for Brooks," *Sporting News*, October 8, 1977.

259. "I hope that . . ." Ibid.

260. Earl Weaver had spent . . . Earl Weaver with Berry Stainback, *It's What You Learn After You Know It All That Counts*.

260. "Never in my . . ." Jim Henneman, "Praises Flow in Auld Lang Syne for Brooks," *Sporting News*, October 8, 1977.

260. "the single most effective . . ." Chuck Thompson with Gordon Beard, *Ain't the Beer Cold* (South Bend, Indiana: Diamond Communications, 1996).

260. "I don't think . . ." Earl Weaver with Berry Stainback, *It's What You Learn After You Know It All That Counts.*

16. Cooperstown

262. "I remember Brooks Robinson . . ." Anthony Castrovince, "Shapiro Learned People Skills from Dad," MLB.com, November 29, 2009.

262. "Good teams put . . ." Phil Jackman, "Listening to 'Old No. 5' Remains Easy Delight for Orioles Watchers," www.sun-sentinel.com, August 21, 1992.

263. "On the air . . ." Chuck Thompson with Gordon Beard, *Ain't the Beer Cold.*

263. "When you retire . . ." Kathy Blumenstock, "Retirement Is Painful for Professional Athletes," *Washington Post*, June 21, 1982.

263. "I really think . . ." Woody White, "Brooks Robinson Glad He's Retired," *Herald-Journal*, June 26, 1985.

264. "I'm a little overwhelmed . . ." AP in *Montreal Gazette*, January 13, 1983.

265. "We grew up . . ." Joseph Durso, "At Cooperstown, the Past Has Its Day," *New York Times*, July 31, 1983.

265. "When Brooks went in . . ." Mike Klingaman, "Brooks Robinson Will Forever Be the Orioles' Third Baseman," *Baltimore Sun*, May 14, 2012.

265. "I can't believe it . . ." Milt Richman, "Brooks Is So Full of Love, You Just Gotta Love the Guy," UPI in *St. Petersburg Times*, August 1, 1983.

266. "I never saw . . ." Fred Down, "Hall Hurrah," UPI in *Deseret News* (Utah), August 1, 1983.

266. "I keep asking . . ." Joseph Durso, "Four Enter Baseball Hall Amid Cheers and Tribute," *New York Times*, August 1, 1983.

266. "Throughout my career . . ." Mike Klingaman, "Brooks Robinson Will Forever Be the Orioles' Third Baseman," *Baltimore Sun*, May 14, 2012.

266. "To be recognized . . ." Fred Down, "Hall Hurrah," UPI in *Deseret News* (Utah), August 1, 1983.

266. At the Hall of Fame ceremony . . . John Steadman, *Days in the Sun.*

272. "reveals many attributes . . ." Roy Firestone, "The Kid Who Never Forgot," www.royfirestone.com, accessed June 4, 2012.

272. "That's what baseball . . ." "Brooks at 70," www.pressboxonline.com, May 24, 2007.

272. "Mrs. Robinson . . ." Ibid.

272. "I went $200,000 . . ." Ibid.

272. "the most magnificent . . ." Chuck Thompson with Gordon Beard, *Ain't the Beer Cold.*

274. "I don't want . . ." David Ginsburg, "Brooks Robinson: Still Loving Baseball at 70," www.usatoday.com, June 14, 2007.

274. "He appreciates minor . . ." Ibid.

275. "Of all the . . ." Thomas Boswell, "Brooks Robinson: A Man of Class Bows Out," *Baseball Digest*, December 1977.

275. "there were TV . . ." Chuck Thompson with Gordon Beard, *Ain't the Beer Cold*.

276. "It wasn't a bother . . ." John Schulian, *Sometimes They Even Shook Your Hand* (Lincoln: University of Nebraska Press, 2011).

276. "My wife says . . ." "Brooks at 70," www.pressboxonline.com, May 24, 2007.

277. "Everywhere I go . . ." David Ginsburg, "Brooks Robinson: Still Loving Baseball at 70," www.usatoday.com, June 14, 2007.

278. "We've got all . . ." Dean Bartoli Smith, "Brooks Robinson Remembered as Young Fan's Hero, at a Time When He Really Needed One," www.baltimorebrew.com, October 28, 2005.

280. "I try to keep . . ." "Brooks at 70," www.pressboxonline.com, May 24, 2007.

280. "He was a man . . ." Michael Olesker, "Robinson's Image Springs Eternal," *Baltimore Sun*, January 13, 1983.

280. "Why? The public . . ." John Steadman, *Days in the Sun*.

281. "I consider myself . . ." "Legends of the Diamond 2," MLB.com, August 20, 2009.

281. "It passed so fast . . ." John Eisenberg, "No Bows for Brooks," baltimoresun.com, September 14, 2005.

281. "Someone asked me . . ." Philip Seaton, "Professional Third Baseman Defined: Arkansas' Brooks Robinson," arkansassports360.com, June 2009.

281. "People are going . . ." Childs Walker, "O's, Brooks: No Rift," baltimoresun.com, June 14, 2008.

282. "I've been very . . ." Peter Schmuck, "B. Robinson Was Treated for Cancer," baltimoresun.com, May 13, 2009.

282. "It was sickening . . ." Fritz Peterson, "All My Friends Are Hurt and Dying," www.baseballhappenings.net, February 7, 2012.

17. Statues

284. "first in the hearts . . ." Pressboxonline.com, October 22, 2011.

285. "To all my . . ." WNST.net, October 22, 2011.

286. "Brooks Robinson was the best . . ." *Sleepless in Seattle*, dir. Nora Ephron, TriStar Pictures, 1993.

287. "In the future . . ." Brooks Robinson and Jack Tobin, *Third Base Is My Home*.

287. "He's doing great . . ." AP, ESPN.com, March 20, 2012.

287. "He's not Brooks Robinson . . ." Jeffrey Paternostro, www.amazinavenue.com, April 12, 2012.

287. "In other words . . ." Paul M. Banks, thesportsbank.net, July 14, 2011.

287. "Lonnie Chisenhall doesn't . . ." Paul Hoynes, *Plain Dealer*, www.cleveland.com, April 15, 2012.

288. "The baseball park . . ." Fay Vincent, *We Would Have Played for Nothing*.

288. "When they talk . . ." Jim Murray, "Baseball's Living Legend: Orioles' Brooks Robinson," *Los Angeles Times*, in *Free Lance-Star*, July 24, 1971.

288. "How many interviews . . ." Roy Firestone, "The Kid Who Never Forgot," www
.royfirestone.com, accessed June 4, 2011.

288. "All major leaguers . . ." Bob Addie, *Sporting News*, June 12, 1976.

288. "Robinson's character is . . ." C. C. Johnson Spink, "A Tribute to Robinson,"
Sporting News, September 11, 1977.

289. "It's fantastic . . ." Ed Linn, "Why Everyone Loves Brooks Robinson," *Sport*, June
1972.

289. "I try to be kind . . ." Brooks Robinson and Jack Tobin, *Third Base Is My Home*.

289. "I've been blessed . . ." Roy Firestone, "The Kid Who Never Forgot," www.royfire
stone.com, accessed June 4, 2011.

289. "I'd like to be . . ." Fay Vincent, *We Would Have Played for Nothing*.

Bibliography

Aaron, Hank, with Lonnie Wheeler. *I Had a Hammer*. New York: HarperCollins, 1991.

Adelman, Tom. *Black and Blue: The Golden Arm, the Robinson Boys, and the 1966 World Series That Stunned America*. New York: Little, Brown, 2006.

Beard, Gordon. *Birds on the Wing*. New York: Doubleday, 1967.

Berney, Louis. *Tales from the Orioles Dugout*. Champaign, Illinois: Sports Publishing, 2004.

Bouton, Jim. *Ball Four*. New York: World, 1970.

Bryan, Mike. *Baseball Lives*. New York: Pantheon, 1989.

Burchard, Marshall, and Sue Burchard. *Sports Hero: Brooks Robinson*. New York: G. P. Putnam's Sons, 1972.

Callahan, Tom. *Johnny U: The Life and Times of John Unitas*. New York: Crown, 2006.

Chafets, Zev. *Cooperstown Confidential*. New York: Bloomsbury USA, 2009.

Corbett, Warren. *The Wizard of Waxahachie: Paul Richards and the End of Baseball as We Knew It.* Dallas: Southern Methodist University Press, 2009.

Eisenberg, John. *From 33rd Street to Camden Yards: An Oral History of the Baltimore Orioles.* New York: McGraw-Hill, 2001.

Epstein, Dan. *Big Hair and Plastic Grass: A Funky Ride Through Baseball and America in the Swinging '70s.* New York: Thomas Dunne Books, 2010.

Falls, Joe. *50 Years of Sports Writing.* Champaign, Illinois: Sports Publishing, 1997.

Gildea, William. *When the Colts Belonged to Baltimore.* New York: Ticknor & Fields, 1994.

Guinn, Norris, and Willis Callaway. *Lamar Porter Field and Memories of Sports in Little Rock During the 1950s.* Little Rock: Self-published, 2009.

Harrison, A. Cleveland. *A Little Rock Boyhood: Growing Up in the Great Depression.* Little Rock: Butler Center for Arkansas Studies, 2010.

Kell, George, and Dan Ewald. *Hello Everybody, I'm George Kell.* Champaign, Illinois: Sports Publishing, 1998.

Klein, Dave. *Great Infielders of the Major Leagues.* New York: Random House, 1972.

LaNier, Carlotta Walls. *A Mighty Long Way: My Journey to Justice at Little Rock Central High School.* New York: Random House, 2009.

Leavy, Jane. *Sandy Koufax: A Lefty's Legacy.* New York: HarperCollins, 2002.

Metro, Charlie, and Thomas Altherr. *Safe by a Mile.* Lincoln: University of Nebraska Press, 2002.

Palmer, Jim, and Jim Dale. *Palmer and Weaver: Together We Were Eleven Foot Nine*. Kansas City, Missouri: Andrews & McMeel, 1996.

Peary, Danny. *We Played the Game: Memories of Baseball's Greatest Era*. New York: Black Dog and Leventhal, 1994.

Pepe, Phil. *Catfish, Yaz, and Hammerin' Hank: The Unforgettable Era That Transformed Baseball*. Chicago: Triumph, 2005.

Robinson, Brooks, and Fred Bauer. *Putting It All Together*. New York: Hawthorn, 1971.

Robinson, Brooks, and Jack Tobin. *Third Base Is My Home*. Waco, Texas: Word, 1974.

Robinson, Eddie, with C. Paul Rogers III. *Lucky Me: My Sixty-Five Years in Baseball*. Dallas: Southern Methodist University Press, 2011.

Robinson, Frank, and Al Silverman. *My Life Is Baseball*. New York: Doubleday, 1968.

Robinson, Frank, and Berry Stainback. *Extra Innings*. New York: McGraw-Hill, 1988.

Rosengren, John. *Hammerin' Hank, George Almighty and the Say Hey Kid: The Year That Changed Baseball Forever*. Naperville, Illinois: Sourcebooks, 2008.

Schulian, John. *Sometimes They Even Shook Your Hand*. Lincoln: University of Nebraska Press, 2011.

Seidel, Jeff. *Baltimore Orioles Where Have You Gone*. Champaign, Illinois: Sports Publishing, 2006.

Staples, Billy, and Rich Herschlag, eds. *Before the Glory: 20 Baseball Heroes Talk About Growing Up and Turning Hard Times into Home Runs*. Deerfield Beach, Florida: Health Communication, 2007.

Steadman, John. *Days in the Sun*. Baltimore: Baltimore Sun, 2000.

Thompson, Chuck, with Gordon Beard. *Ain't the Beer Cold*. South Bend, Indiana: Diamond Communications, 1996.

Vecsey, George. *Stan Musial: An American Life*. New York: Ballantine, 2011.

Vincent, Fay. *We Would Have Played for Nothing: Baseball Stars of the 1950s and 1960s Talk About the Game They Loved*. New York: Simon & Schuster, 2008.

Weaver, Earl, with Berry Stainback. *It's What You Learn After You Know It All That Counts*. Garden City, New York: Doubleday, 1982.

Wilson, Doug. *Fred Hutchinson and the 1964 Cincinnati Reds*. Jefferson, North Carolina: McFarland, 2010.

Zander, Jack. *The Brooks Robinson Story*. New York: Julian Messner, 1967.

Index

DISCARD